My Morning Manna

Volume 1

Ed Nelson

Mile-Hi Publishers, Inc. • P.O. Box 19340 • Denver, Colorado 80219 • (303) 922-5833

To my dear wife, Guyla,
my companion in the Lord's work for 41 years.
Her encouragement to be faithful to the Lord
and His word, as well as her
diligent labor in typing and proofreading,
has made this volume possible.

Preface

During my tenure as pastor of South Sheridan Baptist Church in Denver, Colorado, I was burdened to help our church families with their daily devotions. Therefore, in 1975 I began writing *My Morning Manna*. These devotionals were published monthly (later bi-monthly) by the church for 16 years. Other churches and individuals subscribed to the publication.

Following my resignation from the pastorate of the church, I decided to publish these devotional materials in a book form. This is volume 1 of the devotional books to be published. Nearly all of the devotionals in this volume have been selected from those I have written over the years. In a few cases, I wrote a new one for certain days.

By using this volume of *My Morning Manna*, you will have a guide and help for personal and/or family devotions. By following the Bible readings for each day, you will read through the Bible in a year. From each day's Bible reading assignment, there is a portion called "Family Reading." I endeavored to have this "Family Reading" portion to average about 20 verses per day. Each day's devotional has been written about some or all of the scripture listed for family reading.

I am thrilled that we can share this time together meditating on His word. I trust that *My Morning Manna* will be a help to you in your Bible reading and in having some Bible truth on which to meditate each day.

Ed Nelson

DAILY SCHEDULE
FOR JANUARY

Day	Personal Reading	Family Reading	Title
Jan. 1	❐ Gen. 1–3	❐ Gen. 2	Happy New Year?
Jan. 2	❐ Gen. 4–7	❐ Gen. 7	The Refuge in the Home
Jan. 3	❐ Gen. 8 & 9	❐ Gen. 9:1-19	Complete Rainbow
Jan. 4	❐ Gen. 10–12	❐ Gen. 12	Family Altar
Jan. 5	❐ Gen. 13–16	❐ Gen. 13	Lot's Wrong Choice: The World
Jan. 6	❐ Gen. 17–19	❐ Gen. 17	The God Who Is Enough
Jan. 7	❐ Gen. 20–22	❐ Gen. 22	God Tested Abraham
Jan. 8	❐ Gen. 23 & 24	❐ Gen. 24:1-25	Abraham's Servant—A Picture of a Soulwinner
Jan. 9	❐ Gen. 25 & 26	❐ Gen. 25:19-34	Why Did Esau Despise His Birthright?
Jan. 10	❐ Gen. 27–29	❐ Gen. 27:1-25	Jacob, the Supplanter
Jan. 11	❐ Gen. 30 & 31	❐ Gen. 30:1-24	Beware of Envy
Jan. 12	❐ Gen. 32–34	❐ Gen. 32	Broken to Bless
Jan. 13	❐ Gen. 35 & 36	❐ Gen. 35	Back to Bethel
Jan. 14	❐ Gen. 37–39	❐ Gen. 37:1-27	The Danger of Hatred
Jan. 15	❐ Gen. 40 & 41	❐ Gen. 41:9-16, 33-48, 55-57	Joseph's Exaltation
Jan. 16	❐ Gen. 42–44	❐ Gen. 44	Repentance Essential
Jan. 17	❐ Gen. 45–47	❐ Gen. 46	Faith Versus Fears
Jan. 18	❐ Gen. 48–50	❐ Gen. 50	A Man of Character
Jan. 19	❐ Ex. 1–3	❐ Ex. 1	Redemption
Jan. 20	❐ Ex. 4–6	❐ Ex. 4	What Is That in Thine Hand?
Jan. 21	❐ Ex. 7–9	❐ Ex. 7:14-25; 8:5-7, 16-18; 9:8-12	Satan's Emissaries Defeated
Jan. 22	❐ Ex. 10–12	❐ Ex. 12:1-13, 21-33	The Passover
Jan. 23	❐ Ex. 13–15	❐ Ex. 14	God's Instruction for Victory
Jan. 24	❐ Ex. 16–18	❐ Ex. 16	The Daily Manna
Jan. 25	❐ Ex. 19–21	❐ Ex. 20	The Law and the Altar
Jan. 26	❐ Ex. 22–24	❐ Ex. 23:9-33	God's Leading
Jan. 27	❐ Ex. 25–27	❐ Ex. 25	The Oil for the Lights
Jan. 28	❐ Ex. 28 & 29	❐ Ex. 29:1-21	Total Consecration
Jan. 29	❐ Ex. 30–32	❐ Ex. 32:1-28	Who Is on the Lord's Side?
Jan. 30	❐ Ex. 33 to 35:29	❐ Ex. 33:1-22	The Blessing of His Presence
Jan. 31	❐ Ex. 35:30 to Chapter 38	❐ Ex. 35:30-35; 36:1-8; 38:21-23	God Uses Men

DAILY SCHEDULE
FOR FEBRUARY

Day	Personal Reading	Family Reading	Title
Feb. 1	❐ Ex. 39 & 40	❐ Ex. 40:16-38	The Tabernacle Constructed
Feb. 2	❐ Lev. 1–4	❐ Lev. 2	The Life and Death of Our Lord
Feb. 3	❐ Lev. 5–7	❐ Lev. 5:14-19; 6:1-7	Trespass Offering
Feb. 4	❐ Lev. 8–10	❐ Lev. 10	Taking Spiritual Things for Granted
Feb. 5	❐ Lev. 11–13	❐ Lev. 11:1-8, 35-47	The Fact of Sin
Feb. 6	❐ Lev. 14 & 15	❐ Lev. 14:1-20	The Cleansing of the Leper
Feb. 7	❐ Lev. 16–18	❐ Lev. 17	The Precious Blood of Christ
Feb. 8	❐ Lev. 19–22	❐ Lev. 19	Beware of Talebearing
Feb. 9	❐ Lev. 23 & 24	❐ Lev. 23:1-22	The Feasts of Jehovah
Feb. 10	❐ Lev. 25 & 26	❐ Lev. 25:1-24	The Year of Jubilee
Feb. 11	❐ Lev. 27 & Num. 1	❐ Num. 1:1-4, 16-21, 45-54	Our Pedigree
Feb. 12	❐ Num. 2 & 3	❐ Num. 3:1-16	No Respect of Persons
Feb. 13	❐ Num. 4 & 5	❐ Num. 4:1-20	No Job Too Small
Feb. 14	❐ Num. 6 & 7	❐ Num. 6	The Lord's Blessing
Feb. 15	❐ Num. 8–10	❐ Num. 9:15-23; 10:1-12	The Leading of the Spirit and the Word
Feb. 16	❐ Num. 11–13	❐ Num. 13	Only Believe
Feb. 17	❐ Num. 14 & 15	❐ Num. 15:1-3, 17-24, 32-41	The Wandering Years
Feb. 18	❐ Num. 16–18	❐ Num. 18:1-24	The Lord our Portion
Feb. 19	❐ Num. 19–21	❐ Num. 21:1-19	The Brazen Serpent
Feb. 20	❐ Num. 22 & 23	❐ Num. 22:1-22	A False Prophet
Feb. 21	❐ Num. 24–26	❐ Num. 25	The Danger of Sin
Feb. 22	❐ Num. 27–29	❐ Num. 27	The Claim to Inheritance
Feb. 23	❐ Num. 30 & 31	❐ Num. 30	The Law of Vows
Feb. 24	❐ Num. 32 & 33	❐ Num. 32:1-25	The Sin of Bordering the World
Feb. 25	❐ Num. 34–36	❐ Num. 35:11-34	Cities of Refuge
Feb. 26	❐ Deut. 1 & 2	❐ Deut. 1:1-8, 25-36	Going About in Circles
Feb. 27	❐ Deut. 3 & 4	❐ Deut. 4:1-16, 29-35	A Favored Position
Feb. 28	❐ Deut. 5–7	❐ Deut. 6	The Word in Your Heart
Feb. 29	❐ Deut. 8–10	❐ Deut. 10	God's Requirements

DAILY SCHEDULE
FOR MARCH

Day	Personal Reading	Family Reading	Title
Mar. 1	❑ Deut. 11–13	❑ Deut. 13	Beware of False Prophets
Mar. 2	❑ Deut. 14–16	❑ Deut. 15	God's Anti-Poverty Program
Mar. 3	❑ Deut. 17–21	❑ Deut. 17	America—Beware!
Mar. 4	❑ Deut. 22–25	❑ Deut. 22:8-30	Principles of Separation
Mar. 5	❑ Deut. 26–28	❑ Deut. 28:1-6, 13-19, 50-53, 58-62	Blessings and Curses with Warning of Judgment
Mar. 6	❑ Deut. 29–31	❑ Deut. 30	God's Promises to Israel
Mar. 7	❑ Deut. 32–34	❑ Deut. 32:1-13, 29-36	His People
Mar. 8	❑ Josh. 1–4	❑ Josh. 2	The Scarlet Line
Mar. 9	❑ Josh. 5–7	❑ Josh. 7	God Judges Sin in the Camp
Mar. 10	❑ Josh. 8 and 9	❑ Josh. 8:1-25	Regaining Lost Ground
Mar. 11	❑ Josh. 10–12	❑ Josh. 10:1-25	The Lord Gives the Victory
Mar. 12	❑ Josh. 13–15	❑ Josh. 14	Caleb—God's Great Man
Mar. 13	❑ Josh. 16–19	❑ Josh. 17	Have the Victory Where You Are
Mar. 14	❑ Josh. 20–22	❑ Josh. 22:10-34	Judge Not
Mar. 15	❑ Josh. 23 & 24 & Jud. 1	❑ Josh. 24:1-25	The Right Decision
Mar. 16	❑ Jud. 2–4	❑ Jud. 2:16–3:11	Fighting for God
Mar. 17	❑ Jud. 5–7	❑ Jud. 7	The Sword of the Lord and of Gideon
Mar. 18	❑ Jud. 8 & 9	❑ Jud. 9:1-6, 20-24, 46-57	God Judges Sin
Mar. 19	❑ Jud. 10–12	❑ Jud. 10	Idolatry
Mar. 20	❑ Jud. 13–16	❑ Jud. 16:1-21, 30-31	Where Does Your Strength Lie?
Mar. 21	❑ Jud. 17–19	❑ Jud. 18:1-26	Make Jesus King of Your Life
Mar. 22	❑ Jud. 20 & 21	❑ Jud. 20:1-28	Coming to the End of Ourselves
Mar. 23	❑ Ruth 1–4	❑ Ruth 1:1-14; 2:5-16	Ruth—Deciding for the Lord and Receiving Grace
Mar. 24	❑ I Sam. 1–3	❑ I Sam. 1	A Model Mother
Mar. 25	❑ I Sam. 4–7	❑ I Sam. 6	The Will of God
Mar. 26	❑ I Sam. 8–11	❑ I Sam. 8	Heed the Lord
Mar. 27	❑ I Sam. 12–14	❑ I Sam. 13	Wait on the Lord
Mar. 28	❑ I Sam. 15–17	❑ I Sam. 17:31-54	Victory Belongs to God!
Mar. 29	❑ I Sam. 18–20	❑ I Sam. 18:1-18	The Love of Jonathan
Mar. 30	❑ I Sam. 21–24	❑ I Sam. 24	Vengeance Is God's
Mar. 31	❑ I Sam. 25–27	❑ I Sam. 25:14-39	Vengeance Is God's (Part II)

DAILY SCHEDULE
FOR APRIL

Day	Personal Reading	Family Reading	Title
Apr. 1	❐ I Sam. 28–31	❐ I Sam. 28	Result of Disobedience to God
Apr. 2	❐ II Sam. 1–3	❐ II Sam. 2:8-28	A Fool Died
Apr. 3	❐ II Sam. 4–7	❐ II Sam. 7	Claiming His Promises
Apr. 4	❐ II Sam. 8–11	❐ II Sam. 11	Sin Produces a Hard Heart
Apr. 5	❐ II Sam. 12 & 13	❐ II Sam. 13:3, 15-36	The Results of Sin
Apr. 6	❐ II Sam. 14 –16	❐ II Sam. 16	Beware of Flattery
Apr. 7	❐ II Sam. 17–19	❐ II Sam. 18:9-33	The Tragedy of Rebellion
Apr. 8	❐ II Sam. 20–22	❐ II Sam. 22:1-23	Deliverance
Apr. 9	❐ II Sam. 23 & 24 & I Kings 1	❐ II Sam. 24	Paying the Price
Apr. 10	❐ I Kings 2 & 3	❐ I Kings 3:1-15; 4:29-34	The Wisdom of Solomon
Apr. 11	❐ I Kings 4–6	❐ I Kings 6:1-22	Honoring the Lord First
Apr. 12	❐ I Kings 7 & 8	❐ I Kings 8:46-66	Solomon's Prayer and Blessing
Apr. 13	❐ I Kings 9–11	❐ I Kings 10:1-23	The World Recognizes God's Blessings
Apr. 14	❐ I Kings 12–14	❐ I Kings 13:1-22	Always Obey God
Apr. 15	❐ I Kings 15–17	❐ I Kings 15:1-24	Rely on the Lord
Apr. 16	❐ I Kings 18 & 19	❐ I Kings 19	Victory over Discouragement
Apr. 17	❐ I Kings 20 & 21	❐ I Kings 20:23-43	The Danger of Compromise
Apr. 18	❐ I Kings 22 & II Kings 1	❐ I Kings 22:6-28, 34-37	Preach the Word
Apr. 19	❐ II Kings 2–4	❐ II Kings 2	God's Power
Apr. 20	❐ II Kings 5–7	❐ II Kings 5:1-19	The Healing of Naaman
Apr. 21	❐ II Kings 8 & 9	❐ II Kings 8:1-19	The Depths of Sin
Apr. 22	❐ II Kings 10–12	❐ II Kings 10:11-33	Sin Will Bring Its Fruit
Apr. 23	❐ II Kings 13–15	❐ II Kings 13	May We Long for Victory
Apr. 24	❐ II Kings 16–18	❐ II Kings 17:1-23	Sin Brings Captivity
Apr. 25	❐ II Kings 19–21	❐ II Kings 19:14-37	Miraculous Answer to Prayer
Apr. 26	❐ II Kings 22–24	❐ II Kings 22	The Book
Apr. 27	❐ II Kings 25 & I Chr. 1	❐ II Kings 25:1-10, 21-30	A Daily Supply
Apr. 28	❐ I Chr. 2–4	❐ I Chr. 4:9-10, 21-23, 39-43; Col. 3:1-7, 22-25	Blessings from Chronicles
Apr. 29	❐ I Chr. 5 & 6	❐ I Chr. 5	Sin Brings Reproach
Apr. 30	❐ I Chr. 7–9	❐ I Chr. 7:20-23; 9:17-29;I Tim. 6:9,10	Special Truths for Today

DAILY SCHEDULE
FOR MAY

Day	Personal Reading	Family Reading	Title
May 1	❐ I Chr. 10 & 11	❐ I Chr. 10; 11:1-10	God's Judgment
May 2	❐ I Chr. 12–14	❐ I Chr. 13	Failing to Obey God
May 3	❐ I Chr. 15 & 16	❐ I Chr. 15:1-3, 11-29	Doing a Right Thing in the Wrong Way
May 4	❐ I Chr. 17–20	❐ I Chr. 17:7-27	The Promises of God
May 5	❐ I Chr. 21–23	❐ I Chr. 21:9-30	David's Choice
May 6	❐ I Chr. 24–26	❐ I Chr. 24:1-5; 2 5:1-7; 26:4-12	Using Our Gifts
May 7	❐ I Chr. 27–29	❐ I Chr. 28	David Instructs and Encourages Solomon
May 8	❐ II Chr. 1–4	❐ II Chr. 2	Right Priorities
May 9	❐ II Chr. 5–7	❐ II Chr. 7	Revival
May 10	❐ II Chr. 8–11	❐ II Chr. 10	A Soft Answer
May 11	❐ II Chr. 12–15	❐ II Chr. 12	The Danger of Prosperity
May 12	❐ II Chr. 16–19	❐ II Chr. 16; 17:1-5	Total Reliance
May 13	❐ II Chr. 20–22	❐ II Chr. 21	The Price of Sin
May 14	❐ II Chr. 23–25	❐ II Chr. 23	The King Enthroned
May 15	❐ II Chr. 26–29	❐ II Chr. 26	The Danger of Pride
May 16	❐ II Chr. 30–32	❐ II Chr. 32:1-23	God Delivers
May 17	❐ II Chr. 33–35	❐ II Chr. 33	Parents—Beware!
May 18	❐ II Chr. 36 & Ezra 1 & 2	❐ II Chr. 36	No Remedy
May 19	❐ Ezra 3–6	❐ Ezra 3 & 4:1-5	Standing for God
May 20	❐ Ezra 7–9	❐ Ezra 8:15-36	Looking to God
May 21	❐ Ezra 10 & Neh. 1 & 2	❐ Neh. 1 & 2:1-5	Nehemiah — The Builder
May 22	❐ Neh. 3–5	❐ Neh. 5	Nehemiah's Example
May 23	❐ Neh. 6 & 7	❐ Neh. 6	Stand in the Battle
May 24	❐ Neh. 8–10	❐ Neh. 9	The Curse of Pride
May 25	❐ Neh. 11 & 12	❐ Neh. 12:27-47	Honor Your Leaders
May 26	❐ Neh. 13 & Est. 1 & 2	❐ Est. 1	Moral Standards for Today
May 27	❐ Est. 3–7	❐ Est. 6 & 7	God's Intervention
May 28	❐ Est. 8–10; Job 1	❐ Job 1	Why Serve God?
May 29	❐ Job 2–5	❐ Job 5:1-20	The Rock of Ages When Life's Ship Is Rocked with Trouble
May 30	❐ Job 6–8	❐ Job 7:1-20	Let's Quit Complaining
May 31	❐ Job 9–11	❐ Job 9:13-35	Job's Problem

DAILY SCHEDULE
FOR JUNE

Day	Personal Reading	Family Reading	Title
June 1	❐ Job 12–14	❐ Job 14	After Death—What Then?
June 2	❐ Job 15–17	❐ Job 16	Be Careful to Uplift—Very Slow to Criticize
June 3	❐ Job 18–20	❐ Job 19:7-29	Job's Glorious Hope
June 4	❐ Job 21–23	❐ Job 23	God's Purpose in Trials
June 5	❐ Job 24–28	❐ Job 28	Where Is Wisdom?
June 6	❐ Job 29–31	❐ Job 31:1-28	The Self Life
June 7	❐ Job 32–34	❐ Job 34:1-23	God's Righteous Judgment
June 8	❐ Job 35–37	❐ Job 35	Importance of Attitude
June 9	❐ Job 38 & 39	❐ Job 38:1-23	Man's Unlimited Understanding
June 10	❐ Job 40–42	❐ Job 42	Job Saw Himself!
June 11	❐ Ps. 1–7	❐ Ps. 5	The Blessing of Prayer
June 12	❐ Ps. 8–13	❐ Ps. 10	The Antichrist
June 13	❐ Ps. 14–18	❐ Ps. 18:1-24	Christ, the Center of Life
June 14	❐ Ps. 19–23	❐ Ps. 22:1-22	The Cross
June 15	❐ Ps. 24–29	❐ Ps. 27	Wait on the Lord
June 16	❐ Ps. 30–33	❐ Ps. 33	God—Our Deliverer
June 17	❐ Ps. 34–36	❐ Ps. 34	Constant Praise
June 18	❐ Ps. 37–39	❐ Ps. 37:1-23	Doubt Not God's Wisdom!
June 19	❐ Ps. 40–44	❐ Ps. 42 & 43	A Longing for God
June 20	❐ Ps. 45–49	❐ Ps. 45	Fairest Lord Jesus
June 21	❐ Ps. 50–55	❐ Ps. 51	Sin Forgiven
June 22	❐ Ps. 56–61	❐ Ps. 60 & 61	The Rock That Is Higher Than I
June 23	❐ Ps. 62–67	❐ Ps. 62 & 63	Trusting the Lord
June 24	❐ Ps. 68 & 69	❐ Ps. 69:1-21	The Suffering Christ
June 25	❐ Ps. 70–73	❐ Ps. 71	A Message for All Ages
June 26	❐ Ps. 74–77	❐ Ps. 77	From a Sigh to a Song
June 27	❐ Ps. 78	❐ Ps. 78:1-22, 35-38	Be Ye Steadfast
June 28	❐ Ps. 79–83	❐ Ps. 81	What Might Have Been
June 29	❐ Ps. 84–88	❐ Ps. 84 & 85	Strengthened
June 30	❐ Ps. 89–91	❐ Ps. 91	The Lord Our Habitation

DAILY SCHEDULE
FOR JULY

Day	Personal Reading	Family Reading	Title
July 1	❑ Ps. 92–96	❑ Ps. 95 & 96	Worship Him
July 2	❑ Ps. 97–102	❑ Ps. 97 & 98	Our Souls Preserved
July 3	❑ Ps. 103–105	❑ Ps. 104:1-12, 24-35	Let Us Sing
July 4	❑ Ps. 33 & 106	❑ Ps. 33:1-12; 106:1-23	America—Continue to Honor God
July 5	❑ Ps. 107–109	❑ Ps. 107:23-43	Victory in Time of Trouble
July 6	❑ Ps. 110–115	❑ Ps. 111 & 112	Praise Ye the Lord
July 7	❑ Ps. 116–119:24	❑ Ps. 119:1-24	The Word of God
July 8	❑ Ps. 119:25-104	❑ Ps. 119:57-80	Purpose of Afflictions
July 9	❑ Ps. 119:105-176	❑ Ps. 119:137-160	God's Pure Word
July 10	❑ Ps. 120–131	❑ Ps. 122, 123, 124	The House of the Lord
July 11	❑ Ps. 132–136	❑ Ps. 135	Praising the Lord
July 12	❑ Ps. 137–141	❑ Ps. 139	God's Searching and Knowing
July 13	❑ Ps. 142–147	❑ Ps. 142 & 143	Prayer Needed
July 14	❑ Ps. 148–150; Prov. 1 & 2	❑ Prov. 2	Understanding the Fear of the Lord
July 15	❑ Prov. 3–5	❑ Prov. 4	Guard Your Heart
July 16	❑ Prov. 6 & 7	❑ Prov. 6:1-21	A Walking Mouth and Talking Feet
July 17	❑ Prov. 8–10	❑ Prov. 8:1-21	Wisdom
July 18	❑ Prov. 11–13	❑ Prov. 11:10-31	Giving
July 19	❑ Prov. 14 & 15	❑ Prov. 15:1-21	A Soft Answer
July 20	❑ Prov. 16–18	❑ Proverbs16:13-33	Honey in the Speech
July 21	❑ Prov. 19–21 25-27; 21:11	❑ Prov. 19:1-18,	Knowledge of Him
July 22	❑ Prov. 22 & 23	❑ Prov. 23:1-22	Temptations to Flee
July 23	❑ Prov. 24–26	❑ Prov. 26	Put Out the Fire
July 24	❑ Prov. 27–29	❑ Prov. 27:1-17	A Big Enemy: Envy
July 25	❑ Prov. 30 & 31	❑ Prov. 30:1-20	A Wicked Generation
July 26	❑ Ecc. 1–3	❑ Ecc. 2	Vanity and Rejoicing
July 27	❑ Ecc. 4–7	❑ Ecc. 7:1-22	Truths by Which to Live
July 28	❑ Ecc. 8–12	❑ Ecc. 9	That Which Makes a Joyful Life
July 29	❑ S. of Sol. 1–5	❑ S. of Sol. 4	Christ's Evaluation of His Church
July 30	❑ S. of Sol. 6–8 & Is. 1	❑ Is. 1:1-18	The Prophet of Grace
July 31	❑ Is. 2–6	❑ Is. 5	God's Judgment Coming

DAILY SCHEDULE
FOR AUGUST

Day	Personal Reading	Family Reading	Title
Aug. 1	☐ Is. 7–9	☐ Is. 9	God's Promises Are Sure
Aug. 2	☐ Is. 10–13	☐ Is. 11 and 12	Water from the Wells
Aug. 3	☐ Is. 14–17	☐ Is. 14:1-23	Satan
Aug. 4	☐ Is. 18–22	☐ Is. 19	What About Egypt in Prophecy?
Aug. 5	☐ Is. 23–26	☐ Is. 26	The Mind Resting in the Lord
Aug. 6	☐ Is. 27–30	☐ Is. 28:1-20	Judgment on Apostasy
Aug. 7	☐ Is. 31–35	☐ Is. 33:14-24; Is. 35	The Future Kingdom
Aug. 8	☐ Is. 36–38	☐ Is. 37:1-23	A Personal Relationship with the Lord
Aug. 9	☐ Is. 39–41	☐ Is. 40:10-31	Soaring Like an Eagle
Aug. 10	☐ Is. 42–44	☐ Is. 44:1-20	Keep Yourselves from Idols
Aug. 11	☐ Is. 45–48	☐ Is. 48	Separation from the World
Aug. 12	☐ Is. 49–53	☐ Is. 51	Trusting Him
Aug. 13	☐ Is. 54–58	☐ Is. 55 & 56	The Satisfying Bread
Aug. 14	☐ Is. 59–62	☐ Is. 59	Judgment on All
Aug. 15	☐ Is. 63–66	☐ Is. 65	Faster Than the Telegraph
Aug. 16	☐ Jer. 1–3	☐ Jer. 3	God's Yearning for Backsliders
Aug. 17	☐ Jer. 4–6	☐ Jer. 4:1-22	Break Up Your Fallow Ground
Aug. 18	☐ Jer. 7–9	☐ Jer. 8	What Wisdom Is in Them?
Aug. 19	☐ Jer. 10–13	☐ Jer. 13	Wilt Thou Not Be Made Clean?
Aug. 20	☐ Jer. 14–17	☐ Jer. 17:1-18	The Mystery of Iniquity
Aug. 21	☐ Jer. 18–21	☐ Jer. 20	Jer.'s Victory
Aug. 22	☐ Jer. 22–24	☐ Jer. 23:1-14, 23-30	True and False Prophets
Aug. 23	☐ Jer. 25–27	☐ Jer. 26	A Faithful Prophet
Aug. 24	☐ Jer. 28–30	☐ Jer. 28	A Faithless Prophet
Aug. 25	☐ Jer. 31 & 32	☐ Jer. 32:6-28, 37-41	God's Answer to Jer.'s Puzzle
Aug. 26	☐ Jer. 33–36	☐ Jer. 33:1-22	God's Promise of Blessing
Aug. 27	☐ Jer. 37–40	☐ Jer. 39	Don't Pass Redemption Point
Aug. 28	☐ Jer. 41–44	☐ Jer. 42:13-22; Jer. 43	The Sign of the Hidden Stones
Aug. 29	☐ Jer. 45–48	☐ Jer. 48:1-18, 38-42	Nominal Christians
Aug. 30	☐ Jer. 49 & 50	☐ Jer. 49:7-22	The Sin of Pride
Aug. 31	☐ Jer. 51	☐ Jer. 51:1-14, 25 & 26, 42-49	Babylon Destroyed

DAILY SCHEDULE
FOR SEPTEMBER

Day	Personal Reading	Family Reading	Title
Sep. 1	❐ Jer. 52; Lam. 1	❐ Lam. 1	How?
Sep. 2	❐ Lam. 2 & 3	❐ Lam. 3:22-50	The Goodness of God
Sep. 3	❐ Lam. 4 & 5 & Ez. 1	❐ Ez. 1:1-20	The Glory of God
Sep. 4	❐ Ez. 2–6	❐ Ez. 5	God's Judgment
Sep. 5	❐ Ez. 7–10	❐ Ez. 8 & 9	A Vision of Jesus
Sep. 6	❐ Ez. 11–13	❐ Ez. 11	Needed: A New Heart
Sep. 7	❐ Ez. 14–16	❐ Ez. 16:1-14, 43, 60-63	The Grace of God
Sep. 8	❐ Ez. 17–19	❐ Ez. 18:1-23	Individual Responsibility
Sep. 9	❐ Ez. 20 & 21	❐ Ez. 21:1-7, 18-32	The Right of the Lord
Sep. 10	❐ Ez. 22 & 23	❐ Ez. 22:13-31	God Needs Men
Sep. 11	❐ Ez. 24–26	❐ Ez. 25	The Judgment of the Nations
Sep. 12	❐ Ez. 27–29	❐ Ez. 28	Know the Lord
Sep. 13	❐ Ez. 30–32	❐ Ez. 31	The Pearl of Pride
Sep. 14	❐ Ez. 33–35	❐ Ez. 33:1-20	The Responsibility of Being a Watchman
Sep. 15	❐ Ez. 36–38	❐ Ez. 36:16-38	A New Heart
Sep. 16	❐ Ez. 39 & 40	❐ Ez. 39:1-17 & 25-29	Judgment on Russia
Sep. 17	❐ Ez. 41–43	❐ Ez. 43:1-12, 18-27	The Glory of the Lord
Sep. 18	❐ Ez. 44–46	❐ Ez. 44:1-23	The Cleansed Priesthood
Sep. 19	❐ Ez. 47 & 48; Dan. 1	❐ Dan. 1	God's Great Man: Daniel
Sep. 20	❐ Dan. 2 & 3	❐ Dan. 2:1-28	Prayer and Praise
Sep. 21	❐ Dan. 4–6	❐ Dan. 4:18-37	Danger of Pride
Sep. 22	❐ Dan. 7–9	❐ Dan. 9:1-19	Daniel—Greatly Beloved
Sep. 23	❐ Dan. 10–12	❐ Dan. 11:36-45 & Dan. 12	The Two Resurrections
Sep. 24	❐ Hos. 1–6	❐ Hos. 4:6-11; 5:1-15	God's Judgment Coming
Sep. 25	❐ Hos. 7–12	❐ Hos. 10	Break Up Your Fallow Ground
Sep. 26	❐ Hos. 13 & 14; Joel 1 & 2	❐ Hos. 13 & 14	God's Yearning Tenderness
Sep. 27	❐ Joel 3; Amos 1–4	❐ Amos 1 & 2:1-5	A Bold Prophet Pronouncing Judgment
Sep. 28	❐ Amos 5–9	❐ Amos 7:14-17; & 8	Famine in the Land
Sep. 29	❐ Oba., Jonah, & Mic. 1	❐ Jonah 1 & 2	Salvation Is of the Lord
Sep. 30	❐ Mic. 2–7	❐ Mic. 5	Our Great Shepherd

DAILY SCHEDULE
FOR OCTOBER

Day	Personal Reading	Family Reading	Title
Oct. 1	❑ Nah. 1–3 & Hab. 1–3	❑ Hab. 1:1-17; 2:1-4	Rejoice—No Matter What!
Oct. 2	❑ Zeph. 1–3 & Hag. 1 & 2	❑ Hag. 1	The Danger of Selfish Living
Oct. 3	❑ Zech. 1–7	❑ Zech. 6	The Crowning Day
Oct. 4	❑ Zech. 8–13	❑ Zech. 12 & 13	The Fountain of the Word
Oct. 5	❑ Zech. 14 & Mal. 1–4	❑ Mal. 3	Our Unchanging God
Oct. 6	❑ Mat. 1–4	❑ Mat. 3	Why Was John the Baptist a Great Man?
Oct. 7	❑ Mat. 5–7	❑ Mat. 5:17-48	Christ's Law
Oct. 8	❑ Mat. 8, 9, & 10:1-23	❑ Mat. 9:16-38	New Garments and New Vessels
Oct. 9	❑ Mat. 10:24-42; 11; & 12	❑ Mat. 11:1-19	Be Rid of Doubts!
Oct. 10	❑ Mat. 13 & 14	❑ Mat. 13:1-23	The Parable of the Soils
Oct. 11	❑ Mat. 15–17	❑ Mat. 15:21-39	Faith in Christ
Oct. 12	❑ Mat. 18–20	❑ Mat. 20:1-16, 25-28	The Privilege of Serving Him
Oct. 13	❑ Mat. 21 & 22	❑ Mat. 22:1-22	Do You Have the Wedding Garment?
Oct. 14	❑ Mat. 23 & 24	❑ Mat. 24:1-26	The Character of This Age
Oct. 15	❑ Mat. 25; 26:1-46	❑ Mat. 25:1-22	"Watch Therefore!"
Oct. 16	❑ Mat. 26:47-75 & 27	❑ Mat. 27:1-24	Judas Sold Himself
Oct. 17	❑ Mat. 28; Mk. 1 & 2	❑ Mat. 28	His Presence with Us
Oct. 18	❑ Mk. 3; 4; 5:1-20	❑ Mk. 5:1-20	The New Creature
Oct. 19	❑ Mk. 5:21-43; 6; & 7:1-23	❑ Mk. 5:21-43	Only Believe
Oct. 20	❑ Mk. 7:24-37; 8; 9	❑ Mk. 8:14-38	The Healing of the Blind Man
Oct. 21	❑ Mk. 10 & 11	❑ Mk. 10:23-45	The Deceitfulness of Riches
Oct. 22	❑ Mk. 12; 13; 14:1-16	❑ Mk. 12:28-44	The Secret of True Giving
Oct. 23	❑ Mk. 14:17-52; 15	❑ Mk. 14:26-52	Smitten by God
Oct. 24	❑ Mk. 16 & Lk. 1	❑ Lk. 1:13-38	Believe God's Promises
Oct. 25	❑ Lk. 2 & 3	❑ Lk. 3:1-23	The Ministry of John
Oct. 26	❑ Lk. 4 & 5	❑ Lk. 4:1-22	Turn Your Eyes Upon Jesus
Oct. 27	❑ Lk. 6 & 7	❑ Lk. 7:1-23	When Jesus Meets Death
Oct. 28	❑ Lk. 8 & 9:1-45	❑ Lk. 9:18-42	The Mount of Transfiguration
Oct. 29	❑ Lk. 9:46-62; 10; 11	❑ Lk. 10:21-42	One Thing Needful
Oct. 30	❑ Lk. 12 & 13	❑ Lk. 12:15-34	Beware of Covetousness
Oct. 31	❑ Lk. 14 –16	❑ Lk. 15:1-24	Christ Receives Sinners

DAILY SCHEDULE
FOR NOVEMBER

Day		Personal Reading		Family Reading	Title
Nov. 1	❐	Lk. 17 & 18	❐	Lk. 18:1-17	A Sinner Saved
Nov. 2	❐	Lk. 19 & 20	❐	Lk. 20:27-47	Immortality
Nov. 3	❐	Lk. 21 & 22	❐	Lk. 22:31-53	What Is the Difference?
Nov. 4	❐	Lk. 23 & 24	❐	Lk. 23:1-25	Beware Joining with Others Against Christ
Nov. 5	❐	Jn. 1–3	❐	Jn. 1:1-20	Receiving Him
Nov. 6	❐	Jn. 4 & 5	❐	Jn. 5:1-21	No Man
Nov. 7	❐	Jn. 6 & 7	❐	Jn. 6:22-44	What Would You Answer?
Nov. 8	❐	Jn. 8 & 9	❐	Jn. 8:31-55	Enslaving Sin
Nov. 9	❐	Jn. 10 & 11	❐	Jn. 10:1-21	God Leads
Nov. 10	❐	Jn. 12 & 13	❐	Jn. 12:27-50	Believing Is Commanded
Nov. 11	❐	Jn. 14–16	❐	Jn. 16:12-33	Necessity of Prayer
Nov. 12	❐	Jn. 17; 18; 19:1-16	❐	Jn. 19:1-16	Pilate on Trial
Nov. 13	❐	Jn. 19:17-42; 20 & 21	❐	Jn. 20:1-21	Christ Is Risen
Nov. 14	❐	Acts 1–3	❐	Acts 1	Holy Spirit Power
Nov. 15	❐	Acts 4–6	❐	Acts 4:1-13, 21-31	Filled with the Spirit
Nov. 16	❐	Acts 7 & 8	❐	Acts 8:4-8, 26-40	Model Soulwinner
Nov. 17	❐	Acts 9 & 10	❐	Acts 10:23-48	Three Conversions
Nov. 18	❐	Acts 11–13	❐	Acts 12	God's Work Moves On!
Nov. 19	❐	Acts 14–16	❐	Acts 16:16-40	The Philippian Jailer Saved
Nov. 20	❐	Acts 17–19	❐	Acts 18	Gallio's Indifference
Nov. 21	❐	Acts 20 & 21	❐	Acts 20:17-38	The Word of His Grace
Nov. 22	❐	Acts 22–24	❐	Acts 23:1-13, 21-35	Victory in Service
Nov. 23	❐	Acts 25–27	❐	Acts 27:21-44	Faith Triumphing
Nov. 24	❐	Acts 28; Rom. 1 & 2	❐	Rom. 2:5-29	God's Judgment Begins with His Own
Nov. 25	❐	Rom. 3–6	❐	Rom. 5	Results of Justification
Nov. 26	❐	Rom. 7–9	❐	Rom. 8:1-25	Holy Spirit Power
Nov. 27	❐	Rom. 10–13	❐	Rom. 11:1-14, 26-36	Future of Israel
Nov. 28	❐	Rom. 14–16	❐	Rom. 16	Warning About False Teachers
Nov. 29	❐	I Cor. 1–4	❐	I Cor. 2	The Wisdom of God
Nov. 30	❐	I Cor. 5–8	❐	I Cor. 7:1-24	The Importance of Marriage

DAILY SCHEDULE
FOR DECEMBER

Day	Personal Reading	Family Reading	Title
Dec. 1	❑ I Cor. 9–11	❑ I Cor. 10:1-22	The Majority Did Not Please God
Dec. 2	❑ I Cor. 12–14	❑ I Cor. 14:1-22	Tongues
Dec. 3	❑ I Cor. 15 & 16	❑ I Cor. 16	Duties That Bring Victory
Dec. 4	❑ II Cor. 1–4	❑ II Cor. 1	Blessings in Trials
Dec. 5	❑ II Cor. 5–8	❑ II Cor. 6 & 7:1	Separation: A Must for Christians of All Ages
Dec. 6	❑ II Cor. 9–12	❑ II Cor. 8:20-24 & 9	God's Abounding Grace
Dec. 7	❑ II Cor. 13; Gal. 1–3	❑ Gal. 1	Beware of False Teachers
Dec. 8	❑ Gal. 4–6	❑ Gal. 5	The Battle Every Believer Faces
Dec. 9	❑ Eph. 1:1–4:16	❑ Eph. 3	Unto Him That Is Able
Dec. 10	❑ Eph. 4:17-32; 5 & 6	❑ Eph. 4:17-32	The New Man in Control
Dec. 11	❑ Phil. 1–3	❑ Phil. 2:1-24	One-Mindedness
Dec. 12	❑ Phil. 4; Col. 1 & 2	❑ Col. 2	Walk in Him
Dec. 13	❑ Col. 3 & 4; I Thes. 1 & 2	❑ I Thes. 2	Paul's Burden in Doing God's Will
Dec. 14	❑ I Thes. 3–5; II Thes. 1	❑ I Thes. 5	Always Ready
Dec. 15	❑ II Thes. 2 & 3; I Tim. 1–4	❑ I Tim. 1	The Gospel Defined
Dec. 16	❑ I Tim. 5 & 6; II Tim. 1 & 2	❑ II Tim. 1	Death Abolished
Dec. 17	❑ II Tim. 3 & 4; Titus 1–3	❑ II Tim. 4	Paul's Burden and Glory
Dec. 18	❑ Phile; Heb. 1 –3	❑ Heb. 1 & 2:1-8	God Has Spoken Through Christ
Dec. 19	❑ Heb. 4–7	❑ Heb. 6	Two Classes of Believers
Dec. 20	❑ Heb. 8–10	❑ Heb. 10:1-25	Thankful for His Sacrifice
Dec. 21	❑ Heb. 11–13	❑ Heb. 11:1-22	Faith
Dec. 22	❑ James 1–4	❑ James 1	Count Trials as Joy
Dec. 23	❑ James 5; I Pet. 1–3	❑ I Pet. 2	Growing in the Lord
Dec. 24	❑ I Pet. 4 & 5; II Pet. 1–3	❑ II Pet. 3	Remembering the Word
Dec. 25	❑ I Jn. 1–4	❑ I Jn. 1	The Blessing of Fellowship Through Christ
Dec. 26	❑ I Jn. 5, II & III Jn., & Jude	❑ II & III Jn.	Stand for the Truth
Dec. 27	❑ Rev. 1–4	❑ Rev. 1	Genesis and Revelation
Dec. 28	❑ Rev. 5–9	❑ Rev. 5	The Worthy Triumphant Lamb
Dec. 29	❑ Rev. 10–14	❑ Rev. 11	Singing of Our Reigning King
Dec. 30	❑ Rev. 15–18	❑ Rev. 17	Judgment on Babylon
Dec. 31	❑ Rev. 19–22	❑ Rev. 22	"Even So, Come, Lord Jesus!"

January 1

Read Genesis 1–3
Family Reading: Genesis 2

Happy New Year?

New Year's Day—I like it. My two favorite holidays of the year are New Year's Day and my birthday. The reason I like both of these days so much is that they are days of beginning again. I can look forward to the future and endeavor to make it a time different from the failures of the past. I like the poem—

He came to my desk with quivering lip; the lesson was done.
"Have you a new leaf for me, dear Teacher? I have spoiled this one!"
I took his leaf, all soiled and blotted, and gave him a new one, all
   unspotted,
Then into his tired heart I smiled: "Do better now, my child."

I went to the throne with trembling heart; the year was done.
"Have you a New Year for me, dear Master? I have spoiled this one!"
He took my year all soiled and blotted, and gave me a new one, all
   unspotted,
Then into my tired heart He smiled; "Do better now, my child!"

— Author Unknown

I am glad to have a new year in front of me in which I can endeavor to do better. In today's reading we find that God planted two special trees in a garden: the tree of life and the tree of knowledge of good and evil (v. 9). Adam had a choice. He could choose between life and death. The tree that would bring death was the tree of knowledge of good and evil. God placed it there as a test to Adam and with the warning that he would die if he ate of its fruit.

In Genesis 3 we find that Adam chose the way of disobedience which resulted in death. Then God put him out of the garden so that he could not partake of the tree of life. The only way that we can now have eternal life is to come to Christ, who in Matthew 1 was named Jesus, the One who will save people from their sins. We are all children of Adam. Will we have a good **new year**? That will depend on whether we follow Adam in disobedience or walk with Christ in yieldedness to Him.

Character Verse: *"Happy is the man that findeth wisdom, and the man that getteth understanding."* — *Proverbs 3:13*

Read Genesis 4–7
Family Reading: Genesis 7

The Refuge in the Home

"And the Lord said unto Noah, Come thou and all thy house into the ark; for thee have I seen righteous before me in this generation."
—Genesis 7:1

God told Noah to bring his whole family into the ark. That ark was a beautiful picture of Jesus Christ, who delivers us from God's judgment on sin. The Hebrew word for *pitch* in Genesis 6:14 is *kaphar.* This word is translated *atonement* seventy times in the Old Testament. It is the word used in Leviticus 17:11 — *"For the life of the flesh is in the blood: and I have given it to you upon the altar to make an atonement for your souls: for it is the blood that maketh an atonement for the soul."* The pitch in the ark was a picture of the blood of Christ. That ark pictured Jesus Christ shedding His blood to give us safety in the flood of God's judgment.

Noah was to bring his family into the ark. God wants every believer to be concerned about his family and bring them all into the place of safety in Christ. Oh, the blessing of that family riding high and dry inside the ark all through that terrible flood. This is what God wants for my family and for your family.

This is the principle God is enunciating today. As we live for the Lord and fear Him, we have confidence; and our children will have a place of refuge. Let us abide in Christ so that our walk will be right before our children. Then our homes will be havens of rest and refuge for them.

Character Verse: *"In the fear of the Lord is strong confidence: and his children shall have a place of refuge." — Proverbs 14:26*

January 3

Read Genesis 8 and 9
Family Reading: Genesis 9:1-19

Complete Rainbow

In Genesis 9:12 God gave Noah a token of His covenant. That covenant was that He would not destroy the earth again with a flood (v. 15). The token was a beautiful sight to Noah, and it is a beautiful display to behold even to this day. It is the token of the rainbow.

The rainbow came because there had been a storm. Every rainbow has a cloud as its background. The rainbow is brightest when the clouds are the darkest, but we must always realize that the rainbow can be revealed only when there is a break in the clouds. That rainbow says that the sun has been shining even though there are clouds.

The rainbow is the symbol of God's everlasting love. Read Isaiah 54:9. Sorrow is the dark background on which God paints His tokens of love. His grace can take the teardrops and storm clouds of our lives and turn them into arches of triumph and jewels of glorious luster. We do not know when the storm clouds will come, but we can always be sure that God will give a rainbow. *"For our light affliction, which is but for a moment, worketh for us a far more exceeding and eternal weight of glory" (II Corinthians 4:17).*

The rainbow on earth is only a half circle; but when we get to Heaven, it will be a complete circle. Revelation 4:3 states that John saw a *". . . rainbow round about the throne, in sight like unto an emerald."* The rainbow will be a complete circle and it will be only green, the color representing praise and worship. On earth the bow is bent toward Heaven, not toward earth. It points up to tell us God's wrath was removed at Calvary.

Character Verse: *"But whoso hearkeneth unto me shall dwell safely, and shall be quiet from fear of evil."* — *Proverbs 1:33*

January 4

Read Genesis 10–12
Family Reading: Genesis 12

Family Altar

When Abram came into the land at God's direction (Genesis 12:4, 5), he immediately built an altar (Genesis 12:7). When he moved on to the area between Bethel and Hai, he again built an altar. Abram fellowshiped with God at the altar and was blessed.

But when Abram went down into Egypt (Genesis 12:10-20), he failed to build an altar. While in Egypt he committed an awful sin of lying to Pharaoh about his wife Sarah. Had he built an altar and worshiped, he could have been delivered from this sin. Abram learned his lesson because he returned unto his altar when he went back to the place near Bethel (Genesis 13:4).

Do you need to return to the altar? It is important that you have a daily place of worship and blessing. It was a *must* for Abram. I know it is a *must* in my life. You will also find it to be true in your life.

The most important altar we build is our family altar. This is a daily time when the family meets to read the Bible together and to pray together.

Several years ago I was conducting an evangelistic campaign in Southeastern Colorado. One night I gave an invitation for men to come forward to start a family altar. After the service a man came to me and said he would really like to do this, but that he did not come forward. When I asked why he did not step out on this invitation, he said, "Brother Nelson, we are having a difficult time financially and we just cannot afford to buy any more furniture right now." He had the idea that the family altar was a literal piece of furniture—an altar where the family knelt each day.

Since then I have called it a "family worship time." Family altar should involve reading the Bible and praying together. Let me encourage you to have a family worship time every day.

Bible Truth for Today: *"Except the Lord build the house, they labor in vain that build it: except the Lord keep the city, the watchman waketh but in vain." —Psalm 127:1*

January 5

Read Genesis 13–16
Family Reading: Genesis 13

Lot's Wrong Choice: The World

Abram was a wise man who desired to serve the Lord. When he saw that his herdmen and Lot's herdmen were not getting along together, Abram suggested they separate and go different ways. *"Can two walk together, except they be agreed?" (Amos 3:3).* No! Of course not. If two are going to walk together, they must be agreed. Abram and Lot were brethren going two separate directions, and they could not stay together. In verses ten through thirteen, we see why Lot could not fellowship with Abram:

1. He had an eye open to the world and to its attractions and lusts (v. 10). The plains of Jordan looked lush and green. They were as beautiful as the valleys of Egypt, which is a Bible type of the world. Lot desired the world and was ready to make a decision toward a worldly life. God's command to His children is, *"Love not the world, neither the things that are in the world . . . " (I John 2:15).*

2. Lot made the wrong choices (v. 11). He based his choices on the world and its allurements. Our lives are a result of the choices we make. Lot chose wrong, and he and his family suffered from that time on. Be careful about every choice you make.

3. Lot pitched his tent toward Sodom (vv. 12,13). That was where his heart was. His eye was on the world. His treasure was in Sodom. *"For where your treasure is, there will your heart be also" (Matthew 6:21).*

For two believers to have spiritual fellowship, they must follow I John 1:7— *"But if we walk in the light, as he is in the light, we have fellowship one with another, and the blood of Jesus Christ his Son cleanseth us from all sin."*

Bible Result of Lot's Wrong Choice: *"For that righteous man* [Lot] *dwelling among them, in seeing and hearing, vexed his righteous soul from day to day with their unlawful deeds." —II Peter 2:8*

Read Genesis 17–19
Family Reading: Genesis 17

The God Who Is Enough

There are thirteen years between Genesis 16:16 and Genesis 17:1. As far as the record goes, God was silent in the life of Abram all of those years. In Genesis 16 Abram had resorted to the flesh in an effort to have a son. Because of this, Abram experienced an awful silence from God for thirteen years.

Then God appeared unto Abram as the Almighty God (Genesis 17:1). The name for God in the Hebrew is *El Shaddai, the breasted one.* Just as an infant must rely on its mother's breast for nourishment and strength, so the believer can rely on *El Shaddai* as the strength-giver and the satisfier of his life. God wants to be the Almighty God in each of our lives. He can be just that if we will yield our all to Him.

Someone has translated *El Shaddai* as *The God who is enough.* Amen! I like that. He is enough for my every need. Genesis 17 reveals Him as the One who in grace will meet every requirement in my life. Below I list the things God promised to Abram:

"And I will make my covenant . . ." (v. 2).
" . . . and I will multiply thee exceedingly . . ." (v. 2).
"And I will make thee exceeding fruitful . . ." (v. 6).
"And I will make nations of thee . . ." (v. 6).
"And I will establish my covenant . . ." (v. 7).
"And I will give unto thee . . ." (v. 8).
" . . . and I will be their God . . ." (v. 8).
"And I will bless her . . ." (v. 16).

God does it all. Man can do nothing except receive of the grace of the God who is enough. May we rest on His grace completely.

> *His love has no limit, His grace has no measure,*
> *His pow'r has no boundary known unto men;*
> *For out of His infinite riches in Jesus*
> *He giveth and giveth and giveth again.*

> — *Annie Johnson Flint*

January 7

Read Genesis 20–22
Family Reading: Genesis 22

God Tested Abraham

Abraham's life is marked by four great spiritual crises in which Abraham needed to surrender something that was naturally dear to him. First, he surrendered his native land and family (Genesis 12:1). Second, he was called on to surrender Lot (Genesis 13). Third, he had to relinquish his cherished hope for Ishmael (Genesis 17:17,18). The fourth big test is this one presented in Chapter 22 in which Abraham was asked to surrender Isaac for an offering to the Lord.

The life of every believer will always be a series of tests. It is only by discipline in our lives that God develops Christian character. Abraham had one supreme testing for which the previous ones were training and preparing—when he was called on to offer Isaac. God does not ask for our intellect, our talents, or our money, but our hearts. *"But lay up for yourselves treasures in heaven, where neither moth nor rust doth corrupt, and where thieves do not break through nor steal: For where your treasure is, there will your heart be also" (Matthew 6:20,21).* He wants our hearts, and then He will have all of us.

In this passage God was proving Abraham's faith and faithfulness. When God saw Abraham was going to carry out the orders God had given, He commanded Abraham to refrain from laying a hand on Isaac. Then God said, *" . . . now I know that thou fearest God . . . " (v. 12).*

God will also put us to the test. In verse one God states that He did this *" . . . after these things . . . "* It was after Abraham had received God's blessing that God permitted a test to see if he meant to glorify the Lord.

Bible Truth for Today: *"My brethren, count it all joy when ye fall into divers temptations; Knowing this, that the trying of your faith worketh patience." —James 1:2,3*

January 8

Read Genesis 23 and 24
Family Reading: Genesis 24:1-25

Abraham's Servant—A Picture of a Soulwinner

Genesis 24 recounts the story of the servant going to receive a bride for Abraham's son Isaac. This servant presents a picture of the believer laboring as a soulwinner. Let's note some truths revealed here about soulwinners:

First, the soulwinner is sent by God. Abraham commanded his servant, " . . . *thou shalt go . . . " (v. 4).* The servant was sent; therefore, he pictures the soulwinner.

Second, the soulwinner must be separated to be used of God. Abraham warned the servant, " . . . *Beware that thou bring not my son thither again" (v. 6).* The servant was not to take the son into the far country, just as a successful soulwinner will not engage in worldly activity, thereby dragging Christ into the world.

Third, the soulwinner must be submissive. The servant put his hand under Abraham's thigh and swore to him concerning his seeking a bride for Isaac. He agreed to be obedient to God's direction (v. 9).

Fourth, the soulwinner must be spiritual. This servant knelt down and prayed to God. The Lord honored that prayer and did answer according to the servant's request (v. 11).

Fifth, the soulwinner must be surrendered. This servant trusted the Lord and waited on God for His leadership.

Sixth, the soulwinner needs to be steadfast. He sought for a decision and would not be hindered until he had the decision.

Bible Truth for Today: *"The fruit of the righteous is a tree of life; and he that winneth souls is wise." —Proverbs 11:30*

January 9

Read Genesis 25 and 26
Family Reading: Genesis 25:19-34

Why Did Esau Despise His Birthright?

The last words of Genesis 25 read: *" . . . thus Esau despised his birthright" (v. 24)*. Why did he despise his birthright? Esau was a man of the flesh and not of faith. The birthright involved a spiritual blessing; and Esau revealed his lack of appreciation for spiritual things when he asked, *". . . what profit shall this birthright do to me?" (v. 32)*. There are two facts presented in verse twenty-seven revealing the reasons why Esau despised his birthright:

1. He was a hunter.
   Hunting in the Word of God carries an evil connotation. There are two hunters in the Bible—both evil men: Nimrod and Esau. Nimrod was a rebel, and Esau despised his birthright. Hunting in the Bible involves the idea of hunting for souls. Psalm 140:11 states, *". . . evil shall hunt the violent man to overthrow him."*

2. Esau was also *" . . . a man of the field . . . " (v. 27)*.
   Matthew 13:38 says, *"The field is the world . . . "* Esau's mind was set on the world. It was no wonder that he despised his birthright. Because he loved the world and all of its attractions, he asked, *" . . . what profit shall this birthright do to me?"* Esau was a man who lived for and after the flesh. He could not establish proper values because he was not walking in the Spirit. In Hebrews 12:16,17 God calls Esau a fornicator and a profane person because he loved the world.

Bible Truth for Today: *"Love not the world, neither the things that are in the world. If any man love the world, the love of the Father is not in him."* —*I John 2:15*

January 10

Read Genesis 27–29
Family Reading: Genesis 27:1-25

Jacob, the Supplanter

Genesis 27 is the story of Jacob stealing the blessing from Esau. Esau tells his father, Isaac, that the name *Jacob* suits his brother because Jacob supplanted him twice by taking away his birthright and his blessing (v. 36). The word *supplanter* means one who by trickery or treachery supersedes another. Jacob used trickery to get the blessing.

The whole story of Genesis 27 is an account of fleshly activity and work. Isaac was a man who catered to the flesh. Three times we read that he loved savory meat (vv. 4, 9, and 14). The problem of this chapter arose because Isaac desired flesh and its benefits. Then we see that Rebekah, Jacob's mother, was a schemer and a trickster. She developed the whole wicked scheme of having Jacob dressed in goats' skins and Esau's clothes to deceive Isaac. She led her son to lie and cheat. No wonder Jacob had such a battle with being honest all of his life.

Note some of the wicked deception of Jacob:

1. He used stolen clothes (v. 15).
2. He lied to his father by saying, " . . . *I am Esau thy firstborn; I have done according as thou badest me . . . " (v. 19)*.
3. He repeated the lie in verse twenty-four when he again stated positively that he was Esau. One lie always needs another to cover up the first one.
4. He blamed his sin and wickedness on God. *"And Isaac said unto his son, How is it that thou hast found it so quickly, my son? And he* [Jacob] *said, Because the Lord thy God brought it to me" (v. 20)*. This dreadful wickedness is literally taking God's name in vain to blame sin on Him.

Jacob was dishonest, and he lacked character to make his life right. He built sin upon sin in ruining his life. Each of us must be careful not to allow sin to take root in our lives.

Bible Truth for Today: *"And we know that all things work together for good to them that love God, to them who are the called according to his purpose." —Romans 8:28*

January 11

Read Genesis 30 and 31
Family Reading: Genesis 30:1-24

Beware of Envy

Envy is a bitter foe to spirituality in our lives. As we look at Rachel's life, we see what a dreadful toll envy claimed in her life. Genesis tells us that Rachel envied her sister. Note these warnings from God's Word about envy:

*"A sound heart is the life of the flesh: but **envy the rottenness of the bones**." — Proverbs 14:30*

*"Let us not be desirous of vain glory, provoking one another, **envying one another**." — Galatians 5:26*

In I Corinthians 13:4 we learn that love envies not. Where there is envy, there is no love; and where there is Scriptural love, envy flees.

James begged believers in Christ not to envy: *"But if ye have **bitter envying** and strife in your hearts, **glory not**, and lie not against the truth" (James 3:14).*

Envy always brings other sins in its train. This is exactly what happened with Rachel. She fretted against God. She spoke to Jacob: *" . . . Give me children, or else I die" (v. 1).* Only God can give children. Psalm 127:3 states that *" . . . children are an heritage of the Lord . . . "* Any children we have are gifts from God. How foolish for Rachel to fret. But further she asked for death. I would suppose she was literally threatening to commit suicide. Also, she did not ask for just one child. She insisted on children—more than one. She envied her sister and wanted the blessing her sister had. She should have said, "Lord, I will be content with whatever God sends me." Hebrews 13:5 instructs us to *" . . . be content with such things as ye have: for he hath said, I will never leave thee, nor forsake thee."* Love and contentment will deliver us from envy and all of its companion sins.

Bible Truth for Today: *"Let not thine heart envy sinners: but be thou in the fear of the Lord all the day long." —Proverbs 23:17*

"For wrath killeth the foolish man, and envy slayeth the silly one."

—Job 5:2

January 12

Read Genesis 32–34
Family Reading: Genesis 32

Broken to Bless

Jacob faced one of the biggest tests of his life. Soon he was to meet Esau, who came with four hundred men. Verse seven states that when Jacob learned of his brother's approach, he *" . . . was greatly afraid and distressed . . . "* So he started working on a plan to handle the situation.

It is good to note that Jacob prayed, but his mistake was that he planned before he prayed. His prayer begins at verse nine, but his plan started in verse seven. We ought always to have prayer precede our plans. His prayer was a good prayer. He began by quoting God's promise; and then in verse ten he confessed, *"I am not worthy . . . "* I am sure that his crooked dealings and trickery came before him. And, praise God, our God is full of mercy, always ready to forgive when one comes with a heart broken over sin. Jacob also confessed that he had done much of his work in the strength of the flesh. He prayed, *" . . . with my staff I passed over this Jordan . . . " (v. 10).* Then he prayed for deliverance. This was right, but I wonder if he was totally sincere. He had hardly finished the prayer when he reverted to the plan on which he had been busy before he prayed. Jacob's first thought was always a plan. It is best to pray and then wait on God.

That night something unusual happened. Jacob carried out his plan of dividing his company. Then verse twenty-four states that Jacob was left alone. At that time he was brought into a wrestling match that lasted till daybreak. Many have misunderstood this, thinking it is a testimony of Jacob's earnestness in prayer. No, it does not say Jacob wrestled, but rather, *" . . . there wrestled a man with him . . . "* God was dealing with Jacob to take away his self-trust. For a time Jacob held his own and God saw that He did not prevail against him. Then God touched his thigh. He broke Jacob's strength, and Jacob went from resisting to clinging. Because he held on, Jacob's name was changed to *Israel,* which means, *"prince with God."* Neither Jacob nor anyone else can become the prince with God until he is broken before God. May each of us be willing for God to break us.

Bible Principle for Today: *"The Lord is nigh unto them that are of a broken heart; and saveth such as be of a contrite spirit." —Psalm 34:18*

January 13

Read Genesis 35 and 36
Family Reading: Genesis 35

Back to Bethel

During his sojourn in Haran, Jacob had permitted sin in the flesh to rule his life. In Genesis 31:13 Jacob recounted that the God of Bethel had commanded him to come back to Bethel and to the land of his kindred. He had gone as far as Shalem (Genesis 33:18) and there had settled down. However, Genesis 34 recounts the tragic situation that arose because he had bordered on the edge of the world. Now in Genesis 35:1 God again commands him, " . . . *Arise, go up to Bethel, and dwell there . . .* "

Bethel was the place where Jacob saw the ladder vision and where he met the Lord. Since that experience, he had journeyed a long way and lived in the fellowship of those who knew not the Lord. He had not grown spiritually, and he still carried the problems of his selfish, fleshly nature. He had left his first love and needed to return to the place where he had met God. Jacob needed to heed God's definite command to " . . . *Put away the strange gods that are among you, and be clean . . .* " *(v. 2).* In leaving his first love and backsliding, he had let strange gods come into his life. God wanted him to return to Bethel and honor the Lord.

When he did return, he built an altar and called it *El-beth-el (v. 7).* When he first met God, it was *"Bethel,"* which means *"the house of God."* Now it meant much more. It was *"El-Beth-el,"* which means *"the God of the house of God."* He now had a personal relationship with God, rather than just an experience on which to rely.

Bible Truth for Today: *"Return, ye backsliding children, and I will heal your backslidings. Behold, we come unto thee; for thou art the Lord our God." —Jeremiah 3:22*

January 14

Read Genesis 37–39
Family Reading: Genesis 37:1-27

The Danger of Hatred

The story of Joseph is interesting to young and old alike. This chapter shows the wicked results of envy and hatred. Joseph's brothers hated him because his father had given him what is called in the King James Version " . . . *a coat of many colors*" *(v. 3)*. Literally, it was a coat of many pieces. It was actually a garment that had sleeves. As Jacob gave this coat to Joseph, it was a significant act that showed remarkable distinction for Joseph. This full garment with sleeves came to the ankles. The regular workman's garment was one that came to the knees and had no sleeves, thereby enabling a man to set about his work. This tunic with sleeves clearly marked the wearer as a person of special distinction. It meant that Jacob was placing the birthright on Joseph—the eldest son of Rachel, Jacob's beloved wife. Very likely, Joseph had spent time listening to Jacob tell him the stories about his life and his ancestors. Jacob had a special love for this son and was giving him the privileges of the first born.

The hatred of his brothers was magnified when Joseph had two dreams which he related, indicating that his father, mother, and brothers would bow down to him.

We see something of the character of Joseph when we note in verse thirteen that he immediately obeyed his father in accepting the call to go visit the brethren. When the brothers saw him approaching, they came up with a wicked scheme to murder him. They took off this coat of many pieces—the thing that made them hate him so—and cast him into a pit, and " . . . *sat down to eat bread* . . . " *(v. 25)*. His cries for help were coming out of the pit, but they sat down to eat bread. They had no compassion, no concern. What a dreadful thing is hatred and bitterness when it takes over a life.

Today, examine your life. Has any hatred or bitterness come in against others, particularly against any member of your family? Guard this. It can ruin your life.

Bible Warning for Today: *"Looking diligently lest any man fail of the grace of God; lest any root of bitterness springing up trouble you, and thereby many be defiled."* *—Hebrews 12:15*

January 15

Read Genesis 40 and 41
Family Reading: Genesis 41:9-16, 33-48, 55-57

Joseph's Exaltation

The chief butler had been restored to Pharaoh's household. He was to remember Joseph was still in prison. Somehow the butler forgot until two years later when Pharaoh had a dream. All of this must have been in the will of God. He told Pharaoh about Joseph at just the right time so that Joseph could come and reveal the secret to Pharaoh. God's Word teaches us that His plan will always prove best.

Joseph always exalted the Lord. He told Pharaoh, *" . . . It is not in me: God shall give Pharaoh an answer of peace" (v. 16).* Joseph became the great man that he was because he was humble and willing to submit all to the direction of the Spirit of God.

When a man relies on the Holy Spirit, the world will know that the Spirit of God is in him. Pharaoh asked, *" . . . Can we find such a one as this is, a man in whom the Spirit of God is?" (v. 38).* Pharaoh further recognized that there was none so wise or discreet as Joseph (v. 39).

Following the revealing of the dream, Joseph was exalted. Here he continues to be a picture of our Lord Jesus Christ. He had been in the prison and now is exalted on the right hand of Pharaoh. Pharaoh made Joseph ruler over the land. He gave him the insignia of his office with a ring, vestures of fine linen, and a gold chain around his neck. As he rode in the chariot, everyone was commanded to bow before him. We think of the Lord Jesus Christ, who underwent suffering for us but who someday shall be highly exalted. And every knee shall bow before Him, and every tongue shall confess Him Lord to the glory of God the Father.

Bible Truth for Today: *"Wherefore God also hath highly exalted him, and given him a name which is above every name."*

—Philippians 2:9

January 16

Read Genesis 42–44
Family Reading: Genesis 44

Repentance Essential

As the prime-minister of Egypt, Joseph had been dealing with those who rejected him. These brothers who had sinned by selling Joseph to the Midianites did not realize who this prime-minister was. In dealing with them, Joseph knew there could be no reconciliation without repentance. Joseph had his silver cup placed in Benjamin's sack.

They had not gone far on their journey home when Joseph's steward overtook them and inquired about the cup. They all claimed innocence; and when the cup was discovered in Benjamin's sack, they were shocked in disbelief. With hearts trembling with fear, these brothers were led back to the presence of Joseph. Perhaps the very silver in this cup reminded them of the twenty pieces of silver they received from the Midianite merchantmen when they sold Joseph (Genesis 37:28).

Judah stepped to the front. He was the one who perpetrated the conspiracy to sell Joseph to the Midianites (Genesis 37:26, 27). His conscience was bothering him. He confessed, " . . . *God hath found out the iniquity of thy servants . . . " (v. 16).* Judah had anticipated that the sin would be found out. Nobody is going to get away with sin. God has His way of dealing with those who work contrary to His will. Judah and his brethren had bowed down to Joseph just as God said they would. They now knew how wicked their sin had really been. Judah made the confession of sin and manifested the repentance that was necessary for reconciliation.

Judah offered to become surety for Benjamin—thus giving one more example of Christ taking our place at the cross and becoming our surety. Because of Judah's strong confession, Joseph revealed himself to his brethren (Genesis 45). Before this could happen, God had to bring these men to a place of repentance.

Bible Truth for Today: *"I tell you, Nay: but, except ye repent, ye shall all likewise perish."* —*Luke 13:3*

January 17

Read Genesis 45–47
Family Reading: Genesis 46

Faith Versus Fears

I am sure that as Israel was heading down into Egypt, he had some real fears and questions. In spite of all his sinful and scheming life, Israel was a man of faith. God had given him the new name, Israel, because he was a man of faith. He manifested this faith even as he began his journey toward Egypt. He *" . . . offered sacrifices unto the God of his father Isaac."* He had a spiritual desire to honor the Lord.

In verse one the Scripture uses his name *Israel*. In verse two he is referred to as *Jacob*. Why? In verse one he is manifesting his faith and the new nature by offering sacrifice. In verse two he reveals the old nature because of his fears. We believers today have the same two natures. We have the Jacob nature, the old nature, often called *"the old man."* And then we have the new nature through the new birth, called *"the new man" (Ephesians 4:22-24)*. God wants us all to walk in the energy of the Israel nature and not to succumb to the wiles of the Jacob nature.

God told Jacob not to be afraid (v. 3). God's promise was that He would go with him and bring his posterity back again into the land of promise.

Verse four gives God's promise to Jacob: *" . . . and Joseph shall put his hand upon thine eyes . . . "* Herein was the secret of blessing to Israel. Jacob and his sons and all their families were carried down into Egypt because all their hopes were centered in Joseph. They wanted to be near him, to revel in his glory and in his exaltation. They received a joyous welcome, not because they were Canaanites, not because Abraham was their father, not because of their own family distinction, but simply because they were related to Joseph.

Joseph is the picture of our Lord Jesus Christ. All we have is in Christ because we are His. May we long to be near Him and to rejoice in His glory.

Bible Truth for Today: *"And he is the head of the body, the church: who is the beginning, the firstborn from the dead; that in all things he might have the preeminence."* — *Colossians 1:18*

January 18

Read Genesis 48–50
Family Reading: Genesis 50

A Man of Character

What a difference character makes in a man. In this passage we have a contrast between the character of Joseph and that of his deceitful and conniving brothers. When Jacob died, the brothers were fearful that Joseph would wreak vengeance on them. Humanly speaking, they deserved it. And certainly with the type of character they had, they would have wrought vengeance had they been in Joseph's place. They had done evil to Joseph, and they never forgot that. They could not understand that a man of such character would not hold a bitter spirit over ill treatment.

Instead of being bitter, Joseph told them that what his brothers had done to him was used of God to be a blessing. The Lord had used it in Joseph's life to save many people alive and thereby do great good. Joseph's concern was the will of God, not the flighty fancies of men.

Therefore, Joseph counseled them: " . . . *fear ye not: I will nourish you, and your little ones . . .* " *(v. 21).* He did not hold a bitter spirit but rather forgave them. He left vengeance with God and reacted with kindness to his brothers. Joseph recognized that what others do to us is not nearly so important as how we respond to what they do. Good character traits demand that we not be retaliatory. We can always believe the truth of Proverbs 15:1— *"A soft answer turneth away wrath: but grievous words stir up anger."* Character always stands in sharp contrast to the cheap, gaudy looseness of the world. Joseph's brothers were full of fear because they had not acted according to God's principles. Joseph could stand boldly and sweetly because he had honored the Lord and lived with Biblical character. Oh, that we might have real character as Joseph did.

Character Verses:

"The name of the Lord is a strong tower: the righteous runneth into it, and is safe." —*Proverbs 18:10*

"The spirit of a man will sustain his infirmity; but a wounded spirit who can bear?" —*Proverbs 18:14*

January 19

Read Exodus 1–3
Family Reading: Exodus 1

Redemption

Years ago when I was a boy, there was a leading radio program called "Major Bowes' Amateur Hour." The program featured outstanding amateur talent from across America. One night they had a ten-year-old genius on the program. Major Bowes asked the boy, "Son, what do you think is the greatest truth ever given?" The boy thought a short time and then spoke, surprising Major Bowes and, I am sure, a number of listeners. He said, "Sir, I believe the greatest truth ever presented is **redemption**."

Amen! That boy was right. Redemption—there is no greater truth. Redemption lifts us from the pits of sin into the glory of the Lord Jesus Christ. Exodus begins with moans and groans but ends with glory. This is redemption.

To redeem means to buy back. The Israelites were slaves under Egyptian bondage. God delivered them from their slavery and gave them a land of their own. They were redeemed by God.

God saw men in the bondslavery of sin. He paid the price to buy them back by having His own Son, the Lord Jesus Christ, shed His blood on the cross. We are redeemed through His sacrifice: *"In whom we have redemption through his blood . . ."* (Ephesians 1:7).

In Exodus 1 we see Israel in bondage. Through the first eleven chapters, that bondage grows worse. But in Chapter 12, Israel is redeemed from bondage through the blood of the lamb. That lamb pictures God's Lamb, the Lord Jesus Christ.

> *Redeemed, how I love to proclaim it!*
> *Redeemed by the blood of the Lamb;*
> *Redeemed through His infinite mercy,*
> *His child, and forever, I am.*

Bible Truth for Today: *"Christ hath redeemed us from the curse of the law, being made a curse for us: for it is written, Cursed is every one that hangeth on a tree." — Galatians 3:13*

January 20

Read Exodus 4–6
Family Reading: Exodus 4

What Is That in Thine Hand?

In Exodus 4 God answered the questions that Moses presented to Him in Chapter 3. The first question was, *"Who am I?" (Exodus 3:11).* The second question was, "Who shall I say has sent me?" (Exodus 3:13). Moses felt inadequate for the task of leading Israel out of bondage; yet, God had said, *" . . . bring forth my people . . . out of Egypt" (Exodus 3:10).*

In Chapter 4 God asked Moses, *"What is that in thine hand?" (v. 2).* Moses held a rod, a shepherd's crook. This was not a fancy instrument. In fact, it was a despised tool in Egypt, for shepherds were an abomination to the Egyptians (Genesis 46:34). God was saying to Moses that He did not need a fancy instrument. Instead, He could use that which was despised to do His work. *"But God hath chosen the foolish things . . . the weak things . . . And base things of the world, and things which are despised, hath God chosen . . . That no flesh should glory in his presence" (I Corinthians 1:27-29).*

God is not looking for great talent, but rather for sincere dedication. God uses what we already have, not what we might get.

> *What is that in thine hand, Moses?*
> *Moses answered, "A rod."*
> *God was saying, "Dedicate it to Me.*
> *Use it and I will bless."*
> *What is that in thine hand, David? — A sling.*
> *God used it to defeat Goliath.*
> *What is that in thine hand, Gideon? — A pitcher.*
> *God used it to defeat the Midianites.*
> *What is that in thine hand, Martin Luther? — A parchment.*
> *He nailed it to the door, and the Reformation began.*
> *What is that in thine hand, Bunyan? — A pen.*
> *What great works came out of his prison cell!*

God can use you. Give Him what you have. Dear reader, what is in your hand today?

Bible Truth for Today: *"I beseech you therefore, brethren, by the mercies of God, that ye present your bodies a living sacrifice, holy, acceptable unto God, which is your reasonable service."*

—Romans 12:1

January 21

Read Exodus 7–9
Family Reading: Exodus 7:14-25; 8:5-7, 16-18; 9:8-12

Satan's Emissaries Defeated

"And the magicians could not stand before Moses because of the boils; for the boil was upon the magicians, and upon all the Egyptians." —*Exodus 9:11*

In II Timothy 3:8 we read, *"Now as Jannes and Jambres withstood Moses, so do these also resist the truth: men of corrupt minds, reprobate concerning the faith."* These two names are those of two magicians who worked miracles in Egypt. This verse says that Jannes and Jambres withstood Moses. Satan has many ways of endeavoring to defeat God's work. First, he tries it by open antagonism. In Exodus 1 and 2 we see Satan as a roaring lion endeavoring to destroy the baby Moses. God had the victory, and Satan could not win out. Then Satan endeavored to resist by having Pharaoh stand against Moses. This did not work either. Then we read that Satan used these magicians to withstand Moses. They withstood him, but not by having him put out of the king's palace or having him imprisoned or killed. Rather, they withstood him by duplicating his works.

When Satan does not have the victory as a roaring lion, he comes as an angel of light. (Please compare I Peter 5:8 and II Corinthians 11:13,14.) II Timothy 3 presents one mark of perilous times where men endeavor to duplicate the Lord's works. We see this today with many so-called *"cures"* and *"healings"* by *"miracle workers."* Generally, on investigating their claims, we find that they are not real. Some can be real because Satan has supernatural power.

We can always rest assured that God is going to win out. Satan's magicians are not going to triumph. Exodus 9:11 states that even the magicians had the boils and did not triumph in their withstanding of Moses. It will be so even today. The sorcerers that endeavor to withstand the work of God are going to be clearly manifested, and God is going to triumph. Praise God, He is going to win the battle.

Bible Truth for Today: *"And the God of peace shall bruise Satan under your feet shortly. The grace of our Lord Jesus Christ be with you. Amen."* —*Romans 16:20*

January 22

Read Exodus 10–12
Family Reading: Exodus 12:1-13, 21-33

The Passover

This first Passover pictures Jesus Christ, our Passover. He died on the cross in fulfillment of the type laid down in Exodus 12. The time of the Passover was to be the beginning of months, the first month of the year (v. 2). When we come to Christ and are washed in His blood, we have the real blessing of life, which begins with Calvary. Nothing else is so important as trusting Jesus Christ as our Lord and Saviour.

The Lamb was a type of Jesus Christ as follows:

1. *"Without blemish" (v. 5)*—Christ was the Lamb without blemish and without spot.

2. *"Male of the first year" (v. 5)*—Christ was taken in the prime of His life to die for us.

3. *"Out from the sheep or from the goats" (v. 5)*—Christ became a man to identify Himself with sinners.

4. *"Kept up until the fourteenth day" (v. 6)*—to be sure it was the lamb without blemish. Christ was tested in all points like as we are—yet without sin (Hebrews 4:15).

5. The lamb to be killed in the evening (v. 6) — *"Without shedding of blood is no remission" (Hebrews 9:22)*.

6. Strike the blood on the door posts and lintel (v. 7).

This last part tells us of the application of the blood. Though Christ has shed His blood, we must have it applied to our lives. The blood was in *"the basin" (v. 22), a threshold* or a lowered place to catch water and keep it from going into the house. The father would dip the hyssop in the basin at the bottom of the door and sprinkle it on the two side posts and the lintel. In doing this, he would have used a motion in the form of a cross. All of this pictured the fact that Christ died on a cross for us. The blood has been shed. Have you had it applied to your life?

Bible Truth for Today: *"The next day John seeth Jesus coming unto him, and saith, Behold the Lamb of God, which taketh away the sin of the world." —John 1:29*

January 23

Read Exodus 13–15
Family Reading: Exodus 14

God's Instruction for Victory

In Exodus 14:13 God instructed Israel: *". . . Fear ye not, stand still, and see the salvation of the Lord, which he will show to you today: for the Egyptians whom ye have seen today, ye shall see them again no more for ever."*

First: *"Fear ye not."* This is always God's instruction to His people. God wants His people to trust Him and, therefore, not fear. *"Fear not,"* God said to Abram (Genesis 15:1), to Joshua (Joshua 8:1), to Gideon (Judges 6:23), to the shepherds at Bethlehem (Luke 2:10), and to us today (Luke 12:32). How do we come to this place of not fearing? Isaiah 26:3 has the answer: *"Thou wilt keep him in perfect peace, whose mind is stayed on thee: because he trusteth in thee."*

Second: *"Stand still."* Israel was to realize that she could do nothing without God. Israel was hemmed in and faced a very serious trial. The power of the flesh cannot overcome. Self help is worthless. God must undertake. All that any of us can do in the face of serious testing is to stand still and let God work.

Third: *"See the salvation of the Lord."* This was an act of faith. They could see what God was going to do. The waters actually parted when Israel came to enter the sea. As they stood still, they were seeing by faith what God would do. They, like Moses, were trusting *" . . . as seeing him who is invisible" (Hebrews 11:27).*

In verse fifteen Moses was given a further command. He was to *" . . . speak . . . "* God always wants His man to speak up as he leads God's people. Then He says, *" . . . go forward."* They were to stand still, relying upon God's power and strength to perform the miracle. Then by faith they were to go forward and watch God work. Faith will have us stand still, and then faith will have us go forward.

Thot: Men who *stand still* **before** God *still stand* **for** God!

Bible Truth for Today: *"For their redeemer is mighty; he shall plead their cause with thee."* —*Proverbs 23:11*

January 24

Read Exodus 16–18
Family Reading: Exodus 16

The Daily Manna

Today we will consider the manna that God sent from Heaven for the Israelites as presented in Exodus 16. Verses seven and twenty-one state that they gathered it every morning. From these verses we get the title for this book, *My Morning Manna.*

The manna was given because the Israelites complained that they had nothing to eat in the wilderness. God promised them that He would rain bread from Heaven (v. 4). This manna provided by the Lord as dew from Heaven is a beautiful type of the food God has provided for our souls. This food is His own Word. Let's consider a few ways in which we see this type:

1. The manna was a supernatural gift — from Heaven and not of earth. So it is with the Bible (II Peter 1:21).

2. The manna came right to where the people were.
   It was right at hand, right before their eyes. So it is with the Word of God. It is readily accessible to all of us. Is it not a shame that in countries where it is much more difficult to get the Bible, it is prized more by the people?

3. The manna was to be eaten.
   It was not just to be looked at and admired. It had to be eaten. So the Bible is given to us to study and dig into its treasures.

4. The manna was gathered daily. We need His Word daily.

5. The manna was gathered by stooping.
   It did not grow upon trees. In order to obtain it, the Israelites had to bow down. To understand God's Word, we must come humbly to feed daily on His Word.

Bible Truth for Today: *"And now, brethren, I commend you to God, and to the word of his grace, which is able to build you up, and to give you an inheritance among all them which are sanctified."* — *Acts 20:32*

January 25

Read Exodus 19–21
Family Reading: Exodus 20

The Law and the Altar

Exodus 20 presents the law of God. These ten commandments give God's law, the perfect law that covers every area of life. Each commandment is important and joins with all of the other nine as well as complementing the other nine to make one complete and perfect whole. For example, the tenth commandment, *"Thou shalt not covet . . . "* *(v. 17).* depends on the first, *"Thou shalt have no other gods before me"* *(v. 3).* That person who has the Lord as his only God will not covet, nor will he commit murder, nor commit adultery.

Why even meditate on the Ten Commandments? Are they given to us to save us? No—there is no salvation in the law. It is given to reveal to us that we are sinners. *"Therefore by the deeds of the law there shall no flesh be justified in his sight: for by the law is the knowledge of sin"* *(Romans 3:20).* That is exactly why we need the law. It is God's moral standard for all time and a basis for God's judgment.

One of the failings of the day in which we live is a failure of those in pulpits to teach and preach the law of God. There it stands—as given on Mt. Sinai—not only for Israel in that day but for all people of all ages. And we dare not take away from it or change it. We would be tampering with that which God has given. God warned that men were not to use a tool on stones in God's altar (v. 25). Human wisdom delights to trim and arrange doctrine so it is more congenial to fallen man. But we must leave God's law untouched and God's altar of sacrifice, the cross, untouched. Believe the law and you will see the need for the altar. Take the law that convicts and the sacrifice that saves just as God's Word has given them.

> *Oh, the love that drew salvation's plan!*
> *Oh, the grace that brought it down to man!*
> *Oh, the mighty gulf that God did span at Calvary!*

Bible Truth for Today: *"Now we know that what things soever the law saith, it saith to them who are under the law: that every mouth may be stopped, and all the world may become guilty before God. Therefore by the deeds of the law there shall no flesh be justified in his sight: for by the law is the knowledge of sin." —Romans 3:19,20*

January 26

Read Exodus 22–24
Family Reading: Exodus 23:9-33

God's Leading

God promised to send His angel before Israel to direct and keep them. God has always gone with His people. In the great commission the Lord says, *". . . and, lo, I am with you alway . . . " (Matthew 28:20).* God's purpose in sending His angel before them was to keep them and lead them by His power into the place He had prepared for them. God has done the very same thing for us. He has saved us and kept us by His power and is also leading us to the place He has prepared for us.

The Lord does demand obedience from His people. If they obeyed Him, He would protect them from sickness and harm; He would bless their provisions and meet their need; and He would destroy the enemies before them. God said that He would even send hornets before them to drive out the enemies—but not immediately or all at one time. He said, *"By little and little I will drive them out from before thee, until thou be increased, and inherit the land" (v. 30).*

God's promised victory to His children does not happen hastily but takes time. God promises to drive out the enemies *by little and little.* He wants His children to claim victories, hold them, and then go on to new victories. Had the enemies been driven out immediately, the Israelites would not have had strength to overcome the beasts of the fields. As they grew, they developed strength to handle new victories.

> *All the way my Saviour leads me,*
> *Cheers each winding path I tread,*
> *Gives me grace for ev'ry trial,*
> *Feeds me with the living bread.*
> *Though my weary steps may falter,*
> *And my soul athirst may be,*
> *Gushing from the Rock before me,*
> *Lo! a spring of joy I see.*
> *—Fanny Crosby*

Bible Truth for Today: *"I am crucified with Christ: nevertheless I live; yet not I, but Christ liveth in me: and the life which I now live in the flesh I live by the faith of the Son of God, who loved me, and gave himself for me." —Galatians 2:20*

January 27

Read Exodus 25–27
Family Reading: Exodus 25

The Oil for the Lights

Today we begin reading about the tabernacle. I wish we had time in these daily devotionals to write in detail about the various parts of the tabernacle. Since that is not possible, our only comment will be that the entire tabernacle is a beautiful picture of Jesus Christ. All of the gold in the furnishings speaks of His deity. All of the wood speaks of His humanity. The tabernacle presents Him as the God-man who came to give Himself for our sins.

Twice in Chapter 25 the Lord commands Moses to build the tabernacle exactly according to His specifications (vv. 9,40). God wanted the tabernacle carefully constructed and assembled so that it would be the complete and perfect picture of Christ.

We find God's instructions concerning the golden lampstand (vv. 31-40). This is a picture of Jesus Christ in John 8:12, " . . . *I am the light of the world . . .* " In the tabernacle no light entered. The only light was that from the lampstand. The only light that can lighten our lives in the darkness of sin is the Lord Jesus Christ.

Moses was directed to see that there was oil for the lampstand (v. 6). This piece of furniture was really not a candlestick since it did not hold a candle. Instead, it was a lamp that burned oil. It was absolutely necessary that there be oil provided or the light would go out.

In our lives we need Christ as our Light. But for the light to continue to glow and bless, we need the oil of the Holy Spirit. We have no oil spring within ourselves. We need *"oil for the light"* just as Moses was commanded to provide for Israel (v. 6). The lamps needed to be fed the oil. In our lives we need fresh grace every day to see the need met for us to be His light in the world.

Truth, holiness, joy, knowledge, love—these are all beams of the sacred Light. However, we cannot give them forth unless in private we surrender to the Holy Spirit and have His oil within.

Bible Truth for Today: *"For ye were sometimes darkness, but now are ye light in the Lord: walk as children of light."* —Ephesians 5:8

January 28

Read Exodus 28 and 29
Family Reading: Exodus 29:1-21

Total Consecration

"Then shalt thou kill the ram, and take of his blood, and put it upon the tip of the right ear of Aaron, and upon the tip of the right ear of his sons, and upon the thumb of their right hand, and upon the great toe of their right foot, and sprinkle the blood upon the altar round about."

—Exodus 29:20

The blood of the ram was to be placed on the tip of the right ear, upon the thumb of the right hand, upon the big toe of the right foot of Aaron and his sons. Aaron, the high priest, and his sons, the priests, were to be cleansed for their work. Aaron is the type of Christ as our High Priest. Christ needed no cleansing, but Aaron as the type did need cleansing. We find the same application of the blood for the priests in Leviticus 8 and for the cleansed lepers in Leviticus 14. This application of the blood tells of important areas that need cleansing:

1. The ear—that which we hear. Our ears need to be cleansed and dedicated to God. What we hear has much to do with what we are. *"So then faith cometh by hearing . . ." (Romans 10:17).* Lot vexed his righteous soul by " . . . *seeing and hearing . . ." (II Peter 2:8).*

2. The thumb of the right hand—that which we do. Our works will declare our relationship to God. " . . . *faith without works is dead" (James 2:17, 20).* We must know that by grace we are saved; but when saved, " . . . *we are his workmanship, created in Christ Jesus unto good works . . ." (Ephesians 2:10).* Also, note verses eight and nine.

3. The great toe of the right foot—our walk as believers. The walk also must be consecrated to Christ. We need to walk " . . . *in love . . ." (Ephesians 5:2),* " . . . *as children of light" (v. 8),* and " . . . *circumspectly, not as fools, but as wise" (v. 15).* Our walk must be clean.

May each of us long for total consecration with our hearing, our work, and our walk yielded to Him.

Scriptural Consecration: *"If ye then be risen with Christ, seek those things which are above, where Christ sitteth on the right hand of God."*

—Colossians 3:1

January 29

Read Exodus 30–32
Family Reading: Exodus 32:1-28

Who Is on the Lord's Side?

"Then Moses stood in the gate of the camp, and said, Who is on the Lord's side? let him come unto me. And all the sons of Levi gathered themselves together unto him." —Exodus 32:26

Apostasy had entered the camp. Aaron had made a golden calf as an idol for Israel to worship. He had broken the second commandment which reads: *"Thou shalt not make unto thee any graven image, or any likeness of anything that is in heaven above, or that is in the earth beneath, or that is in the water under the earth. Thou shalt not bow down thyself to them, nor serve them . . . " (Exodus 20:4,5).* When Moses saw the golden calf and the dancing around it, he threw down the two tables of stone that he carried and they broke. This is a picture of James 2:10— *"For whosoever shall keep the whole law, and yet offend in one point, he is guilty of all."* As Moses broke the tables, he showed that Israel in breaking the second commandment was actually guilty of breaking all the law of God.

Moses realized Aaron had led the people astray. They had gone into sin. He threw out this challenge: *"Who is on the Lord's side? let him come unto me."* It was not time for compromise nor for concealment of the sin. Where there is open apostasy, there can be no neutrality because when the question is between God and Satan, neutrality is itself apostasy. Moses knew there must be a separation. He was speaking to God's people. They needed to stand for God and against sin.

Bible Truth for Today: *"Wherefore come out from among them, and be ye separate, saith the Lord, and touch not the unclean thing; and I will receive you, And will be a Father unto you, and ye shall be my sons and daughters, saith the Lord Almighty."* — II Corinthians 6:17, 18

January 30

Read Exodus 33 through 35:29
Family Reading: Exodus 33:1-22

The Blessing of His Presence

Moses wisely said, " . . . *If thy presence go not with me, carry us not up hence" (v. 15).* It would be well for us to say this to the Lord in every enterprise. How many distresses and difficulties would we avoid! How much more peaceful and comfortable should we be in life's journey!

It was a tremendous privilege for Moses to speak with the Lord face to face as with a friend (v. 11). Moses was the man of the law, but he was only so because he had come to know God's grace. God told Moses that he had found grace in the Lord's sight (v. 17). Because of God's grace, Moses could plead for God's faithful leadership.

" . . . *show me now thy way, that I may know thee . . . " (v. 13).* God answered that prayer, " . . . *My presence shall go with thee . . . " (v. 14).* Then Moses said, " . . . *If thy presence go not with me, carry us not up hence" (v. 15).* We should do the same as Moses. Let us ask ourselves, "Is the Lord with us in this pursuit? What is our chief aim?" Stop a moment and consider. Can you expect the presence of God in that which you are doing? Can you honestly lift up a believing heart in prayer to the Lord to accompany you? If you cannot ask Him to go with you, you certainly ought not go. It would have been better for Peter to have stayed in the Lord's presence with a cold body than to have warmed himself at the fire of the high priest's officers.

I read a story of Satan, who had taken over a young Christian's life. When he was asked how he dared to tackle a child of God, he replied, "I found her on my own playground at the movie theater. Therefore, I challenged her as my own servant." Christians have no business on the devil's playground.

The fact that Moses was blessed with the presence of God is manifested in verses twenty-one and twenty-two.

Bible Truth for Today: *"Go ye therefore, and teach all nations, baptizing them in the name of the Father, and of the Son, and of the Holy Ghost: Teaching them to observe all things whatsoever I have commanded you: and, lo, I am with you alway, even unto the end of the world. Amen. —Matthew 28:19,20*

January 31

Read Exodus 35:30 through Chapter 38
Family Reading: Exodus 35:30-35; 36:1-8; 38:21-23

God Uses Men

In Exodus 25–31 God gave Moses the instructions for building the tabernacle. Then in Exodus 35–40 we read about the actual construction of the tabernacle. Moses led the people to build the tabernacle exactly as God had instructed. Why did God give a double account of the tabernacle, first in Exodus 25–31 and then again in Exodus 35–40? Remember that every part of the tabernacle is a type of the Lord Jesus Christ. The Lord gave the account twice, showing us that all which was originally planned in Heaven has been or shall be accomplished on earth.

In the building of the tabernacle, God called a man by the name of Bezaleel to do the work. God called Aholiab to be his assistant in the work. Why were these men called?

First, we see they were called because **they were wise-hearted men**. Exodus 35:35 reads, *"Them hath he filled with wisdom of heart . . ."* Exodus 36:1 states, *"Then wrought Bezaleel and Aholiab, and every wise hearted man, in whom the Lord put wisdom and understanding . . ."* Proverbs states repeatedly that *" . . . the fear of the Lord is the beginning of wisdom."* These men honored the Lord, and He gave them wisdom.

Second, they were called because **they were willing-hearted men**. Exodus 36:2 says, *"And Moses called Bezaleel and Aholiab, and every wise hearted man, in whose heart the Lord had put wisdom, even **every one whose heart stirred him up** to come unto the work to do it."*

Third, they were called because **they were willing-handed men**. A wise heart and a willing heart are proved by willing hands. In Exodus 38:22 God states that Bezaleel *" . . . made all that the Lord commanded Moses."* These men had ability, but they were willing to follow the directions God had given and the leader God had appointed. This gives one big reason for the success of the building of the tabernacle.

Bible Truth for Today: The Type of Man Whom God Uses: God said, *" . . . I have found David the son of Jesse, a man after mine own heart, which shall fulfill all my will."* —Acts 13:22

February 1

Read Exodus 39 and 40
Family Reading: Exodus 40:16-38

The Tabernacle Constructed

The last five chapters present the building of the tabernacle. In Exodus 36–39 God reveals the preparation of all the materials for the setting up of the tabernacle. In Chapter 40 Moses leads in the assembling of the tabernacle.

Please note how often the Scripture records that work was done *"as the Lord commanded Moses."* This phrase is used in verses 16, 19, 21, 23, 25, 27, 29, and 32. Moses was careful to do the work according to the direction of the Lord. Hebrews 3:5 states that Moses was *" . . . faithful in all his house, as a servant, for a testimony of those things which were to be spoken after."* God wanted all to know that Moses carefully and faithfully carried out all the instructions of God. We, too, are to obey completely and faithfully the Word of God. Faithfulness is that which pleases the Lord. *"Moreover it is required in stewards, that a man be found faithful"* (I Corinthians 4:2).

When Moses finished the work, *"Then a cloud covered the tent of the congregation, and the glory of the Lord filled the tabernacle"* *(v. 34).* Again in verse thirty-five God states that *" . . . the glory of the Lord filled the tabernacle."*

Why did God fill the tabernacle with His glory? First, He filled it because Moses and the people had been faithful. Had they failed to obey God completely, there would not have been this glory upon the tabernacle. Second, God filled the tabernacle because every item was anointed (vv. 9-15). God wanted each item anointed because each pictured the person of Christ. The anointing oil pictured the person, the presence, and the power of the Holy Spirit. The tabernacle, being covered with a cloud and being moved as the cloud moved, speaks of the fact that all of the ministry of Christ was under the direction of the Holy Spirit. To be used of God, we also need to be filled with the Spirit.

Bible Truth for Today: *"For Christ is not entered into the holy places made with hands, which are the figures of the true; but into heaven itself, now to appear in the presence of God for us."*

—Hebrews 9:24

February 2

Read Leviticus 1–4
Family Reading: Leviticus 2

The Life and Death of Our Lord

We are now reading in the book of Leviticus. Please do not consider the book dry and uninteresting. I read of a Bedouin woman who found a treasure of one million dollars in the desert sand of El Alamein. You can find spiritual treasure in the book of Leviticus.

In the first five chapters of Leviticus, we find five offerings: the burnt offering, the meal offering, the peace offering, the sin offering, and the trespass offering. All five offerings picture Jesus Christ, who alone can take away sin.

Chapter 2 reveals the meat offering—better translated *"meal"* offering, for there was no meat in it. This meal offering presents the perfect life of Christ. It was made of finely ground flour—no sharp or rough edges. He lived a perfect life in our place and as our example. In the burnt offering of Leviticus 1, we find a picture of Christ dying for our sins. In this meal offering of Leviticus, we have the beautiful picture of the Lord as He lived and walked and served on earth. He lived a perfect life in our place. He died an atoning death for our sins. We must have both the atoning death and the perfect life.

Bible Truth for Today: *"But we see Jesus, who was made a little lower than the angels for the suffering of death, crowned with glory and honor; that he by the grace of God should taste death for every man." —Hebrews 2:9*

February 3

Read Leviticus 5–7
Family Reading: Leviticus 5:14-19; 6:1-7

Trespass Offering

Every sin is a trespass against God, an offense to the very majesty of Heaven. It is a trespass against the holy government of our God. Righteousness demands that amends be paid or the trespasser be shut away from the presence of God. Jesus Christ paid that debt in our place. He is our trespass offering.

The important truth to realize is that even though a person does not know that he has committed a trespass, he is still guilty. Leviticus 5:17 states " . . . *though he wist* [knew] *it not, yet is he guilty, and shall bear his iniquity.*" God's Word is the standard of judgment. God holds man responsible for the light he has been given. How guilty will men be who have the Bible and have never read it!

We note in Leviticus 6:2 that a sin against our neighbor is a sin against the Lord. When he restores, he is to restore more than he took. (Note Leviticus 6:5.) Praise God, when Jesus died, He restored man. The grace of God has been magnified through Him.

Gypsy Smith told a story of a strong man who came into one of his meetings weeping. The man cried, "Oh, sir, my sin is too great ever to be forgiven." Quick as a flash, the preacher said, "But His grace is greater than all your sin." Dr. Towner, the musician for the meetings, heard it and caught the words. He walked home and wrote this song:

> *Marvelous grace of our loving Lord,*
> *Grace that exceeds our sin and our guilt,*
> *Yonder on Calvary's mount outpoured,*
> *There where the blood of the Lamb was spilt.*
> *Grace, grace, God's grace,*
> *Grace that will pardon and cleanse within;*
> *Grace, grace, God's grace,*
> *Grace that is greater than all our sin.*

Bible Truth for Today: *"But if we walk in the light, as he is in the light, we have fellowship one with another, and the blood of Jesus Christ his Son cleanseth us from all sin." —I John 1:7*

February 4

Read Leviticus 8–10
Family Reading: Leviticus 10

Taking Spiritual Things for Granted

Nadab and Abihu were the sons of the high priest. Because they were around spiritual things all of the time, they began to take spiritual things for granted. There was no reality of spiritual things in their lives. One day they decided they could take matters in their own hands and go into the Holy of Holies to offer incense. Leviticus 16:1, 2 seems to imply that they did go behind the veil where only Aaron, the high priest, was to go; and he was permitted to do so only once a year.

God smote both Nadab and Abihu with fire, and they were killed instantly. I believe God permitted them to try to flee from the tabernacle. They got just past the door when they were smitten. Moses commanded his cousins to carry their bodies *from before the sanctuary . . . " (v. 4).* This means they had dashed out of the tabernacle in an effort to flee. But God wanted Aaron and Moses and the camp of Israel to know that no one can treat God's Word and will lightly. Verse three states that " *. . . Aaron held his peace."* He knew these two sons had rebelled at the command of the Lord. He fully realized that the punishment was just. He had no argument with God about it.

How often this same thing happens today. Young people reared in a Christian home take the blessings of the Lord for granted. Far too often this is true of youth in a Christian school. They live with a lukewarm testimony and refuse to yield themselves to Christ. Nadab's name means *"volunteer soldier,"* and Abihu's name means *"worshiper."* Here were two young men who could have been used of God but were killed because they took all of their blessings and privileges from God on a commonplace level.

Character Verse: *"As righteousness tendeth to life: so he that pursueth evil pursueth it to his own death." —Proverbs 11:19*

Read Leviticus 11–13
Family Reading: Leviticus 11:1-8, 35-47

The Fact of Sin

Leviticus is a book of *atonement*. Chapter 16 presents the great day of atonement in Israel. To prepare for that, the previous chapters present various truths. First, there are the offerings in Chapters 1–7 which picture Christ as the sacrifice atoning for sin. Second, Chapters 8–10 tell us about the priests, their clothing, and their ministry.

These are the two necessary ingredients for an atonement: an offering and a priesthood. They take us through Chapter 10. It would seem that since the offering and priesthood have been presented in these first ten chapters, the day of atonement could be given in Chapter 11, but it does not appear until Chapter 16. Instead, God gives five chapters, 11–15, to discuss that which is unclean. The offerings and the priesthood are important, but there is one more truth that must be presented—the fact of sin. That is the truth that is presented in these five chapters.

Though the offerings had been revealed and though the priesthood had been established, the Israelites still needed to understand the reality of sin and the facts of uncleanness. Similarly, though Christ has already been made the offering for sin and though Christ is our High Priest, we still must face the fact of our sin before we can be reconciled to God. Not until we see our sin will we come to God for forgiveness and cleansing.

Chapter 11 presents different marks of uncleanness. If an animal did not have a parted hoof or did not chew the cud, it was unclean. The animal needed to walk right and eat right. To be clean, one must feed on the Word of God and walk with a testimony for God. Two things could not be made unclean. A fountain of water would not become unclean by contact with a dead animal (v. 36). The fountain of water is a picture of the Holy Spirit, and He can never be made unclean. Also, sowing seed would not be contaminated by a dead body (v. 37). Sowing seed speaks of the Word of God. Neither the Holy Spirit nor the Word of God can be defiled. As believers in Christ, we must rely on God's Word and on the Holy Spirit to keep us from sin.

February 6

Read Leviticus 14 and 15
Family Reading: Leviticus 14:1-20

The Cleansing of the Leper

Leviticus 14 presents the ceremony of the cleansing of the leper. The words *"cleanse," "cleansed," "cleansing,"* and *"clean"* appear twenty-four times in this chapter.

The only one who could make the leper clean was the priest. Our High Priest is the Lord Jesus Christ. He is the only One who can cleanse us from the leprosy of sin.

Note the priest's actions: *"Then shall the **priest** command to take . . . " (v. 4); "And the **priest** shall take . . . " (vv. 14, 15); "And the **priest** shall dip . . . " (v. 16).*

If you will read through the chapter carefully and thoughtfully, you will find that all of the action is on the part of the priest, not on the part of the leper. Cleansing comes only by the priest. In verse two we see the leper must be brought to the priest. So the Holy Spirit is the One who woos the sinner to Christ.

The priest went forth to the leper (v. 3). This is exactly what Jesus did: He came from Heaven into the vile world of sin, became a man, and suffered for sin. The priest went out of the camp (v. 3). Jesus Christ suffered outside the gate (Hebrews 13:12, 13).

The priest did everything in connection with the sacrifice. He commanded the materials to be taken (v. 4); he commanded the death of the bird (v. 5); he dipped the living bird in the blood (v. 6); and he sprinkled the blood on the leper (v. 7).

Note that the priest was to *" . . . take for him . . . "* the needs for the sacrifice (v. 4). The leper was not required to pay for the birds, cedar, scarlet, or the hyssop; these were taken for him. In the same way, God has provided in Christ everything necessary for our salvation.

Bible Truth for Today: *"For by grace are ye saved through faith; and that not of yourselves: it is the gift of God: Not of works, lest any man should boast." —Ephesians 2:8, 9*

February 7

Read Leviticus 16–18
Family Reading: Leviticus 17

The Precious Blood of Christ

Chapters 17–22 comprise a section on law for Israel concerning the blood and the place to sacrifice. The animals killed in Leviticus 17 were for the food of the people. The people were to kill a clean animal at the gate of the tabernacle, and its blood and fat were to be used as a peace offering. The Israelite would take the balance of the carcass home for food for his family. God referred to the death of these animals as a sacrifice. This means that **our whole life is holy to God**. "To the saved person, there is no difference between the secular and the sacred" (Bob Jones, Sr.).

"Whether therefore ye eat, or drink, or whatsoever ye do, do all to the glory of God" (I Corinthians 10:31). As this was God's commandment, disobedience brought severe punishment. Verses four and nine state: " *. . . that man shall be cut off from among his people."* In verse ten God says, " *. . . I will even set my face against that soul . . ."* In verse sixteen again God warns that the offender " *. . . shall bear his iniquity."*

Why would the punishment be so severe? It was because this blood pictured the blood of Jesus Christ. I Peter 1:18, 19 states that we are redeemed by " *. . . **the precious blood** of Christ, as of a lamb without blemish and without spot."* Verse eleven gives us the importance of the blood because it is the life. When Jesus shed His blood, He gave His life. Oh, how we need to preach the blood of Christ!

A famous preacher came to Washington, D. C., a number of years ago to begin a new pastorate. One of the fashionable ladies came to him and said, "Doctor, I hope you will not talk too much about the blood as our former pastor did." His enlightening answer was, "Madam, I will not talk too much about the blood." She said, "Oh, I am glad to hear that." And then he added, "You cannot say too much about the blood." Amen. May we love the precious blood of Christ.

Bible Truth for Today: *"And almost all things are by the law purged with blood; and without shedding of blood is no remission."*

—Hebrews 9:22

February 8

Read Leviticus 19–22
Family Reading: Leviticus 19

Beware of Talebearing

Leviticus 19 is a wonderful chapter to read to acquire principles for our lives. The big reason that God gives for having such rules is that He is the Lord our God. Our lives should be lived properly because we are bearing His name. Because He is our Lord, we should be careful to follow these principles.

One important rule is given in Leviticus 19:16—*"Thou shalt not go up and down as a talebearer among thy people . . . "*

Talebearing is a most dreadful sin. Injury comes from it in three directions. The talebearer himself is hurt by doing so; the person who hears it can be harmed irreparably; and the one on whom the tale is told is injured because his good name has been hurt.

Whether the report is true or false, God's Word forbids us to spread it. We ought never try to damage another man's reputation. A brother's good name should be so precious to us that we would not aid the devil in dishonoring the church and the name of the Lord.

Some glory in pulling down their brothers, as if by doing so they raise themselves. The Scripture states plainly: *" . . . speak evil of no man . . . " (Titus 3:2).*

The Bible does give permission to censure sin—and it informs us the method to use. We should rebuke our brother to his face and not rail behind his back. Beware of talebearing!

Character Verse for Today: *"The words of a talebearer are as wounds, and they go down into the innermost parts of the belly."*
—Proverbs 26:22

Read Leviticus 23 and 24
Family Reading: Leviticus 23:1-22

The Feasts of Jehovah

Chapters 23–25 comprise a new section of Leviticus. This is a portion presenting the **holy times** for the nation of Israel. In these three chapters we find a pervading atmosphere of joy, rest, and celebration. This gives a thrilling climax to Leviticus, a book filled with rules and regulations.

Leviticus emphasizes the truth of holiness. Without holiness there can be no approach to God nor any walk with God. Therefore, the Lord gave these holy times in the calendar for Israel so that they would have many days each year devoted to meditation. Their meditation would be on Jehovah—who He is and what He had done for the nation.

Leviticus 23 presents the feasts of Jehovah. We think of a feast as a banquet, but the meaning of the word *"feast"* in Leviticus 23 is different from our modern-day conception of the word. These feasts were appointed times for solemn festivals in Israel.

These feasts present Christ and His work. The Passover presents Christ, God's Lamb, as our Redeemer. The Feast of Unleavened Bread speaks of fellowship with our Lord. The Feast of Firstfruits presents the resurrection of Christ. The Feast of Pentecost (fifty days) was fulfilled in the coming of the Holy Spirit. The Feast of Trumpets presents Christ in His coming, regathering Israel.

Bible Truth for Today: *"But now in Christ Jesus ye who sometimes were far off are made nigh by the blood of Christ." —Ephesians 2:13*

February 10

Read Leviticus 25 and 26
Family Reading: Leviticus 25:1-24

The Year of Jubilee

Israel had a special year every fiftieth year called the year of jubilee. The word *jubilee* is the Hebrew word referring to the blast of the trumpets. That trumpet sound went to every corner of the nation. It was made on the day of atonement, just after the atonement was made. The jubilee was based on the atonement. No one could enjoy its privileges without knowing that he was living on the basis of the atoning sacrifice offered by the priest.

Every Israelite looked forward to the feast of jubilee. All estates and conditions of the people felt the hallowed, refreshing influence of the jubilee. The exile returned home; the captive was made free; the debtor's account was settled; each family had its long-lost member back in fellowship again; every inheritance was returned to its rightful owner. When the trumpet sounded, the manslayer left the city of refuge and returned home; the poverty-stricken family went back to their inheritance.

The year of jubilee reminded both buyer and seller that the land belonged to Jehovah and was not to be sold. In verse twenty-three Jehovah says that " . . . *the land is mine* . . . " Those to whom it was given as an everlasting covenant have the land forever. The year of jubilee becomes a picture of the millennial reign, when Israel will be back in the land, claiming the possession that is theirs by inheritance.

Where is the king who can take the land from the Lord? Which council of nations can take the land away from the people of God? He has said (and His Word stands) that the land is the Lord's. There have been battles and wars fought over this land, but in the end—be sure—*the land is the Lord's.*

Bible Truth for Today: *"Come unto me, all ye that labor and are heavy laden, and I will give you rest."* —*Matthew 11:28*

Read Leviticus 27 and Numbers 1
Family Reading: Numbers 1:1-4, 16-21, 45-54

Our Pedigree

Israel was in the wilderness (v. 1). In fact, the first word in the Hebrew text is the word translated *"wilderness."* Israel had come out of Egypt and crossed the Red Sea, thereby being redeemed from Egypt's slavery and bondage. They were not as yet in the Promised Land of Canaan. Here we have a picture of every believer. When one receives Christ, he is saved from the bondage of the world. Just as the Israelites had a wilderness experience before they entered the land of Canaan, so every believer will have some type of wilderness experience between his salvation and his life of victory in Christ. (Canaan is an Old Testament picture of victory in the Christian life—it is not a valid picture of Heaven as many suppose.) Some believers have a longer wilderness experience than others. Alas! Some live and die in the wilderness and never attain victory in Christ.

God required that those who were ready to go forth to war be numbered. The army was comprised of those men who were twenty years of age and older. God wanted nothing left to chance. God required over 600,000 fighting men, along with the women, children, and elderly, to be properly organized.

In addition to their being numbered, the men also had to declare their pedigrees (v. 18). For an Israelite to be uncertain of his pedigree would have caused undue confusion. If we are to be used of the Lord, we must know our pedigree—we must know that we have been saved. We need to be able to say, " . . . *Now are we the sons of God . . .* " (I John 3:2).

Bible Promise of Assurance: *"These things have I written unto you that believe on the name of the Son of God; that ye may know that ye have eternal life, and that ye may believe on the name of the Son of God."* —I John 5:13

February 12

Read Numbers 2 and 3
Family Reading: Numbers 3:1-16

No Respect of Persons

Numbers 3 opens with a record of Aaron's family. It is the testimony of the awful consequences of sin. Aaron's sons, Nadab and Abihu, offered strange fire before the Lord. Verse four states that they died when they offered this strange fire.

Think of it! Aaron's sons were taken. When these two sons died, the number of Aaron's sons as priests was cut in half. Sin knows no limit. It will wreck the home of the high priest as quickly as any other home. Not only was Aaron's family judged, but also the families of Nadab and Abihu were judged. Verse four says, " . . . *and they had no children . . . "* It was a disgrace in Israel to have no children; so these two men died in disgrace. This was undoubtedly looked upon as a judgment from God.

No sins are left unjudged by God. He will deal with sin wherever it is. If it is in the home of the family of the high priest, God will show no favors. Sin brings judgment. This law cannot be changed.

Not even God's servants will be exempt from judgment. God's law is: " . . . *the wages of sin is death . . . " (Romans 6:23).* And again: " . . . *the soul that sinneth, it shall die" (Ezekiel 18:4).* Regardless of the person involved in sin, God's judgment is sure. *"For there is no respect of persons with God" (Romans 2:11).* Aaron's household? Yes, judgment will come there as soon as anywhere else. God will not tolerate sin.

Our children are affected by our service. If I fail God, my children will also taste the result. Sin will bring judgment in my life that will affect the lives of my children. Parents, beware that you walk with the Lord.

Bible Prayer for Today: *" . . . cleanse thou me from secret faults. Keep back thy servant also from presumptuous sins . . . "*

—Psalm 19:12, 13

February 13

Read Numbers 4 and 5
Family Reading: Numbers 4:1-20

No Job Too Small

In Numbers 3:31 we are told that the Kohathites had the responsibility of " *. . . the ark, and the table, and the candlestick, and the altars, and the vessels of the sanctuary wherewith they minister, and the hanging, and all the service thereof."* What a privilege these Kohathites had: the carrying of the holy things of the tabernacle.

Aaron and his sons were to take the furniture and to cover it. Then the Kohathites were to come in to bear these articles when the tabernacle moved. Numbers 4:15 says: " *. . . the sons of Kohath shall come to bear it: but they shall not touch any holy thing, lest they die . . . "* The Kohathites had a holy and blessed responsibility. Their privilege was that of handling the beautiful golden vessels of the tabernacle. The Gershonites, on the other hand, looked after the rough, unattractive badger skins. The Merarites took care of the seemingly insignificant pins. But all were important. It was just as important to carry the pins as it was to carry the holy furniture. There are no small tasks when connected with the work of the Lord.

The Kohathites had the privilege of handling the lovely golden vessels; however, with that privilege came an awesome responsibility, violation of which could have meant death. In Numbers 4:15 and 20 God warned the Kohathites of the possibility of death if they did not do their job properly. With greater privilege always comes greater responsibility.

Thot for Today: *Everyone is not privileged to do magnificent things, but everyone is privileged to do little things MAGNIFICENTLY!*

February 14

Read Numbers 6 and 7
Family Reading: Numbers 6

The Lord's Blessing

The sixth chapter of Numbers presents the Nazarite vows. Up until this chapter, God has been dealing with the whole camp of Israel. However, in this chapter, He speaks of individual separation and individual dedication.

The Nazarite vow was one of separation. The word *"separation"* appears sixteen times; and the word *"consecrate,"* three times.

The interesting truth is that God's great statement about His blessing on Israel appears in this same chapter (vv. 23-27). What a blessing it is! God promises to bless, to keep, to make His face shine upon, to be gracious unto, and to give Israel peace. He closes the blessing by promising to put His name on Israel and to bless them. Remember that this tremendous blessing was given by God in the very chapter that speaks of individual separation.

C. H. MacIntosh in his book, *Notes on Numbers,* wrote the following on verses twenty-four through twenty-seven:

"What a provision! Oh, that Israel had entered into it, and lived in the power of it! But they did not! They quickly turned aside, as we shall see. They exchanged the light of God's countenance for the darkness of Mount Sinai; they abandoned the ground of grace and placed themselves under law. In place of being satisfied with the portion in the God of their fathers, they lusted after other things. (Compare Psalms 55 and 56.) In place of the order, the purity, and separation to God with which our book opens, we have disorder, defilement, and giving themselves to idolatry."

God's Blessing: *"The Lord bless thee, and keep thee: The Lord make his face shine upon thee, and be gracious unto thee: The Lord lift up his countenance upon thee, and give thee peace."*

—Numbers 6:24-26

February 15

Read Numbers 8–10
Family Reading: Numbers 9:15-23; 10:1-12

The Leading of the Spirit
and the Word

In the last part of Numbers 9 and the first of Numbers 10, we find God's last instruction to Israel before they began to march. In Numbers 10:11,12 we read that God lifted the cloud from above the tabernacle, and the Israelites began their journey. The last instruction God gave before they began to march was this instruction concerning the trumpets. These were to be used to give public notice of assemblies, alarms, and calls to move.

God instructed Moses concerning the making of the trumpets. They were to be constructed of silver, which is a picture of redemption. They were to be of one whole piece, speaking of the unity of the camp. There were several purposes for these trumpets:

1. The calling of the assembly — vv. 2 and 7
2. The announcement of a time to march — v. 2
3. The summoning of the priests — v. 4
4. The call to march — vv. 5 and 6
5. The call to battle — v. 9
6. The call of rejoicing and praise — v.10

By using the trumpets made according to God's specifications, the Israelites had an assurance from God that victory would be theirs. Note " . . . *and ye shall be remembered before the Lord your God, and ye shall be saved from your enemies . . . " (10:9)*. It is God who gives the victory. The trumpets reminded Israel of God's grace and power.

In the verses just before this passage about the trumpets, God discusses the guiding cloud (Numbers 9:15-23). Then He presents the ministry of the trumpets. The cloud pictured the leading of the Spirit. The trumpets speak of the leading of His Word. The prophet giving forth the Word of God is to lift up his voice " . . . *like a trumpet . . . " (Isaiah 58:1)*. The two go hand in hand. We must have the Spirit's direction; but He can lead us only according to the Word of God. If we do not have the trumpet sound of Bible preaching, we will not know the leading of the Holy Spirit.

February 16

Read Numbers 11–13
Family Reading: Numbers 13

Only Believe

The spies of Israel were sent to spy out the land and to bring back a report concerning the land and the people. You may ask: "Why did God send the spies?" God gave Moses the command in Numbers 13:2, *"Send thou men, that they may search the land of Canaan,"* because the Israelites requested it. In Deuteronomy 1:22 God states of Israel: *"And ye came near unto me every one of you, and said, We will send men before us, and they shall search us out the land . . . "* Their sending spies revealed their unbelief, for certainly God knew who was in the land, and He is the One who was leading them. He wanted them to possess the land.

The sending of the spies brought temptation, revealed cowardliness, manifested their unbelief, and resulted in failure. How different the story would have read if they had only gone on in faith, believing God.

The majority of the spies came back with the report that though the land was very good, a land that flowed with milk and honey, the inhabitants were giants that made the Israelites look like grasshoppers. The Israelites simply had no faith that God was able to give the victory.

Thank God, there was a minority report given by Joshua and Caleb. They said: *" . . . Let us go up at once, and possess it* [the land]; *for we are well able to overcome it" (Numbers 13:30).* These two men believed God. They knew that by faith in God's power they could have blessed victory.

> *Only believe, only believe;*
> *All things are possible,*
> *Only believe.*

Bible Truth for Today: *"Take heed, brethren, lest there be in any of you an evil heart of unbelief, in departing from the living God. So we see that they could not enter in because of unbelief."*

—Hebrews 3:12,19

February 17

Read Numbers 14 and 15
Family Reading: Numbers 15:1-3, 17-24, 32-41

The Wandering Years

The key word in the Book of Numbers is *wilderness*. Every Christian will have some type of wilderness experience. However, the children of Israel had an experience that no believer needs to have. It was not simply the wilderness experience, but they had years of wandering, beginning in Chapter 15.

Note a wonderful truth—the grace of God. In Numbers 14 God sent judgment and said that that generation should not come into the land (v. 30). Then in Numbers 15:2 God said: *" . . . When ye be come into the land of your habitations, which I give unto you."* God immediately talked about their being in the land. He repeated this in verse eighteen: *" . . . When ye come into the land whither I bring you."* Because of grace, the believer, though not perfect nor all he ought to be, can know there is a future inheritance. In Numbers 15 Israel was wandering in the wilderness as a judgment of God. At the same time, God was speaking to Israel in full confidence that the next generation would be in the Promised Land.

In verse thirty-eight God told them to wear a fringe of blue on their garments. They were wandering in the wilderness, and this fringe of blue was to remind them of Heaven. They were to do what Colossians 3 tells believers to do: *" . . . seek those things which are above . . . " (v. 1).*

I like this stanza of Thomas Kelly's hymn, *"Praise the Saviour"*:

> *Then we shall be where we would be,*
> *Then we shall be what we should be;*
> *Things that are not now, nor could be,*
> *Soon shall be our own.*

Bible Truth for Today: *"There is therefore now no condemnation to them which are in Christ Jesus, who walk not after the flesh, but after the Spirit." —Romans 8:1*

February 18

Read Numbers 16–18
Family Reading: Numbers 18:1-24

The Lord Our Portion

"And the Lord spake unto Aaron, Thou shalt have no inheritance in their land, neither shalt thou have any part among them: I am thy part and thine inheritance among the children of Israel."
—*Numbers 18:20*

What more could we want than to know that the Lord is our part and our inheritance! What a blessing this is to the believer.

The eighteenth chapter of Numbers instructs the Israelites that they are to give the first of everything to the Lord. In verse twelve, God wants the best of the oil, the vineyard, and the wheat. He asks for the firstfruits so that the priesthood can be sustained by Israel.

Today every believer is a priest. (Read I Peter 2:5, 9.) Therefore, the Levites of the Old Testament are a picture of the believers today. The priesthood was given as a gift of grace to the nation of Israel: *" . . . to you they are given as a gift for the Lord . . . " (v. 6).* Even so, today we have been given the privilege of priesthood by the grace of God. Therefore, we can believe that God will be our portion just as He was the portion of the Levites.

It is a wonderful thing when we can look upon God as being our portion. I think of the early days when families homesteaded the West. They would come to the plot of ground allocated them by the government. Then they would place a small part under cultivation, and the next year they would add some more until at the end of some years they would possess the whole.

So it is with the mighty nature of God. He gives us the privilege of growing in the length and depth and height and breadth of His love. He is over all—our total portion. Thank Him for it today.

Bible Truth for Today: *" . . . but Christ is all, and in all."*
—*Colossians 3:11*

February 19

Read Numbers 19–21
Family Reading: Numbers 21:1-19

The Brazen Serpent

Numbers 21:5-9 is a very important passage of Scripture. Jesus used it as an illustration of the new birth when he talked to Nicodemus in John 3:14. It is a type of salvation in Christ and should be a blessing to us every time we read it. Note the following:

1. The Danger of Discouragement
    Verse four says: " . . . *the soul of the people was much discouraged because of the way.*" This discouragement produced the sin of murmuring that brought God's drastic judgment.

2. The Serious Sin of Murmuring
    "*[T]he people spake against God, and against Moses, . . .*" *(v. 5).* God wants it known for all time that to speak against Him and to speak against His leaders is a serious and wicked sin. He dealt with it on the part of leaders such as Korah in Numbers 16. Now He deals with it on the part of the rank and file of His people. Murmuring actually involves rebelling against God.

3. The Drastic Judgment of God
    " . . . *much people of Israel died*" *(v. 6).* This is a picture of the results of sin in our lives.

4. The Remedy
    A brass serpent was held up before the people. This brass serpent is a type of the fact that Jesus Christ died for our sins. Brass, in the Bible, typifies God's judgment, and a serpent is a picture of sin. Therefore, a brass serpent pictures God's judgment on sin. Just as this brass serpent was lifted up in the wilderness, so Jesus Christ was lifted up on the cross for our sins. The people were healed miraculously by looking and believing. As we look to Calvary and believe on the Lord Jesus Christ, we are saved.

Bible Truth Presented in John: "*And as Moses lifted up the serpent in the wilderness, even so must the Son of man be lifted up: That whosoever believeth in him should not perish, but have eternal life. For God so loved the world, that he gave his only begotten Son, that whosoever believeth in him should not perish, but have everlasting life.*" —*John 3:14-16*

February 20

Read Numbers 22 and 23
Family Reading: Numbers 22:1-22

A False Prophet

Israel had arrived at the place where they would stay until they would cross over Jordan. The wanderings of Israel over, they would now prepare to cross Jordan. However, this did not mean that Satan would cease to attack. He never gives up on God's people. He will constantly attack and endeavor to defeat the work of the Lord.

Beginning here in Numbers 22, Satan used Balaam, a false prophet, in an effort to defeat Israel. In Numbers 21 Satan used fiery serpents, thereby coming as a roaring lion (I Peter 5:8). In Numbers 22 Satan used a false prophet, thereby coming as an angel of light (II Corinthians 11:13-15). It was Satan who was behind the attack.

Balaam is a false prophet. What made him so dangerous was that he had such a strong likeness to a true prophet. He is a picture of the prophet given in Matthew 7:22,23: *"Many will say to me in that day, Lord, Lord, have we not prophesied in thy name? and in thy name have cast out devils? and in thy name done many wonderful works? And then will I profess unto them, I never knew you: depart from me, ye that work iniquity."*

Balaam talked as though he wanted the will of God done, but he was lying the whole time. I believe he knew that he must recognize the Lordship of Christ. However, when he said that he wanted the messengers to tarry overnight so that he could know what the Lord would say, he was lying. God told him: *" . . . If the men come to call thee, rise up, and go with them . . . " (v. 20).* He was to go only if the men came and asked him to go. However, Balaam rose up in the morning and saddled his ass. It does not say that the men came and called him. He was determined to do what he wanted rather than what God wanted him to do. This is the reason God's anger was kindled. Balaam was not a true prophet of God.

Bible Truth for Today: There will be false prophets arise among us today. *"But there were false prophets also among the people, even as there shall be false teachers among you, who privily shall bring in damnable heresies, even denying the Lord that bought them and bring upon themselves swift destruction." —II Peter 2:1*

February 21

Read Numbers 24–26
Family Reading: Numbers 25

The Danger of Sin

In Numbers 25 we read the tragic story of Balaam trying to curse Israel. He was totally unsuccessful. Every time he tried to curse, God turned the curse into a blessing. But what he could not do on the outside with cursing, Balaam did on the inside with counseling to commit sin. In verse one the people began to commit whoredom as a result of Balaam's counsel. *"Behold, these caused the children of Israel, through the counsel of Balaam, to commit trespass against the Lord in the matter of Peor, and there was a plague among the congregation of the Lord" (Numbers 31:16).*

This action is called *" . . . the doctrine of Balaam . . . "* in Revelation 2:14. The doctrine of Balaam was the teaching that God's people could play with sin and not suffer evil consequences. This is totally untrue. Sin will always bring judgment. God brought a plague on the children of Israel in which 24,000 died (25:9).

Satan's method is to attack the children of God. If he cannot defeat them by a curse from without, he will endeavor to defeat them by sin from within. Balaam counseled Balak, King of Moab, to send some beautiful Moabite women into the camp of Israel to lead the Israelite men to sin. What Balaam could not do with the armies of Balak, he was able to do with the women of Moab.

Christians should fear nothing so much as they fear sin. God wants His people to maintain separation from sin so that His blessing can be poured out.

Bible Truth for Today: *"But every man is tempted, when he is drawn away of his own lust, and enticed. Then when lust hath conceived, it bringeth forth sin: and sin, when it is finished, bringeth forth death." —James 1:14,15*

February 22

Read Numbers 27–29
Family Reading: Numbers 27

The Claim to Inheritance

Zelophehad had five daughters but no sons. In Numbers 26 God had given the places of inheritance to the various tribes and families. The family of Zelophehad faced a real problem since there was no law in Israel permitting women to inherit property. These five daughters came to Moses and Eleazar. Moses realized this matter needed to come before the Lord because he was obeying God's law. *"And Moses brought their cause before the Lord" (v. 5).* And God did give him a new law in verses seven through eleven.

These daughters seemed to have no hope of getting a home in the Promised Land. They had reached the border of Canaan but could go no further. The one thing these daughters had was faith. The father's name, *Zelophehad*, meant *"firstborn."* The firstborn always had an inheritance. They believed in the justice and goodness of God. They had faith to believe God would give them an inheritance. They wanted to plant their feet on the highest spiritual ground possible. Yes, they wanted all God had for them. They wanted to be more than servants. Their desire was to have the position and blessing of sons. May we long for the fullness of our privileges as sons of God, " . . . *heirs of God, and joint-heirs with Christ . . . " (Romans 8:17).*

They did have an important plea. In verse three they said that their father was not in the company of Korah, the rebel. That is an excellent plea because they were saying that their father had not become involved in the sin with the others. Sin will always keep us from the fullness of blessing that God has for us. May we be able to come before God with that same blessing of our having kept ourselves from sin. Paul said, *"But I keep under my body, and bring it into subjection: lest that by any means, when I have preached to others, I myself should be a castaway" (I Corinthians 9:27).*

Bible Truth for Today: *"The Spirit itself beareth witness with our spirit, that we are the children of God: And if children, then heirs; heirs of God, and joint-heirs with Christ; if so be that we suffer with him, that we may be also glorified together." —Romans 8:16,17*

February 23

Read Numbers 30 and 31
Family Reading: Numbers 30

The Law of Vows

Numbers 30 is an important chapter which presents God's law concerning vows. Israel was soon to be in the land of Canaan, the land of plenty. They were going to have an abundance they had not previously enjoyed. There would be a tendency to make vows to God out of this abundance. Individuals might make some rash promises which the family could not fulfill.

Vows to Jehovah are serious and solemn. They could be made by anyone, a man (v. 2) or a woman (v. 3), and could be both positive and negative. The *vow* (Hebrew, *neder*), the positive part, involved the presentation of one's property to the Lord. The *bond* (Hebrew, *issar*), the negative aspect, involved abstinence from certain things.

Vows were not made to be broken. Verse two reads, *"If a man vow a vow unto the Lord, or swear an oath to bind his soul with a bond; he shall not break his word, he shall do according to all that proceedeth out of his mouth."* This is taught clearly in the book of Ecclesiastes: *"Be not rash with thy mouth, and let not thine heart be hasty to utter anything before God . . ." (5:2). "Better is it that thou shouldest not vow, than that thou shouldest vow and not pay" (5:5).*

The woman is under the authority of the man. This is contrary to the present-day women's lib movement. Women need to study the Bible and come to the place of submission to the authority of men. Without that submission, there will be nothing but problems in the life of the woman and of the family. The father of a daughter living in his household could veto her vow (vv. 3-5). The husband of a married woman could veto her vow (vv. 10-15). The husband-to-be of an engaged girl could do the same (vv. 6-8). However, a widow's vow would stand because she was acting as the head of a household.

Bible Truth for Today: *"Therefore, my beloved brethren, be ye steadfast, unmoveable, always abounding in the work of the Lord, forasmuch as ye know that your labor is not in vain in the Lord."*

—I Corinthians 15:58

February 24

Read Numbers 32 and 33
Family Reading: Numbers 32:1-25

The Sin of Bordering the World

God planned for Israel to possess the Promised Land: *"But I have said unto you, Ye shall inherit their land, and I will give it unto you to possess it, a land that floweth with milk and honey: I am the Lord your God, which have separated you from other people" (Leviticus 20:24).*

In Numbers 32:1-5 we read that the tribes of Reuben and Gad asked for land on the east side of Jordan because it was good for cattle. Moses warned that they should not stay east of Jordan and let their brethren go to war because this would discourage the hearts of the children of Israel (vv. 6,7). They finally reached a compromise in which Reuben and Gad would go over Jordan to help the rest of the tribes conquer Canaan and then return unto their own land.

Moses warned the men of Reuben and Gad: *"But if ye will not do so, behold, ye have sinned against the Lord: and be sure your sin will find you out" (v. 23).* This sin was the one of not being in the battle for God. Lot committed this sin when he made his wrong choice (Genesis 13). Jacob committed this sin when he bordered the world (Genesis 33:18,19). Lot lost his family and his testimony. Jacob lost his daughter and caused much grief to his whole family. Whenever one begins to border on the world, he loses his testimony for the Lord.

Christians are to be soldiers, willing to fight. Many believers, without realizing it, discourage other Christians simply because they will not go into the battle and stand true for the Lord. Bordering on the world will always bring defeat to the child of God.

Bible Truth for Today: *"Love not the world, neither the things that are in the world. If any man love the world, the love of the Father is not in him."* — I John 2:15

Read Numbers 34–36
Family Reading: Numbers 35:11-34

Cities of Refuge

God made provision for menslayers to have a city of refuge to which to flee. These six cities were strategically placed so that an individual could flee to the city when the need arose. In Hebrews 6:18,19 the truths which the Apostle Paul wrote concerning these cities can be applied to believers today.

These cities of refuge are a picture of Christ:

1. They were appointed by God. Christ is God's Prophet chosen from among the people. *"Him hath God exalted . . . to be a Prince and a Saviour . . . " (Acts 5:31).*

2. They were a protection against a lawful avenger. The avenger of a murdered one had the authority to kill the murderer outside the cities of refuge. The avenger fitly represents the law, which cannot save but has the power to kill. *" . . . by the deeds of the law there shall no flesh be justified in his sight . . ." (Romans 3:20).*

3. The city was to be entered in haste. There was then, and there is today, great danger in delay. Death may overtake the sinner before he gets to the refuge. Escape for thy life. *" . . . behold, now is the day of salvation . . . " (II Corinthians 6:2).* "How shall we escape, if we neglect so great salvation. . . ?" (Hebrews 2:3).*

4. The sinner was to stay in the city of refuge until the death of the high priest. Praise God, our High Priest, Jesus Christ, never dies! We are safe for eternity.

Bible Truth for Today: *" . . . we might have a strong consolation, who have fled for refuge to lay hold upon the hope . . . Which hope we have as an anchor of the soul . . . within the veil; Whither the forerunner is for us entered, even Jesus . . . " —Hebrews 6:18-20*

February 26

Read Deuteronomy 1 and 2
Family Reading: Deuteronomy 1:1-8, 25-36

Going About in Circles

There is an old story about a fellow who saw a merry-go-round for the first time. Fascinated, he decided he just had to have a ride on that contraption. His wife tried to reason with him by telling him he would waste his money. But he would not listen. He bought a ticket and when the merry-go-round stopped the next time, he climbed on one of the mechanical horses. He went around a few times and then the merry-go-round stopped. His wife was nearby as he climbed off the horse. She lamented, "Well, I hope you are satisfied! You have spent your money. You got off right where you got on, and you ain't been nowhere!"

This same thing could have been said to Israel. They had gone round and round in the wilderness wanderings and had been nowhere. In verse two God told them they could have made it in eleven days. Then in verse three He states that it took them forty years. Think of it—forty years to take a journey requiring less than two weeks.

Why did it take so long? God gives the answer in verses twenty-six and twenty-seven. The people rebelled against the commandment of the Lord. They would not believe Caleb and Joshua and move into the land. God judged them for their sins.

Israel not only rebelled but also murmured (v. 27). And this discouraged the whole camp of Israel. As a result, they wandered for forty years until the generation that rebelled had died.

Let's ask ourselves: Do we obey the Lord, or do we walk in circles because we have failed to believe God?

Proverbs for Today: *"But the path of the just is as the shining light, that shineth more and more unto the perfect day. The way of the wicked is as darkness: they know not at what they stumble."*

—Proverbs 4:18,19

February 27

Read Deuteronomy 3 and 4
Family Reading: Deuteronomy 4:1-16, 29-35

A Favored Position

Israel was a specially favored nation. In this fourth chapter of Deuteronomy God reminds them repeatedly of their favored position. Let me list just a few blessings God mentions in this chapter:

1. God destroyed the followers of Baal-peor from among the congregation (v. 3).

2. Moses taught the people God's statutes and judgments, just as the Lord commanded him (v. 5).

3. Israel had the presence of God with her as a nation. *"For what nation is there so great, who hath God so nigh unto them, as the Lord our God is in all things that we call upon him for?" (v. 7).*

4. The Israelites heard the Lord speak out of the midst of the fire, and they continued to live (v. 33).

5. God gave the victory because the Lord loved Israel (v. 37-39).

Since they were such a privileged nation, there were some things God wanted them to guard. They needed to take heed not to forget God's grace and mercy. He warned: *" . . . lest thou forget . . . " (v. 9).* How easy it is for us who have known the blessings of God to forget those blessings. God wants us to remember all that He has done for us — and then remembering, to serve Him with a yielded heart.

God warned them to be careful that they live according to what they heard. We must first hear God's Word so that we can do what we hear. James tells us, *"But be ye doers of the word, and not hearers only, deceiving your own selves" (James 1:22).*

The Believer's Favored Position: *"But ye are a chosen generation, a royal priesthood, an holy nation, a peculiar people; that ye should show forth the praises of him who hath called you out of darkness into his marvelous light." —I Peter 2:9*

February 28

Read Deuteronomy 5–7
Family Reading: Deuteronomy 6

The Word in Your Heart

Deuteronomy 6:6 commands: *"And these words, which I command thee this day, shall be in thine heart."*

The Israelite was to have the Word of God in his heart so that he could teach it to his children and honor it in his home (vv. 7-9). Remember, it reads: *"in thine heart."* It does not read: *"in thine head."*

An account by Dr. Bernard Schneider relates an interesting incident. Once when he gave a man a tract, the man told him he was interested in the Bible and had, in fact, memorized all of it. When Dr. Schneider questioned this, the man challenged him to a duel. He told Schneider to pick any chapter he wanted and they would quote alternate verses. Since Dr. Schneider had just memorized Isaiah 53, he chose that chapter. Surely enough, this man could quote every alternate verse word perfect; and he helped Schneider on some of those over which he stumbled. When they finished, the man kept right on quoting in Isaiah for several minutes. There was no doubt that he had memorized the Bible.

But when Dr. Schneider questioned him, he found that the man had never really trusted the Lord Jesus Christ. He had the Word of God in his head but not in his heart.

The Word of God must be received in the heart if a person is to be saved. And only in the heart can the Word of God deliver from sin. Be sure God's Word is in your heart and not just in your head.

Bible Truth for Today: *"Thy testimonies have I taken as an heritage for ever; for they are the rejoicing of my heart."* —Psalm 119:111

February 29

This page is put here for use on leap year. On the years when there are only twenty-eight days in February, you will need to work extra hard to get caught up right away.

Read Deuteronomy 8–10
Family Reading: Deuteronomy 10

God's Requirements

Moses rehearsed again the requirements that God had for a fruitful and effective life. The same requirements that God outlined for Israel will be those we need today.

1. *" . . . fear the Lord thy God . . . " (vv. 12,20).* This means that we should give Him such reverence as to adore His majesty and acknowledge His authority. The word *fear* means that we should stand in awe as we note His power, His love, and His wrath. All the subsequent things I list below will result in the life that does fear the Lord:

2. *" . . . walk in all his ways . . . " (v. 12).* Everything we do must be conformable to the will of God. We learn His ways by studying His Word.

3. *" . . . love him . . . " (v. 12).* We must be well pleased that He is our God and live daily in the blessed contemplation of communion with Him. We are to fear Him as a great God, and our Lord, and we are to love Him as a good God and our Father and Benefactor.

4. *" . . . serve the Lord thy God with all thy heart . . . " (v. 12).* If we fear Him, and walk in His ways, we will be ready to serve Him with our entire being. This matter of service will manifest our love for Him.

So keep the commandments and statutes of the Lord. This is not difficult because *" . . . his commandments are not grievous" (I John 5:3).* Keeping His commandments is actually for our own good (Deuteronomy 10:13). As we do that which pleases Him, we find it has turned out to be that which was best for us.

Bible Truth for Today: *"For this is the love of God, that we keep his commandments: and his commandments are not grievous."*

—I John 5:3

March 1

Read Deuteronomy 11–13
Family Reading: Deuteronomy 13

Beware of False Prophets

An ever-present danger in the work of the Lord is that of false prophets. God warned Israel about them in Deuteronomy 13.

God's command concerning these false prophets is that God's people have nothing to do with them. They are not to hearken to the words of the prophet (v. 3). But more, they were to put the false prophet to death because his purpose was to lead the people of God astray (v. 5). This passage is very clear in its teaching that God's people must deal definitely and drastically with false prophets. Let's note some statements God gives in this passage:

"And that prophet . . . shall be put to death . . . " (v. 5).

" . . . So shalt thou put the evil away from the midst of thee" (v. 5).

"Thou shalt not consent unto him, nor hearken unto him; neither shall thine eye pity him, neither shalt thou spare, neither shalt thou conceal him: But thou shalt surely kill him . . . " (vv. 8, 9).

"And thou shalt stone him with stones, that he die; because he hath sought to thrust thee away from the Lord, thy God . . . " (v. 10).

So serious is this matter of apostasy, that God said any city that followed after a false prophet was to be utterly destroyed (vv. 15, 16). Only as God's people dealt with apostasy in such a definite and strong manner could they be assured of God's continued mercy and compassion.

Bible Truth for Today: *"Ye shall walk after the Lord your God, and fear him, and keep his commandments, and obey his voice, and ye shall serve him, and cleave unto him."* —Deuteronomy 13:4

March 2

Read Deuteronomy 14–16
Family Reading: Deuteronomy 15

God's Anti-Poverty Program

When our United States of America was founded, brilliant and dedicated men carefully prepared a constitution to cover every primary area of life in a free country. Just so, God gave Israel a "constitution" that was designed to direct, lead, and govern in every aspect of their lives. Since this "constitution" of Israel was divine, it was ideal and complete for Israel. It was adapted for Israel in the Promised Land, but it also has become a basis for proper government in all times.

Two truths underline this Divine Bill of Rights:

1. Its provisions were fair to all members of society.
   All other nations had laws favoring the ruling wealthy class. God provided laws to protect and provide for the helpless and unfortunate.

2. God provided for the difference between the ideal and the real.
   The ideal was that every service and function be performed in the will of God. He knew that sinful man would not always walk in His direct will.

The **ideal** and the **real** are contrasted in Deuteronomy 15:4 and 11. Verse four is the **ideal**: *"Save when there shall be no poor among you . . . ."* Verse eleven is the **real**: *"For the poor shall never cease out of the land . . . "* We need to love the poor, preach the gospel to them as Jesus did, but never expect to reach the ideal. Jesus Himself said, *"For the poor always ye have with you . . . " (John 12:8).* Our responsibility is to reach them with the gospel.

Bible Principle for Today: *"Better it is to be of a humble spirit with the lowly, than to divide the spoil with the proud." —Proverbs 16:19*

March 3

Read Deuteronomy 17–21
Family Reading: Deuteronomy 17

America—Beware!

In Deuteronomy 17:14-20 God gives the responsibility of a king. He knew that the Israelites would desire a king someday, for they would want to be just like the heathen nations around them. God's people have always had the problem of wanting to be like other people. Since God knew His people would ask for a king, He gave instructions concerning a king. If followed by today's rulers, these instructions would make a better king or president. Let's note some of these instructions:

1. He was to be the Lord's choice — v. 15.

2. He was to read the law of God all the days of his life so that he could learn to fear the Lord and to keep the statutes of God— vv. 18, 19.

3. He was not to multiply horses to himself—v. 16.

4. He was not to return to Egypt—v. 16. America today is returning to the bondage from whence she came during the American Revolution.

5. He was not to multiply silver and gold to himself—v. 17.

6. He was not to multiply wives unto himself—v. 17.

In the days of Solomon, we find every one of these rules broken. We do not read of his making a copy of the law and reading therein daily. He did go to Egypt; he did get horses from Egypt; he did have multiplied wives; and he did multiply silver and gold for himself. No wonder Israel became a nation in bondage! America, beware!

Bible Truth for Today: *"Righteousness exalteth a nation: but sin is a reproach to any people." —Proverbs 14:34*

March 4

Read Deuteronomy 22–25
Family Reading: Deuteronomy 22:8-30

Principles of Separation

In Deuteronomy 22:9-11 we have three vital principles of separation in the Christian life.

1. *"Thou shalt not sow thy vineyard with divers seeds . . . " (v. 9)*

   We are not to mix the seed of the Word of God with the worldly seeds of the philosophies of men. The Bible teaches that the seed is the Word of God (Luke 8:11; I Peter 1:23). In Colossians 2:8 God warns: *"Beware lest any man spoil you through philosophy and vain deceit, after the tradition of men, after the rudiments of the world, and not after Christ."* We must sow only with the Word of God and not add to the seed of the Word.

2. *"Thou shalt not plow with an ox and an ass together" (v. 10).*

   In the Bible an ox is a picture of a true servant of Christ. An ass is a type of one who does not believe the Word of God. The Lord does not want His servants to endeavor to work with the ungodly crowd.

3. *"Thou shalt not wear a garment of divers sorts, as of woollen and linen together" (v. 11).*

   God states that His people are not to have mixed clothing. Our clothes are what the world sees. If our clothing does not present the right testimony to the world, our whole testimony will be wrecked.

In II Corinthians 6:14 God gives a clear presentation of the separation of believers from the world: *"Be ye not unequally yoked together with unbelievers . . . "* God's people are to be separated from the world and stand true to Christ.

Bible Truth for Today: *"Wherefore come out from among them, and be ye separate, saith the Lord . . . "*   —II Corinthians 6:17

March 5

Read Deuteronomy 26–28
Family Reading: Deuteronomy 28:1-6, 13-19, 50-53, 58-62

Blessings and Curses with Warning of Judgment

America needs to hear and heed this passage because America is heading down the wrong road in disobeying the Lord and the Bible. God permits famine, violence, and breaking down of sexual distinctions when judgment comes. America, BEWARE!

After God pronounced the curses in verses fifteen through nineteen, He listed many ways these curses would be realized in Deuteronomy 28:20-44. Then in verse forty-five God speaks again of the fact that these curses would come upon Israel and pursue and overtake them because they would not hearken to the Lord.

God lists serious things that would come upon Israel. In verses fifty through fifty-three God states that He would send a powerful nation against Israel who would destroy her land and cause famine to come to the people. Then in verses fifty-nine through sixty-four God says He will afflict Israel with plagues and a scattering of the people. All of this will come as God's judgment if His people refused to obey and honor the Lord (v. 58).

Deuteronomy 27 and 28 present the curses and blessings that could have come from God upon Israel. These curses or blessings hinged upon the obedience of Israel.

If Israel would hearken unto the Lord, God would bless the nation and set it on high above other nations (28:1). It was because of this promise that the Queen of Sheba came to Israel and was amazed at the prosperity of the nation and the blessing of God upon it. In fact, Israel's obedience was sure to bring blessing. *"All these blessings shall . . . overtake thee, if thou shalt hearken unto the voice of the Lord thy God" (v. 2).* Think of it—the person who is faithful to obey the Lord cannot run fast enough to escape the blessing of God upon him!

Bible Truth for Today: *"For the time is come that judgment must begin at the house of God: and if it first begin at us, what shall the end be of them that obey not the gospel of God?"* —*I Peter 4:17*

March 6

Read Deuteronomy 29–31
Family Reading: Deuteronomy 30

God's Promises to Israel

Deuteronomy 30 presents the Palestinian Covenant that God made with Israel. It is an **unconditional promise** of future blessing.

There are seven great promises here. Verse one tells us that Israel will be scattered among the nations. They will be removed from the land because of their unfaithfulness. This promise has been fulfilled.

Verse two states that there will be a future repentance of Israel. They will " . . . *return unto the Lord . . . and obey his voice . . . "* Verse three tells us that the Lord will return and gather Israel from the nations—the first mention in God's Word of Christ's return to earth. Not until Christ returns will the land be blessed and be at peace.

Verses four and five state that Israel will go back to possess the land; then there will be a national conversion (v. 6). Verse seven reveals that the enemies of Israel will be judged. Finally, when the Lord returns, Israel will receive full blessing (vv. 9, 10).

There will be no blessing for Israel in the land until they return in obedience with a new heart which God will give them. Presently, Israel has not returned in obedience to God. The return that is mentioned in Deuteronomy 30 will bring the covenant promise of the future. God gave Israel the opportunity to make the right decision. He set before them life and death, blessing and cursing; then He commanded them to " . . . *choose life, that both thou and thy seed may live" (v. 19).* Their love and obedience were required by God. The Lord Jesus Christ is coming again, and these promises will be fulfilled!

New Testament Promise Fulfilling Deuteronomy 30:3— *"And so all Israel shall be saved: as it is written, There shall come out of Zion the Deliverer, and shall turn away ungodliness from Jacob."*

—Romans 11:26

March 7

Read Deuteronomy 32–34
Family Reading: Deuteronomy 32:1-13, 29-36

His People

Deuteronomy 32:9 says, *"[T]he Lord's portion is his people. . . ."* What a wonderful promise! How are we His people? It is by His **choice**. He chose us and set His love upon us. He chose each of us apart from any goodness in us or any goodness that He could foresee in the future.

Israel was the Lord's not only by choice but also by **purchase**. He had bought and paid for Israel to the very last penny. Therefore, there was no dispute about His title to them. The same is true with us. We *" . . . were not redeemed with corruptible things, as silver and gold . . . But with the precious blood of Christ . . . " (I Peter 1:18, 19).* And as the Lord's portion, we have been completely redeemed. Praise God, there is no mortgage on our inheritance. No suits can be raised in court by others who claim our portion. The price was paid in the open court of God, and the church belongs to the Lord forever. The Bible says, *" . . . The Lord knoweth them that are his . . . " (II Timothy 2:19).*

Israel was Christ's not only by choice and by purchase but also by **conquest**. The Lord fought a battle so that we could be won also. He fought that battle at Calvary; and then He fought another battle—the battle for our own hearts. How often we barred the gates and built our fences against Him. But, praise God, we could look to His cross and realize that He had paid the entire payment in our place. He has conquered us. We should indeed be a captive of His omnipotent love. Think of it! We can never be our own; therefore, we must day by day desire to do His will and show forth His glory.

Bible Truth for Today: *"What? know ye not that your body is the temple of the Holy Ghost which is in you, which ye have of God, and ye are not your own? For ye are bought with a price: therefore glorify God in your body, and in your spirit, which are God's."*
—I Corinthians 6:19, 20

March 8

Read Joshua 1–4
Family Reading: Joshua 2

The Scarlet Line

"And she said, According unto your words, so be it. And she sent them away, and they departed: and **she bound the scarlet line in the window***" (Joshua 2:21).* The spies had been protected by Rahab since she looked upon them as the representatives of the God of Israel. She let them escape from Jericho by this scarlet line. The spies then told her that they would be back to take Jericho and that if she would bind the scarlet line in the window and bring her family inside the house, everyone within the doors of her house would be protected.

This scarlet line speaks of the blood of Christ, the necessary sacrifice for salvation. Rahab depended on the promise of the spies for her preservation and that of her family. Her faith was simple and firm, but very obedient. She tied the scarlet line in the window immediately after the spies left. As nearly as I can calculate, it was somewhere between two and three weeks before the walls of Jericho fell. She left that scarlet line in the window all of that time. Undoubtedly, there were people who would ask her, "Why do you put that scarlet line in the window?" She rested upon the promise of those spies to protect her family.

Today you need to be under the blood of Christ with such a definite trust in His blood that it can be seen as easily by others as this scarlet cord was. But above everything else, it will be seen by the Lord Jehovah, the Avenger, who will see it and pass over. Be sure you have tied the scarlet line in the window of your life. Rahab's house was on the wall and it stood unmoved. My life is part of the wall of humanity; but when destruction smites the race, I shall be secure because of the blood of Christ.

> *Under the blood of Jesus, safe in the shepherd's fold;*
> *Under the blood of Jesus, safe while the ages roll;*
> *Safe though the worlds may crumble;*
> *Safe though the stars grow dim;*
> *Under the blood of Jesus, I am secure in Him.*

Bible Truth for Today: *"And almost all things are by the law purged with blood; and without shedding of blood is no remission."*

—Hebrews 9:22

March 9

Read Joshua 5–7
Family Reading: Joshua 7

God Judges Sin in the Camp

God announced the reason for Israel's defeat at Ai when He said, *"Israel hath sinned . . ." (v. 11).* God will always permit defeat when there is sin in the camp. The Lord said that Israel would not know His victorious presence if she failed to deal with sin in the fellowship. When God spoke of the sin of only one man, Achan, He said that **Israel** had sinned. Many churches do not experience blessing because they have an Achan in the camp. Every child of God should examine his life to be sure he is not causing defeat to God's work by his sin.

God said, *" . . . There is an accursed thing in the midst of thee, O Israel . . . " (v. 13).* That word *accursed* literally means *"a devoted thing."* When Israel was preparing its attack on Jericho, God instructed that they were not to take of the *" . . . accursed thing . . . "*—the *"devoted thing"*—because this action would bring a curse on Israel. Then God said, *"But all the silver, and gold, and vessels of brass and iron, are consecrated unto the Lord . . . " (Joshua 6:19).* These items were to come into the treasury of the Lord. To take them was to be stealing from God. God's drastic dealing with this sin should be a solemn warning to those who steal from God today by failing to tithe faithfully.

Joshua dealt with the sin. Verse twenty-six tells us that the Lord turned from the fierceness of His anger. Today we too must face and deal with sin.

Bible Truth for Today: *" . . . and be sure your sin will find you out."* *—Numbers 32:23*

March 10

Read Joshua 8 and 9
Family Reading: Joshua 8:1-25

Regaining Lost Ground

In Joshua 7 Israel was defeated because of sin, but Joshua dealt with that sin. Joshua 7:26 tells us that the Lord *" . . . turned from the fierceness of His anger . . . "* Then Joshua 8 opens with God promising that He had given Ai into Joshua's hand. The truth is that God longs to bless His people with blessing and victory. When sin is recognized and confessed, God is able to restore and use an individual. Israel did confess sin; therefore, God did give victory over Ai. Joshua and his people did recover lost ground.

After the defeat of Ai, we find Joshua and the Israelites at Mount Ebal (vv. 30-35). It was here that they were taught the way that they would be blessed and the way that they would be cursed. They needed to learn, as do we, that there are laws in the Christian life. Joshua spoke plainly. He gave the blessings and the cursings—the laws of life and of death (literally, the laws of Heaven and of Hell). The Israelites stood, half on one peak and half on the other, and they assented to the Word of God. If they disobeyed, they would die; if they obeyed, they would live.

The law was written on the altar (vv. 31, 32), the very place where the burnt offerings and peace offerings were sacrificed. We have the law, but the power to live a godly life comes only by God. May we yield all to Him to lead a life of victory and blessing.

Bible Principle for Today: *"A poor man that oppresseth the poor is like a sweeping rain which leaveth no food." —Proverbs 28:3*

March 11

Read Joshua 10–12
Family Reading: Joshua 10:1-25

The Lord Gives the Victory

Joshua found that there were five powerful kings marching against Gibeon. Since he had pledged to fight for Gibeon, he immediately began the march against the kings (v. 7). He moved forward with God's promise: *" . . . Fear them not: for I have delivered them into thine hand . . . " (v. 8).*

We read that the Lord *"discomfited"* the enemies (v. 10). He miraculously cast down great stones from Heaven and thereby defeated a sizable contingency of the enemy (v. 11). Again, God performed the miracle of having the sun stand still for a full day (v. 13), thus giving Israel much more time to complete the work of the battle. Joshua and Israel won a great victory.

Then we read God's promise: *" . . . for thus shall the Lord do to all your enemies against whom ye fight" (v. 25).* God gave the victory and promised to continue giving the victory. Note the fear that struck the hearts of the five kings: *"But these five kings fled, and hid themselves in a cave at Makkedah" (v. 16).* Five kings—all in a cave—hiding! They were brought out of the cave, laid down in humility and slain, with the feet of Joshua's captains on their necks (vv. 24-26).

This is what God wants to do with the enemies that stand against us. The enemy may be pride or lust or self. Recognize the enemy and then trust God to give the victory.

Bible Truth for Today: *"But thanks be to God, which giveth us the victory through our Lord Jesus Christ. Therefore, my beloved brethren, be ye steadfast, unmoveable, always abounding in the work of the Lord, forasmuch as ye know that your labor is not in vain in the Lord." —I Corinthians 15:57, 58*

March 12

Read Joshua 13–15
Family Reading: Joshua 14

Caleb—God's Great Man

Caleb is one of the great Bible characters. Great people for God are not complicated people—they are simply those who rest in the Lord. You can read a real man of God like a book. To someone who understands the truths of the Spirit of God, it is easy to discern why a man of God is a great man. If we could learn to follow the Lord as Caleb did, we would have the same results in our lives.

In Joshua 14:11 Caleb stated: *"As yet I am as strong this day as I was in the day that Moses sent me: as my strength was then, even so is my strength now, for war, both to go out, and to come in."* Caleb was eighty-five years old and was still a man of great strength. Joshua 15:14 states that he drove out the three giants, the sons of Anak, from the land. He was still able to win battles. In Joshua 14:12 Caleb asked Joshua to give him the mountain and he would win the victory.

What made Caleb a great man? First, he was a man of faith. Back in Numbers 13 and 14 when the spies went into the land, he disagreed with the majority. That majority measured the giants against their own strength. Caleb, along with Joshua, measured the giants against God. The ten spies trembled; Caleb and Joshua triumphed. The ten had great giants but a little God; Caleb had a great God and little giants. The people cried, "Let us go back into Egypt." Caleb and Joshua said, "Let us go on into the land." Numbers 14:24 states: *"But my servant Caleb, because he had another spirit with him, and hath followed me fully, him will I bring into the land whereinto he went . . . "* Never once did Caleb rebel against Moses. Never once was he found among the grumblers or the unbelievers. Never once did he say, "Let us go back to Egypt." Never once was he found among those who disobeyed God.

Caleb had caught a glimpse of the reward of obedience, and that was sufficient to keep him true for the rest of his life. He had caught a glimpse of the Lord and was determined to be faithful.

Bible Truth for Today: *"But without faith it is impossible to please him: for he that cometh to God must believe that he is, and that he is a rewarder of them that diligently seek him." —Hebrews 11:6*

March 13

Read Joshua 16–19
Family Reading: Joshua 17

Have the Victory Where You Are

Joshua 17:14 is a very interesting and tragic request: The children of Joseph thought that because of their blessing in the past, they were to have special blessings now. They said of themselves, *" . . . seeing I am a great people . . . " (v. 14).* Whenever anyone begins to glory in his own greatness, he will be defeated in his Christian life. *"And Joshua answered them, If thou be a great people, then get thee up to the wood country, and cut down for thyself there in the land . . . " (v. 15).* If they were really great people, they should prove it by their own victories. The fact is that while they were claiming to be a great people, they had not conquered the land. There were still a number of Canaanites who possessed chariots of iron in their land (v. 16).

How typical this is of many folks today who are not satisfied with their lot. They think that they do not have enough opportunity for their gifts. Yet in the sphere that God has given them, the enemy is still deeply entrenched. When folks feel this way, very often the real trouble is in their own lives, not in the situation around them. They have not won the battle where they are.

Faith must strike at the very root of the problem; the dead wood must go (v. 15). God says to those who are dissatisfied and always looking for new opportunities, "What about the trees in your life which mar your vision, block your progress, and rob you of victory? Cut them down!" Determine that you are going to have the victory where you are. When we lay the ax to the root of our sin, it will solve the problem.

Bible Truth for Today: *"To him that overcometh will I grant to sit with me in my throne, even as I also overcame, and am set down with my Father in his throne."* — *Revelation 3:21*

March 14

Read Joshua 20–22
Family Reading: Joshua 22:10-34

Judge Not

The tribe of Reuben, the tribe of Gad, and half the tribe of Manasseh had settled on the east of Jordan. Moses told them that their men would have to come to fight with the rest of Israel to conquer the Promised Land on the west of Jordan. These two and one-half tribes did what Moses asked. Now Joshua told them that they could go back to their families on the east of Jordan.

On the way to their homes, an incident occurred which has important teaching for us today—they built a large altar by Jordan (v. 10). The other tribes became concerned. They thought that these two and one-half tribes were going to start a new place of sacrifice. Without sending anyone to make a proper inquiry concerning this altar, the other nine and one-half tribes determined that this altar represented a rebellion against God. They judged their brethren's motives without knowledge or understanding. On the basis of this wrong judgment, they prepared to go to war. When Phinehas the priest and those who were with him learned that the altar was not to divide but rather to be a witness to the unity of the whole nation of Israel, they were pleased. War was averted and a unity was restored.

This type of thing happens repeatedly today. God's children need to be careful about judging brethren unjustly, thereby bringing division.

Bible Truth for Today: *"Judge not according to the appearance, but judge righteous judgment." —John 7:24*

March 15

Read Joshua 23 and 24 and Judges 1
Family Reading: Joshua 24:1-25

The Right Decision

The book of Joshua is a great book on Christian victory by faith in Jesus Christ. Chapter 24 is somewhat of a summary of the whole book. In verses two through thirteen, Joshua rehearses all of the great things God had done for Israel. In these verses, God states seventeen times that He has done something for Israel.

This is true of us. All that we have is in Christ. *"For we are his workmanship, created in Christ Jesus unto good works . . . " (Ephesians 2:10).*

What we are by the grace of God, we owe entirely to Him. Therefore, we need to do what Joshua 24:14 states: " . . . *fear the Lord, and serve him in sincerity and in truth: and put away the gods which your fathers served on the other side of the flood, and in Egypt; and serve ye the Lord."* We need to determine that because of all He has done for us, we should surrender our lives to serve Him.

Then Joshua asked them to choose whom they would serve. If they were going to serve the other gods, Joshua encouraged them to go ahead and serve them. They, of course, would pay a dreadful price for it.

They had every reason to serve the Lord. Verse thirteen states that God had given them a land for which they did not labor; they lived in cities which they did not build; and they had the privilege of eating of vineyards and olive yards which they had not planted. They should have been anxious to serve the Lord. Joshua warned them about the danger of failing to serve the Lord. Then he told them that regardless of what they decided, his decision was already made. The last part of verse fifteen states: " . . . *but as for me and my house, we will serve the Lord."*

What a decision! It is the decision every one of us must make — that we are going to serve the Lord and lead our homes to serve the Lord. May God help us to do exactly that today.

Bible Truth for Today: *"And whatsoever ye do, do it heartily, as to the Lord, and not unto men." —Colossians 3:23*

March 16

Read Judges 2–4
Family Reading: Judges 2:16–3:11

Fighting for God

The book of Judges presents a major danger that all of God's people face—that of cooling off spiritually and backsliding away from the Lord. Israel corrupted themselves more than their fathers after the judge died. *"And it came to pass, when the judge was dead, that they returned, and corrupted themselves more than their fathers, in following other gods to serve them, and to bow down unto them; they ceased not from their own doings, nor from their stubborn way"* *(Judges 2:19).* They followed other gods and served them and bowed down to them. The judges helped keep Israel walking in the right way. But when the judges died, these Israelites would go back to their own stubborn ways.

Because of Israel's rebellious ways and wicked desires, God announced that He would not drive out all of the inhabitants of the land. Rather, He would leave these pagan nations there as a test to see whether or not Israel would walk in the ways of their fathers.

God wanted Israel to know how to fight. *"Only that the generations of the children of Israel might know, to teach them war, at the least such as before knew nothing thereof" (Judges 3:2).* These Israelites had not known the wars of Canaan. They had a life that was easy without any battles. Judges 3:11 states that the land had rest forty years; then the children of Israel did evil again in the sight of the Lord (Judges 3:12). Somehow when life is too easy, God's people lose their real desire to stand true for God and live for the Lord. David stated in Psalm 144 that God taught his hands to war and his fingers to fight. Pity that poor saint who says he never wants to be involved in a fight. We cannot escape a fight if we are saved. Satan will resist us, and we must fight him. The flesh stands against our spirituality, and God overcomes only through our being willing to fight.

Bible Requirement: *"Wherefore take unto you the whole armor of God, that ye may be able to withstand in the evil day, and having done all, to stand." —Ephesians 6:13*

March 17

Read Judges 5–7
Family Reading: Judges 7

The Sword of the Lord and of Gideon

"And the three companies blew the trumpets, and brake the pitchers, and held the lamps in their left hands, and the trumpets in their right hands to blow withal: and they cried, The sword of the Lord, and of Gideon" (Judges 7:20). Gideon won the victory in Judges 7 in a very unusual manner. It was a victory that only God could give because Gideon and his band were greatly outnumbered. The Midianites and Amalekites were *" . . . like grasshoppers for multitude . . . " (v. 12).* God had Gideon reduce the size of his army until he had only three hundred against a vast multitude.

But, *" . . . If God be for us, who can be against us?" (Romans 8:31).* As believers, we also face overwhelming foes. There is no way to win the victory in our own strength. We must have miraculous power. We need to do the same things Gideon did. The men were to break their pitchers and let the light of the torch shine. Then they were to sound with the trumpets and cry out: *"The sword of the Lord, and of Gideon!"* This is exactly what we must do.

First, we must let our lights shine before men (Matthew 5:16). Men need to see our good works and thus know we have been with Jesus.

Second, there must be the sound, the blowing of the trumpets. This speaks of our blowing the gospel trumpet—giving out the Word of God so that sinners can come to receive Christ.

Third, we must always recognize the truth which Gideon knew — *"The sword of the Lord, and of Gideon!"* It is God's work—we cannot do it alone. But it is also true that as Gideon had to bear the sword, we too must give out the Word of God—the Sword of the Spirit (Ephesians 6:17). Then we will have unusual victory.

Bible Truth for Today: *Stand therefore, having your loins girt about with truth, and having on the breastplate of righteousness; And your feet shod with the preparation of the gospel of peace; Above all, taking the shield of faith, wherewith ye shall be able to quench all the fiery darts of the wicked. And take the helmet of salvation, and the sword of the Spirit, which is the word of God." —Ephesians 6:14-17*

March 18

Read Judges 8 and 9
Family Reading: Judges 9:1-6, 20-24, 46-57

God Judges Sin

Abimelech was a half-brother to the seventy sons of Gideon. He contrived to have these seventy sons slain so that he could be the king over Shechem. Jotham, one of the sons, was not slain because he hid himself. From the top of Mount Gerizim, Jotham cried out a prophecy against Abimelech and the Shechemites. He warned the men of Shechem that if they had not dealt truly with the family of Gideon, fire would come out from Abimelech to destroy the men of Shechem. If the reverse were true, fire would come out from the men of Shechem and destroy Abimelech (vv. 19, 20).

This is exactly what happened: *"Thus God rendered the wickedness of Abimelech, which he did unto his father, in slaying his seventy brethren: And all the evil of the men of Shechem did God render upon their heads: and upon them came the curse of Jotham the son of Jerubbaal"(vv. 56,57).* (*Jerubbaal* is another name for *Gideon.*)

Abimelech thought he was acting on his own when he was made king of Shechem (v. 6). However, God permitted an evil spirit to come between Abimelech and the men of Shechem, and a strong battle ensued between them. *"Then God sent an evil spirit between Abimelech and the men of Shechem; and the men of Shechem dealt treacherously with Abimelech" (v. 23).* The end of it all was that Abimelech destroyed the men of Shechem, and the Shechemites destroyed Abimelech.

The reason for this dual destruction is that God was fulfilling His prophecy. They were destroyed because of their sin. God judges sin. No one gets by with sinning against Almighty God. It may look as though someone is getting away with sin, but be sure the day will come when God will judge that sin. *" . . . be sure your sin will find you out" (Numbers 32:23).*

Bible Truth for Today: *"Though hand join in hand, the wicked shall not be unpunished: but the seed of the righteous shall be delivered."*
—Proverbs 11:21

March 19

Read Judges 10–12
Family Reading: Judges 10

Idolatry

"Go and cry unto the gods which ye have chosen; let them deliver you in the time of your tribulation." —*Judges 10:14*

The book of Judges, as well as the entire history of Israel in the Old Testament, presents the fact that Israel consistently slipped into idolatry. In this chapter we find that they served Baalim, and Ashtaroth, and the gods of Syria, Zidon, Moab, Ammon, and the Philistines (v. 6). This means that they *" . . . forsook the Lord, and served not him" (v. 6).*

God hates idolatry. He told Israel He would not continue to deliver them because they had forsaken Him. *"Yet ye have forsaken me, and served other gods: wherefore I will deliver you no more" (v. 13).*

God warned Israel that there will be a day of tribulation to come when sorrow and distress will seize upon them. In the time of trouble God is a wonderful refuge. It is true today that He is a refuge for us in the time of sorrow and distress. But alas! We have forsaken the Lord, have preferred other lovers to Him, and have chosen other gods beside Him. What a dreadful thought that is! You see, idolatry can be a very real enemy to us today. Paul wept over the Philippians when he said that they had among them enemies of the cross of Christ. *"For many walk, of whom I have told you often, and now tell you even weeping, that they are the enemies of the cross of Christ: Whose end is destruction, whose God is their belly, and whose glory is in their shame, who mind earthly things" (Philippians 3:18, 19).*

In Isaiah 44:20 God says that the person who serves idols *" . . . feedeth on ashes . . . "* What an awful thought to bow down to idols and be literally feeding on ashes and not honoring the Lord.

Just as Israel consistently fell into idolatry, the same thing can happen to us today. Remember God's warning. We can cry to other gods, but they cannot deliver us. Only our God can deliver!

Bible Command for Today: *"Little children, keep yourselves from idols."* —*I John 5:21*

March 20

Read Judges 13–16
Family Reading: Judges 16:1-21, 30-31

Where Does Your Strength Lie?

These four chapters of Judges give the story of Samson. As God's man, he fell into shame and disrepute. Samson, the mighty man of God, became Samson, the man mocked by the Philistines.

Delilah asked him an important question. *"And Delilah said to Samson, Tell me, I pray thee, wherein thy great strength lieth . . . "* *(v. 6)*.

In answering Delilah's request, Samson revealed he did not know where his strength lay. He was a Nazarite, one who was wholly dedicated to God in living for Him and in being separated from the world. In Numbers 6:2 God said the Nazarite was one who would take a vow to separate himself unto the Lord. Samson was a Nazarite from his birth and probably took all the blessings for granted. His life was filled with sin and self-trust. Even as he answers Delilah in Judges 16, we find him lying. Because of his sin, he lost his power. The cutting of his hair was a sign that he was not fully resting on God's promise.

Where did Samson's strength lie? It lay right where your strength lies today—in trusting the revealed Word of God. Samson needed to believe the Lord and to obey God's direction. This is the very thing he did not do. In turning from the plan of God through His Word, Samson revealed his lack of faith in the promise. Faith always considers not so much the greatness of the promise but the Author who is behind the promise. Faith realizes He is the God who cannot lie, the omnipotent God who never changes. Therefore, faith concludes the promise must be fulfilled. Samson's strength lay in trusting the Lord and His Word. The manifestation of his trusting His Word would have been his obedience to that Word.

The believer who walks with spiritual strength is the one who feeds his soul on the Word of God. At the Passover in Exodus 12, immediately following the application of the blood, the Israelite was to feed on the lamb for strength. That is a picture of our feeding on God's Word after we have put our trust in the Lamb, the Lord Jesus Christ.

March 21

Read Judges 17–19
Family Reading: Judges 18:1-26

Make Jesus King of Your Life

This chapter reveals the awful corruptness of the nation of Israel— even that connected with religion. There is nothing more corrupt than corrupt religion. The Danites took Micah's idols and his priest. He asked them, *". . . and what have I more? . . . " (v. 24).* All he had was a religion, but he did not have the Lord.

Like Micah, all these Danites wanted was a religion. All they had to do to get a priest was to offer this man the opportunity to be a priest to more people than just the man Micah. When they offered this priest an enlarged opportunity, he immediately accepted, and his *" . . . heart was glad . . . " (v. 20).* When this young man first came to Micah in Judges 17:10, he took the position because it afforded him food, clothing, and spending money. He was a priest who served only as a job.

All of this tells us that they had no king (v. 1). In fact, this whole section of Scripture emphasizes their having no king. (Read Judges 17:6; 18:1; and 19:1.)

We do not need to follow in their train; we can know the Lord Jesus and crown Him as King of our lives. When we do submit to His Lordship, we will not fall into the trap of corrupt religion.

Bible Truth for Today: *"Now the Spirit speaketh expressly, that in the latter times some shall depart from the faith, giving heed to seducing spirits, and doctrines of devils; Speaking lies in hypocrisy; having their conscience seared with a hot iron." —I Timothy 4:1, 2*

March 22

Read Judges 20 and 21
Family Reading: Judges 20:1-28

Coming to the End of Ourselves

This story of the wickedness in Gibeah is one of the most tragic stories in the Word of God. Because the Levite had cut up the body of his dead concubine and sent pieces throughout all Israel, the whole nation was stirred about the sin that was permitted in a tribe of Israel. The leaders and soldiers of Israel came together in Mizpeh to consider the problem (vv. 1-3). They heard the testimony of the Levite, and this stirred them to action (vv. 4-9).

They acted properly in asking the Benjamites to deliver the guilty people in Gibeah so that they could be put to death. The Benjamites would not deliver the inhabitants of Gibeah (v. 13). Instead, they prepared to go to war. The tribe of Benjamin did not want to face the fact of its sin.

In the balance of the chapter, we read of 65,000 men being killed. Of these, 40,000 were from the tribes that were trying to do what was right. God gave the victory over Benjamin but not until after two defeats in which the 40,000 died. It was after they inquired of the Lord (v. 27) that Israel won the victory. Before this, it appears that they had gone somewhat in their own strength. They had asked about going to battle but had really not sought the Lord's blessing. God permitted them to come to see the futility of their own effort so that they could see the victory in His power. Not until we come to the end of ourselves will we see God's power and victory in our lives.

Bible Principle for Today: *"I am the vine, ye are the branches: He that abideth in me, and I in him, the same bringeth forth much fruit:* ***for without me ye can do nothing."*** *—John 15:5*

March 23

Read Ruth 1–4
Family Reading: Ruth 1:1-14; 2:5-16

Ruth—Deciding for the Lord
and Receiving Grace

Today we are reading the entire book of Ruth. What a pity that we are forced to read through this little book so quickly. This is one of the great masterpieces of all literature, and I wish we could slow down and read it over a period of a week or more. This is a great Old Testament book that presents Boaz as a type of Jesus Christ and Ruth as a type of the bride of Christ.

The first chapter reveals the tragedy of backsliding. Elimelech and Naomi lived in Bethlehem, which means *"the house of bread."* They left Bethlehem and went to Moab, which means *"the place of desire."* They allowed their desires to take them from the place of blessing to Moab. There Elimelech and his two sons died, leaving three widows—Naomi, Ruth, and Orpah.

Naomi had decided she was going back to Bethlehem and offered her two widowed daughters-in-law the privilege of staying in Moab. Orpah acceded to Naomi's offer and stayed in Moab, but not Ruth! She gave herself to the God of Naomi and thus stayed with Naomi.

It is one thing to love the things of the Lord when all is going well, but it is another to stand fast for the Lord in the face of discouragement and difficulty. Ruth was willing to suffer for the Lord's sake. May we have the same attitude Ruth had. Ruth returned with Naomi, and God blessed her in a great way.

Bible Truth for Today: *"I beseech you therefore, brethren, by the mercies of God, that ye present your bodies a living sacrifice, holy, acceptable unto God, which is your reasonable service. And be not conformed to this world: but be ye transformed by the renewing of your mind, that ye may prove what is that good, and acceptable, and perfect, will of God."* —Romans 12:1, 2

March 24

Read I Samuel 1–3
Family Reading: I Samuel 1

A Model Mother

Hannah is a model for all mothers. She rejoiced when God gave her the privilege of motherhood. When she knew she was going to be a mother, " . . . *her countenance was no more sad" (v. 18)*.

Hannah gave her son a home that taught him to serve the Lord. From a human standpoint, we can say that Samuel became the great man that he was because of a godly mother. What made Hannah a model mother?

First, she was a praying mother. She knew what it was to come to God and wait before Him for the blessing. Because she poured out her soul before the Lord, she was able to go in peace and believe that God would grant her request (v. 15).

Second, she trusted the Lord. After she had prayed and fasted, she trusted the Lord to answer her prayer. Verse eighteen states that she ate and was no more sad. When the baby Samuel was born, she named him Samuel, which means, *"asked of God."* She believed God had answered her prayer.

Third, she honored the Lord. After she had weaned the child, she immediately took him to the temple and to the priest. Verse twenty-eight says that she had *"lent"* Samuel unto the Lord. The word *lent* literally means *given*. She gave Samuel to the Lord so that he could be used of God.

Mothers do make the difference in a society. Lord Shaftesbury said: "Give me a generation of Christian mothers, and I will undertake to change the face of English society in twelve months."

Hannah was a praying mother who trusted and honored the Lord. Mothers, give your children to God and trust Him to bless and use them.

Bible Truth for Today: *"Who can find a virtuous woman? for her price is far above rubies."* —Proverbs 31:10

March 25

Read I Samuel 4–7
Family Reading: I Samuel 6

The Will of God

In this chapter we read of the desire of the Philistines to move the Ark of the Covenant. They put it on a cart drawn by two milk cows. There are some good truths we can learn from these cows.

Both of these cows had calves, and the Philistines kept the calves shut up in a pen at home. The two cows left home and took " . . . *the straight way . . . " (v. 12)* to Beth-shemesh. This was a miracle. To get two cows to leave home and head directly in another direction is totally contrary to the nature of cows. And then to get those two cows to leave their calves behind them as they went means that God was intervening in miraculous power. All the way to Beth-shemesh the cows went lowing, crying for their calves. But they did not turn to the right hand nor to the left. They went straight to Beth-shemesh.

Here were two cattle unaccustomed to the yoke, pulling together evenly on the load. They had no driver but pulled together and went straight to Beth-shemesh. This is a miracle of the overpowering hand of God on two brute creatures. In Isaiah 1:3 God says that animals have more sense than rebellious people have: *"The ox knoweth his owner, and the ass his master's crib: but Israel doth not know, my people doth not consider."*

The two animals reveal what should be our attitude about the will of God. They left home, the place of natural desire, and left the calves of their natural affection. They were willing to deny themselves and go forward for God. They turned not to the right hand nor to the left. In the will of God, we are to go straight down the road for God. We must not let natural desires and natural affections influence our lives. To yield to the will of God is not bondage but blessing.

Character Verse: *"In all thy ways acknowledge him, and he shall direct thy paths." —Proverbs 3:6*

Bible Truth for Today: *"In the way of righteousness is life; and in the pathway thereof there is no death." —Proverbs 12:28*

March 26

Read I Samuel 8–11
Family Reading: I Samuel 8

Heed the Lord

There is a fervent desire within every one of us to be like our peers. This chapter reveals this awful wicked tendency. Samuel tried to warn the people of Israel of the danger that would come when they would have a king. The people of Israel told Samuel: " . . . *we will have a king over us; That we also may be like all the nations; and that our king may judge us, and go out before us, and fight our battles" (vv. 19, 20)*. They wanted to be like the rest of the world.

Samuel endeavored to tell them what problems would result. Samuel did convey the message to Israel that their rejection of him was actually a rejection of God (v. 7). The Lord commanded Samuel to tell them the manner of the king:

> He would appoint their sons to be his bodyguards and horsemen (v. 11).
> He would use men to be his servants in the fields (v. 12).
> He would take their daughters to be his bakers (v. 13).
> He would take away their lands and vineyards (v. 14).
> He would tax them by taking one-tenth of their sheep (vv. 15-17).

Samuel prophesied that the day would come that the Israelites would regret that they ever asked for a king (v. 18), but the people would not hearken. They cried out that they wanted a king so that they could be like all of the nations. They thought that with a king they would have someone to fight their battles. They expressed the cry of all men in their desire to have someone they could follow. They manifested a fervent desire for leadership; but at the same time, they rejected the leadership of the Lord.

Men are still the same. They need to learn to rely on the Lord rather than on their own wisdom. It was not long before the Israelites trembled under the leadership of the king just as Samuel had said they would (I Samuel 13:6, 7).

Bible Truth for Today: *"And seekest thou great things for thyself? seek them not: for, behold, I will bring evil upon all flesh, saith the Lord: but thy life will I give unto thee for a prey in all places whither thou goest." —Jeremiah 45:5*

March 27

Read I Samuel 12–14
Family Reading: I Samuel 13

Wait on the Lord

Saul's reign was filled with tragedy. He was a headstrong man who trusted in his own strength rather than in the Lord's might. This thirteenth chapter reveals a big reason for Saul's failure as the king of Israel. Because of Jonathan's victory over the Philistines, the Israelites were held " . . . *in abomination* . . . " *(v. 4)* by the Philistines. Therefore, the Philistines gathered a great army to war against Saul. This brought the Israelites to a time of great distress, and they hid themselves in caves, thickets, pits, etc. (v. 6). Some even fled to the area on the east of the Jordan River.

Then Saul made a big mistake. Samuel had promised to meet Saul in Gilgal in seven days. As Saul tarried, the people trembled in fear because of the imminent threat of the Philistines. The seventh day arrived, and Samuel had not come. In his impatience, Saul did not wait for the seventh day to pass. He decided to act on his own.

God had carefully outlined the duties of the prophet, the duties of the priest, and the duties of the king. Without special permission from God, these leaders were never to be involved in another's duties. The king was to be king but not to take the responsibility of the priest. But Saul ignored what God had commanded, and he decided he would function as his own priest. Had he just waited, Samuel would have kept his appointment. He did arrive the very same day, the seventh day, immediately after Saul had intruded into the priest's office.

In his explanation to Samuel, Saul said, " . . . *I forced myself therefore, and offered a burnt-offering*" *(v. 12)*. I am sure he was sincere, but he was impatient and rash. Because of this, Saul lost the privilege of continuing as king. Samuel told him that he had done foolishly and that another would be given the kingdom (vv. 13, 14).

Bible Truth for Today: *"One thing have I desired of the Lord, that will I seek after; that I may dwell in the house of the Lord all the days of my life, to behold the beauty of the Lord, and to enquire in his temple."* —Psalm 27:4

March 28

Read I Samuel 15–17
Family Reading: I Samuel 17:31-54

Victory Belongs to God!

David won a blessed victory. There are several reasons in this passage for his victory. First, David trusted the Lord. He used the instruments he had and understood. Beyond this, however, his faith and trust were in the Lord. As he approached Goliath, this giant Philistine cursed David by his gods. David did not retaliate with cursing. Rather, he announced publicly that his trust was in the Lord. David said: *". . . I come to thee in the name of the Lord of hosts, the God of the armies of Israel, whom thou hast defied" (v. 45).* Later David wrote in Psalm 20:7— *"Some trust in chariots, and some in horses: but we will remember the name of the Lord our God."*

Second, David told Goliath his defiance was not against Israel only but that Goliath was actually defying Almighty God. The Lord gave the victory because it was literally a battle of Goliath against God.

Third, the Lord uses human instruments. David announced that the battle was God's. He said the Lord would deliver, but the Lord had given the responsibility to David. Though the battle is the Lord's and though the victory comes from Him, God uses human instrumentality to win His battles.

Fourth, God wins the victory so that others may know of His power and might. The reason for the Lord's giving the victory is: *"that all the earth may know that there is a God in Israel" (v. 46).*

> *O for a faith that will not shrink,*
> *Though pressed by every foe,*
> *That will not tremble on the brink*
> *Of any earthly woe!*
> *—W. H. Bathurst*

Prayer and Command for Today: *"But thanks be to God, which giveth us the victory through our Lord Jesus Christ."*
—I Corinthians 15:57

March 29

Read I Samuel 18–20
Family Reading: I Samuel 18:1-18

The Love of Jonathan

In verses one and three we read that Jonathan loved David as his own soul. There is nothing greater in this life than for one Christian to know the deep love of another. What an example these two men are to us today. They had a fervent love for each other. When Jonathan died, David said: *"I am distressed for thee, my brother Jonathan: very pleasant hast thou been unto me: thy love to me was wonderful, passing the love of women" (II Samuel 1:26).*

I want to list a few traits of Jonathan that made him a great man. First, he was a man's man. Some people get the idea that if a man is loving, he is actually a sissy. This is not the case. A real man is one who manifests love to others. For two men to walk together as close friends, the essential requirement will be that they be agreed. The prophet Amos asked the question: *"Can two walk together, except they be agreed?" (Amos 3:3).* Jonathan was a man just like David. He was as skilled with the bow as David was with the sling.

Second, Jonathan was a tender and compassionate man. He showed compassion for David. With his compassion he manifested genuine character. He was willing to forsake his father to take the stand for right in being loyal to David.

Third, Jonathan was submissive. He realized David was to be king. He gave David his robe, his garments, his sword, his bow, and his girdle. These were the items that identified him as a prince and a military leader. He was willing to give them to David, thereby saying that he was surrendering all of his rights so that David could be used of God. Today we need men who are men, who are compassionate, and who are submissive.

Bible Truth for Today: *"A friend loveth at all times, and a brother is born for adversity."* *—Proverbs 17:17*

March 30

Read I Samuel 21–24
Family Reading: I Samuel 24

Vengeance Is God's

I Samuel 24 is filled with Bible truths for the life of the believer.

First, we see the awful result of jealousy in a man's life. Saul was filled with jealousy of David, causing him to take three thousand men to endeavor to kill David. He did all of this even though David had not harmed him. *"For jealousy is the rage of a man: therefore he will not spare in the day of vengeance" (Proverbs 6:34).* Saul permitted his jealousy of David to drive him to frightful depths of determination to see David slain.

But through all of this, David did not permit himself to develop hatred and bitterness. The opportunity to slay Saul was in his hand. He even regretted cutting off a piece of Saul's garment. *"And it came to pass afterward, that David's heart smote him, because he had cut off Saul's skirt" (v. 5).* David did not react to Saul; instead, he left Saul in the hand of God. He begged his servants not to stand against Saul and to be aware of the awful danger of bitterness (v. 7). David vowed that his hand would not be upon Saul, but he would commit Saul to the Lord. *"The Lord judge between me and thee, and the Lord avenge me of thee: but mine hand shall not be upon thee" (v. 12).* David, as a man after God's own heart, manifested God's grace by sparing the life of Saul.

Remember Romans 12:19 — *" . . . it is written, Vengeance is mine; I will repay, saith the Lord."* It is not so important how people act toward me as how I react toward them.

Bible Truth for Today: *"To me belongeth vengeance, and recompense; their foot shall slide in due time: for the day of their calamity is at hand, and the things that shall come upon them make haste."*

—Deuteronomy 32:35

March 31

Read I Samuel 25–27
Family Reading: I Samuel 25:14-39

Vengeance Is God's (Part II)

Note that today we are again considering this important truth that vengeance belongs to God. Why repeat this truth for two days in a row? The answer is simple—it is a very important truth that we all need to know!

I Samuel 25 is another clear illustration of the blessing of leaving vengeance with God. Nabal had mistreated David and his servants; so David decided to destroy Nabal and his men. Nabal's wife Abigail heard of the problem and rushed to meet David. She apologized for any failure on her part to take care of David's servants and pleaded with David not to carry out his plan of avenging himself. She told David that evil had not been found in him all the days of his life, and she warned that he could destroy his relationship with God. She said that God could handle His enemies very easily, for the Lord could sling the enemies as rocks out of a sling (v. 29).

David thanked Abigail for her advice, which kept him from avenging himself. He accepted the food she brought. When Abigail returned home, she found Nabal enjoying a drunken orgy. The next morning when he had sobered up, she told him of the fact that she had kept David from destroying him. Nabal suffered a heart attack and died ten days later.

Then David realized that God had taken vengeance. He said: " . . . *Blessed be the Lord, that hath pleaded the cause of my reproach from the hand of Nabal, and hath kept his servant from evil: for the Lord hath returned the wickedness of Nabal upon his own head*" *(v. 39)*. Oh, what a testimony that vengeance belongs unto God!

Perhaps there have been times when you have felt the urge to take vengeance. God will not bless such efforts. If you have this attitude, first, ask God to forgive you. Second, begin to pray for the one against whom you are vengeful. Third, leave the matter in God's hands.

Bible Principle: *"Dearly beloved, avenge not yourselves, but rather give place unto wrath: for it is written, Vengeance is mine; I will repay, saith the Lord." —Romans 12:19*

April 1

Read I Samuel 28–31
Family Reading: I Samuel 28

Result of Disobedience to God

Saul inquired of the Lord but did not receive His answer (v. 6). In I Chronicles 10:14 the Scriptures state that Saul *"inquired not of the Lord."* The Hebrew indicates that Saul did not sincerely seek the Lord. Apparently, he asked of God but was not willing to follow God's direction. Therefore, God did not give him an answer.

Saul, in turn, tried to seek an answer from the kingdom of darkness. In this we see Saul's insincerity. Saul had outlawed familiar spirits (I Samuel 28:9). However, he had made no sincere effort to get rid of them; and then he sought one himself. In verse ten Saul swore to the witch that he would not enforce his own law! It was no wonder the kingdom was in trouble.

Did Samuel actually appear to Saul? Yes, I believe he did. The witch could not bring Samuel to speak to Saul. By the power of Satan, she could have demons imitate Samuel's voice; but even she was surprised when Samuel actually appeared (v. 12). God overruled what satanic sources were doing and sent his prophet back with a message of doom for Saul. Samuel's message was that the Lord had become Saul's enemy, and the kingdom would be taken from him. Saul's tragic end was announced and settled.

The life of Saul gives us the dreadful story of the results of disobedience to God. He was a man who started with great promise. However, because of an unwillingness to obey the Lord, Saul lost everything.

Bible Command for Today: *"But the God of all grace, who hath called us unto his eternal glory by Christ Jesus, after that ye have suffered a while, make you perfect, stablish, strengthen, settle you."*

—I Peter 5:10

April 2

Read II Samuel 1–3
Family Reading: II Samuel 2:8-28

A Fool Died

According to II Samuel 3:33, David asked a question concerning Abner: " . . . *Died Abner as a fool dieth?"* Surely David and others thought Abner had acted as a fool in not staying in the city of refuge. He could have been safe from the avenger of blood by remaining in the city of refuge.

Abner was not a fool because he was dumb. David considered Abner a military genius. He said of Abner, " . . . *there is a prince and a great man fallen this day in Israel" (II Samuel 3:38).* Abner died as a fool because he lived as a fool. II Samuel 2 tells us some ways in which Abner was a fool. *"It is as sport to a fool to do mischief: but a man of understanding hath wisdom" (Proverbs 10:23).* In II Samuel 2:14 " . . . *Abner said to Joab, Let the young men now arise, and play before us . . . "* What Abner called *play* was the thrusting of each man's sword into another's side. This bloody, murderous game Abner called *"play."* God said a man who makes sport of mischief is a fool.

Abner made a mockery of sin. God says in Proverbs 14:9, *"Fools make a mock at sin . . . "* Abner learned that a man who makes a mockery of sin would be considered a wicked fool. *"The fool hath said in his heart, There is no God . . . " (Psalm 14:1).* The word for *mock* is the same word that is translated in other Scriptures as *scorn.* It refers to someone making fun of a foreigner who talks and dresses differently from the residents. God says that the man who makes fun of the foreigner is a mocker, a derider, a scorner. He imitates the foreigner in his actions and speech and gets laughs out of the crowd. God calls that *mocking.* One who mocks sin is a fool.

Finally, Abner died as a fool because he refused the protection of the city of refuge. He refused to turn to Christ and be saved. Any man who refuses Jesus Christ is deemed a fool by God.

Bible Truth — All Should Flee for Refuge to Jesus Christ.

" . . . who have fled for refuge to lay hold upon the hope set before us: . . . Whither the forerunner is for us entered, even Jesus . . ."

—Hebrews 6:18, 20

April 3

Read II Samuel 4–7
Family Reading: II Samuel 7

Claiming His Promises

*"And now, O Lord God, the word that thou hast spoken . . . **do as thou hast said**" (II Samuel 7:25).*

David was claiming God's promises. His promises were never meant to be thrown aside as wastepaper. He intended that we should use His promises. God's gold is not miser's money. It is mined and minted so that it can be traded. The thing that pleases God most is to see that His promises are put in circulation.

God actually loves to have His children bring a promise before Him and say, *"Lord, do as thou hast said."* Do you realize that we actually glorify God when we claim His promises? Do you think that He will be poorer when He gives you the riches He has promised? Do you suppose that He will lose holiness when He gives you holiness? Or do you think that He could be bankrupted by meeting your needs?

Assurance of salvation comes by claiming His promise that whosoever believes has eternal life. I have believed on Him; therefore, I can claim His promise that I have eternal life.

The same is true with His pardon and forgiveness. Though our sins be as scarlet, they shall be as white as snow (Isaiah 1:18). Faith claims that promise. To fail to claim it is to doubt God's Word. God is anxious to pardon, to cleanse, and to forgive. Let's not show lack of faith by wondering if His promises are really true.

When a Christian notes a promise, if he does not take it to God, he dishonors the Lord. He can and will honor the Lord if he will come boldly before the throne of grace and say, "Lord, I am unworthy and undeserving; but I bring Thy promise before Thee. I have nothing to recommend me but that Thou hast said it." The sun never wearies of shining, and the river never tires of flowing. And God delights in meeting needs. Therefore, take His promise and say, *"Lord, do as thou hast said."*

Bible Truth for Today: *"Call unto me, and I will answer thee, and show thee great and mighty things, which thou knowest not."*

—Jeremiah 33:3

April 4

Read II Samuel 8–11
Family Reading: II Samuel 11

Sin Produces a Hard Heart

The story of David's sin in II Samuel 11 is a frightful revelation of the danger of sin. God had said that David was *" . . . a man after his own heart . . . " (I Samuel 13:14).* Please note that though he was a special man after God's *"own heart,"* he was still a man. It is always essential to remember that the best of men are men at the best. As a man, David sinned grievously against the Lord.

One of the insidious results of sin is that it leaves the heart cold toward God and calloused toward the sin. In verse twenty-five David said to Joab, *" . . . Let not this thing displease thee, for the sword devoureth one as well as another . . . "*

How cold David's heart had become! It did not grieve him that he had committed murder. He should have been broken over the vileness of his sin, but he showed no remorse whatsoever. How deceptive sin is!

David sent word to Joab that he should not let this wicked murder **displease** him. However, God is careful to reveal, *" . . . But the thing that David had done **displeased** the Lord" (v. 27).*

That which displeases God should always displease us. May we learn to hate sin and always be displeased with that which is contrary to God's will and to His Word. I believe David learned his lesson, for later he wrote in Psalm 139:21, 22, *"Do not I hate them, O Lord, that hate thee? . . . I hate them with perfect hatred: I count them mine enemies."*

A Scriptural Attitude About Sin: *"For behold this selfsame thing, that ye sorrowed after a godly sort, what carefulness it wrought in you, yea, what clearing of yourselves, yea, what indignation, yea, what fear, yea, what vehement desire, yea, what zeal, yea, what revenge!"* — *II Corinthians 7:11*

Bible Truth for Today: *"But exhort one another daily, while it is called Today; lest any of you be hardened through the deceitfulness of sin." —Hebrews 3:13*

April 5

Read II Samuel 12 and 13
Family Reading: II Samuel 13:3, 15-36

The Results of Sin

In this thirteenth chapter we find some frightening lessons about sin. First, we see Amnon being influenced by an evil man, Jonadab. This man contrived a scheme whereby Amnon could defile his sister Tamar. This demonstrates the danger of evil companions. Had Amnon not listened to the wicked idea of this evil man, the whole sordid story of II Samuel 13 would probably never have been told. But because of wrong influence, Amnon committed a dreadful sin.

This incident triggered within Absalom a bitter spirit. Verse twenty-two states that " . . . *Absalom hated Amnon, because he had forced his sister Tamar."* Absalom nurtured that bitter spirit and let it breed and grow within his emotions. Bitterness is always something that springs from a hidden root. *"Looking diligently lest any man fail of the grace of God; lest any root of bitterness springing up trouble you, and thereby many be defiled" (Hebrews 12:15).*

Absalom permitted bitterness to cloud his judgment and cause him to commit a rash act. He had Amnon murdered. He was so deceived by his bitter spirit he actually thought that killing Amnon was a valiant act (v. 28). His bitterness then caused him to have broken fellowship. Verse thirty-four tells us that he " . . . *fled . . . "* He was separated from his father and his friends.

Bitterness is wicked. It will destroy the one who believed he had the right to harbor ill will and malice. Beware of lust—the sin of Amnon. And beware of bitterness—the sin of Absalom.

Bible Truth for Today: *"Let all bitterness, and wrath, and anger, and clamor, and evil speaking, be put away from you, with all malice." —Ephesians 4:31*

April 6

Read II Samuel 14 –16
Family Reading: II Samuel 16

Beware of Flattery

In this passage we have two stories that contrast for us reactions that individuals have. In the first four verses, we find David being flattered by Ziba, the false servant of Mephibosheth. Ziba brought him gifts and told David they were for his use. Ziba told David that his master was back in Jerusalem, hoping that the kingdom of Israel would be restored to him. This was, of course, false. We realize this when we read Mephibosheth's testimony in II Samuel 19:25-28.

In verses five through fourteen we find Shimei cursing David. Actually, the cursing of David was a greater blessing than the flattery. He succumbed to the flattery, but he rose to new heights of character under the cursing.

How often does Satan work this way with us. He brings flattery to cause us to fall. May God give us grace to realize there is great danger in flattery and the offering of gifts. God says in Deuteronomy 16:19, " . . . *thou shalt not respect persons, neither take a gift: for a gift doth blind the eyes of the wise, and pervert the words of the righteous.*" This is what happened to David when he accepted the flattery and the gift from Ziba. He gave away all of the right that Mephibosheth had to a liar and a cheat who was simply trying to get Mephibosheth's inheritance by deceptive means. David fell for this line and thereby says to us to beware of the deceitfulness of Satan.

In the book of Proverbs, God gives strong warning concerning flattery: " . . . *therefore meddle not with him that flattereth with his lips*" (20:19). " . . . *and a flattering mouth worketh ruin*" (26:28). "*A man that flattereth his neighbor spreadeth a net for his feet*" (29:5).

Bible Truth for Today: *"The Lord shall cut off all flattering lips, and the tongue that speaketh proud things."* —Psalm 12:3

April 7

Read II Samuel 17–19
Family Reading: II Samuel 18:9-33

The Tragedy of Rebellion

This is the story of the death of Absalom. He was out to kill the anointed king of Israel, his own father David. With deep-seated rebellion against his father and against God, he was determined to have his own way. He rode a mule en route to finding and killing his father. He was rebelling not only against King David but also against the Lord. And God intervened! As Absalom rode under the low-hanging branch of a big oak tree, his long hair (another mark of his pride) caught in the branch; and he was thus lifted off his mule. There he hung between Heaven and earth, as unworthy of either, and as abandoned by both.

I believe God hung him thus in the tree to give warning to all succeeding generations that rebellion against parents is a very wicked sin.

Proverbs 30:17 states, *"The eye that mocketh at his father, and despiseth to obey his mother, the ravens of the valley shall pick it out, and the young eagles shall eat it."*

Absalom died a terrible death. Hanging there by his hair, he was thrust through with darts by Joab and the young men with him. Absalom was given a very disgraceful burial. Verse seventeen states that they cast his body into a deep pit in the woods. They put a great heap of stones on him to symbolize that he should have been stoned as a rebellious son. Absalom had thought of a good burial for his body by building the pillar mentioned in verse eighteen, but he had given no thought to his soul and eternity.

Bible Truth for Today: *"Honor thy father and thy mother: that thy days may be long upon the land which the Lord thy God giveth thee."*
—Exodus 20:12

April 8

Read II Samuel 20–22
Family Reading: II Samuel 22:1-23

Deliverance

II Samuel 22 presents David's song of deliverance. Since the word *salvation* means *deliverance*, this song would be the praise of one who had been saved by the grace of God. This would correspond to our singing, "Since Jesus Came Into My Heart." We who have been saved can sing this same song with David.

David praised the Lord that he had been delivered from all his enemies. David was a man after God's heart but not after man's heart. He had numerous enemies. Please note in verse one that David does not call Saul an enemy. In reading the record, we would believe that Saul was David's chief enemy. David did not hate Saul; he did not count Saul an enemy. However, he realized that his deliverance from Saul was entirely by the power of God.

David said that the Lord was his rock, his fortress, and his deliverer. In the whole song he emphasizes that God is his rock. He asks, " . . . *who is a rock, save our God?" (v. 32).* There is no other Rock on which we can stand except our Lord, the Rock of our salvation. He is our Rock on whom we can stand, our Fortress in whom we can hide, our Shield behind whom we can have protection, our Tower of salvation which can never be battered or destroyed. He delivers us from our enemies and from the evils which would ruin us.

In verse eighteen David says that the Lord delivered him from his enemies, from them that hated him, and from them who were too strong for him. David needed to be delivered from self as well as from Saul, from adulterous thinking as well as from Absalom. All of us need to see that self is an enemy as real as any enemy and more dangerous than enemies outside. Let us ask God to deliver us from SELF!

Bible Truth for Today: *"So then they that are in the flesh cannot please God." —Romans 8:8*

April 9

Read II Samuel 23 and 24 and I Kings 1
Family Reading: II Samuel 24

Paying the Price

David had sinned against God. The prophet Gad offered David three choices of punishment from God. He could choose either seven years of famine, defeat and pursuit by his enemies for three months, or three days of pestilence in Israel. David chose the three days of pestilence, a severe plague. David made this choice because he knew God would send the plague; therefore, he would be literally casting himself into the hand of the Lord. He knew that his enemies would not show the mercy God would show. The plague was severe. Seventy thousand people died.

David prayed, asking God to smite him rather than the people. Then Gad appeared to ask David to offer a sacrifice unto the Lord. God instructed him that the sacrifice was to be offered at the threshingfloor of Araunah. When David endeavored to buy the threshingfloor, Araunah offered to give it to him without any charge. David said: *" . . . Nay; but I will surely buy it of thee at a price: neither will I offer burnt-offerings unto the Lord my God of that which doth cost me nothing . . . " (v. 24)*. David did pay for the threshingfloor; he did present the offering; and because of this offering, the plague was stopped in Israel.

David refused to present an offering that cost him nothing. He realized that a sacrifice must cost something or be worthless. Far too many of God's people are endeavoring to live for the Lord without any cost to themselves. David paid the price. We, too, must pay the price to serve the Lord.

Bible Truth for Today: *"For we which live are always delivered unto death for Jesus' sake, that the life also of Jesus might be made manifest in our mortal flesh." —II Corinthians 4:11*

April 10

Read I Kings 2 and 3
Family Reading: I Kings 3:1-15 and 4:29-34

The Wisdom of Solomon

Solomon's wisdom was given by God. He received wisdom in answer to a prayer that pleased the Lord. Solomon pleased the Lord because he recognized his inadequacies. He was a humble man who prayed, " . . . *I am but a little child: I know not how to go out or come in" (3:7).*

Another thing that pleased the Lord was that Solomon recognized his responsibilities. He knew that the only way he could fulfill his responsibility was to have a miraculous gift of wisdom and understanding from God. He called himself the servant of the Lord.

In his prayer Solomon asked for an understanding heart to judge the people. He recognized that no one without God's strength, wisdom, and understanding could judge the people aright.

Would it not be wonderful if political leaders today would carry the same attitude? So often they have the idea they have been chosen because of their own great ability. If they could recognize that they are totally inadequate except for the power and grace of God, it would make a tremendous difference in the governing of the world today.

The Lord told Solomon that He was pleased with his prayer request. Solomon had not asked for long life nor riches nor the defeat of his enemies. He had asked instead for understanding to discern judgment. What an important prayer this is for all of us to pray! In answering the prayer, God said that He had given Solomon so much wisdom and understanding that there was none like him before and there would never be anyone so wise as he again. I personally believe that there has not been any human so wise as Solomon since that day. According to I Kings 4:32, he authored 3,000 proverbs and wrote 1,005 psalms. As we read the book of Proverbs, we realize what great wisdom God gave him.

Let us ask for a similar need to be met in our lives.

Bible Truth for Today: *"If any of you lack wisdom, let him ask of God, that giveth to all men liberally, and upbraideth not; and it shall be given him." —James 1:5*

April 11

Read I Kings 4–6
Family Reading: I Kings 6:1-22

Honoring the Lord First

God's Word came to Solomon. First, God let Solomon know that He took notice of what Solomon was doing: *"Concerning this house which thou art in building" (v. 12).* There is no work we do for God that goes unnoticed by Him. In each of the letters that the Lord wrote to the seven churches in Revelation 2 and 3, the Lord said, *"I know thy works . . . "* He is observing what we are doing. There is nothing good done for Him but what God has His eye upon the work and the one performing it.

Second, the Lord assured Solomon that if he would be obedient to God—walking in His statutes, executing His judgments, and keeping His commandments—God would bless in a special way. In addition, the Lord promised to dwell among the children of Israel and not forsake them.

God gave Solomon these promises to encourage him. Very likely Solomon realized the same temptations that come to us. We get weary with the expense or care of the work and wish we had never begun. But God promised Solomon the establishment of his family and kingdom. Thus he could realize that he would be abundantly recompensed for all his labors and all the pains associated with the work. An eye to God's promises will always carry us cheerfully through the work.

God promised blessing if Solomon obeyed. However, that implies that the converse is also true. The glory of the temple could and would depart unless Solomon and his people continued to walk in God's statutes. May we labor for God, always remembering our obedience is more important than our labor.

New Testament Truth for Today: *"But seek ye first the kingdom of God, and his righteousness; and all these things shall be added unto you." —Matthew 6:33*

April 12

Read I Kings 7 and 8
Family Reading: I Kings 8:46-66

Solomon's Prayer and Blessing

Solomon had just prayed his prayer beseeching the Lord to forgive the sins of Israel. He had knelt at the altar of the Lord and prayed for Israel. He interceded for his people, knowing that they would sin and that judgment would come as a result. They would be smitten down before the enemy because of sin (v. 33); there would be no rain because of their sin (v. 35); or they would experience famine, pestilence, or plague because of their sin (v. 37). In all of these things, Solomon besought the Lord that if Israel repented, God would forgive and cleanse.

Solomon knew the sinful heart of man and how man will rebel against God. The Lord had given him wisdom in answer to his prayer; therefore, he understood the nature of God's people and knew that they would rebel with a strong inclination to yield to the flesh and sin.

After his prayer, Solomon stood and blessed the people. He announced the blessings which God had given and which He would give to Israel:

1. The Lord had given rest to the nation of Israel according to His promise (v. 56).

2. Not one word of all God's promise had ever failed (v. 56).

3. God would be with Israel and not forsake the nation (v. 57).

4. God is able to incline the hearts of His people to walk in His statutes and ways (v. 58).

The purpose that Solomon gave for having Israel thus live for and bless God was *"That all the people of the earth may know that the Lord is God, and there is none else" (v. 60).* God's purpose always includes giving the witness to those outside the family of God.

Bible Truth for Today: *"If we confess our sins, he is faithful and just to forgive us our sins, and to cleanse us from all unrighteousness." —I John 1:9*

April 13

Read I Kings 9–11
Family Reading: I Kings 10:1-23

The World Recognizes God's Blessings

I always get thrilled when I read I Kings 10. It tells of the visit of the queen of Sheba to Jerusalem. She came to learn from Solomon. I believe she wanted to know more about the Lord whom Solomon served. We read that she came because she had heard of the fame of Solomon " . . . *concerning the name of the Lord . . .* " *(v. 1).* Jesus said that she came " *. . . to hear the wisdom of Solomon . . .* " (Matthew 12:42). She had not come to spy out his land nor to arrange a treaty with him, but rather to learn from his great wisdom.

When she saw the greatness of Solomon's kingdom and the glory of his reign, she told him that she had not believed the reports she had heard. But now she knew that not even the half had been told her. She realized that when a man permits the Lord Jehovah to reign, there will be blessings untold.

The queen recognized that Solomon's men were happy and his servants were happy. When Christ is honored and put in first place, there will be general joy in the midst of the assembly. The queen further recognized that all of this joy and blessing came from the Lord because she said, *"Blessed be the Lord thy God, which delighted in thee, to set thee on the throne of Israel: because the Lord loved Israel for ever, therefore made he thee king, to do judgment and justice"* *(v. 9).*

What a blessing it is when the world can look at God's people and recognize God has blessed them in an abundant way!

Bible Truth for Today: *"But ye are a chosen generation, a royal priesthood, an holy nation, a peculiar people; that ye should show forth the praises of him who hath called you out of darkness into his marvelous light." —I Peter 2:9*

April 14

Read I Kings 12–14
Family Reading: I Kings 13:1-22

Always Obey God

God is dealing with a man of God. At least fifteen times in this chapter he is referred to as *"a man of God."* He spoke as a man of God, fearlessly speaking out against the pagan altar which Jeroboam built at Bethel (v. 2). He prophesied as a man of God, predicting the destruction of the altar at Bethel (v. 3). He witnessed miracles as a man of God, seeing Jeroboam's hand withered (v. 4). He prayed with power as a man of God when he besought the Lord, and the king's hand was restored as it had been before (v. 6). He acted as a man of God when he refused to accept a bribe from Jeroboam (v. 8). He received his orders as a man of God, directly from God (v. 9).

However, he failed as a man of God when he hearkened to another man rather than to the explicit Word of God. A prophet came to him and lied to him (v. 18). The man of God had his orders directly from God. He knew what he was to do, but he hearkened unto man and thus disobeyed God. Disobedience to God is a very serious matter. The prophet told him that since he *" . . . disobeyed the mouth of the Lord, . . . "* and had *" . . . not kept the commandment . . . "* of the Lord, he would die before his time and not be in the place of the sepulchre of his fathers (vv. 21, 22). Because he disobeyed God, a lion killed him in the way (v. 24).

This man of God committed the sin unto death. This is a sin which Christians can commit by their disobedience to God. I John 5:16 states, *" . . . There is a sin unto death . . . "* A Christian must obey the Lord!

Promise for Today: *"And we are his witnesses of these things; and so is also the Holy Ghost, whom God hath given to them that obey him." —Acts 5:32*

April 15

Read I Kings 15–17
Family Reading: I Kings 15:1-24

Rely on the Lord

Our Lord desires complete dedication and yieldedness to Him. Without total surrender to His will and leading, we can get into deep and serious problems. God does not weigh the good we do against the bad to determine our salvation because salvation is a gift of God. The same is true with our Christian life. We have received Christ by faith. We are to live for Him and walk in Him by faith also (Colossians 2:6).

King Asa is a case in point. He began his reign by doing that which was right, but he ended his life in disgrace and ruin. He did not apply Biblical principles to every circumstance of life.

"Asa did that which was right in the eyes of the Lord . . . " (v. 11). He first removed the sodomites from the land; then he removed the idols. He went so far in doing right that he removed his mother from being the queen of Judah. She had made an idol in a grove, and he believed that this disqualified her from being a leader.

But we see definite weaknesses in Asa's life. He did not remove the high places (v. 14). He turned to Ben-hadad for help in his battles with Baasha, king of Israel (vv. 18, 19).

May we learn from Asa's life to be obedient and to rely on the Lord, not on man. God wants complete obedience. Christ needs to be the preeminent One.

Bible Truth for Today: *"Look to yourselves, that we lose not those things which we have wrought, but that we receive a full reward."*

—II John 8

April 16

Read I Kings 18 and 19
Family Reading: I Kings 19

Victory over Discouragement

Though a man of God, Elijah was still open to the temptations of the flesh (James 5:17). In I Kings 19 his flesh manifested itself to hinder his ministry. He became discouraged and asked God that he might die.

Jezebel and Ahab had been wearing down this mighty man of God. He was letting discouragement defeat him. But note that God did not remove Jezebel at this time. God may not remove our problems. He wants us to live in victory over them. But in reality Jezebel was not as big an enemy to Elijah as was his own discouragement.

Elijah is not the only great man who succumbed to testing of the flesh. David defeated Goliath but later said, " . . . *I shall now perish one day by the hand of Saul . . . " (I Samuel 27:1).* All of us may be plagued with discouragement and fear, but we must not let that defeat us.

God had Elijah witness a strong wind, an earthquake, and a fire; however, God was not in any of these. Then the Lord spoke to him in a still, small voice. God often reveals Himself through the silent operation of the Holy Spirit. Those who must have an atmosphere of excitement will have an extorted faith. Elijah was to trust God's quiet workings and wait. This did not mean he would not have excitement. Any man who is mightily used of God before the crowds is a man who has been alone to hear the still, small voice of God. He who is often in God's presence will have victory over discouragement.

Bible Truth for Today: *"I can do all things through Christ which strengtheneth me."* —*Philippians 4:13*

April 17

Read I Kings 20 and 21
Family Reading: I Kings 20:23-43

The Danger of Compromise

Ahab compromised with Ben-hadad, and God told him he would pay for the compromise. Ben-hadad saw that he was losing the battle with Israel. His men suggested the plan whereby he would offer the opportunity of compromise to Ahab. The servants came to Ahab in an attitude of surrender. They suggested that Ben-hadad was Ahab's servant, and they requested that he might live. Ahab immediately called Ben-hadad his brother. When Ahab referred to Ben-hadad as his brother, these servants knew that Ben-hadad would be spared. The servants brought the Syrian king to Ahab, who made a covenant with him.

Ahab was always ready to compromise rather than to stand for that which was right. When any man refers to an enemy of God as "my brother," he has drifted away from God and His Word. The so-called Bible believers today who call the unbelieving enemies of God their brothers will ruin the witness for the Lord.

God used a faithful prophet to pronounce judgment to Ahab. *" . . . Because thou hast let go out of thy hand a man whom I appointed to utter destruction, therefore thy life shall go for his life, and thy people for his people"* (v. 42). God will not permit compromise with His enemies to pass unpunished. Compromise is a most serious sin in the eye of God. In the day in which we live, too often compromise is popular and not considered a serious violation against God. Ahab lost the kingdom and his privilege as king because of the sin of compromise.

Bible Truth for Today: *"Be ye not unequally yoked together with unbelievers: for what fellowship hath righteousness with unrighteousness? and what communion hath light with darkness?"*
                                                    —II Corinthians 6:14

April 18

Read I Kings 22 and II Kings 1
Family Reading: I Kings 22:6-28, 34-37

Preach the Word

Micaiah was a faithful prophet. His message in this passage came to pass. There are several things to note in this passage concerning him:

1. Micaiah did not go along with the rest of the prophets. He was told that the others spoke good unto the king and that he should likewise speak good (v. 13). There will always be the temptation to the prophet of God to be like the rest of the so-called prophets. But a prophet must get his message from God. He cannot simply fit his message to please other men.

2. Micaiah received his message directly from the Lord. *" . . . As the Lord liveth, what the Lord saith unto me, that will I speak"* *(v. 14).* This is the need in the life of every preacher. May God deliver us from preaching anything but the Word of God.

3. Micaiah endured criticism and persecution when he faithfully proclaimed the Word of God. Ahab asked Jehoshaphat, *" . . . Did I not tell thee that he would prophesy no good concerning me, but evil?" (v. 18).* Ahab wanted to hear that which was pleasant. Micaiah was faithful to give him only the Word of the Lord, and for this he was thrown into prison. God has warned us that the time will come when men will not endure sound doctrine but will turn their minds from the truth unto fables. We are in these days today. We need more Micaiahs to pronounce: *" . . . As the Lord liveth, what the Lord saith unto me, that will I speak."*

4. Micaiah took a strong stand against the lying prophets. He would not join them; but instead he stood against them, being ready to speak out and identify their apostasy.

We need some good, old-fashioned Micaiahs among us today.

Bible Truth for Today: *"Preach the word; be instant in season, out of season; reprove, rebuke, exhort with all longsuffering and doctrine."* —II Timothy 4:2

April 19

Read II Kings 2–4
Family Reading: II Kings 2

God's Power

As Elijah was caught up by God, his mantle fell, and Elisha replaced his own clothes with it. When Elisha came to the bank of Jordan, he took the mantle of Elijah and smote the waters, and said: " . . . *Where is the Lord God of Elijah? . . . "(v. 14).* Then when he had smitten the waters, the Bible states that the waters parted, and Elisha went over.

Elisha's faith was in the Lord God, and not in the prophet Elijah. He had honored Elijah and stayed with him; but when Elijah was caught up, Elisha had his faith in the Lord. The mantle that he wore was the same one that Elijah had placed on him in I Kings 19. From that day on, Elisha followed and honored God's prophet. Now he looked to the Lord because he realized that the power Elijah had was not his own but came from the Lord.

Elisha performed twice as many miracles as Elijah did. But Elisha knew that his power did not come from himself; he needed the Lord God of Elijah.

When we lose an Elijah, we do not lose Elijah's God. He has not forsaken the earth. We must always keep our eyes on the Lord and believe Him for His power.

It is important that we want to walk in the step and the spirit of our godly and faithful predecessors. As we realize the power they had, we can ask God for the same power and grace they experienced. Elijah's God will be Elisha's God also. The Lord God of the holy prophets is the same yesterday, today, and forever. However, it will avail us nothing to have the mantles of those who are gone, to have their places and their books, if we do not have their spirit, their power, and their God.

Bible Principle for Today: *"Then he answered and spake unto me, saying, This is the word of the Lord unto Zerubbabel, saying, Not by might, nor by power, but by my spirit, saith the Lord of hosts."*
—Zechariah 4:6

April 20

Read II Kings 5–7
Family Reading: II Kings 5:1-19

The Healing of Naaman

Leprosy is a disease that comes from within and manifests itself on the outside. A sinner's problem is not the acts of sin that he commits but rather the nature of sin within him (Jeremiah 17:9). He needs to be cleansed completely and changed by the power of God.

Naaman had been able to cover his leprosy with his army uniform. Just like self-righteous people today, he hid his sin from the world in order to look respectable. However, no man can hide his sin from God. Before Naaman was healed, he had to strip off all of his clothes and go down into the River Jordan. Not until he was willing to go beyond the facade of his fancy chariot, his respectable uniform, his bags of money, and his retinue of servants and admit that he was a needy leper, could Naaman see the healing miracle of God.

Like many today, Naaman had his own ideas about how to get saved: " . . . *Behold, **I thought**, He will surely come out to me, and stand, and call on the name of the Lord his God, and strike his hand over the place, and recover the leper" (v. 11)*. Regardless of what Naaman thought, he needed to seek the miracle of cleansing in God's way. Today there are those who think that baptism or church membership or good works will save. However, all must go God's way, and He says clearly, " . . . *Ye must be born again"* (John 3:7). Friend, today take God at His Word. Accept what He has said. Believe Him and be sure that you are cleansed from your sin by placing your faith in Jesus Christ.

Bible Truth for Today: *"Jesus answered and said unto him, Verily, verily, I say unto thee, Except a man be born again, he cannot see the kingdom of God." —John 3:3*

April 21

Read II Kings 8 and 9
Family Reading: II Kings 8:1-19

The Depths of Sin

When Elisha told Hazael what he would do, Hazael could not believe it. He did not believe he would ever set the strongholds of Israel on fire, or kill their young men with a sword, or kill little children, or rip up mothers with child. He was shocked that Elisha would even think such a thing; but Elisha was speaking forth the message of God, and God knows our hearts. Not one of us knows the length to which he will go in sin. Proverbs 4:19 reads: *"The way of the wicked is as darkness: they know not at what they stumble."* Hazael did not know all of his potential to commit vile sin.

I Corinthians 10:12 states: *"Wherefore let him that thinketh he standeth take heed lest he fall."* Proverbs 4:23 should challenge us: *"Keep thy heart with all diligence; for out of it are the issues of life."* Again, Jeremiah 17:9 warns us clearly: *"The heart is deceitful above all things, and desperately wicked: who can know it?"* Not one of us can know the potential of horrible sin that exists in our lives. We do not realize the possibility of what we could do if given the right provocation.

"And Hazael said, But what, is thy servant a dog, that he should do this great thing? . . . " (v. 13). Though he could not believe he would do it—yet, within twenty-four hours he had begun by killing the king (v. 15). From that day until he died, Hazael oppressed Israel and resisted God (II Kings 10:32 and 13:4).

Today we need to ask God to reveal how wicked our hearts actually are. Each of us must pray: "Lord, give me grace to be delivered from the depth of sin." Colgate wisely said, "The sin you now tremble at, if left to yourself, you will commit."

Paul's Desire—Our Need Today: *"Was then that which is good made death unto me? God forbid. But sin, that it might appear sin, working death in me by that which is good; that sin by the commandment might become exceeding sinful."* —Romans 7:13

April 22

Read II Kings 10–12
Family Reading: II Kings 10:11-33

Sin Will Bring Its Fruit

Jehu served the Lord with zeal but was not careful about sin in his own life. In verse sixteen, Jehu invited Jehonadab into his chariot so that he could see Jehu's " . . . *zeal for the Lord* . . . " Here he was, serving God with zeal, and yet in verse thirty-two we read that in those very days, the Lord began to cut Israel short. So judgment was falling on Israel, even while the king was manifesting a zeal for the Lord. Today we need to learn from this passage. It is possible—and it is happening today—for a person or a church to allow sin to infiltrate even while a zeal for the Lord is manifested.

Jehu had a zeal for the Lord; but it was only a proud, surface zeal. It was not a deep-seated conviction that affected every area of his life. We can see his sinful attitude when we read of his pride in verse sixteen: *"And he said . . . see my zeal for the Lord . . . "* He manifested that zeal by slaying all that remained of Ahab's family. But then immediately he lied. He announced that he would serve Baal even more than Ahab had done, hiding his real intent of killing all of the Baal priests and destroying their idols.

Certainly it is right to destroy Baalism, but it is not right to do it in a deceptive way. Dr. Bob Jones, Sr., said, "It is never right to do wrong in order to get a chance to do right." Jehu's heart was not right, and he did not intend to live to the glory of God. His motives were not pleasing to the Lord because he did not separate himself from the sins of Jeroboam. (See v. 31.)

Sin was taking its toll. Even while zeal was manifested, the Lord was beginning to cut Israel short. May we remember that God is more concerned about our *being* than He is about our *doing*. While we are *doing*, we must also *be* right.

Bible Truth for Today" " . . . *be ye clean, that bear the vessels of the Lord."* —*Isaiah 52:11*

April 23

Read II Kings 13–15
Family Reading: II Kings 13

May We Long for Victory

Elisha, the prophet of God, had become very ill. Even though Joash, king of Israel, was a man who did evil (v. 11), he did have some conscience. When he heard that Elisha was so ill, he came to him and wept over him, saying, " . . . *O my father, my father, the chariot of Israel, and the horsemen thereof" (v. 14).* In so acclaiming Elisha, Joash was stating that he felt Elisha was needed in the kingdom. He respected his age and realized that Elisha had been as the horses and chariots carrying Israel along. The truth of this is borne out because as soon as Elisha died, the Moabites invaded the land (v. 20). Oftentimes people forget how much a man contributes to the defense of a nation by keeping back the judgment of God.

Elisha commanded the king to take a bow and arrows. He then put his hands upon the king's hands. Elisha was demonstrating to the king that he was to go to war against the nation of Syria and defeat them because the Syrians were oppressing the nation of Israel. It also indicated to the king that he needed to rely on the blessing of God. He could not win the battle without the Lord. He opened the window and was to shoot the arrows eastward toward Syria. Elisha also commanded him to smite the arrows on the ground. The fact that he smote so few times indicated to Elisha that he did not really want to have a total victory over Syria.

This passage teaches that God wants His people zealously to press for the victory that is in the Lord Jesus Christ. In order to do that, we must always take advantage of the blessings at hand. God is ready to give the victory, but we must permit Him to use us.

Bible Truth for Today: *"But thanks be to God, which giveth us the victory through our Lord Jesus Christ."* —I Corinthians 15:57

April 24

Read II Kings 16–18
Family Reading: II Kings 17:1-23

Sin Brings Captivity

Israel, the northern kingdom of Samaria, was carried away captive by Shalmaneser, the king of Assyria. In verses seven through eighteen, God gives the reasons that they were captured. As a result of their sin, God permitted their captivity by the Assyrians.

In verse seven God says that the Israelites were captives in a strange land because of their sin against the Lord. He immediately reminds them that He had brought them up out of Egypt and that they had feared the Lord. God always wants us to meditate on what He has done for us. In Revelation 2:5 He asks Ephesus to *"Remember therefore whence thou art fallen . . . "* Isaiah asked Israel to *" . . . look unto the rock whence ye are hewn, and to the hole of the pit whence ye are digged" (Isaiah 51:1)*. God wants us to remember the awful pit of sin from which He lifted us. Thank God He brought you out of Egypt.

Then God lists the sins that brought them into captivity:

1. *" . . . walked in the statutes of the heathen . . . " (v. 8)*.

2. *" . . . did secretly those things that were not right . . . " (v. 9)*.

3. *" . . . built high places . . . and groves"* for wicked worship of pagan gods (vv. 9-13).

4. Refused to listen to God's message which His prophets delivered (v. 14).

5. Rejected and departed from the Word of God and His commandments (vv. 15,16).

6. *" . . . sold themselves"* over to paganism and idolatry (v. 17).

7. Because of the indictment listed in the previous verses, God removed Israel from the land and permitted them to be placed in captivity (v. 18).

Bible Principle for Today: *"Jesus answered them, Verily, verily, I say unto you, Whosoever committeth sin is the servant of sin."*

—John 8:34

April 25

Read II Kings 19–21
Family Reading: II Kings 19:14-37

Miraculous Answer to Prayer

In this passage we see a wonderful and miraculous answer to prayer. Hezekiah went into the house of the Lord and spread the matter out before the Lord. He prayed a wonderful prayer. First, he magnified and praised the Lord. He exalted the Lord as He who made Heaven and the earth. To Him Hezekiah ascribed all power and glory. Yet Hezekiah recognized God as One who was able and anxious to stoop to the need of His child and give victorious power. Hezekiah pleaded with God to save Israel from the hand of the king of Assyria (v. 19).

The wonderful truth about Hezekiah's prayer is that He asked this request so that all of the kingdoms of the earth might know that Jehovah is the Lord God. There could be no better motive than this in praying for God's victory. We ought to claim His power and victory so that the world can see that He is God.

God tells of the defeat of the Assyrians (vv. 28-37). God said that He would put hooks in their nose and a bridle in their lips and pull them back. Verse thirty-five gives the answer to this prayer and promise. In one night 185,000 Assyrians were killed. Their king, Sennacherib, immediately decided to return to Nineveh.

God answered prayer! It was a believing prayer—prayed in faith. It was a fervent prayer—prayed for purpose. It was a definite prayer—asking God for deliverance. We need this kind of praying today.

Bible Promise for Today: *"Call unto me, and I will answer thee, and show thee great and mighty things, which thou knowest not."*

—Jeremiah 33:3

Bible Truth to Ponder: *"The sacrifice of the wicked is an abomination to the Lord: but the prayer of the upright is his delight."*

—Proverbs 15:8

April 26

Read II Kings 22–24
Family Reading: II Kings 22

The Book

Josiah was a good king. Crowned as king when he was eight years old, he must have had good instructors and advisors to help him to be a king who did that which was right in the eyes of the Lord. In the eighteenth year of his reign, Josiah desired to repair the temple. He sent Shaphan, the scribe, to the high priest to be sure the money that had been collected was being used to repair the house of the Lord. The high priest not only gave Shaphan a good report about the finances but also showed him the book of the law which they had found in the temple.

This was the law as given by Moses. Hilkiah, the high priest, must have been concerned about Israel's failure to obey the law. When Shaphan read the book, he also became concerned, and he read the book to Josiah the king. As Josiah heard these words of God, he became concerned about Israel's disobedience and sin. He realized that the nation was deserving of the judgment of God. He requested that these men who were close to him seek counsel from the Lord about what should be done.

Josiah became concerned when he heard the Word of God. The Bible is the Book that will bring conviction over sin and point a person to turn around. This is exactly what happened to Josiah. Romans 3:20 reads: " . . . *for by the law is the knowledge of sin.*" One big reason God has commanded His preachers to *"Preach the word . . . " (II Timothy 4:2)* is that the Word of God brings conviction of sin. Not until a person is convicted of his sin will he turn to the Lord to trust Christ. When Josiah heard the Word of the Law, he immediately was ready to seek a remedy. He was ready to turn to the Lord for help.

Thot: *God's Word is the mirror that shows us our sin.*

Bible Truth for Today: *"But whoso looketh into the perfect law of liberty, and continueth therein, he being not a forgetful hearer, but a doer of the work, this man shall be blessed in his deed."*

—James 1:25

April 27

Read II Kings 25 and I Chronicles 1
Family Reading: II Kings 25:1-10, 21-30

A Daily Supply

"*And his allowance was a continual allowance given him of the king,* **a daily rate for every day,** *all the days of his life*" (*II Kings 25:30*). Jehoiachin was sent away from the king's palace. He was not given provisions to last him for months to come. He was simply given a daily allowance for each day.

This verse forms a picture of the happy position that the Lord's people hold. God gives us a daily portion. Did you know that is all a man really wants? We do not need tomorrow's supply, for that day has not dawned, and we do not know what our wants would be. The hunger we might suffer next month does not need to be satisfied now, for we do not feel it yet. All we should desire is enough for each day as the day arrives. None of us can eat or drink or wear more than the day's supply of food and raiment. The surplus gives us the problem of having to store it and the anxiety of protecting it against a thief. I can drive only one automobile at a time. Enough is not only as good as a feast; it is all that I can handle and all that I should expect. A craving for more than that is ungrateful. I should pray, "*Give us this day our daily bread.*" I should be thankful for the daily bread and not expect additional supply.

In the areas of spiritual grace, I need a daily supply. I cannot store it up. I need to feed each day, and in His Word a daily portion is provided for us. It is my responsibility to come to the Word and meet that continual allowance that God has for me. I should never go hungry while the daily bread of grace is on the table of mercy.

> Lord, let me no more grow dull to Thy presence,
>   Fill my cold heart with the warmth of Thy love;
> Never again need my poor soul go hungry,
>   Satisfied daily with food from above.
> —Ellen McKay Trimmer

The Right Attitude Toward God's Word: "*O how love I thy law! it is my meditation all the day.*" —*Psalm 119:97*

April 28

Read I Chronicles 2–4
Family Reading: I Chronicles 4:9-10, 21-23, 39-43; Colossians 3:1-7, 22-25

Blessings from Chronicles

The first nine chapters of I Chronicles deal largely with the genealogies and the chronicles of families in Israel. Right in the midst of these genealogies are some verses that speak of God's blessing in lives. We will look at a few of these today.

First, we will note truth concerning Jabez. He was a man honored in the sight of God and therefore honorable before men. He rose above his brethren to a place of distinction. I Chronicles 4:10 records his prayer that God answered. He prayed for God to bless him and enlarge his coast. If we are going to have an enlarged work for God, it is the Lord who must do it. We cannot do it in our own strength. Jabez asked that the Lord's hand might be on him. He also prayed a very important request, that God would keep him from evil. The Lord Himself taught us to pray, " . . . *deliver us from evil . . .* " (Matthew 6:13). We must constantly rely on Him to deliver us from sin. God was pleased with the request of Jabez and answered his prayer.

Second, let us note the faithfulness of some workers in I Chronicles 4:23. Potters were not the very highest grade of workers, but *"the king"* needed potters. Therefore, they dwelt with the king for his work. Think of it! They worked with nothing but clay, but they were serving the king. It does not matter what our work is; if it is for the King, it is royal service. Others took care of the hedges and plants. This was not a service out in front, but they still dwelt with the king.

What a privilege to have fellowship with the Lord! Regardless of our work, if we are serving Him, it is important work. These worked in the dirt or with the dirt, but it was important work just the same. Please never think that any work is lowly work if it is done for the King. We know that our labor for Him is not in vain (I Corinthians 15:58).

Bible Truth for Today: *"And whatsoever ye do, do it heartily, as to the Lord, and not unto men; Knowing that of the Lord ye shall receive the reward of the inheritance: for ye serve the Lord Christ."*

— Colossians 3:23, 24

April 29

Read I Chronicles 5 and 6
Family Reading: I Chronicles 5

Sin Brings Reproach

Reuben was Jacob's firstborn son. This meant that he held the birthright; but because he committed adulterous sin, he lost the privilege and right of the firstborn. The double portion was given to the tribe of Joseph (vv. 1, 2). The dominion part of the birthright was given to the tribe of Judah (v. 2). Judah was also given the privilege of being the chief ruler. The first ruler of Judah was David. The eternal ruler is Jesus Christ, the Lion of the tribe of Judah. In Genesis 49:10 the dying patriarch Jacob spoke of the scepter.

The breaking of the seventh commandment, *"Thou shalt not commit adultery" (Exodus 20:14),* carries with it serious judgments. Adulterous sins leave an indelible stain upon a man and his family. *"But whoso committeth adultery . . . destroyeth his own soul. A wound and dishonor shall he get; and his reproach shall not be wiped away" (Proverbs 6:32, 33).*

Reuben's reproach was not wiped away. However, though the tribe was degraded, God blessed it with material prosperity and valiant men (v. 18). They trusted God in battle and saw great victory (vv. 20-22).

But even then the reproach abode upon them. Having had victory over pagan nations, they fell into their idolatry (v. 25), bringing their early captivity (v. 26). Today we can praise the Lord that in this age of grace God forgives *all* sin, and a sinner can accept Christ and live to glorify God thereafter.

Bible Truth for Today: *"But if we walk in the light, as he is in the light, we have fellowship one with another, and the blood of Jesus Christ his Son cleanseth us from all sin."* —I John 1:7

April 30

Read I Chronicles 7–9
Family Reading: I Chronicles 7:20-23; 9:17-29; I Timothy 6:9,10

Special Truths for Today

From I Chronicles 7 and 9 we will note two special truths today:

1. The Danger of Covetousness
   In I Chronicles 7:20-23 we read that ten sons of Ephraim were slain by the men of Gath. The reason for their murder was the fact that they had come to steal the cattle from these Gathites. Ephraim, their father, mourned because " . . . *it went evil with his house*" *(vv. 22, 23).* His sons caused problems because of their covetous spirit. Covetousness is a wicked sin. God teaches us that covetousness is the root of all evil and will cause one to be pierced through with many sorrows (I Timothy 6:9, 10).

2. The Importance of Serving the Lord
   In I Chronicles 9:17-29 we find that there were Levites whose work was that of being a porter. There were 212 men so chosen (v. 22) with chief porters over them (v. 26) to whom they were accountable. To be a porter seems a lowly office. Undoubtedly many today would say it is too lowly an office for them. David said: " . . . *I had rather be a doorkeeper in the house of my God, than to dwell in the tents of wickedness*" *(Psalm 84:10).*

The work of these porters was important. They had the responsibility opening the doors each morning, of keeping out the unclean, and of moving the ministering vessels. Every labor is important in God's work. May each believer reading this today decide he will faithfully do what God gives him to do.

Bible Truth for Today: *"And he said unto them, Take heed, and beware of covetousness: for a man's life consisteth not in the abundance of the things which he possesseth."* —*Luke 12:15*

May 1

Read I Chronicles 10 and 11
Family Reading: I Chronicles 10 and 11:1-10

God's Judgment

Our family reading for today reveals the transfer of leadership from King Saul to King David. In verses thirteen and fourteen, we find God's statement concerning Saul's death—his death came because of the judgment of God. Truths about God's judgment are important for us to know. We will note some truth from these two verses.

1. Sin will find the sinner out (Numbers 32:23). *"So Saul died for his transgression which he committed against the Lord . . ."* *(I Chronicles 10:13)* No one gets away with sin. God is not mocked. He that soweth to the flesh shall of the flesh reap corruption.

2. No man's greatness can exempt him from the judgment of God. Saul, as king, still had to face the judgment of God.

3. Saul's basic sin was disobedience. He died because he did not keep the Word of the Lord. His transgression was a result of his disobedience to the Word of God. God is referring to the time when Saul failed to obey the Word of God in destroying the Amalekites (I Samuel 15).

4. Consulting with witches is a wicked sin. *" . . . also for asking counsel of one that had a familiar spirit, to enquire of it"* *(v. 13).* God is always displeased when one seeks the occult for help. Judgment is sure on those involved in occult practices. God states very clearly that because Saul sought the witch and not the Lord, God slew him (v. 14).

Thot: *" . . . prepare to meet thy God . . . "* *—Amos 4:12*

May 2

Read I Chronicles 12–14
Family Reading: I Chronicles 13

Failing to Obey God

I Chronicles 13 gives an interesting story of how God's anger was kindled when His people did not obey Him. David had a noble goal. He wanted to bring the ark to Israel. I believe his mistake came when he sought the advice of the people rather than the will of God. Verse four states: *"And all the congregation said that they would do so: for the thing was right in the eyes of all the people."* They, too, wanted the ark brought up, but they were not willing to obey God in every detail.

Verse seven tells of the mistake they made: *"And they carried the ark of God in a new cart out of the house of Abinadab: and Uzza and Ahio drove the cart."* They undoubtedly felt that it was nice to honor the ark by placing it on a new cart, but that is not what God had ordered. Back in the book of Numbers, God had said that the ark must be carried on poles held on the shoulders of the Levites. In fact, God had designated that the tribe of the Kohathites alone were to carry the ark and the holy furniture (Numbers 4). The Kohathites were not to touch the furniture; they were only to carry it. The high priest and his sons were the ones who were to cover the furniture and prepare it for carrying. The Kohathites were warned in Numbers 4:15 that if they touched any of the furniture, they would die.

By placing the ark on a cart, David and the people were disobeying God. They were endeavoring to do the right thing, but they were not doing it God's way. It is important to do God's work in God's way. We need to study the Word of God constantly to be sure that we are obeying the Lord and performing His work according to His will.

When the oxen stumbled and the ark almost fell off the cart, Uzza put forth his hand to hold the ark. He was immediately killed by God. Thus His Word makes it clear that we are to be careful to do God's work in God's way.

Proverb for Today: *"There is a way which seemeth right unto a man, but the end thereof are the ways of death."* — *Proverbs 14:12*

May 3

Read I Chronicles 15 and 16
Family Reading: I Chronicles 15:1-3, 11-29

Doing a Right Thing in the Wrong Way

Yesterday we saw the trouble that came to Israel because they did the right thing in a wrong way. It was right to bring the ark of the covenant back to Israel, but David had it carried on a new cart—a method that was contrary to what God had ordered. Because of doing it in a wrong way, one of the men, Uzza, was killed by God.

Now, in this fifteenth chapter, it appears that David had received some instruction concerning carrying the ark. In verse two he said: *" . . . None ought to carry the ark of God but the Levites: for them hath the Lord chosen . . . "* Apparently, he had read Numbers 4 and other passages that Moses had written. David now had determined to obey the Word of God.

He then appointed Levites to do the work. He called for the priests and Levites to sanctify themselves. He announced and confessed in verse thirteen: *"For because ye* [the Levites and priests] *did it not at the first, the Lord our God made a breach upon us, for that we sought him not after the due order."* Then David had the ark taken in the proper manner. Joy came to Israel because they did it in the proper manner (16:28).

Today we need to obey the Word of God. How blessed it is to study the New Testament and then to do His will as revealed in the New Testament. The reason so many of our churches lack the joy of the Lord is that we fail to study the Word and then obey what God has laid down for us. It is important to do the right things and then to do them in the right way.

> *And we believe Thy Word,*
> *Though dim our faith may be;*
> *Whate'er for Thine we do, O Lord,*
> *We do it unto Thee.*
> *—William W. How*

Bible Truth for Today: *"And whatsoever ye do, do it heartily, as to the Lord, and not unto men."* — *Colossians 3:23*

May 4

Read I Chronicles 17–20
Family Reading: I Chronicles 17:7-27

The Promises of God

In I Chronicles 17:1 David stated that he desired to build a house for the Lord. How often God does for His servants what they desire to do for Him! David desired to build the Lord a house. When God's servants are not accepted one way, they are another. A servant of the Lord does not get upset when the Lord puts him off from the work of his desire. He learns to do God's will, bow before God's will, and praise God for His will. When Nathan brought the message to David that God was going to establish Israel, we read in verse sixteen that David came and sat before the Lord. He humbly asked, " . . . *Who am I, O Lord God, and what is mine house, that thou hast brought me hitherto?"* He then began one of the great prayers of the Word of God. I believe David felt he could not do otherwise. The Lord wants us to come before Him in prayer and supplication. Because God is faithful in His giving and in His grace toward us, this should compel us to set aside special times of prayer and asking.

In his prayer David realized how great God is and what great things He had done for His people. God had promised David that He would build him a house and establish his throne forever (v. 12). That promise will be kept by God. We can know that God will have the throne of David in the land of Israel. Even today we look forward to that day when that throne will be established in the millennium, and we will be in the presence of the Lord.

David closed his prayer with a great statement: *"Now therefore let it please thee to bless the house of thy servant, that it may be before thee for ever: **for thou blessest, O Lord, and it shall be blessed for ever***"(v. 27).* David's greatness hinged on the fact that he relied on God's blessing, not on his own. He believed the promises of God and rested on them. The secret to blessing and power is to claim God's promises and rely on His will and His work to be accomplished.

Bible Principle for Today: *"Being confident of this very thing, that he which hath begun a good work in you will perform it until the day of Jesus Christ." —Philippians 1:6*

May 5

Read I Chronicles 21–23
Family Reading: I Chronicles 21:9-30

David's Choice

David had sinned. In I Chronicles 21:1 we read that Satan had stood against Israel by provoking David to number Israel contrary to the will of God. God smote Israel, and David realized it was because of his sin. In verse eight he confessed his sin and asked God to remove the iniquity. It is a serious sin in the sight of God for anyone to disobey the will of God. Far too many of God's people do not recognize what a serious sin it is to step out of the will of God. David faced the fact of the seriousness of this sin and confessed it.

The Lord sent the prophet Gad to speak to David, " . . . *Choose thee" (v. 11).* The choices he offered David were three years of famine, three months of destruction by his enemies, or three days of pestilence from the Lord. David chose the three days of pestilence because that would come from and be under the direct guidance of the Lord. David gave us his reason for such a choice—that he knew how great are the mercies of the Lord. He did not want to fall into the hand of man but rather into the hand of the Lord because of God's grace that could be manifested in His mercy.

The Lord sent the pestilence. Also, He sent an angel to destroy Israel. But David was right. God in His mercy changed His mind and stopped the pestilence and commanded the destroying angel to withdraw.

David made a wise choice because he understood the character of God. How we all need to thank God for His grace and His abundant mercy. We have been saved by His mercy—delivered from the awful penalty of Hell. Daily in our lives His mercy protects and keeps us. May God give us grace to rest all on His great mercy.

Bible Truth for Today: *"Let thy mercies come also unto me, O Lord, even thy salvation, according to thy word."* —*Psalm 119:41*

May 6

Read I Chronicles 24–26
Family Reading: I Chronicles 24:1-5; 25:1-7; 26:4-12

Using Our Gifts

In these chapters we see that God had a work for every Israelite. God has given each of His children something we can use for the Lord. Romans 12:5-7 teaches this truth clearly:

"So we, being many, are one body in Christ, and every one members one of another. Having then gifts differing according to the grace that is given to us, whether prophecy, let us prophesy according to the proportion of faith; Or ministry, let us wait on our ministering: or he that teacheth, on teaching."

God has given each believer a gift of grace. The believer needs to exercise whatever gift God has given him to the glory of God and for the blessing of the saints. In these verses in Chronicles, God commanded every individual to use his ability for the blessing of the whole camp of Israel. Their ability also became their responsibility. They were to use their ability to serve the Lord, with blessing to all.

The Lord is looking for strong men. He states that God blessed Obed-Edom with sons and grandsons who were strong (26:4-9). God will find strong men today only as they take time to be in His Word and gain strength from it. The Israelites had various responsibilities. Some offered sacrifices; others took care of the tabernacle; still others acted as porters or singers. In the same way, today each believer has a responsibility in which he is to be faithful. May we become strong through His Word so that we can do the work God wants us to do.

Bible Truth for Today: *"As every man hath received the gift, even so minister the same one to another, as good stewards of the manifold grace of God."* *—I Peter 4:10*

May 7

Read I Chronicles 27–29
Family Reading: I Chronicles 28

David Instructs and Encourages Solomon

David had come to the closing time of his life. The Lord had told him that he could not build the temple but that Solomon his son would have the privilege of building it. In Chapter 28 David spoke to the people, informing them of God's will for Solomon his son. Then he also gave Solomon encouragement and direction in moving forward to accomplish the work.

The first instruction he gave Solomon was to *" . . . know thou the God of thy father, and serve him with a perfect heart and with a willing mind . . . " (v. 9)*. This is good advice for anyone serving the Lord. First, he must come to know God. This can only be done as he studies God's Word and as he waits before the Lord in prayer. The heart must be made right. As we study His Word, He gives us instruction to understand the Lord and to know the way we are to walk before Him. Our heart must be submissive, and our mind must be yielded to Him. David warned Solomon that the *" . . . Lord searcheth all hearts, and understandeth all the imaginations of the thoughts . . . " (v. 9)*. God knows our spirit and the direction of our emotions. We need to submit daily to His grace and let Him control our lives.

Apparently, Solomon had some problem with being fearful and weak. In verse ten David commanded, *" . . . be strong, and do it."* Again in verse twenty, *"And David said to Solomon his son, Be strong and of good courage, and do it: fear not, nor be dismayed: for the Lord God, even my God, will be with thee . . . "* All of us need encouragement in serving the Lord. David knew that God would be with his son and that victory would come as he yielded to the Lord. May we today take heed that we are yielded to Him so that He can use us. Let us *" . . . be strong, and do it."*

Bible Truth for Today: *" . . . Be strong and of good courage, and do it: fear not, nor be dismayed: for the Lord God, even my God, will be with thee . . . "* —*I Chronicles 28:20*

May 8

Read II Chronicles 1–4
Family Reading: II Chronicles 2

Right Priorities

Solomon established the right priorities. Verse one reads: *"And Solomon determined to build an house for the name of the Lord, and an house for his kingdom."* Please note that Solomon determined first *"to build an house for the name of the Lord."* Second, he planned to build *"an house for his kingdom."*

Millions miss these priorities altogether. They plan and think only of their own house and give no thought to building a house for the Lord. They are busy with the business, pleasure, and cares of this life and give no thought to eternity and that which pleases the Lord. However, the day will come when they will regret their choice.

Many others place their priorities exactly backward. They are willing to consider a house for the Lord, but they build first their own house for their kingdom. What a mistake! God's plan is revealed in Matthew 6:33—*"But seek ye first the kingdom of God, and His righteousness; and all these things shall be added unto you."*

When Elisha turned to follow Elijah, he destroyed his plow so that he would not have something to draw him back to the worldly pursuits. But he established the right priority when he did this. He first killed the yoke of oxen so that he could offer sacrifice to God, and then he broke up his plow.

When we seek first the kingdom of God, we can be sure the Lord will keep His end of the promise in Matthew 6:33—*"and **all these things** shall be added unto you."*

The *"all these things"* in this verse refer to Matthew 6:32, which speaks of things we eat, things we drink, and clothes we wear. These necessary things will be provided by God as we learn to trust Him.

It is fit that He who is first should be served first. First a temple—then a palace.

Oh—what a difference there would be in our lives if we honored the Lord first in all things! Let's seek Him first and watch His blessings be poured out.

May 9

Read II Chronicles 5–7
Family Reading: II Chronicles 7

Revival

"If my people, which are called by my name, shall humble themselves, and pray, and seek my face, and turn from their wicked ways; then will I hear from heaven, and will forgive their sin, and will heal their land" (II Chronicles 7:14). This is a great verse on revival. The blessing of revival hinges on God's people—*"If **my people**."* God wants to bless the nation through the people of God.

The thrill of II Chronicles 7 is that God's presence had come to be manifested right in the midst of His people. *" . . . and the glory of the Lord filled the house" (v. 1)*

Solomon had prayed for the nation in the sixth chapter. Following his prayer, the seventh chapter begins with the statement: "[Now] *when Solomon had made an end of praying, the fire came down from heaven, and consumed the burnt-offering and the sacrifices . . . "* The fire coming down from Heaven speaks of two things:

First, it speaks of God's acceptance of the sacrifice. This is true with the sacrifice of Moses and Aaron in Leviticus 9:24. It is also the case with the sacrifice of Gideon in Judges 6:21. And, we see it is true again in the sacrifice of Elijah in I Kings 18:38.

Second, it speaks of the sanctification of the Spirit when we read of the tongues of fire in Acts 2:3.

Therefore, the fire falling tells us that God is pleased with the sacrifice of Christ on the cross. God wants His fire to cleanse our souls and set us apart for Him. His fire needs to burn the lust and corruption out of our lives. When we walk with God, the fire will surely do its work in our lives. The two Emmaus disciples asked after they had been with Jesus, *" . . . Did not our heart burn within us . . . ?" (Luke 24:32)*

It is when the fire is consuming that which hinders our testimony and when God's glory fills our lives that we are ready for revival. We can see the blessing of revival and His fullness come again and again if we will obey II Chronicles 7:14—humble ourselves, pray, seek His face, and turn from our wicked ways.

May 10

Read II Chronicles 8–11
Family Reading: II Chronicles 10

A Soft Answer

Jeroboam led a host of Israelites in their request of Rehoboam to make their servitude lighter than it had been under King Solomon. King Rehoboam requested three days to consider it. During this time he asked for counsel. He first sought counsel from the older men who had stood before Solomon. Their advice was that Rehoboam be kind to Jeroboam and his group and speak good words unto them. They told Rehoboam that if he followed this plan, Jeroboam and the Israelites would be servants forever.

But Rehoboam did not heed the advice of these older men. Instead he asked counsel from younger men. Their advice was to answer Jeroboam and his crowd roughly, saying that he would treat them harder and more severely than did Solomon. Because he answered them in such a harsh manner, Rehoboam saw Jeroboam lead a rebellion and split the kingdom. How different history would have been had he followed the advice of the old men.

Proverbs 15:1 reads: *"A soft answer turneth away wrath: but grievous words stir up anger."* This a Bible principle that all of us should heed constantly. Rehoboam found that because he used grievous words, he stirred up anger and caused a rebellion that brought the division of the kingdom. Verse nineteen states that *" . . . Israel rebelled against the house of David unto this day."*

The truth of Proverbs 15:1 is important for each of us. We need to learn it and practice it daily. Remember that *"a soft answer"* does not mean that we should not be firm in our conviction. We must hold our position on what we believe, but we need to do it in a way that does not turn the hearer from listening.

> Be swift, dear heart, in saying
> The kindly word;
> When ears are sealed, thy passionate pleading
> Will not be heard.

Character Verse: *"A soft answer turneth away wrath: but grievous words stir up anger."* — *Proverbs 15:1*

May 11

Read II Chronicles 12–15
Family Reading: II Chronicles 12

The Danger of Prosperity

King Rehoboam backslid. The account is given in this twelfth chapter of II Chronicles. He was king of the southern kingdom, which did not go into apostasy as deeply nor as quickly as the northern kingdom. The southern kingdom remained true to the Lord much longer than did the northern kingdom. But it, too, eventually went into captivity for its apostasy.

Rehoboam had walked with God. We find this truth recorded in II Chronicles 11:17—*"So they strengthened the kingdom of Judah, and made Rehoboam the son of Solomon strong, three years: for three years they walked in the way of David and Solomon."*

What caused Rehoboam to backslide from this good position? This twelfth chapter reveals the answers to this question. First, in his prosperity and blessing, he forgot the Lord. Proverbs 1:32 gives us this wisdom: *" . . . the prosperity of fools shall destroy them."* And Job adds in Job 15:21—*" . . . in prosperity the destroyer shall come upon him."* II Chronicles 12:1 reads: *"And it came to pass, when Rehoboam had established **the kingdom**, and had strengthened himself, he **forsook** the law of the Lord, and all Israel with him."*

Second, he did not prepare his heart to seek the Lord (v. 14). What a contrast there is between Rehoboam and Ezra, who *" . . . had prepared his heart to seek the law of the Lord, and to do it, and to teach in Israel statutes and judgments" (Ezra 7:10)!*

Why did Rehoboam do evil? As we saw in verse fourteen, it was because he did not prepare his heart to seek the Lord. Heart preparation would have required that he humble himself. But Rehoboam had a problem with pride. In this twelfth chapter we find that he humbled himself when he faced the prophecy of Shemaiah (vv. 6, 12). But then again in verse thirteen he strengthened himself and thus felt no need to turn to the Lord. May we ever anxiously seek the Lord.

Bible Truth for Today: *" . . . feed me with food convenient for me: Lest I be full, and deny thee, and say, Who is the Lord? . . . "*

— Proverbs 30:8, 9

May 12

Read II Chronicles 16–19
Family Reading: II Chronicles 16 and 17:1-5

Total Reliance

Our reading from II Chronicles today deals with the lives of King Asa and his son, King Jehoshaphat. Both of these men desired to do what was right in the sight of the Lord. It is repeatedly said of Asa that he did what was right in the eyes of the Lord his God (II Chronicles 14:2). He fulfilled God's will by destroying the high places and the idolatrous worship. He was zealous for the Lord to do His will in every area.

Asa was warned that he must not forsake the Lord. The prophet Azariah told him, " . . . *The Lord is with you, while ye be with him; and if ye seek him, he will be found of you; but if ye forsake him, he will forsake you" (II Chronicles 15:2)*. Because of Azariah's encouragement, Asa " . . . *took courage, and put away the abominable idols . . . " (II Chronicles 15:8)*.

But in Chapter 16 we see Asa changing. He became afraid of Baasha, king of the northern kingdom. Rather than seeking the Lord, Asa sought the help of Ben-hadad, the king of Syria. God never wants us to run to the world to get help in our spiritual battles, but this is exactly what Asa did. God reminded Asa that though the Ethiopians were a huge host, Asa and Judah were able to defeat them through their reliance on the Lord. Since Asa had now forsaken this simple and total reliance on the Lord, Hanani, the prophet, told him he would have wars. God wants us to continue to rest on Him and His grace and strength.

II Chronicles 16:9 is a great verse of Scripture: *"For the eyes of the Lord run to and fro throughout the whole earth, to show himself strong in the behalf of them whose heart is perfect toward him. Herein thou hast done foolishly: therefore from henceforth thou shalt have wars."* It would be good for Christians to memorize this verse and quote it often.

Bible Truth for Today: *"As for God, his way is perfect: the word of the Lord is tried: he is a buckler to all those that trust in him."*

— Psalm 18:30

133

May 13

Read II Chronicles 20–22
Family Reading: II Chronicles 21

The Price of Sin

Jehoram did not follow in the footsteps of his father or his grandfather but allowed his wife, a daughter of Ahab, to lead him astray. *"And he walked in the way of the kings of Israel, like as did the house of Ahab: for he had the daughter of Ahab to wife: and he wrought that which was evil in the eyes of the Lord" (v. 6).*

Following the wickedness of his heart, Jehoram began his reign in pride in an effort to strengthen himself. To accomplish this, he had all of his brothers and any others who might be a threat to his kingdom slain (v. 4). In addition, he led Israel into idolatry (v. 11).

Be certain that God does not sit by idly when such vile men bear wicked rule. The heart of the king is still in the hand of the Lord (Proverbs 21:1). The Lord used Elijah to warn Jehoram that judgment would come. That judgment, as announced by the prophets, involved a dreadful plague upon the people of Israel, upon the king's family, and upon Jehoram himself. In addition, the Lord stirred up the Philistines and the Arabians to plunder the king's palace and family.

The tragedy of a sinful life is shown, for when Jehoram died, he *" . . . departed without being desired . . . " (v. 20).* People were glad he was gone. At the end of a life of selfishness, he found that he had no friends. Sin takes an awful toll. May we each determine to live for the Lord.

Bible Truth for Today: *"Wherefore lay apart all filthiness and superfluity of naughtiness, and receive with meekness the engrafted word, which is able to save your souls." —James 1:21*

May 14

Read II Chronicles 23–25
Family Reading: II Chronicles 23

The King Enthroned

Joash was made king. He was the rightful heir to the throne and should have been king. Queen Athaliah in her wicked plans had endeavored to kill all of the king's sons and thus obliterate the godly line. But Jehoshabeath stole young Joash and hid him. He was spared death and years later was made king of Judah.

Athaliah was a wicked woman who hated God and His work. She did not want royal seed of David to possess the throne. When she saw Joash crowned king, she became angry and cried, *"Treason, Treason" (v. 13).* The daughter of Omri, she was the sister of the wicked King Ahab. She had been around her sister-in-law Jezebel and had learned the methods of a wicked woman. She would go to any length to defeat God's work.

When she cried, *"Treason,"* Jehoiada the priest ordered that she be killed. Upon seeing her killed, Jehoiada made a covenant with the people that they would serve the Lord (v. 16). With that the Israelites destroyed the altars of Baal and broke the idols. This was a great revival. There was a real cleansing of the nation of Israel.

In verse twenty-one we read that *" . . . all the people . . . rejoiced: and the city was quiet, after that they had slain Athaliah with the sword."* God wants His people to deal with sin and wickedness. When sin is judged, there will be rejoicing in the land. Then the real King can come to the throne as did Joash in verse twenty.

God wants each of us to judge sin in our lives so that Christ can be enthroned. Not until we deal with any Athaliah in our lives can we have the rightful king on the throne. And not until then can we have the joy of the Lord a great reality in our lives.

The Lord's Question for Today: *"And why call ye me, Lord, Lord, and do not the things which I say?"* — *Luke 6:46*

May 15

Read II Chronicles 26–29
Family Reading: II Chronicles 26

The Danger of Pride

Uzziah became king as a very young man. Because he did that which was right in the sight of the Lord (v. 4), God wonderfully blessed and used him. He saw victories in battles and accomplished much in improving the land of Israel. He built many towers for defense. He dug many wells for watering the herds of cattle that dotted the countryside. Because he loved farming, he had many vineyards throughout the land.

Uzziah developed an excellent army of defense. Verse thirteen states that his army of soldiers made war with mighty power. He prepared the instruments of war to be used in defensive and offensive war. Also, the nation under his leadership built special engines of war to fight the battles.

Uzziah became a famous king. The last part of verse fifteen says, " . . . *his name spread far abroad; for he was marvelously helped, till he was strong."* Suddenly in this passage there is a change. *"But when he was strong, his heart was lifted up to his destruction . . . "* *(v. 16).* What a tragedy! Here is a man who was helped by God to become strong. His very strength then led him away from simple trust in the Lord.

Pride is a very dangerous enemy to spiritual growth. Uzziah became proud of his strength. He thought he was the one who had made himself strong, and he forgot that God gave him the strength. When he was strong, he let his heart be lifted up to his destruction.

I have seen it true in so many ways. A preacher depends on the Lord for his blessing and strength. Then he may start to believe he did it himself. When he believes he did the work, he immediately will see the seeds of his own destruction at work. This is true in the ministry, a business, or a home. Every one of us must be careful to give God the glory in every area of his life. Always honor the Lord for all of His blessings and goodness.

Proverb for Today: *"Pride goeth before destruction, and an haughty spirit before a fall."* — *Proverbs 16:18*

May 16

Read II Chronicles 30–32
Family Reading: II Chronicles 32:1-23

God Delivers

Hezekiah did that which was right in the sight of the Lord. He rested by faith in what God could do. When Sennacherib set siege against Jerusalem and then railed against God, Hezekiah instructed his people to be strong and courageous. He asked the people not to be afraid nor dismayed because of the king of Assyria. Though Sennacherib's army was much larger, Hezekiah stated that Israel had more with them than did Assyria. Then in verse eight Hezekiah explained how he could make such a statement that there are more with Israel than with Sennacherib: *"With him is an arm of flesh; but with us is the Lord our God to help us, and to fight our battles . . ."*

Sennacherib continued to rail on the Lord God of Israel and to speak against the Lord. He and his army spoke against God as though He were just another idol to which people bow down to worship. Hezekiah was greatly burdened because of this, and he joined with Isaiah in praying to God. And the Lord sent a miracle in answer to prayer.

Verse twenty-one gives that answer to prayer: *"And the Lord sent an angel, which cut off all the mighty men of valor, and the leaders and captains in the camp of the king of Assyria. So he returned with shame of face to his own land. And when he was come into the house of his god, they that came forth of his own bowels slew him there with the sword."*

It was God who delivered Hezekiah. Both he and all of the inhabitants of Jerusalem recognized that God had done it. Because of what God had accomplished, they brought gifts unto the Lord and to Hezekiah. When God's people see what God has done, they are ready and willing to give generously to the Lord. The needs of Hezekiah's kingdom were met because God's people realized the blessing and victory God had given.

Bible Truth for Today: Our God *"is able to do exceeding abundantly above all that we ask or think . . . "*   *— Ephesians 3:20*

May 17

Read II Chronicles 33–35
Family Reading: II Chronicles 33

Parents—Beware!

In Chapter 33 we see some outstanding truths about the effect of parents in the lives of their children. Manasseh was an ungodly king. The evil he did was like to the abominations of the heathen. Yet his father, Hezekiah, was an outstanding and good king. How can this be explained? Why would a good king like Hezekiah have a son who became such a wicked king like Manasseh? I believe the answer is found in II Kings 21:1—*"Manasseh was twelve years old when he began to reign, and reigned fifty and five years in Jerusalem. **And his mother's name was Hephzi-bah**."* I believe God put that comment here to reveal that Manasseh's mother had much to do with his lack of character. God speaks of the *"law of thy mother" (Proverbs 1:8 and 6:20).* A good mother has a law that guides the children to become the adults they should be. *Hephzi-bah* means *this mother.*

Then, too, we see the result of a wicked king like Manasseh. Amon " . . . *did that which was evil in the sight of the Lord, as did Manasseh his father: for Amon sacrificed unto all the carved images which Manasseh his father had made, and served them"(v. 22).* The next verse (v. 23) makes the interesting comment that Amon *". . . humbled not himself before the Lord, as Manasseh his father had humbled himself . . . "* Manasseh had lived in wickedness. But when he was in affliction under the king of Assyria, he humbled himself. It was good he humbled himself then, but he was too late. He had already made such an impact on his son that Amon went on in sin and did not recover from it. Oh, how important in the life of our children is the way we live as adults.

> *Father, as this boy looks up to me*
> *For guidance, and my help implores,*
> *I bring him now in prayer to Thee;*
> *He trusts my strength and I trust yours.*
> *—M. W. Brabham*

Bible Truth for Today: *"And, ye fathers, provoke not your children to wrath: but bring them up in the nurture and admonition of the Lord."* *— Ephesians 6:4*

May 18

Read II Chronicles 36 and Ezra 1 and 2
Family Reading: II Chronicles 36

No Remedy

This is a great chapter on the perennial apostasy of Israel. The nation of Israel was taken into captivity because of her continual backsliding and apostasy. Israel had been given promises of God's blessings if she had only continued to live for the Lord. Israel refused to live for God, and finally God dealt in judgment by taking Israel into captivity.

The last five words of II Chronicles 36:16 give an awful statement by God: *". . . till there was no remedy."* Israel continued in her resistance to God and her rebellion against God until there was no remedy. Is that not a dreadful thought? Man can go so far in his rebellion against God that finally God says there is no remedy. Then God brings judgment. In this case in II Chronicles 36:17 God states: *"Therefore he brought upon them the king of the Chaldees, who slew their young men with the sword in the house of their sanctuary, and had no compassion upon young man or maiden, old man, or him that stooped for age: he gave them all into his hand."* God gave the nation of Israel into captivity. And He let the king of Babylon take all of the riches of the treasures of the land.

Yes, God's people can go on in sin until God says there is no remedy. God gave Israel into captivity. He brought them under the dominion of an ungodly nation because they had continued in their rebellion and resistance till there was no remedy for them. *"But they mocked the messengers of God, and despised his words, and misused his prophets, until the wrath of the Lord arose against his people, till there was no remedy"* (v. 16). Even though God sent prophets to them, the Bible says that they mocked and misused His prophets. This continued until the wrath of the Lord arose against his people, till there was no remedy. Beware that you walk with God and not despise His Word.

Character Verse: *"He, that being often reproved hardeneth his neck, shall suddenly be destroyed, and that without remedy."*

— Proverbs 29:1

May 19

Read Ezra 3–6
Family Reading: Ezra 3 and 4:1-5

Standing for God

In Ezra 3 we read of the foundation being laid for the new temple. First, the men established an altar. Jeshua, the priest, realized that if anything were going to be accomplished, there must be worship of the Lord. Second, they kept the feast of tabernacles (v. 4). They were very careful to follow God's directions and worship Him. They had built the altar and had had the feast before they laid the foundation of the temple. Third, they presented their money. They saw that the needs were supplied before they began to build. They were faithful in their worship and in their stewardship. Therefore, God gave them the privilege of starting the temple.

After laying the foundation, they praised the Lord. Verse eleven states that they sang together in praising and in giving of thanks. Their hearts were right with God, and they were endeavoring to do the work of the Lord.

Then in Chapter 4 we read that the enemy comes against them. You can always be sure that when something is being done for God, Satan will stir up adversaries. In this case, there were inhabitants in the land who did not want to see the temple built. Chapter 4 is a revelation of their opposition. The first step in their opposition was to endeavor to get the Israelites to amalgamate with them. This will always be an attempt of Satan. He would like to have people believe that if they will join in with an ecumenical movement, they will be pleasing the Lord. Nothing could be farther from the truth. God wants His people to be separated from the religions of the people around.

We must constantly be on guard about this subtle attack of the enemy. There are those who would say, "Let us join hands," who are really the enemies of the gospel of Christ. We must take our stand, believing and obeying the Bible.

Bible Truth for Today: *"Be sober, be vigilant; because your adversary the devil, as a roaring lion, walketh about, seeking whom he may devour." —I Peter 5:8*

May 20

Read Ezra 7–9
Family Reading: Ezra 8:15-36

Looking to God

"For I was ashamed to require of the king a band of soldiers and horsemen to help us against the enemy in the way: because we had spoken unto the king, saying, The hand of our God is upon all them for good that seek him; but his power and his wrath is against all them that forsake him." — *Ezra 8:22*

Ezra was leading the Israelites up to Jerusalem. They were carrying a very valuable cargo with gold, silver, and valuable vessels. Along the way they could easily have faced bands of robbers who would take away all of these valuable items needed for their work in Jerusalem. Ezra needed the blessing of God. In verse twenty-one he proclaimed a fast so that they might seek from God a right way for them, for their children, and for the substance which they carried. Thank God for Ezra's desire to see God's work accomplished according to His will.

Ezra considered the possibility of asking the king of Persia for soldiers and horsemen to form a convoy to protect them on the road. But since Ezra had given the king a testimony that *" . . . the hand of our God is upon all them for good that seek him, . . . "* he felt his profession of faith would seem hypocritical to the heathen king. He could not bring himself to lean on an arm of flesh in a work that he knew was of God. So the caravan set out with no visible protection, guarded by the Lord, who is the sword and shield of His people.

Verse thirty-one gives the result. *"Then we departed from the river of Ahava on the twelfth day of the first month, to go unto Jerusalem: and the hand of our God was upon us, and **he delivered us from the hand of the enemy, and of such as lay in wait by the way.**"*

Character Verse: *"Commit thy way unto the Lord; trust also in him; and he shall bring it to pass."* — *Psalm 37:5*

May 21

Read Ezra 10 and Nehemiah 1 and 2
Family Reading: Nehemiah 1 and 2:1-5

Nehemiah — The Builder

Nehemiah is an important book in the Bible. It gives us the many keys to Christian victory. It is a book of revival and of working for God. The key word in the book is *so*. As you read through the book, I suggest you underline two words: the word *so* and the word *work*. *So* is used thirty-two times and reveals that Nehemiah was a man of action and leadership. He was a layman from a well-to-do family and had become a cupbearer in the king's palace. But above everything else, he was a man who was anxious to serve and honor the Lord.

He learned from his brother, Hanani, that the Jews in Jerusalem were in a sad state. They were in great affliction and reproach with the walls of Jerusalem broken down and the gates burned with fire (1:3). Deeply earnest is Nehemiah, this man of God, as he pleads with Jehovah for the state of Jerusalem and its inhabitants. Nehemiah 1:4 states that he sat down and wept, and mourned, and prayed, and fasted. He pleaded with God in verses five through eleven. He ended his prayer: *"O Lord, I beseech thee, let now thine ear be attentive to the prayer of thy servant, and to the prayer of thy servants, who desire to fear thy name . . . "* Nehemiah was greatly used of God because he knew how to pray. Note his quick prayer in Nehemiah 2:4. The book opens and closes with prayer. Nehemiah's prayer included a confession of the sin of Israel. Nehemiah 1:7 records his prayer: *"We have dealt very corruptly against thee . . . "* Anyone used of God must always be ready to face sin and let God deal with it.

Nehemiah became the great builder. He built because he trusted the Lord and loved Him and His work. Today we need builders. We have too many destroyers. It is easy to tear down, but it takes hard work to build. May each of us be a spiritual leader like Nehemiah, building for God.

Bible Truth for Today: *"For we are laborers together with God: ye are God's husbandry, ye are God's building."* — *I Corinthians 3:9*

May 22

Read Nehemiah 3–5
Family Reading: Nehemiah 5

Nehemiah's Example

Yesterday we centered our devotional thought in the fact of Nehemiah as a spiritual leader. Today I want to go further in this vein and think of Nehemiah's example to the people of Israel.

The most dangerous enemies of the work of the Lord are those enemies who work from within. Satanic opposition is dangerous and dreadful. But as bad as is Satan's opposition, there is something worse. That is an enemy who works from within. This includes discouragement to the people of God. In Chapter 5 we have another enemy from within: the greed and unconcern on the part of the leaders of the Jews. They had forced the Jews to mortgage their lands and give the money as tribute so that the leaders could maintain a higher life style. The people had become slaves to a wicked system of a governmental bureaucracy.

Nehemiah, as the appointed governor of Judah, rebuked these self-centered leaders and commanded that the property of the people be restored. He publicly shook out his lap and announced that he wanted God to shake empty those Jews who did not live for the Lord. The people expressed agreement with Nehemiah.

Then Nehemiah revealed the type of man he was. He himself as the governor lived unselfishly. He did not eat the bread and wine of the governors so that he would not have to tax the people. He states that the previous governors had taken from the poor to meet their need (v. 15). Because he feared the Lord, Nehemiah did not embrace the high life style of the other governors.

Nehemiah served the Lord with all of his heart. His book is a classic on service for Christ. One big reason Nehemiah could write such a book is that he was a man who honored the Lord and refused to live for self. He not only served the Lord with his deeds but also served the Lord by his example. Let's build our example around the truth of the Word of God.

Bible Principle: *"For even hereunto were ye called: because Christ also suffered for us, leaving us an example, that ye should follow his steps."* —I Peter 2:21

May 23

Read Nehemiah 6 and 7
Family Reading: Nehemiah 6

Stand in the Battle

Nehemiah was engaged in a great work; his God was with him and gave him success. Enemies and even friends united against him. By wicked words, by craft, and by strategy, they tried to dishearten and deter this man of God from going on with God's work. Opposition is the lot of him who would serve the Lord. Courage is his honor. Perseverance is his jewel.

Look at Nehemiah, this man of God. He faced the opposition but never let it stop him. Verse nine records his prayer— " . . . *O God, strengthen my hands.*" Instead of fleeing from his work, he fled unto his God. Faith inspired prayer, and prayer brought courage. Then he could cry boldly, " . . . *Should such a man as I flee? . . .*" *(v. 11)*.

Here was a man greatly used of God. He stood with courage and would not move. Should such a man flee? Oh, no! Nehemiah despised such cowardice. He said he would stay with the work. Let men order their battles however they will, Nehemiah would trust in the Lord and rely on His direction.

The greatest discouragement that comes to any one of us is that which we experience when we feel friends have turned against us. Nehemiah experienced this heartache when suddenly he realized that Shemaiah, his friend, had been hired by Tobiah and Sanballat to lure him off the wall and into the temple. But this man of God let nothing deter him. He held to his course and stuck by his job.

Because Nehemiah was faithful and would not flee, we read the words, *"So the wall was finished . . ." (v. 15).* That verse would never have been written had Nehemiah fled. Let's stand true to the Lord and His Word.

Bible Command for Today: " . . . *having done all, to stand. Stand therefore . . .* " *—Ephesians 6:13,14*

May 24

Read Nehemiah 8–10
Family Reading: Nehemiah 9

The Curse of Pride

Nehemiah was a man of God. He had keen discernment into the problem that caused the nation of Israel its problems. In this ninth chapter, he recorded the confession of the priests and Levites. This chapter is worthy of your careful reading and meditation. Beginning at verse six in our family reading for today, we find the men praising the Lord. Before they confessed anything to Him, they praised Him for His majesty, His creation, His calling, and His leading.

They praised the Lord for His direction of Abraham and Moses. Then they spoke of His leading the Israelites out of Egypt to Sinai. There it was that God gave Israel the great truths of His law—a law given for their benefit and blessing. Not only did God give them a law to live by, but He also provided for their physical needs and saw that they were cared for.

After they enumerated all of the great things God had done for them, they changed the tone of their conversation with God. They said, *"But they and our fathers dealt proudly, and hardened their necks, and hearkened not to thy commandments" (v. 16).*

Following that verse, we find a listing of many problems that Israel faced. They wandered in the wilderness forty years; then they were delivered. But they continued to backslide and face problems in serving the Lord. What was the key to all of their sin and problems? I believe we find the answer in the very first part of verse sixteen—*"But they and our fathers dealt **proudly** . . . "*

The priests and Levites enumerated many sins and much disobedience. Then we read again in verse twenty-nine: *" . . . yet they dealt **proudly**, and hearkened not unto thy commandments . . . "* Pride was the key to all of their sin. It is a key in our lives to all that hinders and hurts our testimony. Day by day we need to obey the admonition given in I Peter 5:6—*"Humble yourselves therefore under the mighty hand of God . . . "*

Bible Truth for Today: *"Thou hast rebuked the proud that are cursed, which do err from thy commandments."* —*Psalm 119:21*

May 25

Read Nehemiah 11 and 12
Family Reading: Nehemiah 12:27-47

Honor Your Leaders

Nehemiah 12 recounts the dedication of the walls around Jerusalem. This was a high point in the lives of these Israelites. They had worked long and hard at building the walls. The dedication marks the culmination of their labor and the rejoicing that accompanied their thrill over a job well done.

First, Nehemiah presented a long list of names. These were those who had labored in coming to Jerusalem and rebuilding the temple and the walls. It is always good to look at the lives of great spiritual men who have gone before us and led us in the right way. We are encouraged by their noble examples.

Nehemiah wanted the people to know who their leaders were. The New Testament commands us:

"Remember them which have the rule over you . . . "— Hebrews 13:7

"And we beseech you, brethren, to know them which labor among you, and are over you in the Lord, and admonish you; And to esteem them very highly in love for their work's sake . . . "
—I Thessalonians 5:12, 13

Nehemiah led the people to know and respect their leaders. Because of this, there was great rejoicing in the camp of Israel. Today all of us should honor those who lead us in the work of the Lord.

Bible Truth for Today: *"Render therefore to all their dues: tribute to whom tribute is due; custom to whom custom; fear to whom fear; honor to whom honor." —Romans 13:7*

May 26

Read Nehemiah 13 and Esther 1 and 2
Family Reading: Esther 1

Moral Standards for Today

The book of Esther presents history contemporary with that of Nehemiah. The difference is that Esther records events that took place with the Jews who remained in Persia, while Nehemiah speaks of those who returned to Jerusalem. The object of the book of Esther is to record for us the wonderful deliverance of God's people when Haman was planning their total extinction. We realize that God takes care of His own.

In the next two days, please note how God, in His sovereignty, protected His people, the Jews. But now—let's look at some moral truths in Chapter 1:

First, the Persian society did not force people to drink liquor. Verse eight states that " . . . *none did compel . . .* " anyone to drink, but rather the drinking was " . . . *according to every man's pleasure.*" Wine had a very serious effect on King Ahasuerus. After drinking for seven days, according to verse ten, the king's heart was merry and he called for a very immoral act by the queen. The Bible states, *"Wine is a mocker, strong drink is raging: and whosoever is deceived thereby is not wise" (Proverbs 20:1).* The king experienced this awful, devastating effect of alcohol. However, the society did not require everyone to drink. In America today the law does not say we have to drink, but peer pressure forces strong drink on many. I have heard so-called Christians say, "I do not drink . . . only socially." Friend, please don't try to justify your wrongdoing by saying that you are doing it for friendship. You are no less a man or woman because you refuse to take liquor.

We see another important moral truth in this chapter. The queen refused to do what the king requested. He was literally requesting her to show her nude body to all of those decadent men, totally irrational after seven days of drunken orgy. She refused.

Today we need to hold our stand against liquor and its wicked results. Also, we must stand against the female nudity displayed on every hand.

May 27

Read Esther 3–7
Family Reading: Esther 6 and 7

God's Intervention

These two chapters are some of the most thrilling reading in all of literature. Though God's name is never mentioned in the book of Esther, His presence and providence are manifested throughout the book. In Chapters 6 and 7 we certainly see God's miraculous intervention in the life of Mordecai, and through him, in the Jewish nation.

Haman designed and built the gallows on which Mordecai was to be hanged. He planned to have Mordecai killed the very next day. But God would not let the king sleep that night. He had the king read in the Chronicles that Mordecai had saved the king's life. At the very moment the king had received a strong desire to honor Mordecai, Haman appeared so that the king could ask him, " . . . *What shall be done unto the man whom the king delighteth to honor? . . .* " *(v. 6).* Haman, thinking that the king was desirous of honoring him, suggested the great honor that he was forced to bestow on Mordecai: *"Let the royal apparel be brought which the king useth to wear, and the horse that the king rideth upon, and the crown royal which is set upon his head . . . that they may array the man withal whom the king delighteth to honor . . . " (Esther 6:8, 9).*

He not only honored Mordecai with the honor he thought he himself would receive, but he also was hanged on the very gallows he had built for Mordecai. God intervened. Man proposes but God disposes. No man can successfully win against God's purpose and plan.

The wise men and his wife warned Haman: " . . . *If Mordecai be of the seed of the Jews, before whom thou hast begun to fall, thou shalt not prevail against him, but shalt surely fall before him" (Esther 6:13).* Even these unsaved Gentiles had come to realize that the Jews were God's people and that God would do miracles on their behalf.

Proverb for Today: *"There are many devices in a man's heart; nevertheless the counsel of the Lord, that shall stand."*

— Proverbs 19:21

May 28

Read Esther 8–10 and Job 1
Family Reading: Job 1

Why Serve God?

Job was an outstanding man. Verse one says that "[he] *was* *"perfect and upright, and one that feared God, and eschewed* [hated] *evil."* His neighbors considered him to be a good, moral, honest man. Also, God considered him a man of character, honesty, and integrity. Further, the Word of God says that he *feared God.* This means that he was a man who reverenced Jehovah and wanted to honor Him. He was also one who hated evil.

Verse one states that Job was *perfect.* This does not mean that he was sinless. In Job 9:20 he said, " *. . . if I say, I am perfect, it shall also prove me perverse."* So Job himself knew that he was not sinless. He was sincere and loved the Lord with all of his heart.

Some dreadful things happened to Job. His servants were killed and beasts of burden were stolen by the Sabeans. Fire fell from Heaven and burned up his sheep and the shepherds. The camels were stolen, and a great wind destroyed his house, killing his sons and daughters. Also, Job was stricken with boils all over his body.

Why did this happen to Job? Satan appeared before God and asked a question, " *. . . Doth Job fear God for nought?" (v. 9).* Satan was saying that Job feared and served God just because God rewarded him, built a hedge about him, and blessed him. God permitted Satan to attack Job to prove that Job did not serve God for reward but out of a heart of love. Job showed this love after the destruction of his property and his children. God said concerning him, *"In all this Job sinned not, nor charged God foolishly" (Job 1:22).*

Why was Job serving God? He was not serving God for reward. He was serving God because he *loved* Him and *wanted* to serve Him. What a difference this makes! Today we need more of God's people like Job who serve the Lord in spite of circumstances.

Bible Truth for Today: *"Behold, we count them happy which endure. Ye have heard of the patience of Job, and have seen the end of the Lord; that the Lord is very pitiful, and of tender mercy."*

— James 5:11

May 29

Read Job 2–5
Family Reading: Job 5:1-20

The Rock of Ages When Life's Ship Is Rocked with Trouble

Job had some friends who endeavored to comfort him. They spoke much truth, but it appears they did not have a deep experience themselves. Eliphaz was the first of the friends to speak. Much of what he said was true. He said: *"Although affliction cometh not forth of the dust, neither doth trouble spring out of the ground" (v. 6).* He is saying that the testings of life are not by accident. They do not just happen. They are to be expected. He goes on in verse seven to say, *"Yet man is born unto trouble, as the sparks fly upward."* Trouble came into the world as a result of the sin of Adam. Just as the sparks fly upward from a flame, by the laws of nature, so we can be certain of trouble, by the laws of God.

Eliphaz did not stop at that. He then told Job what to do with his troubles, and this again was very true. In verse eight he said: *"I would seek unto God, and unto God would I commit my cause."* That is easy to say; and I must confess, I wonder if Eliphaz was right. We should follow Lamentations 3:32—*"But though he cause grief, yet will he have compassion according to the multitude of his mercies."*

A young English preacher took a walk one afternoon. He came to a gorge made out of the limestone which was two-and-a-half miles long. As he was walking through the gorge, he was enjoying the scenery, not paying any attention to the clouds that were gathering. Finally, he looked up and noted the dark clouds in the sky. He tried to hasten home, but the storm overtook him. The rain came in heavy sheets, and the young minister found shelter in the cleft of a great limestone and watched the rain pour down. Deeply impressed about his protection in the rock, he took a pencil and paper from his pocket and penned these words:

> "Rock of ages, cleft for me,
> Let me hide myself in Thee."

This experience in the storm was the inspiration that caused Augustus M. Toplady to write that great hymn of hope, faith, and love.

May 30

Read Job 6–8
Family Reading: Job 7:1-20

Let's Quit Complaining

In Chapters 6 and 7 we have Job's answer to Eliphaz. In Job 6:12 he confessed how perplexed he was in his trials. He asked, *"Is my strength the strength of stones? or is my flesh of brass?"* He was literally saying, "This is more than I can take. I am not made of stone or brass. I am a man—with weaknesses and failings." Sometimes God lets us go through bitter experiences so that we will come to the end of ourselves and rely on Him.

Job was weakening some in his stand. This is revealed in Job 7:11—*"Therefore I **will not** refrain my mouth; **I will speak** in the anguish of my spirit; **I will complain** in the bitterness of my soul."*

It is hard to believe, but there it is in the Word of God. Job had become so weak spiritually that he boldly announced he was going to complain.

Dr. J. Allen Blair relates the following: "One of the strangest war incidents I have ever read was about the arrest, trial, and imprisonment of a serviceman who was called *A Discourager*. He struck no blow for the enemy. He was not disloyal to his country. He was just a discourager at a very critical time. The fate of the company hung in the balance. He would go along the lines and say discouraging words to the men on duty. The court martial judged it a crime to speak disheartening words at such an hour. And so it was that he was sentenced to a year's imprisonment."

A Christian should not be a complainer. But I am afraid that there are far too many Christians today who act as though they have a calling to complain. Of course, all complaining is really against God. If I really believe Romans 8:28, I will trust the Lord—no matter what takes place. Paul wrote Timothy: *" [But] godliness with contentment is **great gain"** (I Timothy 6:6)*. Let's learn to trust the Lord.

Bible Truth for Today: *"And we know that all things work together for good to them that love God, to them who are the called according to his purpose." —Romans 8:28*

Read Job 9–11
Family Reading: Job 9:13-35

Job's Problem

Job's trouble was similar to that of many believers today. He looked at his sin rather than at the grace and mercy of God. If we look to ourselves, we can name any number of reasons why God should not help us. But if we look to God and recognize Him as the God of all grace, then we shall find deliverance.

In verse two of this ninth chapter Job asks, " . . . *how should man be just with God?"* Then he speaks of the greatness of God, and then he asks whether he would have opportunity to present a plea to God.

One of Job's problems was his doubting. In verse sixteen he states that if God were to answer his prayer, he would still not believe. He would continue to believe that God is great enough to overcome Job's insignificance. Job recognized the futility of self-justification; for he states in verse twenty that if he justified himself, his own mouth would have to condemn him. Job knew that self-justification would never work.

He also recognized the brevity of life. In verses twenty-five and twenty-six he states that his days are swifter than a post, fleeing away rapidly as the swift ships and as an eagle hastening to the prey.

Job's biggest problem was that he did not know he had a mediator to plead his case. Job was searching for one righteous enough to go into the presence of God and yet human enough to bless needy sinners. He wished he had a *"daysman" (v. 33).* A daysman is a go-between. Praise God, we have our Daysman in Jesus Christ. He can fulfill verse thirty-three by laying one hand on God and one hand on me. We have a privilege today in that we have a Mediator who is the one standing between us and God.

Bible Truth for Today: *"For there is one God, and one mediator between God and men, the man Christ Jesus."* —*1 Timothy 2:5*

June 1

Read Job 12–14
Family Reading: Job 14

After Death—What Then?

Job 14:14 presents a very good question for all to ponder: *"If a man die, shall he live again? . . . "* What happens after death? That is a very good question. Everyone needs to face that question. Where will I be after I die?

Job did not wonder if he would die. He states that all the days of man's appointed time will he wait till his change come (v. 14). Job knew he would be changed someday. He knew he would depart this life and face eternity.

Neither did Job question whether he himself would be with the Lord. In Job 19:26 he said, *"And though after my skin worms destroy this body, yet in my flesh shall I see God."* He knew he himself was going to be with the Lord. Therefore, he did not wonder whether he would live again.

The question this verse asks is one that each one of us needs to ask. Since I am going to die, am I prepared? If I were to die today, would I live again in Heaven, or would I suffer eternal death in Hell? If I were to die today, where would I be? These are some of the most important questions you could ever ask yourself.

The story is told of a wealthy landlord who had a man who endeavored to keep him happy. One day he handed the servant his bejeweled walking cane with the words, "Fool, you can keep this until you meet a bigger fool than you." Sometime later the lord called his fool to his bedside and told him he was taking a long trip. The fool asked, "Will you be gone a week?" "No, longer than that." "A month?" "Oh, no, much longer than that." "A year perhaps?" "No! Longer than that. In fact, the trip I am taking is one from which I will never return." "Well," said the fool, "for such a long trip, you must be adequately prepared." "No," replied the lord, "I have made absolutely no preparation." The fool handed his lord the walking cane and said, "I have now found a fool bigger than I—one who is not prepared to die."

Bible Truth for Today: *"And as it is appointed unto men once to die, but after this the judgment."* —Hebrews 9:27

June 2

Read Job 15–17
Family Reading: Job 16

Be Careful to Uplift—Very Slow to Criticize

In this sixteenth chapter Job, God's tested servant, replies to Eliphaz, *"I have heard many such things . . . " (v. 2)*. He was saying, "I have heard this before. You so-called friends of mine are saying the same things again and again." Job's friends seemed to have the same theory that they repeated. Job called them *"miserable comforters" (v. 2)*. They offered Job no solution to his problems and yet continued to heap upon him a heavier burden.

Job said, *"I also could speak as ye do . . . " (v. 4)*. If those men had been in Job's place, he could have treated them as they were doing to him. In verse five Job said he would not treat them as they had treated him, but he said he would strengthen them and endeavor to assuage the grief. In this Job is manifesting a Christ-honoring attitude. It is easy to condemn our brother, note his faults, and be critical. The child of God should always be loving and kind.

Someone has said that the person who kicks continually soon loses his balance. If we knew all the facts, we would not be so critical. Too often we set ourselves up as judges and severely condemn when we do not have all the facts.

A man was getting a shoeshine in a barbershop. The boy who was shining his shoes was terribly slow. The man became exasperated and spoke to the boy harshly, "Can't you do this any faster?" The boy looked up at the man, his eyes filled with tears. The man softened: "Oh, excuse me, son. I did not mean to hurt you." The boy replied, "Sir, it is not what you said that made me cry. The tears were already there. You see, my mother died last night, and I am here this morning only because I want to buy a bouquet of flowers for her grave. My eyes were so filled with tears that I could hardly see your shoes. That is the reason I am so slow."

If that man had only known the facts, he would have acted far differently. If you and I knew the circumstances involved in other lives, we would be far less critical—and a whole lot happier.

Bible Truth for Today: *"Pleasant words are as an honeycomb, sweet to the soul, and health to the bones."* —*Proverbs 16:24*

June 3

Read Job 18–20
Family Reading: Job 19:7-29

Job's Glorious Hope

Job 19:25-27 is an outstanding confession of the Word of God. Job knew they were important words for he introduced them by saying in verses twenty-three and twenty-four: *"Oh that my words were now written! oh that they were printed in a book! That they were graven with an iron pen and lead in the rock for ever."*

Job wanted his words recorded in an enduring manner for all to read. That is exactly what has happened. Thousands of grave markers made out of rock bear the words, *" [For] I know that my redeemer liveth . . . " (v. 25).* Countless books have been written about this great confession. Job knew that he was making a confession to be remembered and revered through the ages.

It was a great confession because it came out of the hopelessness that Job faced. His friends had reproached him as a hypocrite and condemned him as a wicked man; but he appealed to his creed, his faith, and his hope for comfort. No matter what happened to the body, he knew he would experience resurrection.

Job's faith was real because he did not place it just in some fanciful ideas. Rather he placed it in a person. He confessed, *"For I know that my redeemer liveth . . . "*

The Redeemer here is the Lord Jesus Christ, the One who will stand in the latter days as the resurrected, conquering Son of God. Job had his faith in Christ and in the truth that Christ would rise from the dead. He believed that His Redeemer would arise and in the power of His resurrection Job would arise also. Disease could wrack his body; even death could take his body and let it be eaten by worms. Yet Job knew that through his Redeemer's resurrection, he would live again. Job had this hope centuries before Christ came to earth. How much more should you and I have this hope who today have heard the glorious story and believed on the Lord Jesus Christ.

Bible Truth for Today: *"Yet a little while, and the world seeth me no more; but ye see me: because I live, ye shall live also."*

—John 14:19

June 4

Read Job 21–23
Family Reading: Job 23

God's Purpose in Trials

To me Job 23:10-12 is one of the great and thrilling portions of Scripture. Think on these verses with me this morning: *"But he knoweth the way that I take: when he hath tried me, I shall come forth as gold. My foot hath held his steps, his way have I kept, and not declined. Neither have I gone back from the commandment of his lips; I have esteemed the words of his mouth more than my necessary food."* Job said that in spite of the trials that came, he knew that God was with him. He said, *"Oh that I knew where I might find him! that I might come even to his seat!" (v. 3).* In verses eight and nine Job confessed that he had trouble finding the Lord. If he went forward or backward, to the right or the left, he could not surely perceive the Lord.

Then having said all these things, Job's faith came to the surface and he rose above his circumstances with the confession: *"But he knoweth the way that I take . . . "* In spite of his anguish of spirit and his bitter words, Job had not turned against God. Though He seemed to lose sight of Him, he did not renounce the Lord.

Why does God permit such trials? The answer is—the trials bring out the gold. What a purifying effect the experience of testing produces. If a man has any faith in his soul, testing will discover it; if he has a tiny grain of living hope, testing will bring it to light; if he has a particle of love, testing will extract it from the ore.

"That the trial of your faith, being much more precious than of gold that perisheth, though it be tried with fire, might be found unto praise and honor and glory at the appearing of Jesus Christ" (I Peter 1:7).

Bible Principle for Today: *"Beloved, think it not strange concerning the fiery trial which is to try you, as though some strange thing happened unto you: **But rejoice**, inasmuch as ye are partakers of Christ's sufferings; that, when his glory shall be revealed, ye may be glad also with exceeding joy."* —I Peter 4:12, 13

Read Job 24–28
Family Reading: Job 28

Where Is Wisdom?

In the twenty-second chapter Job told about the wicked man who heaps up silver and who glories in his riches. Now in Chapter 28 he tells us of something that is much more valuable than riches. There is a treasure far greater than that which a man can hold in his hand: it is that treasure which he can receive in his heart.

Job speaks of wisdom. In verse twelve he asks, *"But where shall wisdom be found? and where is the place of understanding?"*

Job answers his own question first by stating where wisdom will not be found. It is not found in earthly life (v. 13). Timothy wrote that the widow who lives for earthly pleasure is dead while she liveth (I Timothy 5:6).

Ask the miner or the sailor if he found wisdom deep in the earth or out at sea, and he will have to answer, "No!" (v. 14). And then Job gives five verses (vv. 15-19) to show that wisdom cannot be bought with the riches of the world.

In verse twenty-eight Job gives the answer. He reveals that God is speaking to man. *"And unto man he said, Behold, the fear of the Lord, that is wisdom; and to depart from evil is understanding."* God gives wisdom. He lets us apply the fear of the Lord to our lives so that we have understanding, which results in our departing from evil. *"Evil men understand not judgment: but they that seek the Lord understand all things" (Proverbs 28:5).*

Bible Truth for Today: *"Wisdom is the principal thing; therefore get wisdom: and with all thy getting get understanding."*

—Proverbs 4:7

June 6

Read Job 29–31
Family Reading: Job 31:1-28

The Self Life

We have been reading many passages giving Job's answers to his friends. Verse forty of Job 31 ends the words of Job. He had said everything he was going to say—and he had said plenty! Though he was a good and great man, he had the problem of honoring self.

I have reread Chapters 29, 30, and 31 of Job. I circled every word that was a first person personal pronoun referring to Job. I circled the words *I, me, my, mine*, etc. In these three chapters I counted 199 times that Job refers to or speaks of himself. This means that he referred to himself at least an average of twice in every verse of these chapters.

Job was a good man. Our reading today in Chapter 31 reveals this. He said of himself:

1. That he guarded what his eyes looked at and what his mind meditated on (v. 1).

2. That he endeavored not to walk in vanity or deceit (v. 5).

3. That he did not get involved in adulterous sin (vv. 9, 10).

4. That he treated his servants right (v. 13).

5. That he gave to the poor (vv. 16-22).

6. That he did not live for his wealth (vv. 24, 25).

And we could go on with the list. He was a good man. He lived a good life, but the tragedy was that he lived it for himself rather than for the glory of God. All we do should be for the glory of God. I believe Job underwent these dreadful periods of testing because he lived for self. God wanted to purify Job so that he would live only and always to please God and to bring glory to Him.

Bible Truth for Today: *"Whether therefore ye eat, or drink, or whatsoever ye do, do all to the glory of God."* —I Corinthians 10:31

June 7

Read Job 32–34
Family Reading: Job 34:1-23

God's Righteous Judgment

Elihu has been presenting outstanding truths to Job. Here he emphasizes that God's government is righteous and impartial. *"Therefore hearken unto me, ye men of understanding: far be it from God, that he should do wickedness; and from the Almighty, that he should commit iniquity" (v. 10).*

God's government is righteous, first, because God is righteous. *"Yea, surely God will not do wickedly . . . " (v. 12).* God cannot so much as think evil. *" . . . for God cannot be tempted with evil, neither tempteth he any man" (James 1:13). " . . . God is light, and in him is no darkness at all" (I John 1:5).*

Second, God's government is righteous because of His wonderful care for the children of God. A proper understanding of verses fourteen and fifteen could be, "If God should withdraw His life-giving Spirit and His breath from me, and cause His heart to return to Himself or set His heart upon Himself, all flesh would perish together, and man turn again to dust." God is the Source of all life. He cares for us; we must rely on Him.

Third, God's government is righteous because of His greatness and wisdom. All things are in God's hands, and God knows and understands everything (Job 34:16-23).

> *. . . Wert Thou not holy, Lord,*
> *Why should I come to Thee?*
> *It is Thy holiness that makes*
> *Thee, Lord, so meet for me . . .*
> *Wert Thou not righteous, Lord,*
> *I dare not come to Thee;*
> *It is righteous pardon, Lord,*
> *Alone that suiteth me.*
> *—H. Bonar*

Bible Truth for Today: *"And Abraham drew near, and said, Wilt thou also destroy the righteous with the wicked?"* *—Genesis 18:23*

June 8

Read Job 35–37
Family Reading: Job 35

Importance of Attitude

It seems to me that Elihu was a proud man; but at the same time, he was a very capable and wise man. He did put his finger on a key to the problem Job was having. Job had been crying out for God to make Himself known, but there had been no answer. Elihu said in Job 35:13—*"Surely God will not hear vanity, . . . "* Elihu said it was because people cry out to God (v. 9) but do not ask, *" . . . Where is God my maker, who giveth songs in the night?" (v. 10).* He states in verse twelve that *" . . . There they cry,"* but they do not get an answer. Because of this, Elihu said, *"Surely God will not hear vanity, neither will the Almighty regard it" (v. 13).*

God searches out men's hearts; and when He finds their attitudes and motives are right, He can work on their behalf. God wants us to be sure our attitude is right and to be sure our motive is right.

"All the ways of a man are clean in his own eyes; but the Lord weigheth the spirits" (Proverbs 16:2).

All of us have a tendency to come to our own rescue and then justify ourselves when we face problems. Remember that God not only hears our words but also examines our hearts.

*"Therefore judge nothing before the time, until the Lord come, who both will bring to light the hidden things of darkness, and **will make manifest the counsels of the hearts**: and then shall every man have praise of God" (I Corinthians 4:5). "For the ways of man are before the eyes of the Lord . . . " (Proverbs 5:21). "I the Lord search the heart, I try the reins, even to give every man according to his ways, and according to the fruit of his doings" (Jeremiah 17:10).*

Oh, how important it is for us always to have the right attitude about and toward God, regardless of the circumstances about us.

Bible Truth for Today: *"The fining pot is for silver, and the furnace for gold: but the Lord trieth the hearts."* —*Proverbs 17:3*

June 9

Read Job 38 and 39
Family Reading: Job 38:1-23

Man's Unlimited Understanding

The friends of Job have been speaking from their own human wisdom. Job has been answering them—also often with his human reasoning. In Job 38 the Lord Himself begins to speak to Job and his friends.

He speaks in particular to Job, calling upon him to be valiant and bold as he faces the truth of his case. He challenges Job to gird up his loins like a man. We have the same challenge given in I Corinthians 16:13—*"Watch ye, stand fast . . . quit you like men, be strong."*

Then God asks Job a series of questions. Job did not understand his sufferings. The questions asked were given to reveal man's ignorance of divine chastisement because man has only limited wisdom. God begins by asking, *"Where wast thou when I laid the foundations of the earth? . . . " (v. 4).*

How limited is our understanding? As men, we do know the effect; but how little we know of the cause. In this connection the Lord asked several questions about creation. There would be no way to understand this world and this universe if we did not believe that God created everything.

Man does not have the ability to create nor to understand God's power in creation. In fact, man cannot even fathom the treasures of the snow or the treasures of the hail. Something as tiny as a snowflake God can use to stop cities, snarl armies, and defeat nations. God states that He has reserved the snow and hail against the day of trouble and against nations in battle and war (v. 23). Just a tiny snowflake, created by God—and yet what treasure is hidden therein!

Bible Truth for Today: *"That be far from thee to do after this manner, to slay the righteous with the wicked: and that the righteous should be as the wicked, that be far from thee: Shall not the Judge of all the earth do right?" —Genesis 18:25*

161

June 10

Read Job 40–42
Family Reading: Job 42

Job Saw Himself!

Throughout the book of Job, we find Job defending himself and declaring his righteousness. His three friends had counseled with him and had tried to convince him of his sin. It was after all his human friends dealt with him that Jehovah began to talk directly with him in the thirty-eighth chapter. The Lord's message was one that presented the Lord and who He is. He challenged Job to realize the greatness, the glory, and the grace of Jehovah.

In his answer to the Lord in Chapter 42, Job made a great confession: *"I have heard of thee by the hearing of the ear: but now mine eye seeth thee. Wherefore I abhor myself, and repent in dust and ashes" (vv. 5, 6).*

When Job actually saw himself, he no longer could plead his own righteousness. He saw who he was and saw his own need before the Lord. He said, *"I abhor myself."* God's desire for every one of us is that we could literally see ourselves and come to the end of ourselves. In verse three Job admits that the first words Jehovah spoke to him in Job 38:2 are the words that pierced to the core of his heart. *"Who is he that hideth counsel without knowledge? . . . "* Job confessed that he had been justifying himself by saying, *" . . . therefore have I uttered that I understood not; things too wonderful for me, which I knew not" (42:3).*

This brought Job to the place of a penitent seeking the Lord. He admitted his sin. He confessed that when he saw himself as he really was, he had to repent in dust and ashes. As we see the glory and majesty of the Lord, we will see ourselves as needy and helpless.

Verse ten states that the Lord turned the captivity of Job when he prayed for his friends. It is extremely important that we pray for our friends rather than judge them and condemn them. May God give us grace today to see ourselves as God sees us and to pray for those who have disagreed with us.

Bible Truth for Today: *"Every branch in me that beareth not fruit he taketh away: and every branch that beareth fruit, he purgeth it, that it may bring forth more fruit." —John 15:2*

June 11

Read Psalms 1–7
Family Reading: Psalm 5

The Blessing of Prayer

Psalm 5 shows God's people surrounded by evil and sin. There are bloody and deceitful men who speak lies (v. 6). (The word *"leasing"* means *"lying."*) What is the refuge for the child of God in such circumstances?

The refuge for the child of God is prayer. He can call upon Jehovah in the day of trouble and perplexity. David, a man of meditation, called on God to *"Hearken unto the voice of my cry, my King, and my God: for unto thee will I pray" (v. 2).*

David not only relied on prayer but also relied on the blessing of God when he attended the house of God. *"But as for me, I will come into thy house in the multitude of thy mercy: and in thy fear will I worship toward thy holy temple" (v. 7).*

The two must go together: prayer and attendance in the house of God. Without these, no believer is able to stand against the enemies of the Lord. It is the comfort of the godly that in their hatred of evil they are on God's side. They are in fellowship with Him for He hates evil and they hate evil with Him. The godly can look forward to the day when they will be in His house forever.

When I pray in a right spirit, under the leadership of the Holy Spirit, in the name of Jesus Christ, and in a right relationship to my fellow men, there are two things that happen: (1) Some spiritual blessing will flow to someone in need, and (2) Some evil spirit or force will be checked.

Bible Prayer Promise for Today: *"The sacrifice of the wicked is an abomination to the Lord: but the prayer of the upright is his delight."*
                                                                    —Proverbs 15:8

June 12

Read Psalms 8–13
Family Reading: Psalm 10

The Antichrist

Psalm 10 is a very clear picture of the wicked. We can apply it to the attitude and actions of wicked men of all generations. They persecute the poor and stand against the Lord.

However, this psalm is more than an application to wicked *men*. It is talking about a wicked *man*. Note verse eighteen: " . . . *the man of the earth may no more oppress.*" The one to whom this refers is an individual. Thirty times the pronouns *he* and *his* are used, showing that the wicked is an individual. Twice in verse six this wicked man refers to himself as *I*. He is also called the *"evil man" (v. 15).* I believe this individual is the Antichrist.

He is the beast which has two horns like a lamb and is indwelt by the dragon Satan (Revelation 13:11-18). The Apostle Paul calls him *"that Wicked"* one (II Thessalonians 2:8).

In this tenth psalm we have a picture of the moral character of Antichrist. We see his boasting spirit and his covetousness (v. 3). We find that he hates God and will not have anything to do with Him (v. 4). He says, " . . . *I shall not be moved . . .* " *(v. 6).* He is determined to take his stand against God and everything that is right and decent.

Psalm 10 is a record of the way he will persecute the remnant of Israel. The cries of those being persecuted are the cries of Israel during the tribulation period. Oh, what a dreadful day that will be! I believe the appearance of Antichrist is very close at hand. Christ will appear the second time before the appearance of the Antichrist. Let us say, " . . . *Even so, come, Lord Jesus" (Revelation 22:20).*

> Some golden daybreak, Jesus will come;
> Some golden daybreak, battles all won,
> He'll shout the victory, break through the blue,
> Some golden daybreak, for me, for you.

Bible Truth for Today: *"And lead us not into temptation, but deliver us from evil: For thine is the kingdom, and the power, and the glory, for ever. Amen." —Matthew 6:13*

June 13

Read Psalms 14–18
Family Reading: Psalm 18:1-24

Christ, the Center of Life

The psalmist confesses that he has made the Lord the very center of his life. Psalm 18 is filled with the relationship between the Lord and David. As you read the psalm, please note the times the pronouns are used referring either to the writer or to the Lord. It is a psalm revealing the definite and close personal relationship between the Lord and His servant.

In David's testimony he begins with: *"I will love thee, O Lord, my strength" (v. 1).* Then he states in verse two what the Lord means to him. He does not talk about experiences. Rather, he speaks of the Lord and His reality in David's life.

There are many professed Christians who have never learned the secret of a godly Christian life. Multitudes center their lives in experience rather than in the Person of the Lord Jesus Christ. In this psalm David reveals that he had found the secret of a normal spiritual experience. It is not found in self—it is found in the Lord.

Christ must become the center and the circumference of the Christian life. Therefore, David said, *"The Lord is my rock, and my fortress, and my deliverer . . . " (v. 2).*

The Lord is not only the center of my life; He is Life itself. David said the Lord was his Rock. A rock is a foundation. And Paul said that no man could have any other foundation than Jesus Christ (I Corinthians 3:11).

> *O safe to the Rock that is higher than I,*
> *My soul in its conflicts and sorrows would fly;*
> *So sinful, so weary, Thine, Thine would I be;*
> *Thou blest "Rock of Ages," I'm hiding in Thee.*
> *Hiding in Thee, Hiding in Thee,*
> *Thou blest "Rock of Ages," I'm hiding in Thee.*
> *—William O Cushing*

Bible Truth for Today: *"And he is the head of the body, the church: who is the beginning, the firstborn from the dead; that in all things he might have the preeminence." —Colossians 1:18*

June 14

Read Psalms 19–23
Family Reading: Psalm 22:1-22

The Cross

Psalms 22-24 form a trilogy in the book of Psalms. Psalm 22 speaks of Christ on the cross; Psalm 23 presents Christ, our Shepherd; and Psalm 24 speaks of Christ, the reigning King. Someone has said that all three psalms present the Lord as our Shepherd in the three aspects given in the New Testament.

John 10:11—Jesus said, *"I am the good shepherd: the good shepherd giveth his life for the sheep."* This is presented in Psalm 22 as we see the sufferings of Christ on the cross.

Hebrews 13:20—*"Now the God of peace, that brought again from the dead our Lord Jesus, that great shepherd of the sheep . . ."* He is the Great Shepherd in Psalm 23, looking after, watching over, and providing for His sheep.

I Peter 5:4—*"And when the chief Shepherd shall appear, ye shall receive a crown of glory that fadeth not away."* The Shepherd becomes the King in Psalm 24, to whom we answer at the judgment.

The key to all three psalms is in Psalm 22, the presentation of the cross of Christ. Psalm 22 is the clearest presentation of the suffering and anguish of Calvary to be found anywhere in the Word of God. It is because Christ suffered that we can trust Him and see our lives resting wholly on Him.

> *Alas, and did my Saviour bleed?*
> *And did my Sovereign die?*
> *Would He devote that sacred head*
> *For such a worm as I?*
>
> *Well might the sun in darkness hide,*
> *And shut his glories in,*
> *When Christ, the mighty Maker, died*
> *For man the creature's sin.*

Bible Truth for Today: *"Who his own self bare our sins in his own body on the tree, that we, being dead to sins, should live unto righteousness: by whose stripes ye were healed."* —I Peter 2:24

June 15

Read Psalms 24–29
Family Reading: Psalm 27

Wait on the Lord

It may seem an easy thing to wait, but it is one of the most difficult things for any of us to do. As Christian soldiers we seem not to learn to wait without years of teaching. Moses had to go to the backside of the desert for forty years to learn that he must not act in haste.

In Psalm 27:13 David said, *"I had fainted, unless I had believed to see the goodness of the Lord in the land of the living."* He had a natural tendency to run ahead and then faint when he did not see things happening properly. Thus it is with all of us.

There will always be hours of trial when we will anxiously desire to serve the Lord and yet know not what we ought to do. In that case, what should we do? Should we get disturbed and vexed? Should we fly back in cowardice and say we do not understand? No—the answer is simply to wait. We need to wait in prayer. We need to call upon God and spread the case before Him. We must tell Him our difficulty and plead for His promise of aid.

We must also wait in faith. We simply must believe that God will do what is His will at the right time. While waiting, we should not criticize God but rather bless Him. We should never do what Israel did when they said, "We wish we could go back to Egypt from whence we came." Oh, may we never slip into that. May we be thankful that we have been saved and that we have the opportunity to go forward for the Lord Jesus Christ.

Bible Truth for Today: *"Trust in the Lord with all thine heart; and lean not unto thine own understanding. In all thy ways acknowledge him, and he shall direct thy paths."* —Proverbs 3:5, 6

June 16

Read Psalms 30–33
Family Reading: Psalm 33

God—Our Deliverer

In Psalm 33:12 God promises, *"Blessed is the nation whose God is the Lord; and the people whom he hath chosen for his own inheritance."*

While Israel lived for the Lord, the nation had the blessing of God manifested through all of her national life. But when Israel departed from the Lord, her people were dispersed throughout the world. God blesses a nation that honors Him and forsakes that country that turns away from Him.

We must never forget the truth that God does not need man's strength in order to deliver a nation.

A king must learn to trust the Lord and not a **host**. *"There is no king saved by the multitude of an host . . . "(v. 16).*

A king must learn to trust the Lord and not a **hero**. *" . . . a mighty man is not delivered by much strength"* (v. 16).

A king must learn to trust the Lord and not a **horse**. *"An horse is a vain thing for safety: neither shall he deliver any by his great strength"* (v. 17).

We must learn to turn only in the Lord. *"Our soul waiteth for the Lord: he is our help and our shield"* (v. 20).

> A mighty fortress is our God,
> A bulwark never failing;
> Our helper He, amid the flood
> Of mortal ills prevailing.
> For still our ancient foe
> Doth seek to work us woe;
> His craft and pow'r are great,
> And, armed with cruel hate,
> On earth is not his equal.
> —Martin Luther

Bible Truth for Today: *"Who delivered us from so great a death, and doth deliver: in whom we trust that he will yet deliver us."*

—II Corinthians 1:10

June 17

Read Psalms 34–36
Family Reading: Psalm 34

Constant Praise

David announced in Psalm 34:1 that he would " . . . *bless the Lord at all times: his praise shall continually be in my mouth."* This is the way to real and abiding spirituality.

Paul stated in Philippians 4:4, *"Rejoice in the Lord alway: and again I say, Rejoice."*

True spirituality manifests itself in praising the Lord. We reveal His grace in our lives if we praise Him at all times—in good days and evil days, in days of prosperity and in days of loss; in days of blessing and in days of adversity; in days of health and in days of illness—at all times.

In verse two David amplifies this by stating that his soul shall glory in the Lord. If we desire to please the Lord, let us make Him our boast, our glory. This gives true peace for restless hearts.

Then David gives the cause for His rejoicing in the Lord. Verse four reveals that David had experienced a great deliverance. Great fears had surrounded him. When he sought Jehovah, He answered David, and deliverance from all his fears followed.

Jehovah saves the afflicted who call upon Him, and the Angel of Jehovah is also there for protection and deliverance. Verse seven reads, *"The angel of the Lord encampeth round about them that fear him, and delivereth them."* Verses eight and nine exhort us to taste and see that Jehovah is good, to fear Him; and the assurance is that those who do this shall not want. In verse ten he states that the young lions with all their natural strength lack and suffer hunger; but the person who has refuge in Jesus shall not want any good thing.

Bible Truth for Today: *"O taste and see that the Lord is good: blessed is the man that trusteth in him."* —*Psalm 34:8*

June 18

Read Psalms 37–39
Family Reading: Psalm 37:1-23

Doubt Not God's Wisdom!

To many people, there is a riddle they cannot solve or understand. They wonder why wicked people will prosper and the righteous will abide under afflictions. Men fret over this and question God's authority and wisdom. Psalm 37 is a strong answer to this riddle.

In this psalm God instructs us not to look at the present but to look to the future. The day will come when the wicked will be cut down and removed. The psalmist says this will not be far off, for in verse two he says *"[For] they shall soon be cut down . . . "* and in verse ten—*"For yet a little while, and the wicked shall not be . . . "* God wants His people to trust Him and to know that He, the Judge of all the earth, will do right.

God deals very strongly with the sins of fretting, envying, and worrying. He begins the psalm by commanding, *"Fret not thyself because of evildoers . . . "* To fret is to worry; to worry is to sin. To look at the prosperity of the wicked and envy his position is doubting the wisdom and providence of God.

Never forget: those cattle that are having it easy and getting fat are the ones that are being prepared for the slaughter. Why should I envy their position?

God gives several admonitions to Christians in this psalm. It would be well for Christians to meditate on the psalm and to memorize sections of it.

Note a few of the admonitions: we are to trust in the Lord; to delight ourselves in the Lord; to commit our way unto Him; to rest in the Lord; and to wait patiently for Him.

Let's encourage each other to trust in the Lord.

Bible Promise for Today: *"Trust in the Lord, and do good; so shalt thou dwell in the land, and verily thou shalt be fed."* —Psalm 37:3

June 19

Read Psalms 40–44
Family Reading: Psalms 42 and 43

A Longing for God

Psalms 42 and 43 go together. David was in straits of difficulties and trials. He announced, *"As the hart panteth after the water brooks, so panteth my soul after thee, O God" (v. 1).* The hart, a deer, pants for water when it is being chased or hunted. David felt like a hunted man, and he panted for the water brooks in knowing the Lord. The water brooks for the child of God are found in His precious Word, the Bible. We need to come to the water of the Word of God and be refreshed and cleansed.

David said his soul thirsted for God—for the living God. This One, the living God, is the One who answers prayer. I know He lives for He took my prayer and gave me an answer today. Oh, to be close to Him in prayer that day by day we know Him as the living God. *"My soul thirsteth for God, for the living God: when shall I come and appear before God?" (v. 2).*

David recognized that his only hope was in God. Three times in Psalms 42 and 43 he repeated this verse: *"Why art thou cast down, O my soul? and why art thou disquieted in me? hope thou in God: for I shall yet praise him for the help of his countenance" (Psalm 42:5).*

The psalmist commanded that a believer should hope in the Lord. When the trials and burdens get too heavy, we need to place our hope in God and praise Him for the help of His countenance. He is always ready to smile upon us and lead us through the deep and dark waters. David states that God will show His lovingkindness in the morning and His song in the night. *"Yet the Lord will command his loving-kindness in the daytime, and in the night his song shall be with me, and my prayer unto the God of my life" (v. 8).*

Bible Truth for Today: *" . . . hope thou in God: for I shall yet praise him for the help of his countenance."* —*Psalm 42:5*

June 20

Read Psalms 45–49
Family Reading: Psalm 45

Fairest Lord Jesus

Psalm 45 is a song of praise to our Lord Jesus Christ. Special singers were appointed to sing this psalm. Our King Jesus deserves to be praised with the sweetest and most skillful music of the best-trained singers. Charles Spurgeon says of the subject of this psalm: "Some here see only Solomon and Pharaoh's daughter—they are short-sighted; others see both Solomon and Christ—they are cross-eyed; well-focused spiritual eyes see here Jesus only, or if Solomon be present at all, it must be like those hazy shadows of passers-by which cross the face of the camera and therefore are dimly traceable on the photographic landscape."

In verse one he says, " . . . *I speak of the things which I have made touching the king . . .* " This King is the Lord Jesus Christ. The psalmist says that he is writing concerning the King, and his tongue is the pen of a ready writer. In verse two it seems that the Lord Jesus appeared right before him. Verse one is a preface to what he is going to say about Christ. In verse two he springs forth with praise from a heart that is full of love. The Lord Jesus reveals Himself when we are in an attitude of praise and love for Him. As we pour forth our affections, we usually come to know Him in a new way.

The psalmist cried, *"Thou art fairer than the children of men . . . "* *(v. 2)* The Hebrew word for *fairer* is really a double word. It really means: *"Beautiful, beautiful art thou."* The Lord Jesus is so emphatically lovely that our words must be doubled, strained, yea exhausted before He can be described.

Why is He fair? He is fair because grace is poured into His lips. Therefore, God hath blessed Him forever (v. 2).

Meditation on Christ for Today: *"Thou lovest righteousness and hatest wickedness: therefore God, thy God, hath anointed thee with the oil of gladness above thy fellows."* *—Psalm 45:7*

June 21

Read Psalms 50–55
Family Reading: Psalm 51

Sin Forgiven

This psalm is the record of David's prayer of repentance after his dreadful sin of adultery with Bathsheba. Psalm 32 presents David after he had realized God's forgiveness and cleansing. There he shouted, *"Blessed is he whose transgression is forgiven . . . " (v. 1).* There is no joy like that which a backslider receives when he knows for sure his sin is forgiven by God. Also, in Psalm 32 David tells of God's hand heavy upon him. It was during this dreadful drought experience that David prayed Psalm 51.

Please note some truths David realized as he prayed. Then apply these truths to your own heart.

1. He acknowledged his sin as against God (vv. 3, 4).

2. He knew he was born with a sinful nature (v. 5).

3. He realized that the biggest sin in his life was deceit. Truth in the inward parts is an acid test of character (v. 6).

4. He plainly called his sin *"bloodguiltiness" (v. 14).* He was referring to the death of Uriah. Though he did not actually kill Uriah, he planned it in his heart and, therefore, was guilty of murder.

5. He cried out to God for cleansing (vv. 7-10).

6. He knew he needed the ministry of the Holy Spirit (v. 11).

7. He realized he had lost the joy of his salvation (v. 12).

8. He knew that he could not be a soulwinner until he was thoroughly right with God (v. 13).

Bible Truth for Today: *"There is therefore now no condemnation to them which are in Christ Jesus, who walk not after the flesh, but after the Spirit." —Romans 8:1*

June 22

Read Psalms 56–61
Family Reading: Psalms 60 and 61

The Rock That Is Higher Than I

David prayed, " . . . *when my heart is overwhelmed: lead me to the rock that is higher than I" (Psalm 61:2).* David wrote this sixty-first psalm when he was in flight from Absalom, looking toward home again. David's heart was wrapped in gloom because he was away from the Holy City and Sanctuary. The geographical distance was not great; but because of his deep longing to be in the Holy City, it seemed to him that he was at the *"end of the earth" (v. 2).* He longed for the blessing of the Sanctuary and deliverance from his present distress.

Each of us needs to pray that same prayer. We must learn always to turn to the Rock that is higher than we are. That Rock is our Lord and Saviour Jesus Christ. " . . . *for they drank of that spiritual Rock that followed them: and that Rock was Christ" (I Corinthians 10:4).* And we know that " . . . *their rock is not as our Rock, even our enemies themselves being judges" (Deuteronomy 32:31).*

How can you and I be led to the Rock that is higher than we?

First, we must come to the Word of God. It points us to Christ so that we can rest on His sure foundation.

Second, we need to attend the services of a Bible-preaching church to learn of Him and His all-sufficient grace. As we rest on His grace, we find His strength as the Rock to deliver us from the overwhelming odds of the world and Satan. Attendance in church and thereby fellowship with God's people and instruction in God's Word is an absolute necessity in our lives to deliver us from the wiles of the evil one. Who is there that has not felt overwhelmed? May we pray with David, " . . . *lead me to the rock that is higher than I . . . "(v. 2).*

Bible Truth for Today: *"For thou hast been a shelter for me, and a strong tower from the enemy." —Psalm 61:3*

June 23

Read Psalms 62–67
Family Reading: Psalms 62 and 63

Trusting the Lord

Note Psalm 62:5—*"My soul, wait thou only upon God; for my expectation is from him."* This is the believer's privilege—to wait upon God and receive his expectation from the Lord. If he looks to the world, he will find that that is a poor *"expectation"* indeed. But if he looks to God for the supply of his wants, whether in spiritual or temporal blessings, his *"expectation"* will not be in vain. Constantly he may draw on the bank of faith and find his need supplied out of the riches of God's lovingkindness. I would rather have God for my banker than all of the Rockefellers or Gettys or Hunts.

God warns of the danger of riches: *" . . . if riches increase, set not your heart upon them" (62:10).* It is only when God becomes a definite reality in a life that everyone and everything else is given its correct value.

We are exhorted to *"wait"* on the Lord. *"Truly my soul **waiteth** upon God . . ." (v. 1). "My soul, **wait** thou only upon God . . ." (v. 5).* To *"**wait**"* on God is to trust Him and Him alone. The one who waits on Him sees Him as his Rock, his Salvation, and his Defense.

They that trust in the Lord must trust in Him alone. You cannot trust in the Lord and rest upon the arm of flesh at the same time. Someone has said, "He that stands with one foot on a rock and another foot upon quicksand will sink and perish as quickly as he that stands with both feet upon quicksand." When the Lord is your Rock, you have both feet upon the Rock. And then I always like to remember that blessed statement given by a dear old black lady: "I may tremble on the Rock, but the Rock never trembles under me."

What is our expectation? Praise God, it is that our every need will be met here and now. But more—our expectation is that someday we will be with Him and we shall be like Him, *" . . . for we shall see him as he is" (I John 3:2).*

Bible Truth for Today: *"And if children, then heirs; heirs of God, and joint-heirs with Christ; if so be that we suffer with him, that we may be also glorified together." —Romans 8:17*

June 24

Read Psalms 68 and 69
Family Reading: Psalm 69:1-21

The Suffering Christ

Psalm 69, prophesying the death of the Messiah, is filled with a preview of the agony of Christ on the cross. Who but the Lord Jesus Christ could say, *"They gave me also gall for my meat; and in my thirst they gave me vinegar to drink" (v. 21)?* This was literally fulfilled as Christ died for us on Calvary.

Spurgeon wrote: "If any enquire, 'Of whom speaketh the psalmist this? of himself, or of some other man?' we would reply, 'Of himself and of some other man.' Who that other is, we need not be long in discovering; it is the Crucified alone who can say, *'In my thirst they gave me vinegar to drink.'* His footprints all through this sorrowful song have been pointed out by the Holy Spirit in the New Testament, and therefore we believe, and are sure, that the Son of man is here." Yes, we see Jesus Christ in His agony and suffering for us as we read this psalm.

He begins with *"Save me, O God; for the waters are come in unto my soul" (v. 1).* The mob cried, *"He saved others; himself he cannot save . . . " (Matthew 27:42).* They were right. He came to give His life a ransom for many; and, therefore, He could not save Himself. He said, *"I sink in deep mire . . . " (v. 2).* Everything gave way under this Sufferer. He could get no foothold for support. He suffered alone in your place and mine. He knew what it was to bear the reproach. He gave all that we might be redeemed.

Psalm 69:20 tells us that Jesus Christ, under great reproach and heaviness, was pitied and comforted by none. Our Saviour suffered alone for us.

> He took my sins and my sorrows,
> He made them His very own;
> He bore the burden to Calv'ry,
> And suffered and died alone.
> —Charles H. Gabriel

Bible Truth for Today: *"Reproach hath broken my heart; and I am full of heaviness: and I looked for some to take pity, but there was none; and for comforters, but I found none." —Psalm 69:20*

June 25

Read Psalms 70–73
Family Reading: Psalm 71

A Message for All Ages

The psalmist must have written Psalm 71 in later life. He prays that the Lord will not cast him off in old age (v. 9). He confesses, *"Now also when I am old and grayheaded . . ."* (v. 18).

One of the problems of life is that we fail to keep our perspective right in every period of our lives. We see far too many people growing old and growing sour. They fail to keep a sweet spirit. This psalm teaches us that in every period of life we need to trust the Lord and thereby have the right outlook on life.

I am sure you have heard the statement, "Life begins at forty." At forty life is at least half gone. A person without Christ can be trying to live in a fool's paradise by saying, "Life begins at forty." The fact is, real life begins only when we trust Christ as Saviour and Lord. Without Him, no period of life will be all God meant it to be.

Here the psalmist states that his trust is in the Lord (v. 1). Because he had put his trust in the Lord, he could look back and write: *"O God , thou hast taught me from my youth: and hitherto have I declared thy wondrous works"* (v. 17).

The Christian should not live in the past. He should rejoice in all that the Lord has taught him over the years and apply these truths and principles to problems he meets each day.

The closer a man walks with God, the more sin he sees. Likewise, the farther he walks from God, the less sin he sees. It is as he walks with God, trusts in His Word, and leaves his hope in the Lord, that a man can grow to the place of having the right view of life. Each day should become a challenge where we look to the future and rest in the Lord. This does not mean that a person will be spared trials and difficulties. Even this psalmist had to say, *"Thou . . . hast showed me great and sore troubles . . ."* (v. 20). In spite of the troubles, he could have hope and grow old sweetly because his trust was in the Lord.

Bible Truth for Today: *"But it is good for me to draw near to God: I have put my trust in the Lord God, that I may declare all thy works."*
—Psalm 73:28

June 26

Read Psalms 74–77
Family Reading: Psalm 77

From a Sigh to a Song

Psalm 73 begins the third section of the book of Psalms. It is known as the Leviticus section, emphasizing the holiness of God; and it comprises Psalms 73–89. The first eleven of these psalms are attributed to Asaph: Psalms 73–83. This man Asaph was a Levite, who was the chief of David's musicians (I Chronicles 16:5). In II Chronicles 29:30 we find Asaph's name placed alongside King David's as an author of psalms which the Israelites sang. Asaph was not only a songwriter but also a prophet. Through his psalms, he gave Israel instruction for trying events.

In Psalm 77 he writes concerning the trial of their captivity. In verses one through nine, he utters the **sigh** of a nation or an individual troubled; then in verses ten through twenty he gives the **song** that can come to the heart that trusts the Lord. The first nine verses present the **trouble**; and the last section, the **triumph**. The subject of the first part is the **Present National Disaster**, while that of the last section is the **Past National Deliverance**.

This is true in the life of every believer. If we will just get our eyes off our present burdens and place them on present blessings, we can and will enjoy the victory. It is wonderful to follow the injunction of Psalm 77:11, 12—*"I will remember the works of the Lord: surely I will remember thy wonders of old. I will meditate also of all thy work, and talk of thy doings."*

All of life is a mixture of tears and gladness. None of us are spared tears, and I believe all of us have some measure of joy. However, the deepest praise is often offered from the midst of tears. We are forced by circumstances to go into the presence of God and cry unto Him.

Bible Standard for Today: *"I will meditate also of all thy work, and talk of thy doings."* —*Psalm 77:12*

June 27

Read Psalm 78
Family Reading: Psalm 78:1-22, 35-38

Be Ye Steadfast

The Israelites were not steadfast in their covenants with God. Psalm 78:37 reads: *"For their heart was not right with him, neither were they steadfast in his covenant."* The Israelites regularly received the blessings from the Lord, but they did not walk steadfastly with Him. There are a number of reasons given for their lack of steadfastness. Let us look at just a few.

First, they did not stay in the battle. Verse nine says that they *" . . . turned back in the day of battle."* The Christian life is not one of lying on a bed of roses. There are fights and battles in which to be engaged. Praise God, we do not fight in our own strength. These Israelites sinned by not staying in the fight.

Second, they refused to keep the covenant of God (v. 10). They began with cowardice and then saw that grow to rebellion.

Third, verse eleven states that they forgot His works and His wonders that He had showed them. They never remembered what God had done for them.

Fourth, they lacked faith. Verse twenty-two states that *" . . . they believed not in God, and trusted not in his salvation."* Their lack of faith produced a lack of character that would make them be steadfast. *"But without faith it is impossible to please him . . ."* *(Hebrews 11:6).*

Psalm 78 is a tragic account of the backsliding of God's people. They lacked faith and then forgot all of His blessings. May God give us grace daily to remember all of His blessings and then walk steadfastly with Him. Thank God for His compassion. *"But he, being full of compassion, forgave their iniquity, and destroyed them not: yea, many a time turned he his anger away, and did not stir up all his wrath"* *(Psalm 78:38).*

Bible Command for Today: *"Therefore, my beloved brethren, be ye steadfast, unmoveable, always abounding in the work of the Lord, forasmuch as ye know that your labor is not in vain in the Lord."*

—I Corinthians 15:58

June 28

Read Psalms 79–83
Family Reading: Psalm 81

What Might Have Been

It is always a sad thing when those delivered from Egyptian bondage go into Babylonian captivity. This is exactly what happened to the nation of Israel. Asaph was a man who recorded the history of Israel in song. In Psalm 80:8 he recorded that God had brought a vine out of Egypt. God planted that vine—Israel—and blessed it.

In Psalm 81:10 we find Asaph reminding the people that the Lord God is the One who brought them out of the land of Egypt. Had they only trusted the Lord, He would have blessed and met their need. Then he records the sad news in verse eleven: *"But my people would not hearken to my voice; and Israel would none of me."* The result of such backsliding and rebellion is given in verse twelve: *"So I gave them up unto their own hearts' lust: and they walked in their own counsels."* What a tragedy!

In verse thirteen He states: *"Oh that my people had hearkened unto me, and Israel had walked in my ways!"* If they had walked with God, He would have soon subdued their enemies and turned His hand against their adversaries (v. 14). They would not have needed to go into captivity in Babylon. The haters of the Lord should have come under the control of the Spirit of God, and the time of Israel should have continued without having to go into captivity (v. 15).

Verse sixteen gives a very good summary of what God could have done: *"He should have fed them also with the finest of the wheat: and with honey out of the rock should I have satisfied thee."* What a privilege Israel had! By their rebellion and resistance to God, they lost it all. Oh, **what might have been**!

Is this true in your life? Things might have been different if you had been more obedient to the Lord. I trust that each of you today will promise God you are going to be faithful so that all God would want in your life could be fulfilled.

Requirement for All Believers: *"Moreover it is required in stewards, that a man be found faithful."* —*I Corinthians 4:2*

June 29

Read Psalms 84–88
Family Reading: Psalms 84 and 85

Strengthened

Psalm 84 presents the victory that comes to a soul yielded to the Lord. Verse five says that the man is blessed who has his strength in the Lord. He trusts in the Lord for his power and sustenance.

Then in verse six the psalmist tells of another blessing that comes to this man. The valley of Baca is the valley of dryness or of testing and trial. But this man who trusts in the Lord for His strength turns the valley of dryness into a well so that the rain fills the pools. He can face the temptations and the trials, knowing that the Lord in whom he trusts will give the victory.

Think of it. This man turns the valley of dryness into a well. God does not say that he finds some water for his own refreshment in the valley. Instead, Scripture states that this man turns that valley into a well. The well is there not only to furnish him refreshment, but also to provide for a future dweller or traveler. God permits our experiences, not only to reveal His strength and grace to meet our particular need, but also to leave a well to comfort someone else on down the road. Spurgeon has written: "Many a night of weeping has been a well digged by a pilgrim for himself and has proved quite as useful to others. Travelers have been delighted to see the footprint of man on a barren shore, and we love to see the waymarks of pilgrims while passing through the vale of tears."

Notice also that the well fills from the rain, which means the blessings come down from Heaven. We rely on the Lord, our strength, and He meets all the needs in our lives. God's grace rains down from Heaven to give us new strength for each day.

And that is what verse seven tells us: *"They go from strength to strength . . . "* He is saying: "They grow stronger and stronger." The trials of the valley of dryness are not meant to defeat or destroy us. Instead, they are permitted so that we will have new strength for the journey. We look to Him, our strength, and we receive the rain of grace from above to meet our every need.

Bible Truth for Today: *"I can do all things through Christ which strengtheneth me." —Philippians 4:13*

June 30

Read Psalms 89–91
Family Reading: Psalm 91

The Lord Our Habitation

Psalm 91 deals with the believer's rest in the Lord. He who dwells in the secret place of the Most High is assured he will abide under the shadow of the Almighty (v. 1). In verse nine God states that the believer rests in the Lord as his habitation.

In the wilderness the Israelites were consistently exposed to changes. When the pillar moved, they moved; when it stopped, they stopped. Each night it would stop, and they would pitch their tents. But the next morning ere the sun had risen, the trumpet would sound and the ark would be lifted; and soon they were on their way again. They had very little time to rest before they again heard the call, "Away! This is not your rest; you must still be moving." They were never very long in one place. Oases with their wells and palm trees could not detain them.

Moses wrote this psalm. He was with the Israelites daily in the wilderness. He realized they were constantly moving, but he said, "Though we are always changing and moving, we do have a refuge and a habitation." *"Lord, Thou hast been our dwelling place in all generations" (90:1).*

Though constantly on the move, the Israelites' abiding place was with God. His cloudy pillar was their roof-tree, and its flame by night their household fire. The Christian rests in the Lord as his habitation and refuge. He knows no change with regard to God. He may be rich today and poor tomorrow. He may be sick today and well tomorrow. He may have reason to rejoice today and experience distress tomorrow. But there is absolutely no change in his relationship to God. The Lord loved me yesterday, and He loves me today. No matter what happens, I still am in Him. Let joys be withered or hopes blasted or prospects blighted, I have lost nothing of what I have in Him.

Bible Truth for Today: *"Jesus Christ the same yesterday, and today, and for ever." —Hebrews 13:8*

July 1

Read Psalms 92–96
Family Reading: Psalms 95 and 96

Worship Him

Psalm 95 could be called "The Psalm of the Provocation." It is quoted twice in the book of Hebrews as a warning to the Jewish Christians that they should not falter in the faith and thus despise God's promise as their forefathers had done. David begins the psalm by speaking of the greatness of our God and the fact that He is worthy of our worship and song. *"O come, let us sing unto the Lord: let us make a joyful noise to the rock of our salvation. Let us come before his presence with thanksgiving and make a joyful noise unto him with psalms. For the Lord is a great God, and a great King above all gods" (vv. 1-3).*

The psalmist shows how great our God is. He is Creator, for He made the sea and formed the dry land. He holds all things together and maintains all. David is also careful to show that this God is our God, and we are the sheep in His pasture. He is great above all gods; yet He cares for us.

There is a requirement for His people. They have this great God, worthy of worship, but they must be willing to hear His voice. Failure to hear His voice can bring hardness of heart that will grieve the heart of the Lord. What is the remedy? Verse six tells us to worship Him. We must bow before the Lord, not before a crucifix, not before an image. *"O come, let us worship and bow down: let us kneel before the Lord our maker" (Psalm 95:6).*

Bible Truth for Today: *"This people draweth nigh unto me with their mouth, and honoreth me with their lips; but their heart is far from me." —Matthew 15:8*

July 2

Read Psalms 97–102
Family Reading: Psalms 97 and 98

Our Souls Preserved

Though Psalm 97 is written in the present tense, it is presenting the future. It is the psalm of the kingdom and is written about these future events, using the present tense as though these events were actually transpiring. In the mind of God, when He decrees an event, the certainty of the event is so apparent that He may speak of it in the present tense, though it may not actually be fulfilled for several thousand years.

He begins the psalm by stating that the Lord reigns. He then states that the world will rejoice when the Lord does reign. Today men are making promises that they have the answer to the world's needs of peace, prosperity, and happiness. Actually, no man can bring universal peace until Christ returns to establish His kingdom.

We have a wonderful truth given to us when the psalmist states, " . . . *he preserveth the souls of his saints . . .* " *(v. 10)*. A saint, according to the New Testament, is any person who has put his faith and trust in the Lord Jesus Christ as His Saviour. To be a saint simply means that a person has been set aside for the Lord. If you have received Christ, you are His saint for you belong to Him.

To preserve is to keep. The Lord will keep His saints. We do not keep ourselves! How glad we should be about that, for if salvation depended on our keeping and our preserving, it would not last very long. We simply need to believe God's Word and trust Him for His keeping power. *"Ye that love the Lord, hate evil: he preserveth the souls of his saints; he delivereth them out of the hand of the wicked"* *(Psalm 97:10).*

Bible Truth for Today: *"And I give unto them eternal life; and they shall never perish, neither shall any man pluck them out of my hand. My Father, which gave them me, is greater than all; and no man is able to pluck them out of my Father's hand."* *—John 10:28, 29*

July 3

Read Psalms 103–105
Family Reading: Psalm 104:1-12, 24-35

Let Us Sing

The life of the Christian should be typified by singing. In fact, the Apostle Paul tells that a song in the heart is a sign of the spiritual Christian. *"Speaking to yourselves in psalms and hymns and spiritual songs, singing and making melody in your heart to the Lord" (Ephesians 5:19).* *"Let the word of Christ dwell in you richly in all wisdom; teaching and admonishing one another in psalms and hymns and spiritual songs, singing with grace in your hearts to the Lord" (Colossians 3:16).* It is good for us to remember the things of God and to sing.

First, Moses sang when God triumphed over his enemies. *"Then sang Moses and the children of Israel this song . . . The Lord is my strength and song, and he is become my salvation: he is my God, . . . and I will exalt him" (Exodus 15:1, 2).* We should sing praise to God for his deliverance from our enemies. *"He delivereth me from mine enemies: yea, thou liftest me up above those that rise up against me: thou hast delivered me from the violent man. Therefore will I give thanks unto thee, O Lord, among the heathen, and sing praises unto thy name" (Psalm 18:48, 49).*

Second, the Scriptures show that singing comes from the Christian who has confessed his sin (Psalm 51:14). There is nothing so wonderful in the Christian life as having a pure heart before God. When God removes that sin, our hearts should open up to praise God.

A third reason why we should sing is to be a testimony to the world of the mercy of God. Mankind cries for peace, but they find none. The world is torn with strife. Christians have the answer, and we should proclaim it.

Finally, we shall one day sing a new song (Psalm 144:9). It is the song of the redeemed in Heaven (Revelation 5:9). There is coming a day when all believers shall be with the Lord, and we will sing praise unto our Redeemer.

Bible Truth for Today: *"I will sing unto the Lord as long as I live: I will sing praise to my God while I have my being. My meditation of him shall be sweet: I will be glad in the Lord."* —Psalm 104:33, 34

July 4

Read Psalms 33 and 106
Family Reading: Psalms 33:1-12; 106:1-23

America—Continue to Honor God

Today I varied the reading schedule so that we could go back and read again Psalm 33. Today we celebrate the signing of the Declaration of Independence. Americans can properly be thankful that this Declaration came to be. The Declaration includes references to God and His power. In the first paragraph of the Preamble, there is a reference to *"Nature's God."* In the second paragraph we read: *"We hold these truths to be self evident, that all men are created equal, that they are endowed by their Creator . . . "*

In the last two paragraphs of the Declaration, we find an appeal to *"the Supreme Judge of the world"* and a *"reliance on the protection of Divine Providence."*

We could cite many references in historical documents during the settling of America and the colonial days that refer to the need for a nation to recognize God. I personally believe Psalm 33:12 gives the reason for the blessings bestowed on America, blessings unparalleled in the history of Gentile nations: *"Blessed is the nation whose God is the Lord; and the people whom he hath chosen for his own inheritance."*

God has blessed; but today America, with all of her material blessings, is making the tragic mistake of turning from God. Psalm 106:13-23 warns us that we must not forget God's blessing and fail to wait for His counsel. Read Psalm 106 and pray for America to repent and come back to God.

Bible Truth for Today: *"And he gave them their request; but sent leanness into their soul."* —Psalm 106:15

July 5

Read Psalms 107–109
Family Reading: Psalm 107:23-43

Victory in Time of Trouble

Psalm 107:28 gives us a wonderful promise: *"Then they cry unto the Lord in their trouble, and he bringeth them out of their distresses."*

God is ready to deliver us from our troubles. If He permits us to continue to face the problems, as Job did, it is because He has a purpose and wishes to bring us forth as gold. In verse twenty-eight He promises to bring the righteous out of their distress, if they cry unto Him for His help.

Four times in Psalm 107, God records these words: *"Oh that men would praise the Lord for his goodness, and for his wonderful works to the children of men!" (vv. 8,15,21,31).* We need to see all that He is doing and we, too, would praise Him.

The Lord reminds us beginning in verse twenty-three that men who go to sea may face difficult days. Storms can beset them until they reel to and fro like a drunken man. But when they cry unto the Lord in their trouble, His promise is that He will bring them out of their distresses. This reminds us of Jonah. He rebelled and resisted God. From the belly of the great fish, Jonah prayed and the Lord spake unto the fish, and it vomited up Jonah (Jonah 2:10). Isaiah says of the wicked: *"But the wicked are like the troubled sea, when it cannot rest, whose waters cast up mire and dirt. There is no peace, saith my God, to the wicked" (Isaiah 57:20, 21).*

Storm can follow storm. But praise God, when one sincerely cries out unto the Lord, He delivers by His grace. He can command today as He did when He was on earth, *" . . . Peace, be still . . . " (Mark 4:39),* and there will be a great calm.

> No water can swallow the ship where lies
> The Master of ocean and earth and skies;
> They all shall sweetly obey My will;
> *Peace, be still! Peace, be still!*

Read Psalms 110–115
Family Reading: Psalms 111 and 112

Praise Ye the Lord

Three psalms begin with the command, *"Praise ye the Lord . . ."* *(Psalms 111, 112, and 113).* The psalmist resolves to praise the Lord; and, surely, no one could find a worthier occupation. In Psalm 111:1 he states that he will praise the Lord with his whole heart. Real praise must be whole-hearted praise, for half-hearted praise would be no praise at all. And the psalmist says he will offer this praise in private, *" . . . in the assembly of the upright . . . "*—that is, as an upright man he will join with other upright men in praising the Lord. He will also offer his praise in public, *" . . . in the congregation."*

Psalm 111 lays emphasis on the work and the works of the Lord. He states in verse two that these works are great and are *"sought out of all them that have pleasure therein."* God *"is a rewarder of them that diligently seek him" (Hebrews 11:6).* The Lord said, *" . . . seek, and ye shall find . . . " (Luke 11:9).* Mental laziness never yet led to spiritual illumination. Someone has said that "to see much of God's work, we must sweat our brain." But no one will seek and find God's truth who does not *have pleasure therein.* If we delight in the Word of the Lord as given in Psalm 1, we also shall find pleasure in all His works. His works are listed in verses two through eight of Psalm 111. Then He announces in verse nine that *" . . . holy and reverend is his name."* The Name of the Lord expresses all that He is personally and all that He is to us.

Psalm 112 adds that which the believer has in Christ. He has every need supplied and every victory provided. How we must praise Him for His grace and goodness.

Bible Truth for Today: *"Great is the Lord, and greatly to be praised in the city of our God, in the mountain of his holiness."*

—Psalm 48:1

July 7

Read Psalms 116–119:24
Family Reading: Psalm 119:1-24

The Word of God

Psalm 119 exalts the Word of God as His revelation to men. As you read through this psalm, meditate on its wonderful meaning. There are seven words used in this psalm to express God's divine revelation. These words are used repeatedly, with the outline of the psalm following the twenty-two letters of the Hebrew alphabet. Someone has said this psalm becomes the alphabet of the Christian life.

The seven words that are used repeatedly in this psalm to refer to God's inspired, holy, complete, and divine revelation are as follows:

1. God's Law (used 23 times)—They are enacted by Him as our Sovereign and will make the best law for our lives.

2. His Testimonies (used 22 times)—Solemnly declared to the world, they are sure beyond any argument.

3. His Commandments (used 22 times)—They are given with authority and lodged with us as a trust.

4. His Precepts (used 21 times)—They are the very best recommendation for a godly, useful life.

5. His Word (used 43 times)—Christ, the Eternal Word, is seen all the way through the written Word.

6. His Judgments (used 19 times)—They become basic for the Judge and for the judgment of men.

7. His Statutes (used 21 times)—These are fixed and cannot be changed.

Bible Truth for Today: *"Open thou mine eyes, that I may behold wondrous things out of thy law."* —Psalm 119:18

July 8

Read Psalm 119:25-104
Family Reading: Psalm 119:57-80

Purpose of Afflictions

In verse sixty-five the psalmist states, *"Thou hast dealt well with thy servant, O Lord, according unto thy word."* Then twice in the next seven verses he speaks of being afflicted. Is it possible that one could say, *"Thou hast dealt well with thy servant,"* when that servant has been afflicted? It is possible. David said it. He felt God had dealt well with him even though he had been afflicted. How could he say this? The answer is in verse seventy: *" . . . I delight in thy law."*

When a person delights in God's law, he will experience blessing regardless of his circumstances. When God's law becomes a delight, then surrender to every purpose of God is a delight and blessing. For this reason David could say, *"Thou art good, and doest good . . . "* *(v. 68)*. He believed in God's goodness no matter what the trial.

In verse seventy-one David said: *"It is good for me that I have been afflicted; that I might learn thy statutes."* God has a purpose in affliction. With David, His purpose was that David could learn His statutes. Praise God! When affliction comes, we should simply ask, "Lord, what is it that Thou dost want to teach me?"

> *Set apart—to bear the fragrance*
> *Of His blessed Name,*
> *And with Him to share the sufferings*
> *Of a cross of shame.*
>
> *Set apart—with Him to suffer*
> *O'er a world undone,*
> *And to stand in fiercest conflict*
> *Till the fight is won.*
> — *Selected*

July 9

Read Psalm 119:105-176
Family Reading: Psalm 119:137-160

God's Pure Word

The word *pure* in verse 140 carries with it the idea of refining, as when gold is purified in the refiner's fire. Someone has written concerning the Word of God: "It is absolutely perfect, without the dross of vanity and fallibility which runs through human writings. The more we try the promises, the surer we shall find them."

Pure gold is a wonderful substance. I have heard that it is so fixed that if an ounce of it were set in the eye of a glass furnace for two months, it would not lose a single grain. Those who handle gold coin or bouillon say that they need to weigh the gold at regular intervals because pieces of it seem to chip off, and then there is a certain amount of deterioration. The reason that this takes place is that the gold is not pure gold. Even so the best writings of man still have some dross and imperfection in them. But God's Word is beyond anything that can tear it down.

The Bible has stood the fires of all of its enemies through the centuries. In spite of all the attacks on it, it is just as valid, just as sure, just as pure, just as blessed today as the day it was written or spoken. Hebrews 4:12 says that it is " . . . *sharper than any two-edged sword . . . "* and though it is cut over the years, it is just as sharp. This verse says that it is pure as pure gold that has stood the refiner's fire.

This is the reason that verse 142 can state: *"Thy righteousness is an everlasting righteousness, and thy law is the truth."* God's Word brings righteousness. This righteousness is that which stands the test of time and carries us through.

Why is God's Word a pure word—pure as gold? Verse 160 adds this: *"Thy Word is true from the beginning: and every one of thy righteous judgments endureth for ever."* What a wonderful, blessed Book is the Bible! Let us read its promises and believe its truths.

Bible Truth for Today: *"More to be desired are they than gold, yea, than much fine gold: sweeter also than honey and the honeycomb."*

—Psalm 19:10

July 10

Read Psalms 120–131
Family Reading: Psalms 122, 123, 124

The House of the Lord

David said: *"I was glad when they said unto me, Let us go into the house of the Lord" (v. 122:1).* David's heart was in the worship of God, and he was delighted when others invited him to go where his desires had already gone. We should be faithful ourselves and also invite others to the house of the Lord to worship and fellowship together!

To every Jew, the city of Jerusalem symbolized the very peak of joy. That city was *" . . . compact together" (v. 3).* It was here in Jerusalem that all of the history of the Jewish people found its roots. God said that it was to be a **place** of worship! *"But unto the **place** which the Lord your God shall choose out of all your tribes to put his name there, even unto his habitation shall ye seek, and thither thou shalt come" (Deuteronomy 12:5).*

God had a **place** for His people to come. It was the place where they were to bring their tithes and offerings and to worship the Lord. The God of the Old Testament is the God of the New Testament. The God who had a place in the Old Testament has a place in the New Testament. That **place** today is the local church.

Because we can come to the house of the Lord, we can say with the psalmist David, *"Pray for the peace of Jerusalem . . . " (122:6).* And further, because we go to the house of the Lord, we can know that *"Our help is in the name of the Lord, who made heaven and earth" (Psalm 124:8).*

How wonderful it is to look forward to being in the presence of the Lord of Heaven. Wolfgang Schuch, the martyr of Lothareng, Germany, upon hearing the sentence that he was to be burned at the stake, began to sing Psalm 122. It was a joy for him to come to the house of the Lord. Let us rejoice that we can attend the local church on Sundays and serve the Lord Jesus. May we be faithful in our attendance and in our giving tithes and offerings in the local church.

Bible Truth for Today: *"Not forsaking the assembling of ourselves together, as the manner of some is; but exhorting one another: and so much the more, as ye see the day approaching." —Hebrews 10:25*

July 11

Read Psalms 132–136
Family Reading: Psalm 135

Praising the Lord

Psalm 135 begins with the word *Hallelujah* and ends with the word *Hallelujah*. In the King James version that one word is translated, *"Praise ye the Lord."* This is a psalm of praise. Psalm 134 is the last of the Psalms of Ascent. These fifteen psalms—from Psalm 120 through Psalm 134—were sung as the Israelites came to the temple for worship. Psalm 135 begins a new group of psalms: the songs of experience for the believer.

The first word for a believer to express in his spiritual experience is *Hallelujah*. There is no better way to walk daily with the Lord than to walk praising Him. Someone has called this the envelope psalm. The first section of the psalm in verses one to three calls for praise, and the last section in verses nineteen to twenty-one again emphasizes praise. Between these two sections God encloses reasons for praise.

The word for praising in verses nineteen to twenty-one is *bless*. That comes from the Hebrew word *barak*. It is related to the word *berek*, which means *knee*. Literally, the word *bless* means *to bend the knee*.

Who is to be involved in praise? Verse two says two groups should praise the Lord. The first group are the priests—those who stand in the house of the Lord. The second group are those in the courts of our God. These would be the people. In other words, all of God's people should praise the Lord since all are His servants.

Today let's ask God to teach us to praise Him. It is good and it is pleasant to praise the Lord. We praise the Lord in our daily living to glorify Him. We praise Him by attending services where His Word is proclaimed. We praise Him by our participation in His work by giving and serving.

Bible Truth for Today: *"Rejoice in the Lord, O ye righteous: for praise is comely for the upright." —Psalm 33:1*

July 12

Read Psalms 137–141
Family Reading: Psalm 139

God's Searching and Knowing

Psalm 139 is one of the most notable of God's sacred songs. David was facing many enemies. He delighted in God's presence. He sings of God's omniscience and then of His omnipresence. Nothing can soothe the heart in time of trial like a realization that God knows and understands.

The psalm begins and ends with God's searching and God's knowing. *"O Lord, thou hast **searched** me, and **known** me" (v. 1).* *"**Search** me, O God, and **know** my heart . . . " (v. 23).* God has searched us in the past. The original word for *search* meant *to dig*, as looking for precious metals. David knew that God had searched him—but he still wanted God to do some searching in the future.

David prayed, *"Search me, O God, and know my heart . . . "* David wanted everything to be right in the sight of God. David was under severe stress. But he knew that God knew. What a blessing! God does know. David said there was not a thought he had, not a way he walked, and not a word he spoke but what God knew.

Then David spoke not only of God's omniscience, but also of His omnipresence. He could not flee, if he wanted to, from the presence of God. There is no place where he could hide from God. Even if he took the wings of the morning, traveling at the speed of light, 186,000 miles per second, he could not hide. Andrew Bonar wrote: "Whither, then? Not to Heaven . . . not to Hell . . . not to any part of creation, for His providence is at work there in every sparrow that lights on the ground. What a comforting thought to a believer! If God's eye is on me, then I am blessed, though I be obscure, and though I suffer unheeded by man."

Bible Prayer for Today: *"Search me, O God, and know my heart: try me, and know my thoughts: And see if there be any wicked way in me, and lead me in the way everlasting."* —*Psalm 139:23, 24*

July 13

Read Psalms 142–147
Family Reading: Psalms 142 and 143

Prayer Needed

These two psalms speak much of David's praying. He cried to the Lord and poured out his heart before God. David knew what it was to pray. Far too often today God's people really do not know what it is to pray and hold on to God. I am amazed at a story Dr. Harry Ironside told, and yet I realize how applicable it is today.

Dr. Ironside was visiting a group of believers in a western state who had some very peculiar ideas. Every week they gathered for the study of the Bible, but they never had a prayer meeting. He asked them, "Do you never have a prayer meeting?" One brother answered, "Oh, no, we have nothing to pray for." Dr. Ironside asked how they could feel they had nothing to pray for. His answer was, "We have *'all spiritual blessings in heavenly places in Christ'*; so we do not need to pray for spiritual blessings. Physically, we have everything we need. We have all the land we need. We do not need to pray for money because we have plenty to keep us going. We do not need to pray for wives since we are all married. Because we have nothing to pray for, we just give God thanks."

Dr. Ironside asked them to pray for him—but they said they could do that at home. Some time later Dr. Ironside became quite ill in Minneapolis. A year later he came back to the same western city. The same brother told him, "When we heard you were ill, we met twice a week to pray for you. But when we received news that you were well again, we stopped praying."

Dr. Ironside asked, "Why did you stop? When flat on my back, I did not have any trouble with the devil; but when strong and well, I have to go out and face the foe, and I need prayer far more."

A simple, interesting story—but it is so typical of many of us. We need to pray consistently to see the Lord overcome the flesh and the devil in our lives.

Bible Promise for Today: *"Ask, and it shall be given you; seek, and ye shall find; knock, and it shall be opened unto you."*

—Matthew 7:7

July 14

Read Psalms 148–150; Proverbs 1 and 2
Family Reading: Proverbs 2

Understanding the Fear of the Lord

Proverbs 2:1-6 is a very important passage in the Word of God. The secret that so very many have sought is made known—how can we find the knowledge of God? In verse five He states: *"Then shalt thou understand the fear of the Lord, and find the knowledge of God."* How do we reach this place? The Christian does not need to be scholarly or profound to understand the Scriptures and the truth. He simply needs to be hungry for the truth and be willing to search for it. A careless reading of the Scriptures does not produce wisdom and knowledge. First, the ears must be inclined to hear the Word of God (v. 2). *"So then faith cometh by hearing, and hearing by the word of God" (Romans 10:17).* A man opens his ear to hear the Word, and then he must apply his heart to receive understanding. The Word of God is that which gives wisdom and understanding, but the individual must give himself to receive it.

In verse one the writer wants the young man to receive the words and hide God's commandments with him; then he will have wisdom and knowledge.

Even among those who value the precious Word of God, diligent Bible study seems on the wane. Reading books about the Bible is quite different from searching the Word for oneself.

The Lord gives wisdom as we yield to Him. There must be a willingness to work and to search. The one who cries after knowledge and lifts up his voice for understanding will be the one to understand the fear of the Lord and find the knowledge of God (v. 3). Seeking knowledge and wisdom needs to be just as important to us as seeking silver is to the miner. We need to dig into the Word of God, endeavoring to get the truths from it for our own lives.

When wisdom does enter into a man, he will see deliverance from evil (vv. 10-12). God's Word cleanses and delivers us.

Bible Truth for Today: *"For the Lord giveth wisdom: out of his mouth cometh knowledge and understanding."* —Proverbs 2:6

July 15

Read Proverbs 3–5
Family Reading: Proverbs 4

Guard Your Heart

"Keep thy heart with all diligence; for out of it are the issues of life." —*Proverbs 4:23*

The advice of the writer of Proverbs is to keep the heart with all diligence. The word for *diligence* here is *to guard or build a fence about to protect.* Everyone needs to guard his heart with such diligence as this.

Unless we give diligence to this purpose, vanity can prevail in our minds until we are not used of God. Error can come to the understanding, and we can develop a rebellion in our will against the blessed will of God. If we do not guard our hearts, our affections may be set upon objects other than the Lord. When this happens, we can be left to grieve over a hard heart and an absent God. Satan rejoices when a believer is thus defeated. Darkness seems to prevail and spiritual depression sets in.

I find that I must regularly and consistently check to be sure my heart is walking with the Lord. I cannot let my attitude and my conscience become hardened to the grace of God. As I write this, only this last week, I had to check on my attitudes because they had gone astray.

Therefore, I must pray that the Lord will stir my soul to give *"all diligence."* We shall not be saved for our diligence, but those of us who are saved may escape many snares and evils when we are diligent to guard the heart. Proverbs 13:4 says: " . . . *the soul of the diligent shall be made fat."* The diligent here feed upon heavenly truth—upon God's grace and love; then their souls seem to prosper and be in health. The careless ones trifle with God, however, and their own souls seem to fill with dejection and distress.

Let us take the admonition of this verse: *"Keep thy heart with all diligence; for out of it are the issues of life."*

Bible Command for Today: *"My son, attend to my words; incline thine ear unto my sayings."* —*Proverbs 4:20*

July 16

Read Proverbs 6 and 7
Family Reading: Proverbs 6:1-21

A Walking Mouth and Talking Feet

In Proverbs 6:12, 13 we find Solomon's introduction of the character of a wicked man. It is interesting that verse twelve states that the wicked walks with his mouth. And then in verse thirteen he speaks of the wicked speaking with his feet.

How does one walk with his mouth? Solomon says the wicked walks with a *"froward"* mouth—that is, with a crooked, perverse, distorted mouth. How does this person walk? His walk is perverse to the Word and will of God. His mouth is a primary manifestation of what he is. It is as though he were literally walking with his mouth because he is going absolutely contrary to the Word of God.

Verse thirteen states that " . . . *he speaketh with his feet* . . . " How do men speak with their feet?

They speak rage and anger by stamping the feet.

They speak hatred and murder by moving to a place to inflict harm or to kill.

They speak laziness and sluggardliness. Compare the firm step of the successful business man with the shuffling wiggle of the loafer. How much bad character is expressed in the statement: "He is a tramp!"

Men speak perverseness when they walk as women, with prissy feet.

Think of it—the mouth walks and the feet talk. May we manifest grace with our lips and character with our feet.

Bible Command for Today: *"This I say therefore, and testify in the Lord, that ye henceforth walk not as other Gentiles walk, in the vanity of their mind." —Ephesians 4:17*

July 17

Read Proverbs 8–10
Family Reading: Proverbs 8:1-21

Wisdom

In this eighth chapter of Proverbs we have a definite change from the previous chapters. In Chapters 4, 5, 6, and 7 God gives warnings to the young man about the danger and folly of sin. In this chapter we turn from the contemplation of evil to meditate on the ways of wisdom.

Proverbs 8 presents wisdom as a person. Any anointed eye and mind will perceive Christ in this chapter as the wisdom of God. *"But of him are ye in Christ Jesus, who of God is made unto us wisdom, and righteousness, and sanctification, and redemption." (I Corinthians 1:30).* We find personal affections ascribed to wisdom. Wisdom has hate (Proverbs 8:13); wisdom manifests love (8:17); and wisdom rejoices (8:30, 31). All of these are attributes of a person and are praises of the Lord Jesus Christ.

What does wisdom do? She cries out from high places. Praise God that wisdom does get into high places. Gladstone, the great Christian, became prime minister of England. President Calvin Coolidge was a dedicated Christian.

Verse two states that wisdom also cries by the way in the places of the paths. These are the crossroads, where the crowded paths of ordinary, everyday life meet. The Lord is calling from every area of life.

What a difference between wisdom's call in Proverbs 8 and the harlot's call in Proverbs 7. Wisdom calls from the high places for all to see; the harlot calls in the dark night where none can see (Proverbs 7:9). Wisdom beckons in the busy crossroads; the harlot does so in the obscure street corner trying to deceive (Proverbs 7:8).

Wisdom and sin are still calling today. Which one are you heeding?

Bible Truth for Today: *"Wisdom is the principal thing; therefore get wisdom: and with all thy getting get understanding."*

—Proverbs 4:7

Read Proverbs 11–13
Family Reading: Proverbs 11:10-31

Giving

In verse twenty-four God gives a principle of the Christian life about which the world knows nothing. In fact, the principle is so different from the world's concept that men of the world cannot fathom the truth.

God states, *"There is that scattereth, and yet increaseth . . . "* *(v. 24).* He is speaking of a Christian who is generous. The more he scatters, the more he increases. Many people today follow the theory, "We must take care of *No. 1.*" This wicked attitude of the world is always to be concerned about self. They are afraid to scatter, for they do not know how their own needs will be met.

The same is true in the matter of Christian growth. The soul who is willing to give out that which he has will find that his knowledge increases. Pity those poor souls who never give out. It is sure that they are going to miss the blessing.

The principle also applies to giving and to stewardship. He who gives to meet the need of others will find his own needs met.

It is amazing but true: God will always honor the one who scatters. The universe is built on the principle of giving. The sun and clouds give. The rivers give.

Above all, the Lord Jesus Christ gave Himself that we might be redeemed. *"For God so loved the world, that he gave . . . "* *(John 3:16).* It is because He gave that we have eternal life through His grace.

Bible Promise for Today: *"Give, and it shall be given unto you; good measure, pressed down, and shaken together, and running over, shall men give into your bosom. For with the same measure that ye mete withal it shall be measured to you again."* *—Luke 6:38*

July 19

Read Proverbs 14 and 15
Family Reading: Proverbs 15:1-21

A Soft Answer

"A soft answer turneth away wrath: but grievous words stir up anger." —*Proverbs 15:1*

It is impossible for a man to estimate aright the power for good or for evil that lies in the tongue. A kindly, gracious word will often disarm the most ill-tempered and wrathful man; while a sharp, cutting remark has frequently separated for years friends dear to each other.

It is sometimes considered unmanly by many not to resent an insult, and to allow wrathful words to pass unchallenged. It actually takes much more true character to meet an angry man in quietness of spirit, and to return cool, calm words for heated, hasty ones, than it does to give railing for railing, or malice for malice. We all need to emulate our Saviour in this, *"Who, when he was reviled, reviled not again; when he suffered, he threatened not; but committed himself to him that judgeth righteously"* (I Peter 2:23).

A man who does not know how to control his spirit will use grievous words. These will always stir up anger. A gracious demeanor will go far toward cooling angry passions of another; but grievous words will just add fuel to the flame.

This proverb is a good one to use constantly in our homes and in our church relationships. A soft answer on the part of a husband or wife will go a long way to solving difficult problems. The same is true with parents. A father or mother needs to be mature enough to have a soft answer so that he or she can turn away wrath. But far too often the parent permits grievous words to flow forth and thus stirs up anger. If Proverbs 15:1 were practiced in our lives, we would find a complete transformation in all of our relationships.

Thot: *It is not so important how others act to me, as it is how I react to them.*

July 20

Read Proverbs 16–18
Family Reading: Proverbs16:13-33

Honey in the Speech

From Proverbs 16, I want you to think about the blessed truth of speaking kind words.

Verse twenty-one states: *" . . . and the sweetness of the lips increaseth learning."* Do you want to be able to instruct someone? Do it with sweetness. Use kind words.

Verse twenty-four reads: *"Pleasant words are as an honeycomb, sweet to the soul, and health to the bones."*

Oh, how kind words can be a blessing! They can actually bring health to the body. The individual who speaks caustically can expect that his speech will cause sickness—in his life and in the life of others. But pleasant words will bring health.

Verse thirty-two says: *"He that is slow to anger is better than the mighty; and he that ruleth his spirit than he that taketh a city."*

Speech reveals the attitude of the heart. Bitterness and malice will be revealed by the speech. The child of God must guard his speech to be sure that he is speaking with sweetness. But he cannot straighten out the speech if the heart is all twisted with sin.

Did you know that a little honey in the speech will do a lot to brighten the day and lighten the load for someone else? Why not try it today!

> *If I had known in the morning*
> *How wearily all the day*
> *The words unkind would trouble my mind*
> *I said when you went away,*
> *I had been more careful, darling,*
> *Nor given you needless pain,*
> *But we vex "our own" with look and tone*
> *We may never take back again.*

Bible Truth for Today: *"Let your speech be alway with grace, seasoned with salt, that ye may know how ye ought to answer every man."* —Colossians 4:6

July 21

Read Proverbs 19–21
Family Reading: Proverbs 19:1-18, 25-27; 21:11

Knowledge of Him

Today's reading, Proverbs 19, gives us a very important truth. Verse two states: *"Also, that the soul be without knowledge, it is not good; and he that hasteth with his feet sinneth."*

Solomon opens that verse with the word *"also"*; that means he is continuing the truth from verse one. There he speaks of a perverse person who is a fool. He said that this man is perverse in his lips. In other words, his speech is not good. In verse two he carries the truth on to show the source of this fool's perverse ways. That source is that the soul is without knowledge.

No wonder Paul prayed, *"That I may know him, and the power of his resurrection, and the fellowship of his sufferings, being made conformable unto his death" (Philippians 3:10).*

Paul wanted knowledge. He desired to know Christ. But how do we get this knowledge of Him? It comes only as we have the knowledge of His Word. Without this knowledge, our hearts will be wrong and our lips perverse.

For this reason God said twice in Proverbs 19 that *"a false witness shall not be unpunished, and he that speaketh lies shall not escape (perish)" (vv. 5 and 9).* This is why in this chapter we are repeatedly warned of the danger of riches and the curse of slug-gardliness.

There is a need that our hearts be changed by the knowledge of Christ through the knowledge of His Word. We need to be saved, but then we need to go on to increase in knowledge. *"Hear counsel, and receive instruction, that thou mayest be wise in thy latter end" (Proverbs 19:20).*

Bible Truth for Today: *"Cease, my son, to hear the instruction that causeth to err from the words of knowledge."* —*Proverbs 19:27*

July 22

Read Proverbs 22 and 23
Family Reading: Proverbs 23:1-22

Temptations to Flee

We find two dreadful temptations that men face in Proverbs 23:1-5. The first temptation is that of gratifying the flesh. Verse one warns: *"When thou sittest to eat with a ruler, consider diligently what is before thee."* This is the temptation to gratify the flesh with the delights of luxurious eating—we may call it "gourmet" eating today. Most of us face this temptation often. Verse two states that if a person is *"given to appetite,"* he would be wise to resist the temptation of luxurious eating as if he were putting a knife to his throat. The expression *"given to appetite"* means something more than just being hungry. It deals with craving for *"dainties."* If there is no appetite, then there will be no temptation. Also, if the appetite be strong but the table is not spread with *dainties*, there will be no temptation. With all of our culinary skills and restaurants catering to appetites, this temptation comes before us often. Bishop Hall wisely wrote: "If I see a dish to please my appetite, I see a serpent in that apple, and will strengthen myself in a willful denial."

The second temptation is to labor to be rich (v. 4). This is the temptation to covetousness. If God gives riches, we should thank Him and endeavor to use them wisely for His glory. But to give ourselves relentlessly just to gain wealth is to set our eyes on something that will fly away. We believers are going to have Heaven, and *that* before long. How foolish to let worldly riches draw us from the eternal lasting riches in Christ Jesus.

Bible Command for Today: *"But thou, O man of God, flee these things; and follow after righteousness, godliness, faith, love, patience, meekness. Fight the good fight of faith, lay hold on eternal life, whereunto thou art also called, and hast professed a good profession before many witnesses."* — I Timothy 6:11, 12

July 23

Read Proverbs 24–26
Family Reading: Proverbs 26

Put Out the Fire

Proverbs 26 has several verses that deal with gossip and improper use of the lips. Verse twenty reads: *" . . . where there is no talebearer, the strife ceaseth."* The writer is speaking of contention in this passage. He compares contention to a fire. The fire needs fuel to keep going. That fuel is supplied by the talebearer. When there is no fuel to add to the fire, it goes out; so where there is no talebearer, the strife and contention cease.

We constantly hear loud cries that we need to make our buildings safer in case of fire. We are to use smoke detectors, sprinkling systems, and other safety devices. Fire chiefs and safety experts have joined together in America, asking for effective ways to stop fires.

There is a fire doing much more damage, but we hear so few voices crying out to have it stopped. That is the fire spoken of in James 3:6—*"And the tongue is a fire, a world of iniquity: so is the tongue among our members, that it defileth the whole body, and setteth on fire the course of nature; and it is set on fire of hell."*

The tongue can be the wood or the burning coals to keep the fire of contention burning. In fact, the talebearer can cause the fire to burn with incendiary heat. It can be like gasoline thrown on a fire. This fire destroys as it reveals hatred and deceit (vv. 24, 26), abominations in the heart (v. 25), and hidden wickedness (v. 26). The talebearer leaves deep wounds that go into the innermost part of the life (v. 22).

Let us each put out this fire today. Ask God to deliver you from a talebearing tongue.

Bible Prayer for Today: *"Set a watch, O Lord, before my mouth; keep the door of my lips."* —Psalm 141:3

July 24

Read Proverbs 27–29
Family Reading: Proverbs 27:1-17

A Big Enemy: Envy

Proverbs 27 has much to say about friendship. At least seven verses refer directly to friendship—the truths that can build friendship and the things that can destroy it. In this context of speaking about friendship, God asks the question in verse four: " . . . *who is able to stand before envy?*" This awful sin of envy can destroy any friendship and destroy any life.

God states that wrath is cruel. It is not that temporary flash of impulse that comes and then disappears. Absalom held his wrath within him for two years—but it did vent itself in terrible things when he released its cruelty (II Samuel 13:22,23). Wrath produces anger which will overflow and do much harm.

Yet even though this overflowing anger is terribly cruel, it can be appeased. Esau hated his brother, but his wrath was turned into brotherly love. He witnessed the presence and power of God.

Envy is something worse than wrath or anger. Where envy appears, reason does not seem to help. Reason is not water to quench the flame but becomes oil to spread the flame. Anger is produced by an offense. An angry person can be reasoned with. But envy is produced by another's prosperity or by favor received by another. Envy is related to pride, the most dangerous enemy within the human breast. Satan lost his first estate because of envy. Cain killed Abel because of envy.

Guard relentlessly against this awful jealousy. Let's rejoice in another's prosperity—in another's blessings. Envy appears in our churches constantly—yea, even in the ministry.

God asks: " . . . *who is able to stand before envy?*" The answer is obvious: "No one." Ask God to humble you today and deliver you from this terrible enemy of the soul.

Bible Principle for Today: *"For where envying and strife is, there is confusion and every evil work."* —*James 3:16*

July 25

Read Proverbs 30 and 31
Family Reading: Proverbs 30:1-20

A Wicked Generation

Proverbs 30 is a wonderful passage of Scripture, which reveals some great truths. In verses eleven to fourteen, God speaks of a wicked generation. This generation is spoken of in four ways, and all of these speak of the moral and spiritual state of the last days.

First, we read of *" . . . a generation that curseth their father and doth not bless their mother (v. 11).* How true this is of our generation today! The third chapter of II Timothy cites disobedience to parents as one of the marks of the last days (v. 2).

Second, we read of a generation *" . . . pure in their own eyes . . . "* (v. 12). Verse five states that *"Every word of God is pure . . .* If this generation would read and heed the Word of God, they would realize how impure they are. They have never seen themselves as sinners, filthy in God's sight, and therefore they think themselves quite pure. In John 9:41 Jesus said: *" . . . If ye were blind, ye should have no sin: but now ye say, We see; therefore your sin remaineth."* The generation that is pure in their own eyes are sinful in God's sight; those sinful in their own sight can become pure in God's eyes.

Third, this generation has lofty eyes (v. 13). Again II Timothy 3 describes this generation: *" . . . boasters, proud, blasphemers, . . . heady, highminded . . . " (vv. 2-4).* Man loves to boast, failing to consider that *"Pride goeth before destruction, and an haughty spirit before a fall" (Proverbs 16:18).*

Fourth, we reach the inevitable climax. This generation, filled with pride, clean in their own sight, becomes a violent, ruthless generation. We see it surrounding us today. Let's keep our homes so that the influence of such a generation does not wreck our families.

Bible Truth for Today: *"Professing themselves to be wise, they became fools." —Romans 1:22*

July 26

Read Ecclesiastes 1–3
Family Reading: Ecclesiastes 2

Vanity and Rejoicing

Ecclesiastes 2 speaks of the vanity of life. Life does not have to be vain and empty. There can be rejoicing if one will put his trust in the Lord Jesus Christ.

In Ecclesiastes the word *"vanity"* appears thirty-six times. The word means *that which is fleeting or transitory.* Life is very transitory, and each person must realize that he needs to live with eternity's values in view, not just for the things this world can offer. It is futile to rely on human effort to accomplish any fullness in our lives. The author of Ecclesiastes gives us several things that will only prove to be vain and empty:

First—mirth and pleasure are vain (v. 1). An individual who lives just for laughs and wine will find no permanent satisfaction there (vv. 2, 3).

Second—possessions and things are vain (vv. 4-11). Solomon had all of these as listed in this passage. They included houses, gardens, pools, servants, and treasures; but he could positively say that these did not give rest or satisfaction.

Third—wisdom can be vanity (vv. 12-17). The wise man and the fool both die the same way. Solomon said that trusting in his wisdom would be vain and foolish.

Fourth—Solomon felt this vanity so much that he wondered what would happen with his successor. He worked all this time, and then to see the fruit of his labor destroyed by his successor would be heart-rending. However, Solomon said this surely could happen. No wonder Solomon cried: *"Vanity of vanities . . . all is vanity"* (1:2).

Bible Truth for Today: *"Turn away mine eyes from beholding vanity; and quicken thou me in thy way." —Psalm 119:37*

July 27

Read Ecclesiastes 4–7
Family Reading: Ecclesiastes 7:1-22

Truths by Which to Live

The first six chapters of Ecclesiastes present the vanity of all things. Now, beginning with Chapter 7, we receive counsel for the days of suffering that come because of vanity. Here we find some of the best wisdom for a good life that can be found in all literature.

Solomon emphasizes that the sorrow and perplexity of life cannot be escaped. We are dying men and women in a world of deterioration, decay, and change. But God's truth can give joy and meaning to life. Below are five truths that will lead to a happier and more successful life. There are others, but space does not permit us to give them.

1. Choose to give thought; reject the frivolity of life (vv. 1-4). Solomon says, *"It is better to go to the house of mourning, than to go to the house of feasting . . . " (v. 2)*. Going to a funeral causes one to give thought to his spiritual condition.

2. Hear rebuke rather than the song of fools (vv. 5-8). We are far better off to listen to criticism from one with wisdom than to listen to the mindless songs of the foolish world.

3. Be slow to anger (v. 9). Remember, anger marks a fool.

4. Accept God's will for each day, and don't complain (vv. 10-14). Yearning for the good old days is not realistic. Even to inquire about them and long for them is foolish (v. 10).

5. Choose godliness; avoid self-righteousness and sensual living (vv. 15-22).

Proverb for Meditation Today: *"The words of a talebearer are as sounds, and they go down into the innermost parts of the belly."*

—Proverbs 26:22

July 28

Read Ecclesiastes 8–12
Family Reading: Ecclesiastes 9

That Which Makes a Joyful Life

How much sadness there is in the world today! Even among Christians there is not the joy and happiness there should be. Ecclesiastes 9 gives us a recipe for living that is very important.

In the first seven verses the writer discusses the problem of evil men seeming to triumph over those who want to do right. He speaks of the fact that the man in the world supposes that when he dies, everything is ended. It appears there is no real retribution on earth. The wicked can go his way and never seem to be judged.

The question comes then: "Is there really any reason to live righteously?" Oh, yes, there is! The preacher then gives the reader a recipe for a life of joy. He instructs the righteous to go right on living day by day (v. 7). He gives the following instructions:

1. Eat and drink with joy and a merry heart (v. 7).

2. Recognize that God is the Judge (v. 7).

3. Keep the garments white—that is, live a holy life (v. 8).

4. Have a joyful home life. Here is a great command: *"Live joyfully with the wife whom thou lovest all the days of the life of thy vanity . . . " (v. 9).* Every child of God needs to determine that he is going to do all he can to make his home life a blessing.

5. Do the work before you with all of your heart (v. 10).

Bible Command to Be Holy: *"Depart ye, depart ye, go ye out from thence, touch no unclean thing; go ye out of the midst of her; be ye clean, that bear the vessels of the Lord." —Isaiah 52:11*

July 29

Read Song of Solomon 1–5
Family Reading: Song of Solomon 4

Christ's Evaluation of His Church

The Lord's admiration of His church is very wonderful, and His description of her beauty is very glowing. She is not merely fair but *"all fair" (vv. 1, 7)*. The Lord Jesus views the church as being in Himself, washed in His sin-cleansing blood, clothed in His merit and righteousness, and filled with beauty and comeliness. Nor is His bride barely lovely; she is superlatively so. The Lord styles her as the *"fairest among women" (1:8; 5:9; 6:1)*.

Think of our position as believers and members of His body. We have a positive righteousness that was given us when we were *"accepted in the beloved" (Ephesians 1:6)*. If the Lord Jesus could exchange His bride for any or all of the queens that make up the royalty and nobility of earth, He would not because He puts His bride first and foremost. We who are in His bride really are "somebodies" in His sight. As the moon outshines the stars, His church is the *"fairest among women."*

To His statement that His bride is *"all fair,"* the Lord adds the negative: " . . . *there is no spot in thee" (v. 7)*. Think of it! No spot. Certainly He knew that a critical world would try to show that this bride has some defects. He answers before they can speak, "She has no spot."

A spot is a tiny blemish and can be easily removed. But He announces that she has even been delivered from that. Had He said that she would have no horrible deformity or no hideous scar or no deadly ulcer, we might have marveled. But He said, *"no spot."*

His love is wonderful. The church has strayed, has grieved His Holy Spirit. But He does not allow her faults to affect His love. He may chide, but it will be with tenderness. He loves His church! He loves us! May we rejoice in the wonderful privilege of being in His church, under His grace, and bound to His love. And may we live to manifest Him, our perfect Redeemer, to a needy world.

Bible Truth for Today: *"Husbands, love your wives, even as Christ also loved the church, and gave himself for it." —Ephesians 5:25*

July 30

Read Song of Solomon 6–8 and Isaiah 1
Family Reading: Isaiah 1:1-18

The Prophet of Grace

Today we begin our reading of the Prophets. We usually divide these books into two sections—the Major Prophets and the Minor Prophets. We call Isaiah, Jeremiah, Ezekiel, and Daniel the Major Prophets; we refer to the twelve books from Hosea through Malachi as the Minor Prophets. This division is made only on the basis of the length of the books, not on the importance of the prophets.

All of these prophetic books have special messages for the divided kingdoms of Judah and Israel. They deal with sin in the nation and in the hearts of the people. Warning Israel of her backslidden condition, the prophets invited her to return.

The message of Isaiah is the first one of the prophetic books. Some have called him the chief of the writing prophets. He must have prophesied almost sixty years. Isaiah is particularly the prophet of redemption, giving many wonderful truths about salvation.

As we read Isaiah in the next several days, take time to meditate on his message. Please make special note of our Bible Truth for Today—Isaiah 1:18. After God had given the sins and failings of the people, this verse gives hope to the nation. And the verse can be applied in any life because Christ has shed His blood to pay for our sins. God is able to forgive all sins. Make sure today that your sins have been forgiven.

Bible Truth for Today: *"Come now, and let us reason together, saith the Lord: though your sins be as scarlet, they shall be as white as snow; though they be red like crimson, they shall be as wool."*

—Isaiah 1:18

July 31

Read Isaiah 2–6
Family Reading: Isaiah 5

God's Judgment Coming

The vineyard of Isaiah 5 is the nation of Israel; the choicest vine is the house of Judah (v. 7). God said that the well-beloved (Jehovah) had a vineyard planted in a very fruitful hill. The Lord did everything possible for the vineyard. He fenced it, gathered out the stones, planted it with the choicest vine, and built a tower in the midst of it.

God looked for fruit, but He did not find good fruit. It brought forth wild grapes that were no fruit. The words *wild fruit* are a very modest translation. Literally, it means *rotten fruit or spoiled fruit.*

This is a picture of Israel. She was not true fruit unto the Lord but rather *wild fruit*. When God looked for judgment, He found only oppression and defeat. God said that Israel would be laid waste. It would not be pruned nor cared for as a vineyard that would bring forth fruit. Briers and thorns would come up in the vineyard. All of this is represented by the sin, unbelief, and apostasy of the nation of Israel.

God said He would command the clouds that there be no rain. Wherever sin has come in, God says there is a dreadful dryness about the work; and God says there must be judgment. For this reason, He pronounces the woes upon Israel. The word *woe* means *the curse of God.* He pronounces these curses because of the sin of Israel and Judah. The cry *woe* is repeated six times, with three definite judgments listed.

Israel is but a small stage of what God will do with all of mankind someday. Judgment is sure, *"Because he hath appointed a day, in the which he will judge the world in righteousness by that man whom he hath ordained; whereof he hath given assurance unto all men, in that he hath raised him from the dead" (Acts 17:31).*

God will keep this appointment of judgment as He promised.

August 1

Read Isaiah 7–9
Family Reading: Isaiah 9

God's Promises Are Sure

Isaiah 8 tells of an awful day to come in the land of Israel because of her disobedience to the Word of God. There will be trouble, darkness, and dimness of anguish on earth, and Israel will be driven to darkness (Isaiah 8:22). This condition is caused by Israel's turning from the simplicity of believing the law and testimony (Isaiah 8:20).

Then God begins Chapter 9 with the word, *"Nevertheless . . . "* Things were very bad, but not so bad as they had been. Israel could say as Paul said in II Corinthians 4:9, that they were *"Persecuted, but not forsaken . . . "* God promised three things to Israel:

First, He promised them a *" . . . great light . . . "* (Isaiah 9:2). He was looking forward to the day of the gospel message of Jesus Christ. When the Lord Jesus came to the borders of Zebulun and Naphtali, Matthew records it was the fulfillment of Isaiah's prophecy that the people should see a great light (Matthew 4:13-16).

Second, He promised them a great joy. This joy also comes through the Messiah, our Lord Jesus (Isaiah 9:3).

Third, He promised a deliverance from bondage (Isaiah 9:4, 5).

Following these promises, the Lord reveals who is He that shall undertake and accomplish these great things. It is the child to be born, the son to be given. Without a doubt, He is referring to the Lord Jesus. He is the Child that was born, born as a child, the son of the woman. But when Isaiah speaks of the Son, he does not say He will be born but rather, He will be given. The Son is from eternity. He could not be born. He took a human body, and that body could be born. This is the Lord Jesus, who is the mighty God and the Prince of Peace. Isaiah spoke of Him as though He had already been born. So sure was Isaiah that this miracle would take place that he said a *"child is born"* and a *"son is given."* He knew this One was coming.

Bible Truth for Today: *"For whatsoever things were written aforetime were written for our learning, that we through patience and comfort of the scriptures might have hope."* —Romans 15:4

August 2

Read Isaiah 10–13
Family Reading: Isaiah 11 and 12

Water from the Wells

I remember as a boy the joy in going out to the well and getting a cold cup of water. Our well was over 265 feet deep, and the water it gave was soft, cold, and refreshing. There is nothing better than a cold drink of water from a good well when one is thirsty.

God promises that with joy His people shall *" . . . draw water out of the wells of salvation" (Isaiah 12:3).* In the millennial reign there will be much praise of the Lord and His grace because *" . . . God is my salvation; I will trust, and not be afraid: for the Lord JEHOVAH is my strength and my song; He also is become my salvation" (v. 2).* Certainly we have much about which to sing. God is good, and His grace is sufficient. The water in the wells of salvation comes because of His grace.

God shows poor sinners their need of Jesus and their thirst for righteousness. Then He shows them this living water, its freeness, freshness, and sweetness. He supplies each one with a bucket of faith to draw with joy and drink with pleasure. This river runs all the way from Genesis 3 throughout the Scripture. It is pictured in the everlasting love of the Father, the rich grace of Jesus Christ the Son, and the wonderful joy that the Holy Ghost gives. Yet it is but one fountain of grace flowing from the oneness of God and is communicated to us out of the fullness of Jesus Christ.

This fountain is ever free, full, and inexhaustible. Therefore, we ought always to rejoice in the Lord our Saviour.

Bible Truth for Today: *"But whosoever drinketh of the water that I shall give him shall never thirst; but the water that I shall give him shall be in him a well of water springing up into everlasting life."*

— John 4:14

August 3

Read Isaiah 14–17
Family Reading: Isaiah 14:1-23

Satan

Isaiah 14 gives us a picture of Satan. He was once in Heaven, a brilliant, powerful creation of God. But he fell and became a power in the earth. The first chapter of Job reveals that he is moving up and down in the earth, walking to and fro (v. 7). How do we explain the evil that is in the world? It comes from this source—the vile personality of Satan.

Satan was filled with self. In Isaiah 14:13 he said, " . . . *I will exalt my throne above the stars of God . . . "* The same fact about Satan is revealed when God says in Ezekiel 28:17, *"Thine heart was lifted up because of thy beauty . . . "*

Evil in the world came from selfishness. It was born of self-desire. It came from Satan's self-occupation with his own creature beauty, ignoring his dependence on his Creator for all. To live to the glory of God, we must put an end to selfishness. Certainly self-occupation must be over. Complacent self-occupation is filled with grave danger.

The remedy for self-occupation is the filling of our thoughts with the Lord Jesus—His beauty, His perfection, and His love. It is in this that we will find safety, joy, blessing—yes, and true holiness.

Satan revealed his selfish pride in the following statements: *"I will sit . . . " (v. 13); "I will ascend . . . I will be like the most High" (v. 14).* For us to be delivered from Satan's wiles, we must beware of pride in our own lives.

Bible Truth for Today: *"Finally, my brethren, be strong in the Lord, and in the power of his might. Put on the whole armor of God, that ye may be able to stand against the wiles of the devil."*

—Ephesians 6:10, 11

August 4

Read Isaiah 18–22
Family Reading: Isaiah 19

What About Egypt in Prophecy?

This nineteenth chapter of Isaiah contains the most important prophetic utterance concerning Egypt that we find in the Old Testament. It centers on two great themes:

1. Destruction for Egypt (vv. 1-15)
    A threefold disaster will come to Egypt. There will be *political disaster* that will involve a civil war. Verse two states that Egyptians will fight Egyptians. Because of this civil war, verses three and four reveal that Egypt will turn to occult practices. God will permit Egypt to come under the *" . . . hand of a cruel lord; and a fierce king shall rule over them, . . . " (v. 4).* This cruel lord and fierce king will be the Antichrist. An *economic disaster* will then be caused by the drying up of the Nile River (vv. 5-10). With the Aswan Dam now in place, we can see the possibility of the drying up of the Nile River. Finally, there will be an *intellectual disaster* (vv. 11-15). Verse eleven states that Egypt's wisest advisers will be "stupid."

2. Deliverance for Egypt (vv. 16-25)
    The Egyptians in five cities will speak the *"language of Canaan" (vv. 18-20).* That would be Hebrew. This means there will be an alliance with Israel. In addition, Egypt will swear to the Lord of hosts (v. 18). Egypt will turn from the religion of Islam to the Lord Jehovah. Please note some other truths in this chapter concerning Egypt—truths which space does not permit here. Praise God, He is the Lord and deals with nations according to His will.

Bible Truth for Today: *"Yea, all kings shall fall down before him; all nations shall serve him." —Psalm 72:11*

August 5

Read Isaiah 23–26
Family Reading: Isaiah 26

The Mind Resting in the Lord

Isaiah 25 ends by telling us of the city of Moab. He says it shall be trodden down, the fortresses of the high fort broken down and ground into the dust.

Isaiah 26 refers to the land of Judah as a *"strong city."* Instead of walls of brick and mud and mortar, this strong city has for its walls and for its bulwarks salvation. The prophet says, *"We have a strong city . . . " (v. 1).* This city is not strong in walls of huge stones; it has a wall much stronger than that. The strong wall is Jehovah's *"salvation."* That salvation comes through the Name of Jesus. That Name means *"salvation,"* and it is a strong tower indeed. A church and a home that have for walls *"salvation"* have a bulwark placed by the Lord which is impregnable to every assault of any foe.

Verse three has been the stay of many a stricken heart in time of trouble: *"Thou wilt keep him in perfect peace, whose mind is stayed on thee: because he trusteth in thee."* Another rendering says: "Thou keepest in peace, a peace that is perfect, without one ripple of anxiety, the mind of the one leaning hard upon Thee."

Please note the strong emphasis is on an individual's trust in the Lord. This has to be a personal relationship if the individual is to receive personal benefits.

He says the *"mind is stayed on thee."* The word for *"mind"* means *"that which is formed."* This would reveal that this mind comes from the very depths of the heart. With every part of his being, the one who trusts in the Lord is relying on the Son of God.

Verse four has a blessed truth for our daily living: *"Trust ye in the Lord for ever: for in the Lord JEHOVAH is everlasting strength."* This *everlasting strength,* according to the Hebrew, means *"the Rock of Ages."*

Bible Promise for Today: *"Thou wilt keep him in perfect peace, whose mind is stayed on thee: because he trusteth in thee."*

—Isaiah 26:3

August 6

Read Isaiah 27–30
Family Reading: Isaiah 28:1-20

Judgment on Apostasy

This is a prophetic passage for our meditation. Verse sixteen speaks of the foundation stone laid in Zion, *" . . . a tried stone, a precious corner stone . . ."* This speaks of the Lord Jesus Christ. I Peter 2:6-8 and Matthew 21:42 reveal that Christ is that stone.

Who is the *"overflowing scourge"?* It involves those who are exactly opposite and in opposition to the Lord. This overflowing scourge would seem to be that which is in contact with the spirit world but also in contact with the physical world. Those who will be affected by the overflowing scourge are the rulers in Jerusalem (v. 14). There is to be some kind of covenant between these rulers and some Antichrist workers. God will test this covenant, only to find it a refuge of lies.

When God tests, He uses judgment and righteousness. The overflowing scourge could well involve demonic activity and the work of the occult. Satan reveals his hatred of all that is of God by bringing persecution of His people. Verses twenty and twenty-one speak of the total inadequacy of all human schemes when God intervenes. The apostates had made a comfortable bed for themselves, as they assumed; it is too short for them to stretch themselves upon it. Their covering is too narrow to comfort and envelop them.

Jehovah is active in what Scripture calls His strange work—His work of judgment on Antichrist and his followers. The judgment of false teachers lingers not, and their damnation slumbers not (II Peter 2:3). Judgment is sure. *"The Lord shall rise up . . . he shall be wroth . . . he will bring to pass" (Isaiah 28:21).* The Lord is coming. Prophecy will be fulfilled. We need to pray, *" . . . Even so, come, Lord Jesus" (Revelation 22:20).*

Bible Truth for Today: *"The Lord knoweth how to deliver the godly out of temptations, and to reserve the unjust unto the day of judgment to be punished." —II Peter 2:9*

Read Isaiah 31–35
Family Reading: Isaiah 33:14-24 and Isaiah 35

The Future Kingdom

In Isaiah 33 we see the tribulation period, a dreadful time when the earth shall mourn and languish (Isaiah 33:9). Through all of this horrible tribulation, we find that Jerusalem shall stand. It will be the city of the coming king (v. 17), and God promises the stakes of Jerusalem shall never be removed (v. 20). Instead, out of the great tribulation will remain Jerusalem, the city of broad rivers and streams, for those who rely on the Lord (v. 21).

Chapter 34 presents the terrible campaign of Armageddon. This is the final battle during this great tribulation period. It is literally a battle between the forces of Christ and those of the Antichrist. Verse eight refers to it as the day of the Lord's vengeance. It is the *"sword of the Lord"* that is active in the battle (v. 6). This is the final bloody campaign just before the kingdom age.

Then we come to Chapter 35—the millennial kingdom with its blessing upon all the world and upon the nation of Israel in particular. In this chapter we have the desert land blooming. In the previous chapter we found a populous and fruitful country turned into a wilderness of terror. In this chapter we have the wilderness turned into a fruitful and good land. Wonders shall be wrought in the kingdom of nature as well as the kingdom of grace. The eyes of the blind shall be opened; the deaf shall hear; the lame shall leap; and the dumb shall sing. The barren lands shall bring forth fruit. It will be a great time. And the earth shall know the way of the Lord, for God shall make a highway of holiness. What a wonderful day to look forward to!

Thot: *The return of the Lord is not some sort of theory for us to engage in academic discussion. Rather it is our Blessed Hope for our daily living.*

August 8

Read Isaiah 36–38
Family Reading: Isaiah 37:1-23

A Personal Relationship with the Lord

Our family reading portion for today is a thrilling passage. I always enjoy reading of Hezekiah's confrontation with Rabshakeh, the general of Sennacherib's army. Rabshakeh brashly spoke against God and His power in Isaiah 36:13-21. He spoke in such a wicked manner again in Isaiah 37:10.

God delivered the nation of Israel. The last three verses of this thirty-seventh chapter tell how God fought for Israel, turning the Assyrians back from Jerusalem and causing Sennacherib's own sons to mutiny and murder their own father.

Hezekiah needed to grow in and through this experience. He requested Isaiah to intercede with God on behalf of Israel. Hezekiah referred to God as Isaiah's God but not as his own. In verse four he said, *"It may be the Lord thy God will hear the words of Rabshakeh, whom the king of Assyria his master hath sent to reproach the living God, and will reprove the words which the Lord thy God hath heard: wherefore lift up thy prayer for the remnant that is left."* He referred to the Lord as the Lord **thy** God—that is, as Isaiah's God, but not as the Lord **our** God. All of us must come to a definite personal relationship with God. Hezekiah knew Isaiah had such a relationship, but he did not actually rely on his own personal relationship with the Lord.

But when Rabshakeh again announced his wicked intentions concerning Israel, Hezekiah went personally to the Lord in prayer (vv. 9-14). Hezekiah prayed unto the Lord himself and told God of Israel's needs. He spoke of his relationship and that of the nation (vv. 15-20). It was this prayer that God answered, beginning at verse twenty-one and going on through the remainder of the chapter. Remember, you and I can have a personal relationship with the Lord. By presenting ourselves to Him in regular, consistent prayer, we can see God give the victories.

Invitation for Today: *"Let us therefore come boldly unto the throne of grace, that we may obtain mercy, and find grace to help in time of need." —Hebrews 4:16*

August 9

Read Isaiah 39–41
Family Reading: Isaiah 40:10-31

Soaring Like an Eagle

Isaiah 40:31 states that " . . . *they that wait upon the Lord shall renew their strength; they shall mount up with wings as eagles; they shall run, and not be weary; and they shall walk, and not faint."*

It is said of the eagle that he mounts up toward the sun, and that of all birds he is the one which can gaze upon the sun without shrinking eye. So it is with faith in our souls. The Lord's people are the only ones who can look by faith upon the *"Sun of Righteousness"* by reading and studying His precious Word. When our blessed Lord Jesus is so revealed to the believer, the soul begins to mount up with wings as eagles, soaring higher and higher, till someday we come into the very presence of God.

Have you ever had the experience of your spirit seeming to soar as though it were on eagles' wings? Have you had those blessed communications with the Lord through prayer and His Word that lead you to high mountains of faith? Oh, when we rise to such heights, we find delight in the Lord Jesus and know His grace and love flowing through us. Sometimes we are so fastened down to this earth, this waste howling wilderness (Deuteronomy 32:10), that we are like a bird with a broken wing who cannot mount higher. We get swallowed up in the world, forgetting God and godliness. Oh, how we need to be delivered from these chains and fetters, seeing earthly cares drop off and our wings given us anew so that we can soar above the world and its temptations. We need to fix our eyes on things above, not on things of the earth (Colossians 3:1-4). This is the way of the eagle—looking up and soaring higher. Praise God, those who wait upon the Lord can have that experience.

Bible Principle for Today: *"Wait on the Lord: be of good courage, and he shall strengthen thine heart: wait, I say, on the Lord."*

—Psalm 27:14

August 10

Read Isaiah 42–44
Family Reading: Isaiah 44:1-20

Keep Yourselves from Idols

God is jealous for His glory to be realized and revered. He proclaims to Israel that there is no God beside Him (v. 8). Then He discusses the evils and vanity of idolatry. Throughout the Word of God, He repeatedly warns of the wickedness and vanity of idolatry:

1. The graven image has no life, cannot be God, and certainly should not be worshiped. " . . . *they see not, nor know* . . . " *(v. 9).* *"They have not known nor understood: for he hath shut their eyes, that they cannot see; and their hearts; that they cannot understand" (v. 18).*

    "They have mouths, but they speak not: eyes have they, but they see not: They have ears, but they hear not: noses have they, but they smell not: They have hands, but they handle not: feet have they, but they walk not: neither speak they through their throat. They that make them are like unto them; so is every one that trusteth in them."—Psalm 115:5-8

2. The graven images are the product of men's hands and craftsmanship. The blacksmith works (v. 12), and the carpenter fashions (v. 13) to produce the idol; but it is the work of men's hands, and therefore it cannot be God.

3. The same tree that a man burns to give heat and bake bread is the tree he uses to make a graven image so that he can pray to it. He speaks to this tree, ascribing personality to it, " . . . *thou art my god."* He worships this tree, asking it to deliver him (v. 17).

4. The one who worships idols feeds on ashes. The idol cannot deliver; it cannot help. Yet millions are bowing down to idols today—even here in America.

Bible Command for Today: *"Little children, keep yourselves from idols."* — *I John 5:21*

August 11

Read Isaiah 45–48
Family Reading: Isaiah 48

Separation from the World

God challenges His people to arise and *"Go ye forth of Babylon, flee ye from the Chaldeans . . . " (v. 20).* In every era the people of God have met with a great principle of evil. Sometimes that principle is embodied in a city; sometimes, in a confederation; and other times, in a conspiracy of darkness. Always it is the same spirit under different forms; always it is the deification of the human against the divine; always it is pride and vainglory against moral values; and always it is man's effort in man's strength against God's power.

The great system of Babylon has always been strange. The walls of ancient Babylon held millions within the city. Babylon today is enclosing millions in a great world system. Babylon has various meanings, but today I am going to use Babylon as a picture of the world.

God said that His people should come out of Babylon. God always wants His people to be separated from the world and all of its attractions. Listen to God's command in II Corinthians 6:17— *"Wherefore come out from among them, and be ye separate, saith the Lord . . . "*

In Isaiah 48:13 and 17 God identifies Himself as the Creator, as Israel's Redeemer, and as Israel's God. Had Israel hearkened to God's commandment, her peace would have been as a river, and her righteousness as the waves of the sea. Israel had followed the ways of Babylon and had no peace. God's command today is to come out of Babylon. Hear the command of Revelation 18:4— *"And I heard another voice from heaven, saying, Come out of her, my people, that ye be not partakers of her sins, and that ye receive not of her plagues."* Unless God's people come out of the world today, they will have no peace.

Bible Principle for Today: *"Wherefore come out from among them, and be ye separate, saith the Lord, and touch not the unclean thing; and I will receive you, And will be a Father unto you, and ye shall be my sons and daughters, saith the Lord Almighty."*

—II Corinthians 6:17, 18

Read Isaiah 49–53
Family Reading: Isaiah 51

Trusting Him

This fifty-first chapter teaches us to trust the Lord. The last part of Isaiah 51:5 states, *"And on mine arm shall they trust."*

To trust Him, we must first of all hearken unto His word.

Verse 1 — *"Hearken to me . . ."*

Verse 4 — *"Hearken unto me, my people; and give ear unto me, O my nation . . ."*

Then in order to trust Him, we must recognize He is the righteous One and He is the Rock. *"Hearken to me, ye that follow after righteousness . . . look unto the rock . . ."* *(v. 1).*

Often it is the storm that drives us to trust in Him. Verse six speaks of the heavens vanishing *" . . . away like smoke . . ."* and the earth waxing *" . . . old like a garment . . ."* What a blessed storm it is that wrecks us on a Rock like this!

Many times we do not go to God because of the multitudes of friends and duties. But when a man is so poor, so friendless, so helpless that he has nowhere else to turn, he flies to the arms of the Lord and is blessedly clasped within them. When troubles come, we learn more of the Lord than at any other time.

The weak man needs the Everlasting Arms. The strong man is weak because he trusts his own strength rather than the Lord. Let's trust in His arms.

Bible Truth for Today: *"Therefore the redeemed of the Lord shall return, and come with singing unto Zion; and everlasting joy shall be upon their head: they shall obtain gladness and joy; and sorrow and mourning shall flee away."* *— Isaiah 51:11*

August 13

Read Isaiah 54–58
Family Reading: Isaiah 55 and 56

The Satisfying Bread

There are things which money cannot buy. It would be completely absurd to try to pay for these things with gold or silver. They are absolutely without price. Therefore, they elude the rich, who have supposed that money is the only medium of exchange. The rich find it difficult to think of wealth other than that used in the market.

What are these things that are without price? They are contained in a Person, and that One is the Lord Jesus Christ, the Suffering One of Isaiah 53. It is impossible to have them unless we enter into a living union with Him.

It was necessary for God to call to the attention of the Jewish people these possessions that cannot be bought. The life of the Jews had become luxurious in Babylon. They had acquired wealth and sold their spiritual appreciation for worldly considerations. Now there was serious danger that they would lose sight of the spiritual needs in their lives. God needed to remind them of two truths:

First, they had to realize that the immortal thirst of the soul could not be quenched by water which has its source in the earth (55:1). Second, they had to recognize that the hunger of the soul could not be satisfied with bread baked in the world's ovens (55:2). All the wealth of the world cannot make a single meal for the soul and the spiritual life. The Lord invited them to hearken diligently and eat that which satisfies spiritual needs (55:2). God said that the way to have this soul-satisfying water and food is to incline the ear and hear the message of the Word of God (55:3).

God's invitation is to receive His grace. Thereby He makes an everlasting covenant with His people and assures forgiveness and life. He is ready to pardon abundantly. All we need to do is to receive the water of life and the bread which He offers.

Bible Command for Today: *"Seek ye the Lord while he may be found, call ye upon him while he is near."* — *Isaiah 55:6*

August 14

Read Isaiah 59–62
Family Reading: Isaiah 59

Judgment on All

Israel had sinned. God invited them to come back, but they simply continued on in their form of religion without any power. In Isaiah 58:3 we read that they fasted without results. They asked, *"Wherefore have we fasted?"* God wanted them to know that it was not His fault that they failed. Isaiah 59:1,2 states: *"Behold, the Lord's hand is not shortened, that it cannot save; neither his ear heavy, that it cannot hear: But your iniquities have separated between you and your God, and your sins have hid his face from you . . . ."*

Has God failed? Has He forgotten to be gracious? No! He never changes. His power is the same as it has always been. The cause of the problem was the sin of Israel. In their formalistic religion Israel carried on a religious front, but there was no relationship to the Lord. In verse five God declares they hatch cockatrice eggs that induce death when eaten. They are like a spider's web. That web is meant to catch a prey. These are the hypocrites who have a form of godliness but deny the power thereof (II Timothy 3:5).

The spider's web is a marvel of skill. And that is exactly what a deceiver's religion is. He takes a barefaced lie and makes it out as true. The spider is different from the bee. It does not suck pollen from the flowers to make its deposit. The web comes from within the spider. And the religion of a hypocrite is only of his own making. Deceivers find their trust and hope within themselves. They lay their own foundation and hew out their own pillars. They are not willing to build their house on the grace of God.

A spider's web is very frail. It may be curiously made, but it is not built to stand. The broom can soon demolish it. God wants the hypocrite exposed for what he is—a deceiver. God brings judgment. Even those who try to depart from evil, God will judge (v. 15). Men grope, but there is none to deliver. What a tragic condition for the nation of Israel!

Proverb for Today: *"The righteousness of the perfect shall direct his way: but the wicked shall fall by his own wickedness."*

—Proverbs 11:5

August 15

Read Isaiah 63–66
Family Reading: Isaiah 65

Faster Than the Telegraph

"And it shall come to pass, that before they call, I will answer; and while they are yet speaking, I will hear." — *Isaiah 65:24*

I have assigned a longer passage than usual for our family reading today. In these last chapters of Isaiah it is very difficult to divide a chapter.

The story is told of the construction of the first telegraph line in the Shetland Islands. A man who was considered rather simple-minded stood looking at the wires being mounted on poles. A businessman said to him, "What a wonderful thing this new invention is! When it is finished, we will be able to send a message 200 miles or more and get an answer back within an hour!" The slightly retarded man did not seem impressed. "There is nothing very great about that," he answered. "There isn't?" asked the man. "Can you tell me of anything better or faster?" The other man, though simple-minded but well grounded in Scripture, referred to Isaiah 65 and asked, "Did you ever hear of an answer before the message is sent?" The businessman looked dumbfounded, thinking this was just a meaningless comment. He little realized how true that statement was.

God, who knows and reads our hearts, also knows our needs. Often while we are yet speaking, the blessing is already on the way. Our prayers are sent faster than any telegraph message and immediately reach God's ears. I Peter 3:12 teaches the same truth as Psalm 34:15—*For the eyes of the Lord are over the righteous, and his ears are open unto their prayers . . . "* What a privilege we have of coming to the Lord and knowing that He is ready and anxious to hear. Before we even ask, He has heard and answered. He knows our needs and will meet them.

Bible Promise for Today: *"And all things, whatsoever ye shall ask in prayer, believing, ye shall receive."* —*Matthew 21:22*

August 16

Read Jeremiah 1–3
Family Reading: Jeremiah 3

God's Yearning for Backsliders

Jeremiah wrote, pleading with a backslidden nation to return to the Lord. The truths that God presented concerning a backslidden nation also apply to churches and individuals today:

First, we realize that God is merciful and even anxious to bring a backslider back to Himself. In verse twelve God states, *" . . . I am merciful . . . and I will not keep anger for ever."* By His very nature, God longs for backsliders to return from their backslidden condition and turn to the Lord.

Second, the requirement that God gives for a backslider to be restored is that he acknowledge his iniquity. Verse thirteen gives God's command to acknowledge the iniquity and the transgression. Iniquity is the sin nature within that causes a person to transgress against the Lord. The backslider must admit the wrong attitude of his heart and the wrong actions he has committed.

Third, the backslider is to turn back to the Lord. God commands in verse fourteen, *"Turn, O backsliding children . . . "* The backslider is not only to acknowledge his sin but also to turn away from it and turn back to the Lord. This is repentance—turning away from sin and turning to the Lord. Naomi not only realized that Moab was bad for her but also arose that she might return from Moab to Bethlehem (Ruth 1:6). The prodigal son not only saw the pigpen in which he was living but also arose to return to his father (Luke 15:20). The backslider must see the pigpen he is in, and then he must arise and turn back to serving the Lord.

God promises to restore the one who does turn. In Psalm 23 David claimed this when he said of the shepherd: *"He restoreth my soul . . . "* In Jeremiah 3 God promised that because He is married to the child of God, He will restore the backslider who returns. He will give the backslider a pastor to feed him and grace to strengthen him.

Promise: *"Return, ye backsliding children, and I will heal your backslidings . . . "* —*Jeremiah 3:22*

August 17

Read Jeremiah 4–6
Family Reading: Jeremiah 4:1-22

Break Up Your Fallow Ground

"For thus saith the Lord to the men of Judah and Jerusalem,
Break up your fallow ground, and sow not among thorns."
—Jeremiah 4:3

Fallow ground is not virgin soil. Ground which has never been plowed is virgin soil, but fallow ground is that which has been plowed and cultivated. It has produced a crop and then has been allowed to lie idle during a growing season. In the big wheat country of eastern Colorado and Kansas, farmers purposely leave a section of their ground fallow every year. As one travels through that country he will note a strip of land growing wheat and then a strip of plowed but unseeded land. These farmers have learned that by letting the ground lie idle every other year, the land produces more than it would if it were sown every year. That strip of unseeded ground is called *"fallow ground."* A good farmer knows that he must keep the weeds out of the fallow ground or he will lose the moisture content of the land. He is careful to till the land to kill the weeds. By breaking up the fallow ground, it will be usable.

Israel had been used of God. The nation had known the Lord but now was in a backslidden condition. Therefore, it was like fallow ground, for it was producing no fruit. Jeremiah called on the nation to break up the fallow ground and not to sow among thorns. Those thorns of cares and riches and pleasures of this life need to be plowed under so that they do not destroy the possibility of fruitbearing (Luke 8:14). It is foolish to sow good seed among the thorns of worldliness and carelessness. Yet how many today try to do that very thing. They want to have the seed of the Word placed in among thorns of their worldly existence. But thorns will choke out the little plants. God says the ground must be turned over so that the thorns can be destroyed and the seed bear fruit. Those who are saved but are backslidden are fallow ground. Those of you in this condition need to plow under the thorns of sin so that the seed of the Word of God can bear fruit.

August 18

Read Jeremiah 7–9
Family Reading: Jeremiah 8

What Wisdom Is in Them?

Jeremiah 7–10 presents the message Jeremiah delivered from the gate of the temple (Jeremiah 7:2). In this message he warns Judah of its serious and dangerous spiritual neglect that was developing into complete apostasy. The temple services had become mere ritual. Men were worshiping the queen of Heaven and other gods (Jeremiah 7:18).

God diagnosed Israel's problem as one of perpetual backsliding (8:5). They refused to return to God. They held fast to their deceit in going away from God. There was no repentance of wickedness but everyone turned to his own course, not endeavoring to follow God (v. 6).

Though they boasted of their wisdom, they did not have the discernment of the migratory birds. *"Yea, the stork in the heaven knoweth her appointed times; and the turtle and the crane and the swallow observe the time of their coming; but my people know not the judgment of the Lord" (v. 7).*

It was the same with the scribes. *"How do ye say, We are wise, and the law of the Lord is with us . . . " (v. 8)?* God said that His law seemed to be in vain. Please note that the Word does not say they denied the law because it is not always denied by those who bow politely away from obeying it. While they profess they love it, they walk in disobedience to it. These are always the most dangerous people in the work of the Lord. The closer one is to the truth, the more dangerous is his unbelief. For us to be right, we must not only profess belief in the truth but also manifest obedience to the truth.

Real wisdom comes from God and His Word. In verse nine God says of the so-called wise men: *" . . . lo, they have rejected the word of the Lord; and what wisdom is in them?"*

Bible Truth for Today: *"Horror hath taken hold upon me because of the wicked that forsake thy law." —Psalm 119:53*

August 19

Read Jeremiah 10–13
Family Reading: Jeremiah 13

Wilt Thou Not Be Made Clean?

Jeremiah ends this thirteenth chapter with a very important question: *"[W]ilt thou not be made clean . . . ?"* It opens with God's command to Jeremiah to gird himself with a linen girdle. The clothing in that day consisted of a short-sleeved undergarment that reached to the knees. The outer garment was a mantle. These loose-fitting garments were girded at the waist so that the clothing would not hamper a man at work. The girdle becomes a sign of service. Jesus told His servants to have their loins *"girded about" (Luke 12:35)*. In John 13 the Lord is the girded Servant, washing His disciples' feet. Believers are to have their " *. . . loins girt about with truth . . . " (Ephesians 6:14)*.

The sign of the linen girdle was to reveal that Israel had been the servant of Jehovah, though a faithless servant. Jeremiah was to take the girdle to the Euphrates, the river of Babylon, and bury it—a sign to Israel that because of her faithlessness to the Lord, she would be taken captive in Babylon. The girdle was there " *. . . many days, . . . "* indicating a lengthy captivity (v. 6). When it was removed, it *"was marred, it was profitable for nothing" (v. 7)*.

The application is easily made. Only real and genuine self-judgment, not captivity, could change the state of the people's hearts. Israel had been called to cleave unto the Lord so that they might be His people (v. 11). But Israel would not hear the Lord; therefore, Israel was as the girdle, " *. . . good for nothing"* (v. 10).

God then gives the parable of the bottle (v. 12), showing their emptiness, not filled with the joy of the Lord but with the drunkenness of self-confidence that leads to their destruction.

The remainder of the chapter reveals that Israel needs a cleansing. The captivity would not break her. Jeremiah ends the chapter, asking, " *. . . wilt thou not be made clean . . . ?"*

Christians need to be sure their hearts are clean. It is so easy for a child of God to excuse his sin rather than to face it, humble himself, and let God cleanse him. Is your heart clean before God, or do you excuse sin in your life and continue on in resistance to God? Today read I John 1:9 and apply it to your life.

August 20

Read Jeremiah 14–17
Family Reading: Jeremiah 17:1-18

The Mystery of Iniquity

"The heart is deceitful above all things, and desperately wicked: who can know it?" —*Jeremiah 17:9*

Jeremiah states that the man will be cursed who trusts in man and makes flesh his arm (v. 5). He also states that the man is blessed that *"trusteth in the Lord, and whose hope the Lord is" (v. 7).*

The reason that we are to trust the Lord instead of man is, *"The heart is deceitful above all things, and desperately wicked . . . "* The sin of our fallen nature is very mysterious. The *"mystery of iniquity"* in II Thessalonians 2:7 is referring to the Antichrist, but there is a sense in which the mystery of iniquity is very real in every human life. We have the mystery of iniquity just as we have the mystery of godliness (I Timothy 3:16). Both of these mysteries have lengths and depths and breadths which no person can ever understand. We will never be able to understand all of the mystery of godliness, but neither can we understand the mystery of iniquity that dwells within our own beings. Sometimes sin seems to sleep, and at other times it seems to awaken with renewed strength.

Day by day as we grow in the Lord, we face the knowledge of these two mysteries. In the spiritual knowledge of both of them—the mystery of sin and the mystery of salvation, we come to a proper understanding of spiritual truth. It is because of these two mysteries that we have some paradoxes in the Christian life, such as: the stronger we grow, the weaker we are (II Corinthians 12:9, 10); the more we possess, the less we have (II Corinthians 6:10); and the more we are like a little child, the greater we become in the kingdom of Heaven (Matthew 18:4).

Bible Truth for Today: *"Blessed is the man that trusteth in the Lord, and whose hope the Lord is."* —*Jeremiah 17:7*

August 21

Read Jeremiah 18–21
Family Reading: Jeremiah 20

Jeremiah's Victory

The prophet Jeremiah had been faithful to preach the Word of the Lord. In this twentieth chapter he had been placed in prison by Pashur, the governor and son of the priest. The next day, when Pashur brought Jeremiah from the prison, this faithful prophet continued to speak forth the truth boldly. He warned Pashur that God's judgment would come and that he and his house would be taken into captivity and die there.

Faithfulness to the Lord and His Word can bring real persecution and tribulation. Jeremiah experienced this. In verse ten he stated that he " . . . *heard the defaming of many, fear on every side . . .* " He said that those who knew him were waiting to take revenge on him.

Under such harassment, Jeremiah became weary and even spoke against the Lord. In verse seven he wrote: " . . . *I am in derision daily, every one mocketh me.*" So weary was he of all this that he cried out in despair: " . . . *I will not make mention of him, nor speak any more in his name. But his word was in mine heart as a burning fire shut up in my bones, and I was weary with forbearing, and I could not stay*" *(v. 9)*.

Jeremiah thought that he could turn from the Lord. However, God's Word would not let him; he found that he had to speak the truth.

Praise God, this prophet did not stay down in the slough of despond. He began to praise the Lord. In verse thirteen he wrote: *"Sing unto the Lord, praise ye the Lord: for he hath delivered the soul of the poor from the hand of evildoers."* God had the victory in Jeremiah's life. He looked to the Word of God and came out triumphant for the Lord.

We, too, need to spend time in God's Word or we will collapse under the attacks of the world.

Bible Truth for Today: *"Princes also did sit and speak against me: but thy servant did meditate in thy statutes."* —Psalm 119:23

August 22

Read Jeremiah 22–24
Family Reading: Jeremiah 23:1-14, 23-30

True and False Prophets

In this passage we have another view of the wicked days in which Jeremiah lived and prophesied. He tells us that the religious leaders were leading the people down the road to destruction. Verse eleven states that both prophet and priest were profane. They did not obey the Lord, and they turned from righteousness to bearing false prophecies. Their ways were slippery ways in the darkness. They not only walked in this way of darkness but also committed adultery, lied, and strengthened the hands of men in wickedness.

"Mine heart within me is broken because of the prophets; all my bones shake; I am like a drunken man, and like a man whom wine hath overcome, because of the Lord, and because of the words of his holiness."—Jeremiah 23:9

Jeremiah did not have any jealousy of others in the prophetic office, but his soul was deeply moved by the lying seers who led God's people astray. These dreadful conditions existed in Samaria and also in Judea. The most serious problem, however, was that this sin and rebellion was in Jerusalem. These false prophets had so deceived the people that Jerusalem had become like Sodom and Gomorrah (v. 14).

What is the answer? The answer then and the answer always is to preach the Word of God. It is the Word of God that can meet every challenge.

"Is not my word like as a fire? saith the Lord; and like a hammer that breaketh the rock in pieces?" *—Jeremiah 23:29*

Amen! God's Word is just that. It does not matter how difficult the problem is. God's Word is powerful and can bring souls to a place of repentance. Let us be sure to use the Word of God and to trust it to bring the fruit.

Bible Truth for Today: *"Have not I written to thee excellent things in counsels and knowledge, That I might make thee know the certainty of the words of truth; that thou mightest answer the words of truth to them that send unto thee?"* *—Proverbs 22:20, 21*

August 23

Read Jeremiah 25–27
Family Reading: Jeremiah 26

A Faithful Prophet

Jeremiah is one of my heroes. This faithful prophet always stood true to the Lord. He was mightily used of the Lord because he preached the Word God commanded him to preach. Verse two tells us that God's commandment to him was, " . . . *Stand in the court of the Lord's house, and speak unto all the cities of Judah, which come to worship in the Lord's house, all the words that I command thee to speak unto them; diminish not a word.*" God uses men who fill this order that He gives to *"speak . . . all the words that I command."*

God gave Jeremiah the promise that if the people did not hearken to His words, judgment would come from God. It was Jeremiah's statement of what God promised that upset the prophets. They did not want to hear the Word of God. Therefore, they announced to Jeremiah, " . . . *Thou shalt surely die" (v. 8)*. All the people gathered against Jeremiah in the house of the Lord. Verses twelve and thirteen reveal Jeremiah's bold answer: " . . . *The Lord sent me to prophesy against this house and against this city all the words that ye have heard. Therefore now amend your ways and your doings, and obey the voice of the Lord your God; and the Lord will repent him of the evil that he hath pronounced against you.*"

Praise God for a man like Jeremiah. He did not let the whims and fancies of the people change his message. He stood on the Word of God and preached its truth without regard to the consequences. Any prophet who is faithful to God must of necessity be a man who boldly preaches the whole counsel of God. As he speaks boldly, he warns people of their sins. Jeremiah called on them to repent of their sins by amending their ways and obeying the voice of the Lord.

Bible Truth for Today: *"I will speak of thy testimonies also before kings, and will not be ashamed." —Psalm 119:46*

August 24

Read Jeremiah 28–30
Family Reading: Jeremiah 28

A Faithless Prophet

In Chapter 28 we find a false prophet, Hananiah, standing against God's prophet Jeremiah. We note some things about false prophets.

First, Hananiah prophesied good things. In verse three he stated that within two years Nebuchadnezzar would be defeated and all of the vessels of the Lord's house restored to Jerusalem. False prophets like to give people that which they want to hear. Certainly this type of prophecy did not offend the people at all. They were glad to know that their bondage would be over. But it was not a true prophecy.

Second, Hananiah tried to please the people. He even went so far as to break the yoke of wood that was around Jeremiah's neck. He thought Jeremiah would be glad to be released from that yoke. But God spoke to Jeremiah saying, I will change their yoke from one of wood to one of iron. Hananiah, trying to please the people, was bringing a false prophecy.

Third, in Hananiah's prophecy there is nothing about repentance or turning from sin. This was the message Israel needed. They did not need to hear good things to tickle their ears; they needed to hear truthful things to point them to the Lord and bring them to repentance from sin.

The chapter ends with Jeremiah speaking frankly to Hananiah the message the Lord gave him. Jeremiah said that God would cast off Hananiah from the earth and that Hananiah would die that year because he had taught rebellion against the Lord. This prophecy was fulfilled. Hananiah preached that which people wanted to hear, but it was not the message God wanted delivered. Today we have false prophets among us giving messages that will please us but that are not the message from the Lord. We can be sure there will be false teachers, and we need to be on guard concerning them.

Bible Principle for Today: *"But there were false prophets also among the people, even as **there shall be false teachers among you.**"*
—II Peter 2:1

August 25

Read Jeremiah 31 and 32
Family Reading: Jeremiah 32:6-28, 37-41

God's Answer to Jeremiah's Puzzle

Jeremiah was puzzled. He could not understand what God was doing. The Lord had told Jeremiah to purchase the field that belonged to his cousin. Jeremiah had obeyed God and purchased the field. God had told Jeremiah to give the evidences of purchase to Baruch, who was to place them in an earthen jar for protection in the days ahead. The Lord said this was to be a sign of the fact that even though Nebuchadnezzar would capture the land, God would restore the land to Israel again.

Jeremiah could not understand why God would have him buy the land, only to see the Chaldeans take it away. He prayed, asking God how this could be. In his prayer he praised the Lord for His greatness. He also recounted God's dealings with the nation of Israel in bringing them out of Egypt and into the Promised Land. Jeremiah confessed the Lord as One who is great and greatly to be praised. He said of God: *"Great in counsel, and mighty in work: for thine eyes are open upon all the ways of the sons of men: to give every one according to his ways, and according to the fruit of his doings" (v. 19).*

God's answer to Jeremiah was that He was the God of all flesh and there is nothing too hard for Him. The Lord then stated that He would bring judgment upon Israel for their sins. This judgment would be revealed by Israel's being taken captive by the Chaldeans. Yet in spite of their captivity, Israel would be delivered and restored to their land. God permitted Nebuchadnezzar to attack the land to bring it under bondage. At the same time, He had Jeremiah buy the land as a prophecy that the nation would be restored to their homeland.

God answered Jeremiah's questions. God had a purpose, though Jeremiah could not understand it. Thank God, Jeremiah obeyed even when he did not understand. God used Jeremiah because he was willing to obey Him.

August 26

Read Jeremiah 33–36
Family Reading: Jeremiah 33:1-22

God's Promise of Blessing

"Call unto me, and I will answer thee, and show thee great and mighty things, which thou knowest not." —*Jeremiah 33:3*

This verse was given in connection with God's promise that He would restore Israel to its land. He promised that His covenant with David would never be broken (vv. 20, 21). God will keep His covenant, and His people Israel will be restored to the land for the kingdom blessing.

Jeremiah 33:3 promises that God will do great and mighty things which cannot even be imagined. Another translation reads, "great and difficult things." Someone has said that it literally speaks of "great and fenced in things"—things that are humanly impossible to reach. Those who expect to receive such blessings must continue in prayer, believing God. Promises in the Bible are not given to supersede prayer but to encourage us to pray. Those who pray and take His promises for their pillows will find that the Father will do for them things which humanly they cannot understand.

The remainder of the chapter tells exactly what He will do. He says, *"And I will cause the captivity of Judah and the captivity of Israel to return, and will build them, as at the first" (v. 7).* He also promises that He will *" . . . cleanse them from all their iniquity . . . " (v. 8)* and put them back in the land with the voice of joy and gladness, with the voice of the bridegroom, and the voice of the bride (v. 11). To the Israelites of that day, that would have sounded impossible; but if **we** call unto Him, He is going to do great and mighty things of which **we** have not even thought. How wonderful it is to rest on the promises of God!

Today let's claim Jeremiah 33:3. Someone reading this needs to claim this for your own life. Memorize the verse and then believe it. God will use it in your own life to be a blessing.

Bible Promise for Today: God *" . . . is able to do exceeding abundantly above all that we ask or think, according to the power that worketh in us." —Ephesians 3:20*

August 27

Read Jeremiah 37–40
Family Reading: Jeremiah 39

Don't Pass Redemption Point

Through Jeremiah God had repeatedly warned Judah that they would be taken captive by Nebuchadnezzar and the Babylonian empire. Jeremiah 39 is the climax of all that Jeremiah had warned would happen. Jerusalem fell and was broken up (v. 2). The siege by the Chaldeans had lasted eighteen months except for the brief respite when Nebuchadnezzar withdrew his troops to meet those sent by the king of Egypt. There were eighteen months of suffering on the part of the besieged inhabitants. Yet through it all there was a hardness of heart and a complacent self-righteousness that kept these Jews from turning back to the Lord. Our God has told us we can go too far in resistance against Him until there is *"no remedy" (II Chronicles 36:16,17)*. The king and his associates tried to flee, but they were captured in the plains of Jericho.

Just above Niagara Falls, there is an insignificant headland called "Redemption Point." No boat that has once gone beyond that point has ever been rescued from destruction. In our lives as individuals and in the life of a nation, there is also a "Redemption Point" beyond which we cannot go without destruction. The people of Jerusalem continued on in their sin until they had gone too far, and there *"was no remedy."* May each of us live in the realm of confessed sin with a desire to walk wholly with God so that we never pass "Redemption Point."

Bible Truth for Today: *" . . . behold, **now** is the accepted time; behold, **now** is the day of salvation."* —*II Corinthians 6:2*

August 28

Read Jeremiah 41–44
Family Reading: Jeremiah 42:13-22 and Jeremiah 43

The Sign of the Hidden Stones

Jeremiah warned God's people in Jeremiah 42:19 that they should not go into Egypt. The Israelites wanted to go to Egypt and thereby escape their responsibility. They said in Jeremiah 42:14 that the reason they wanted to go to Egypt was that they could escape war, would not hear God's trumpet, and would have no hunger for bread.

Actually, all three of these desires should prove a blessing rather than a hindrance in the life of a child of God. Egypt is a picture of the world. When a person comes to the Lord, he gets into a battle and can expect to hear the trumpet of God. When he goes back to Egypt, back into the world, he thinks he is getting away from the fight and away from the trumpet of alarm. This is not where God wants His people. God's command is, *" . . . Go ye not into Egypt . . . " (v. 19).*

Men who are not walking with God cannot understand His command as given by Jeremiah. They will hearken to a false prophet such as Azariah, who said that Jeremiah was prophesying falsely (Jeremiah 43:2). Therefore, they took Jeremiah and went into Egypt. But, praise God, the Lord does not desert His man. In Jeremiah 43:8 we read that the Word of the Lord came to Jeremiah. God can speak through His prophet, regardless of circumstances.

Jeremiah took stones from the brick kiln next to Pharaoh's palace. He hid those stones and then announced that Nebuchadnezzar would set his throne on top of those stones. He was saying that God's people, trying to flee God's judgment by going into the world, will find that God's judgment pursues them there. How often are believers fooled to think that by fleeing into the world they will escape. No God's judgment will come. The only sensible thing to do is to prepare for that day by surrendering to the Lord. Oh, how wise it would have been for God's people to have heeded the counsel of Jeremiah.

Bible Truth for Today: *"Love not the world, neither the things that are in the world. If any man love the world, the love of the Father is not in him." — I John 2:15*

August 29

Read Jeremiah 45–48
Family Reading: Jeremiah 48:1-18, 38-42

Nominal Christians

God called Jeremiah and commissioned him to be a prophet to the nations (Jeremiah 1:5). In the first forty-five chapters, Jeremiah deals primarily with Judah and Israel. He had spoken to the rebellious men of Judah and warned them about their sin, but God's call had gone beyond the nation of Israel. Jeremiah had been called to be a prophet to the nations. Jeremiah gave *"the word of the Lord . . . against the Gentiles" (46:1)*. Nine different nations and peoples, all surrounding the land of Palestine, are mentioned in Jeremiah 46–51. They are Egypt (46:2-28); Philistia (47); Moab (48); Ammon, Edom, Syria, Kedar, and Elam (49); and Babylon (50 and 51).

These nations typify some who have a direct influence on the work of God today. Egypt speaks of the world. Philistia represents those who border on the world.

Today's reading centers on Moab. The Moabites picture that large group today who think they are religious but who have no genuine profession. In many nations of the world, they are actually called *Nominals*. They are *nominal* Christians; i. e., Christians in name only. Moab was an illegitimate child, and the nation claimed a birth it did not have. So every person claiming to be a Christian but not having been born again is actually not in the family.

These people are marked by a careless, indifferent attitude. *"Moab hath been at ease from his youth . . . " (v. 11)*. He has no desire to live to honor the Lord. He trusts in his works and does not rest on the Lord (v. 7). When he does the work of the Lord, he is deceitful and unwilling to get into the fight; he holds back his sword from blood (v. 10).

Today, be sure you are really saved and not just a *nominal* Christian.

Bible Warning for Today: *"I know thy works, that thou art neither cold nor hot: I would thou wert cold or hot. So then because thou art lukewarm, and neither cold nor hot, I will spue thee out of my mouth." —Revelation 3:15, 16*

August 30

Read Jeremiah 49 and 50
Family Reading: Jeremiah 49:7-22

The Sin of Pride

I have had the privilege of visiting Petra in Jordan. It is referred to as the beautiful rose-red city. It is considered to be one of the outstanding tourist attractions of the world. A city was carved out of towering red rocks in the canyon.

Petra was the capitol of Edom. This prophecy in Jeremiah dealt with the people of Edom and particularly with the fortress city of Petra. God addresses the people, " . . . *O thou that dwellest in the clefts of the rock, that holdest the height of the hill . . . " (v.16).* Having their city cut into the rocks and hills, the dwellers of Petra thought that their city was an impregnable fortress. But God warned them that judgment would come and make desolate the city and the land.

God brings judgment because of sin. In verse fifteen God said He would make the nation " . . . *small among the heathen, and despised among men."* In verse sixteen He makes reference to the basic sin of Edom—that sin of pride. He speaks of " . . . *the pride of thine heart . . . "* God spoke through the prophet Obadiah concerning Edom: *"Though thou exalt thyself as the eagle, and though thou set thy nest among the stars, thence will I bring thee down, saith the Lord" (Obadiah 4).*

Proverbs 16:18 states: *"Pride goeth before destruction, and an haughty spirit before a fall."* The truth of this Scripture was literally proved by the downfall of Edom. A proud nation fell and has never risen again.

Thot: "Pride is the root of every sin. We need to see that above everything we must be saved from pride and self-will."

—Andrew Murray

August 31

Read Jeremiah 51
Family Reading: Jeremiah 51:1-14, 25 and 26, 42-49

Babylon Destroyed

Jeremiah was a faithful preacher, not a manpleaser. He knew that because of Israel's sin, the nation would be under the control of Nebuchadnezzar. This had already taken place. But now he also knew that the same God who brought judgment on Israel because of her sins would render more drastic judgment on Babylon because of her wickedness.

The promises of judgment on Babylon appeared impossible of fulfillment, but they were fulfilled to the letter. Babylon was the city that held the glory of all the earth. Now Jeremiah prophesies that this great city, this mighty city, would be destroyed. In fact, so severe was the judgment which God promised that He said Babylon would be destroyed and never rebuilt. Verse twenty-six promised, *"And they shall not take of thee a stone for a corner, nor a stone for foundations; but thou shalt be desolate for ever, saith the Lord."* Men would have said such a destruction would be impossible, but God's Word will always stand. God promised: *" . . . I will fill thee with men, as with caterpillars; and they shall lift up a shout against thee"* *(v. 14).* He told how the city would be filled. In verse thirty-two he stated that the passages would be stopped. The kings of the Medes diverted the river and walked in the bed of the river right into the city. God's Word was fulfilled to the letter. That which men thought was impossible, God prophesied and fulfilled completely.

The Bible is the Word of God. Men may scoff at it, but all of its predictions come true, for it was written by inspiration of God.

Bible Truth for Today: *"The kings of the earth set themselves, and the rulers take counsel together, against the Lord, and against his anointed, saying, Let us break their bands asunder, and cast away their cords from us." —Psalm 2:2, 3*

September 1

Read Jeremiah 52 and Lamentations 1
Family Reading: Lamentations 1

How?

Jeremiah opens Lamentations with questions that are actually exclamations. Note that there are exclamation marks at the end of the statements in Lamentations 1:1 rather than question marks. If someone else had written *Lamentations* he might have had to phrase these statements as questions. Jeremiah was broken and distressed over what had happened to Jerusalem, but he knew why it had happened. Here he is lamenting the awful state of Jerusalem.

"How doth the city sit solitary, that was full of people! how is she become as a widow! she that was great among the nations . . . how is she become tributary!"

How can it be? A city once great—going into captivity? Can it happen to any great city or any great nation? Yes, it can, and history is replete with examples. Our own United States can easily become one more example in history.

In verse eight Jeremiah answers the question of how it could happen: *"Jerusalem hath grievously sinned; therefore she is removed: all that honored her despise her, because they have seen her nakedness . . . "*

Jeremiah is broken over what he has seen in Jerusalem. In verse sixteen, he states that he weeps over the terrible condition of Jerusalem. One big reason he weeps so sorely is that he cannot find those who are concerned. In verse twelve he asks, *"Is it nothing to you, all ye that pass by? . . . "* The tragedy was that people were not concerned. We see the same thing in America today. Our nation is plunging down, but our people show so little concern. America, wake up!

Bible Principle for Today: *"In the fear of the Lord is strong confidence: and his children shall have a place of refuge."*

—Proverbs 14:26

September 2

Read Lamentations 2 and 3
Family Reading: Lamentations 3:22-50

The Goodness of God

This third chapter of Lamentations is an outstanding poem. The first twenty-one verses speak of the sufferings and persecutions that Jeremiah had known. In these verses, he becomes a picture of the Lord Jesus Christ. *"I am the man that hath seen affliction by the rod of his wrath" (v. 1).* That certainly is a type of the Lord Jesus, who took God's wrath in our place on the cross. In the first twenty-one verses, Jeremiah gives a very vivid picture of what Christ endured for us, all pictured in the suffering that Jeremiah endured at that time.

Beginning in verse twenty-two, an entirely different note is struck. There is an exalted strain of joyous confidence. That strain is continued down to verse thirty-six. In the place of complaining that his woes were greater than he deserved, he justifies God and gratefully acknowledges that justice has been tempered with grace. *"It is of the Lord's mercies that we are not consumed, because his compassions fail not. They are new every morning: great is thy faithfulness" (vv. 22, 23).* Any true believer will give this same testimony. One who loves the Lord will always say that his chastisement is not too severe and will never believe that any part of chastisement is undeserved. No self-judged believer ever yet failed to own that he was far from receiving the full reward of his deeds.

Praise God, in all of the chastisement that a believer will have, he can be confident that verse thirty-one is a reality: *"For the Lord will not cast off for ever."* He may be called to sit alone, as in verse twenty-eight; to partake of the dust, as in verse twenty-nine; and to stand with his Saviour in giving his cheek to the smiters, as in verse thirty; but he can be confident that verse thirty-one is a reality, that *"the Lord will not cast off forever."*

Bible Truth for Today: *"The Lord is good unto them that wait for him, to the soul that seeketh him." —Lamentations 3:25*

September 3

Read Lamentations 4 and 5 and Ezekiel 1
Family Reading: Ezekiel 1:1-20

The Glory of God

We come today to the prophecy of Ezekiel. This is a tremendous book and oftentimes considered to be one that is difficult to understand. As we go through this book, I ask you to meditate upon various chapters and endeavor to get some real blessing thereby.

Ezekiel was a priest, and many believe that he had been taught by Jeremiah. He began his ministry when he was thirty years of age. It began with a vision of the glory of God.

Ezekiel saw a cloud coming and fire enfolding itself—that is, it was probably a cloud that came flashing continually with lightning. From that cloud he saw emerge four living creatures. These four creatures had four different faces: on one side, the face of a man; on another, the face of a lion; on another, the face of an ox; and on another, the face of an eagle. In Revelation 4:7, 8 we find the same vision. This passage in Revelation reveals that these creatures are the highest of all principalities and authorities in the heavenly places. Therefore, this vision is to Israel and to us a picture of God. In the center of this four-square cherubim was a fire, representing the glory of Almighty God, flashing forth (v. 13). These cherubim had great wheels full of eyes. They could move in any direction.

These four cherubim represent the oneness of God. The eyes in the wheels represent the omniscience of God. The cherubim represent the omnipotence of God. The lightning-like rapidity with which they move represents the omnipresence of God. As all the cherubim move, the wheels move with one direction, with one life, with one power, and with one motion. What a privilege to know this God personally! He is worthy " . . . *to receive glory and honor and power . . .* " *(Revelation 4:11).*

Our Attitude Toward This Great God: " . . . *This was the appearance of the likeness of the glory of the Lord. And when I saw it, I fell upon my face , and I heard a voice of one that spake."*

—Ezekiel 1:28

September 4

Read Ezekiel 2–6
Family Reading: Ezekiel 5

God's Judgment

In this chapter we have the sign by which the complete destruction of Jerusalem is set forth. The fact that Ezekiel performed this sign on himself indicates how dear the problem of Jerusalem was to his own heart. He considered what was done to Jerusalem as done to himself. Please note the sign:

First, he was to shave off the hair of his head and beard. Jerusalem had been the head, but having degenerated, had become as the hair. When the hair grows thick and long, it is but a burden which a man wishes to cut off. He states, " . . . *This is Jerusalem . . .* " *(v. 5).* Just as Ezekiel was to cut off the hair of his head, so God says He will *"execute judgments in the midst of thee* [Jerusalem] *in the sight of the nations" (v. 8).*

Second, he was to weigh the hair and divide it into three parts. This pictures the exact directing of God's judgments. The cutting of the hair reveals that Israel no longer held a Nazarite position—one of separation unto the Lord.

Third, he was to dispose of the hair so that all would be either destroyed or dispersed (v. 2). Some of the Jews in Jerusalem would be destroyed; others would be dispersed throughout the world. Verse two reveals that some would be destroyed by fire, others by sword, and still others would be scattered.

Fourth, there would be a few hairs that would be placed in Ezekiel's garments, picturing the godly remnant who would be true to Jehovah.

In these few verses we have a picture of what God said would happen to the nation of Israel, and it has been fulfilled. Oh, how much more wonderful it would have been had Israel hearkened unto the Word of God! But instead, they defiled the sanctuary and God brought judgment. America needs to take heed to the message of judgment that God has given!

Bible Principle: *"For if we would judge ourselves, we should not be judged." —I Corinthians 11:31*

September 5

Read Ezekiel 7–10
Family Reading: Ezekiel 8 and 9

A Vision of Jesus

The section beginning with Chapter 8 is a series of visions concerning the judgment that would come upon Judah and Israel (8:1 and 9:9), and particularly Jerusalem (9:4). Ezekiel was in Babylon, taken there in the captivity. It may be that some of those Jews taken captive with him in Babylon had hopes that someday they could go back to Jerusalem and find that the Israelites there had not continued in sin. Instead, they were told through Ezekiel's prophecy that the inhabitants of the homeland had stubbornly continued in their sins.

Chapter 8 tells of an *"image of jealousy"* that Israel permitted— an idol before which the Israelites were bowing (vv. 3, 5). Then God told Ezekiel to dig by the door of the court and he would find even more terrible abominations. There he saw in his vision a wicked secret cult (vv. 9-13). The abominations were in the private devotions as well as the public worship of the Israelites (v. 12). In addition, God warned Israel about the worship of Tammuz, a Babylonian god that was an imitation of Jesus Christ, in that he was supposed to have died and risen again (v. 14). Also, there was sun worship (v. 16). Then God said that this idolatry was not a light thing and that He would deal in furious judgment (vv. 17, 18).

Thus Chapter 9 begins with God ordering judgment to be carried out. In his vision Ezekiel saw six men with slaughter weapons in their hands; but right in the midst of those men, Ezekiel also saw a man clothed in linen with an inkhorn by his side. Linen indicates high rank and special service. I believe this One who did not have a destroying weapon was an Old Testament revelation of the Lord Jesus Christ. He was to pass through Jerusalem and mark those who were burdened about the judgment. This Man said, *" . . . I have done as thou hast commanded me" (v. 11)*. This is exactly what our Lord said in John 17:4— *" . . . I have finished the work which thou gavest me to do."* Praise God for another glimpse of our Lord Jesus in the Old Testament—God's grace and mercy in the midst of judgment.

Bible Truth for Today: *"Then said I, Lo, I come (in the volume of the book it is written of me,) to do thy will, O God." —Hebrews 10:7*

September 6

Read Ezekiel 11–13
Family Reading: Ezekiel 11

Needed: A New Heart

Ezekiel had been prophesying concerning the wickedness of the nation of Israel and the fact that God's wrath would be poured upon the inhabitants, especially upon the city of Jerusalem. Ezekiel 11 presents the truth that God would judge the wicked men that were princes of the land. Then God said the day would come when He would restore Israel to the land (vv. 14-25). God told them that He would fulfill one requirement in their lives so that they could be back in the land and not have all of the abominable things in their lives.

This requirement is given in verses nineteen and twenty:

"And I will give them one heart, and I will put a new spirit within you; and I will take the stony heart out of their flesh, and will give them an heart of flesh: That they may walk in my statutes, and keep mine ordinances, and do them: and they shall be my people, and I will be their God."

This is the need in any nation. There must be a heart given by God. For this reason the Lord Jesus said, " . . . *Ye must be born again" (John 3:7).* Today we hear much talk about changing the environment. The problem is not the environment; it is the heart.

Think of Adam and Eve. They were in a perfect garden, not a bad environment; however, they let sin come in to cause their fall.

Our politicians are constantly talking about what they think will straighten America out. The best thing to straighten America out is to reach souls and have them accept Jesus Christ as Lord and Saviour. Then lives will be changed and they will help change America. America's problem is a heart problem. This land needs a new heart given by God in the lives of our people.

Bible Prayer for Today: *"Let my heart be sound in thy statutes; that I be not ashamed." —Psalm 119:80*

September 7

Read Ezekiel 14–16
Family Reading: Ezekiel 16:1-14, 43, 60-63

The Grace of God

Ezekiel 16 is the longest chapter in the book. It is an important chapter in that it reveals what God did for Israel and what Israel did to God. It presents the **grace of God** and a picture of God's people **leaving their first love.**

Israel's Lost Condition. In the first five verses, God tells what Jerusalem was. She was in her sins and abominations without any hope. She did not belong to the Lord. Here we have a picture of the lost sinner (Ephesians 2:11, 12).

God's Grace Manifested. In verse six God came to this poor lost people and said, " . . . *Live* . . . " Then He made it perfectly clear by adding: " . . . *yea, I said unto thee when thou wast in thy blood, Live.*" God came to me as a poor lost sinner and gave me the same command. Praise God, through the new birth and by His grace, I was given life. Israel did not receive life because of her merit, but because of the matchless, marvelous grace of God.

Note what God did when He acted toward Israel in grace:

First, He clothed Israel (v. 8). Second, He entered into a covenant with Israel—this would be a marriage covenant (v. 8). Third, He washed Israel (v. 9). Fourth, He gave Israel the Holy Spirit (v. 9)— " . . . *I anointed thee with oil.*" Fifth, He gave Israel the garments of salvation and the ornaments of marriage (vv. 10-13). This tells us that Israel partook of the divine nature.

But Israel Left Their First Love. Verse fifteen states that Israel trusted in the beauty she had, rather than resting on the promise of God. Verse forty-three reads: *"Because thou hast not remembered the days of thy youth . . . "* Israel forgot God's grace and left her first love, as did the church in Ephesus (Revelation 2:4).

God's Grace for the Future. God reveals that in the future, even in spite of Israel's sin, He will deal with her in grace (vv. 60-63).

Bible Truth for Today: *"For by grace are ye saved through faith; and that not of yourselves: it is the gift of God."* —Ephesians 2:8

September 8

Read Ezekiel 17–19
Family Reading: Ezekiel 18:1-23

Individual Responsibility

One of the great principles of the Bible is presented in this chapter: judgment is according to individual conduct. Apparently the Israelites were using a proverb which said that the people of Israel were suffering because of their fathers' sins. Note the statement given in verse two. God said He did not want such a proverb used any longer (v. 3). In verse four He stated: *" . . . the soul that sinneth, it shall die."* Following that, He gave illustrations of this. One of the illustrations was that of a son who sees his father's sin and decides he does not want to live like that (v. 14). Verse seventeen states clearly: *" . . . he shall not die for the iniquity of his father, he shall surely live."* Verse twenty states it definitely again: *"The soul that sinneth, it shall die. The son shall not bear the iniquity of the father, neither shall the father bear the iniquity of the son: the righteousness of the righteous shall be upon him, and the wickedness of the wicked shall be upon him."* God states it clearly that each one has individual responsibility.

Then beginning in verse twenty-one, He speaks of the wicked man who decides to turn from his wicked ways. The Lord states that he can live and his transgressions will not be mentioned—they can be pardoned. For God asks the question in verse twenty-three, *"Have I any pleasure at all that the wicked should die? . . . and not that he should return from his ways, and live?"* God does not delight in the death of the wicked; His pleasure is that the wicked turn from his evil way and live.

Therefore, God invites the Israelites to repent and turn from their transgressions in verses 30-32. He states again at the close of the chapter, *"For I have no pleasure in the death of him that dieth . . . "* God longs for souls to turn to Him; that is why He gave His Son. He is waiting for you today to let Him have His way in your life.

Bible Principle for Today: *"The Lord is not slack concerning his promise, as some men count slackness; but is longsuffering to us-ward, not willing that any should perish, but that all should come to repentance." —II Peter 3:9*

September 9

Read Ezekiel 20 and 21
Family Reading: Ezekiel 21:1-7, 18-32

The Right of the Lord

"I will overturn, overturn, overturn, it: and it shall be no more,
until he come whose right it is; and I will give it him."

— Ezekiel 21:27

There is One who will come, *" . . . whose right it is . . . "* There
is a King who has a right to the throne and to the allegiance of His
subjects. He has a right to all that they offer and all that they have.

How did He gain this right?

First, He gained this right by the gift of the Father. Jesus said,
"All that the Father giveth me shall come to me . . . " (John 6:37). In
His prayer in John 17, Jesus repeatedly referred to those who are
saved as those whom the Father had given Him. Therefore, since the
Father gave us to the Son, the Lord Jesus has a right to all that we are.

Second, He has this right because He has purchased and redeemed
us with His own blood. He laid down His life for us, thereby buying
us and establishing a right to our lives by completely paying the price.

He exercises this two-fold right every time He lays a solemn
claim on any one of the people whom He has purchased. The Lord is
not satisfied with merely having a right to the persons of His dear
people; He must have their hearts and their affections as well. He
wants to reign and rule in their lives so that He can be King and Lord
there.

Ezekiel 21 not only talks about the Lord having a right to our
lives but also refers to the fact that He will come as King and exercise
His right to rule the world. Praise God, our King is coming!

Bible Truth for Today: *"Whether therefore ye eat, or drink, or what-*
soever ye do, do all to the glory of God."

— I Corinthians 10:31

September 10

Read Ezekiel 22 and 23
Family Reading: Ezekiel 22:13-31

God Needs Men

"And I sought for a man among them, that should make up the hedge, and stand in the gap before me for the land, that I should not destroy it: but I found none." — *Ezekiel 22:30*

God said that He sought for a man that should make up the hedge and stand in the gap for Him. The tragedy is He did not find a man. Israel was in a dreadful condition. Especially was this true in the city of Jerusalem. In verse two God calls Jerusalem the *"bloody city"* with *"all her abominations."* In the remainder of the chapter, God repeatedly emphasizes the fact that Jerusalem was a bloody city, shedding blood. God warned of judgment that would come. In verse fifteen He warned that the inhabitants of Jerusalem would be scattered among the heathen. Throughout the rest of the chapter God speaks of the wickedness and sin of Jerusalem and the nation of Judah. The country was in sad condition, and God's hope was that He could find a man who could lead.

Always remember that God works through men. God did not seek a committee or a board—He sought for a man. His heart was broken because He did not find a man who was willing to be used. Oh, how God longs for souls to be willing to let Him use them for His glory.

I believe today it is true that God seeks for men and does not find them—men who are willing to sacrifice and surrender everything to the Lord Jesus Christ. Our nation and this world need men who will mean business for God.

Remember, today you can do something for the Lord. You may say, "Why, I am only one." But I say to you, "Remember that you are **one**." God uses individuals. He is seeking for them today. Won't you let God speak to you about what He wants you to do in His work? Let Him have control of your life and you will be amazed what He can accomplish through you.

Bible Principle for Today: *"I beseech you therefore, brethren, by the mercies of God, that ye present your bodies a living sacrifice, holy, acceptable unto God, which is your reasonable service."*

— Romans 12:1

September 11

Read Ezekiel 24–26
Family Reading: Ezekiel 25

The Judgment of the Nations

In these chapters God promised to judge nations according to their attitude toward His people Israel and His city Jerusalem. God tells Babylon He will judge that nation because the king " . . . *set himself against Jerusalem . . . " (24:2)*. God judged Tyre because they had " . . . *said against Jerusalem, Aha, she is broken that was the gates of the people . . . " (26:2)*. In Chapter 25 God gave repeated warnings because various nations had spoken against Jerusalem and Israel. This should make nations that oppose Israel today take heed. God's Word says He will judge them on the basis of their attitude toward Israel. Let's note some of these judgments.

In Ezekiel 25:3 God told the Ammonites He would bring judgment " . . . *Because thou saidst, Aha, against my sanctuary, when it was profaned; and against the land of Israel, when it was desolate; and against the house of Judah, when they went into captivity . . . . "* God warned in verses six and seven that because they had clapped their hands and stomped their feet with all their despite against the land of Israel, there would be a stretched-out hand from God, and the Ammonites would be delivered as a spoil. Ammon today is Jordan; the capital of Jordan is Amman. It is the center of the area that the Ammonites inhabited. Because they resisted Israel, they experienced God's judgment, and Jordan is desolate.

God warned Moab in Ezekiel 25:8. In verses twelve to fourteen He warned Edom: " . . . *Because that Edom hath dealt against the house of Judah by taking vengeance, and hath greatly offended . . . I will also stretch out mine hand upon Edom . . . . "* Any nation that resists Israel is going to experience the judgment of God.

Tyrus is a prime example of how severely God judges. He warned that the city would be removed and the waves of the sea would lap over where the city had been. Chapter 26 tells that judgment came to Tyrus because they resisted Israel. God's judgment is definite. He will fulfill His promise. Certainly nations need to be on guard against a wrong attitude about Israel, God's people.

September 12

Read Ezekiel 27–29
Family Reading: Ezekiel 28

Know the Lord

A characteristic phrase of the book of Ezekiel is *"they shall know that I am the Lord."* In Ezekiel 26:6 God says of Tyre: *" . . . they shall know that I am the Lord."* God told Tyre that He would judge them. In Ezekiel 28:2 He explains why: *" . . . Because thine heart is lifted up, and thou hast said, I am a God, I sit in the seat of God, in the midst of the seas; yet thou art a man, and not God, though thou set thine heart as the heart of God."* Tyre was to know that she was not God but that there is a God in Heaven. God told Edom He would make them know He is God by the vengeance He would send (Ezekiel 24:14). God's judgment reveals that He is the Lord God.

God announces three times that Zidon would know that He is the Lord God (28:22-24). This would be revealed by God's judgments on her. One thing God held against Zidon was that she was a *"pricking brier"* unto the house of Israel (v. 24). God will hold nations accountable for the way they have treated the Jews. Hitler and his Nazi cohorts learned this truth the hard way. God does not let a ruler nor a nation get by with despising His chosen nation Israel. (Note also Ezekiel 25:3, 4; 12:12, 13, 15.) God said in Genesis 12:3—*" . . . I will bless them that bless thee, and curse him that curseth thee . . ."* God reveals the fulfillment of this in Ezekiel 25–28.

Israel will know that God is the Lord (Ezekiel 28:26). God will reveal this to Israel by preserving them and restoring them to the land. He wants all the world to know that He is the Lord God. Let us make Him Lord of our lives.

> *I shall know Him, I shall know Him,*
> *And redeemed by His side I shall stand.*
> *I shall know Him, I shall know Him,*
> *By the print of the nails in His hand.*
> *—Fanny Crosby*

Bible Truth for Today: *" . . . yea, they shall dwell with confidence, when I have executed judgments upon all those that despise them round about them; and they shall know that I am the Lord their God."*
—Ezekiel 28:26

September 13

Read Ezekiel 30–32
Family Reading: Ezekiel 31

The Pearl of Pride

In Ezekiel 31 we read of the pride that plagued Egypt. In yesterday's reading we saw the danger of pride in Tyre. Pride is a dreadful enemy, and in verse two God asks Pharaoh, the king of Egypt, this question, " . . . *Whom art thou like in thy greatness?*" Then God answers the question by stating that Egypt was like the king of Assyria. This king was overthrown by the power of God through the Babylonians, and God predicted that Egypt would have the same fate.

Really, none of us have anything of which to be proud. The king of Assyria really had no right to be proud since everything he had was given to him. Verse four states that he was made great by the waters of the sea and the waters of the rivers. His tree grew great, and then fowls of the heaven came to lodge in it. Verse nine states that he was fair because God made him that way.

The same was true of Egypt. Pharaoh was great because of God's provision—the river of Egypt. God warned Pharaoh to recognize that any greatness he had received had come from God. This is true in each of our lives. The individual who begins to get proud will be defeated. God told Pharaoh, " . . . *yet shalt thou be brought down with the trees of Eden unto the nether parts of the earth . . .* " *(v. 18)*.

Note these verses: *"Humble yourselves therefore under the mighty hand of God, that he may exalt you in due time" (I Peter 5:6)." "Submit yourselves therefore to God. Resist the devil, and he will flee from you" (James 4:7).* Attacks of Satan come with pride. Attacks of Satan are defeated as we humble ourselves.

Proverb for Today: *"Commit thy works unto the Lord, and thy thoughts shall be established." —Proverbs 16:3*

September 14

Read Ezekiel 33–35
Family Reading: Ezekiel 33:1-20

The Responsibility of Being a Watchman

What a responsibility it is to be a watchman! When Cain answered the Lord in Genesis 4, he insolently asked, " . . . *Am I my brother's keeper?"* He is a picture of the unsaved who are strangely and definitely unconcerned with the needs of others. This attitude of Cain must never be characteristic of the attitude of the child of God. We are always to consider it our primary concern that the spiritual needs of others be met. The time is short and we need to be busy in His service.

As believers we should act as watchmen. In Ezekiel 33:2 God says that Israel was to take a man as a watchman. If, when he saw the sword coming, he would warn the people, then they could not blame him for their destruction. But if he failed to warn the people, their blood would be upon his hands. Every child of God is a watchman to warn someone else. We need to be faithful to warn others to turn from their sin and trust the Lord Jesus Christ.

Ezekiel was a faithful watchman. He endeavored to warn Israel. He had done so consistently. Israel still failed and Jerusalem fell, but the blood was not on the hands of Ezekiel.

You and I are watchmen. Have we been faithful? Have we been faithful to warn others who are living in sin and going on the broad road to destruction? How important it is to warn others and not let them go into destruction!

In this passage we find two people who have responsibility. There is the responsibility of the watchman and there is the responsibility of the hearer. Verse eleven tells us that God has " . . . *no pleasure in the death of the wicked."* He wants the watchman to warn, but He also wants the hearer to listen. If the hearer fails to heed the warning, he will die in his iniquity, but the watchman has delivered his soul from responsibility. If the hearer listens, he shall live by the will of God.

Character Verse: *"Whoso despiseth the word shall be destroyed: but he that feareth the commandment shall be rewarded."*

—Proverbs 13:13

September 15

Read Ezekiel 36–38
Family Reading: Ezekiel 36:16-38

A New Heart

One who is born again has a new heart, lives under a new government with his laws coming from the Word of God, serves a new Master, is influenced by a new love, is actuated by a new reverential fear, and is animated with new delights and joys.

II Corinthians 5:17 explains and defines this new heart: *"Therefore if any man be in Christ, he is a new creature: old things are passed away; behold, all things are become new."*

In Ezekiel 36 God tells us what He planned to do for Israel. In verse twenty-two He announces that the message is to Israel. Then in verse twenty-six He states that of all the things He will do for Israel, one of them is that He will give Israel a new heart. *"A new heart also will I give you, and a new spirit will I put within you: and I will take away the stony heart out of your flesh, and I will give you an heart of flesh"* (v. 26).

This is God's promise to Israel. But it is exactly what He does for everyone who trusts Him by faith and is *"born again."* Only God can change a heart. And you can be assured that He will give a new heart to that person who trusts in the Lord. A new heart means a change of life.

Martin Luther said: "A Christian is a new creature in a new world."

Everything should be new to the child of God. We have a new heart and a new spirit. That new heart will lead us into a life of blessing and victory. Some believer may say, "I believe I have a new heart, but my experience points me the other way. I find within me some desires to sin and do wrong." Yes, that is very typical. The Bible teaches that we have an old man and a new man. We are to put off the old man, and we are to put on the new man (Ephesians 4:22-24).

Bible Truth for Today: *" . . . ye have put off the old man with his deeds; And have put on the new man, which is renewed in knowledge after the image of him that created him."* —Colossians 3:9, 10

September 16

Read Ezekiel 39 and 40
Family Reading: Ezekiel 39:1-17 and 25-29

Judgment on Russia

Ezekiel 38 and 39 give us the prophecy against Gog, the northern European power headed by Russia, moving down to the Middle East. God says that the final battle will be *" . . . upon the mountains of Israel" (v. 2)*. There Russia will be defeated and *" . . . fall upon the mountains of Israel, thou, and all thy bands, and the people that is with thee . . . " (v. 4)*. God says that the fire will extend to the isles (v. 6)—the coast lands and the islands of the Mediterranean. Though the judgment on the enemies will occur in Israel, the catastrophe will extend to the ends of the earth to accomplish the purpose of God.

This is going to be such a vast destruction that it will take seven years to burn all of the instruments of warfare that were brought into the land (v. 9). There will be a dreadful odor of putrefaction all over the land until men will want to stop the noses (v. 11). It will take seven months to bury all of the bodies (v. 12). What a dreadful time is coming after the church has been caught up to be with the Lord. Events are moving toward the fulfillment of this right now. Russia is allied with Iran (Persia of Ezekiel 38:5) and is constantly stirring the pot of war against Israel.

Be sure to keep your eyes on the land of Palestine. It is there where final great battles will take place. As things shape up today, it appears that the coming of the Lord is not far away. We each need to be prepared. You can be ready by having your faith in Jesus Christ as Lord and then by living in obedience to His Word.

Bible Truth for Today: *"And now, little children, abide in him; that, when he shall appear, we may have confidence, and not be ashamed before him at his coming." —I John 2:28*

September 17

Read Ezekiel 41–43
Family Reading: Ezekiel 43:1-12, 18-27

The Glory of the Lord

The last section of the prophecy of Ezekiel speaks of the future glory that will come to the nation of Israel. This section, comprising nine chapters from Ezekiel 40 through 48, presents the temple of Israel during the millennial kingdom. To read these last nine chapters of Ezekiel in their literal force is to learn that God has glorious plans in view *for* Israel and *through* Israel for all the earth.

In the temple there is no reference to the Ark of the Covenant. Actually, the glory of the Lord fills all of the temple. In all of the references to the millennial temple, not only in Ezekiel, but also in all of the prophets, there is no reference to a king because Christ is the King. In the millennial age, the world will see fulfillment of what Paul prophesied when he wrote, " . . . *Christ is all, and in all"* *(Colossians 3:11)*.

Do not forget that predictions of blessings never carry with them assurance. Individual blessing comes from a personal response of faith in the Lord Jesus Christ, our living Saviour. Blessings to the individual are to " . . . *them that believe on his name" (John 1:12)*.

In Chapter 43 Ezekiel speaks of the glory of God. This glory filling the house was something new to Ezekiel since in the first part of the book he gave much space to the departing of the Shekinah glory from the temple. Ezekiel was heartbroken over God's abandonment of His house because he knew that it meant Israel's ultimate destruction. Ezekiel 10:19 and 11:23 state that the glory of the Lord was lifted above the city. Now in Ezekiel 43 the glory of the Lord will return and fill the house. When this takes place, Israel is cleansed and her abominations put away. As Israel sees her sins and is ashamed, God promises great blessings (vv. 9-12).

It is the Lord who is this glory. The second verse tells of His voice and His glory. His presence in that day fills the house and the earth with His glory and majesty.

Bible Prophecy for Today: *" . . . The kingdoms of this world are become the kingdoms of our Lord, and of his Christ; and he shall reign for ever and ever." —Revelation 11:15*

September 18

Read Ezekiel 44–46
Family Reading: Ezekiel 44:1-23

The Cleansed Priesthood

God warns that the uncircumcised in heart and flesh should not continue as Levites and priests (v. 9). The reference is to those priests who apostasized during all the periods when idolatry was rife in Israel. During the millennial age when righteousness will rule, mercy will not be lacking because the priests will not be excluded from all types of ministry. They will lose the dignity of higher services but will have the privilege of being ministers at the gate of the outer court.

The ministry of the priest will be to teach the people the difference between the holy and profane. This is given in verse twenty-three, a very important verse for those who minister in the work of the Lord: *"And they shall teach my people the difference between . . . the unclean and the clean."* The Lord reiterates that the priests' inheritance is in the Lord (v. 28). They can expect to live from the offerings of the people and rest in the promise of God.

The fact that man is estranged from God is something dreadfully sad in itself. God is robbed of fellowship and love that rightfully belong to Him. There is something equally as tragic, or maybe worse, and that is the fact that God is denied the glory in service that should be His from those who have been redeemed by His blood. Let us render to Him the service we owe Him with love and gratitude.

Bible Truth for Today: *"Having therefore these promises, dearly beloved, let us cleanse ourselves from all filthiness of the flesh and spirit, perfecting holiness in the fear of God."* — *II Corinthians 7:1*

September 19

Read Ezekiel 47 and 48 and Daniel 1
Family Reading: Daniel 1

God's Great Man: Daniel

One of the most thrilling characters of the Old Testament is Daniel. He was a man who lived all out for the Lord—even while he was a teenager. In Chapter 1 Daniel was probably sixteen or seventeen years old. As a teenager " . . . *Daniel purposed in his heart that he would not defile himself with the portion of the king's meat, nor with the wine which he drank . . . " (v. 8).* Therefore, he asked the prince of the eunuchs, who was in charge of developing these Israelites, that he might not defile himself. He was determined that his life was going to be lived for the glory of God.

In Ezekiel 14:14 Daniel, as a living man, is recognized as an outstanding spiritual man, possessing power with God; and he is listed with two men who had lived years before. He, Noah, and Job are listed as three men so righteous that they could be expected to hold back the judgment of God. The fact that Daniel is listed, while he was still living, tells us of the holy life he must have been living. He began this holy life back when he was a teenager.

No man has ever been more greatly used than Daniel. The reason for his widely used testimony was the fact that he was totally yielded to the Lord. He was a man of faith whose name, *Daniel*, meant *"God be my Judge."* He, by faith, purposed in his heart that he would live for the Lord and would not defile himself.

Because he made such a commitment to God, Daniel became a man with an unusual testimony. For example, please read Daniel 6:4, 5. I give a partial quote: *"Then the presidents and princes sought to find occasion against Daniel concerning the kingdom; but they could find none occasion nor fault . . . Then said these men, We shall not find any occasion against this Daniel . . . "*

Can you imagine it? Here is Daniel, in a high public position. They could examine all the records, all his speeches, and all his actions. And they could not find one single occasion, error, or fault. Why? How do you explain this? It is a direct result of his vow as a teenager that he would not defile himself. He lived for God and had a testimony that rang true. Praise God for a man like Daniel.

September 20

Read Daniel 2 and 3
Family Reading: Daniel 2:1-28

Prayer and Praise

Daniel believed in praying and seeking the mind of the Lord. He believed that God could give him the wisdom to show Nebuchadnezzar his dream. He approached Arioch, the captain of the king's guard, who was in charge of the mass slaying of the wise men of the land. He then had opportunity to approach the king, who gave him time to receive an answer.

Daniel immediately asked his three companions to pray, requesting God to reveal this truth to him. The answer came. God is faithful to keep His promise, and Daniel was faithful to praise the Lord. He blessed the Lord by praising: *"Blessed be the name of God for ever and ever: for wisdom and might are his" (v. 20).* Daniel's praise revealed his humble spirit and his proper attitude concerning the Lord. He loved the Lord with all his heart and said, *"I thank thee, and praise thee, O thou God of my fathers, who hast given me wisdom and might, and hast made known unto me now what we desired of thee . . ." (v. 23).*

Daniel not only praised the Lord in his own private devotions but also testified publicly concerning God's faithfulness. He told the king, *"But there is a God in heaven that revealeth secrets, and maketh known to the king Nebuchadnezzar what shall be in the latter days . . ." (v. 28).* God longs for every one of His children to seek Him and His direction. Then when we have received His answer to our prayer, we should humbly praise Him and testify to others of His miraculous grace.

Prayer Promise for Today: *"Hitherto have ye asked nothing in my name: ask, and ye shall receive, that your joy may be full."*

—John 16:24

Read Daniel 4–6
Family Reading: Daniel 4:18-37

Danger of Pride

This passage presents an unusual story with an excellent lesson for us all. Nebuchadnezzar took the glory of his kingdom for himself as though he had done it. He asked in verse thirty: *" . . . Is not this great Babylon, that I have built for the house of the kingdom by the might of my power, and for the honor of my majesty?"* Nebuchadnezzar had known better than this. At least he had said in Daniel 2:47 that Daniel's God *" . . . is a God of gods, and a Lord of kings."* Again in Daniel 3:29 he announced that no god could deliver like the God of Shadrach, Meshach, and Abednego. How soon had he forgotten that the God of the Hebrews is the Lord of kings! He was anxious to take the glory for himself.

Nebuchadnezzar was actually no different from any of us. All of us have an innate desire to get glory for ourselves and to fail to honor the Lord. In Jeremiah 45 we find that Baruch had this problem. God spoke to him: *"And seekest thou great things for thyself? seek them not: for, behold, I will bring evil upon all flesh . . . " (v. 5).* The reason that we have this problem is found in Jeremiah 17:9, *"The heart is deceitful above all things, and desperately wicked: who can know it?"* We have a sinful nature that would love to glorify self above the Lord.

Nebuchadnezzar became insane. He acted like a beast of the field. But one day his sanity returned, and then he gave the glory to God.

In Daniel 4:34 and 37 he made some wonderful statements about God. Then he stated that God was able to abase the proud. Nebuchadnezzar had to be knocked down in order to come to his proper senses.

Bible Truth for Today: *"I am the Lord: that is my name: and my glory will I not give to another, neither my praise to graven images."*

— Isaiah 42:8

September 22

Read Daniel 7–9
Family Reading: Daniel 9:1-19

Daniel—Greatly Beloved

Gabriel told Daniel, " *. . . thou art greatly beloved . . . " (vv. 23).* Why would God make such an outstanding statement about Daniel? The name *Daniel* means *God is my judge.* Everything about Daniel's life manifested the fact that he believed God was his judge. When a man believes that he is going to answer to God for his words and actions, his life will be different.

Daniel realized by study that there would be seventy years of desolation for Jerusalem (v. 2). He immediately sought God in prayer and supplication. Certainly, as God's greatly beloved man, he carried a heavy burden concerning the sins of God's people. Note his confession: *"We have sinned, and have committed iniquity, and have done wickedly, and have rebelled . . . Neither have we hearkened unto thy servants . . . Yea, all Israel have transgressed thy law . . . " (vv. 5, 6, 11).*

One reason Daniel realized Israel's sin was the fact that he also recognized God's holy attributes. Note what Daniel realized concerning the character of God:

Faithfulness of God—" *. . . keeping the covenant and mercy to them that love him . . . " (v. 4).*

Righteousness of God—*"O Lord, righteousness belongeth unto thee . . . " (v. 7). " . . . for the Lord our God is righteous in all his works which he doeth . . . " (v. 14).*

Mercy and Forgiveness of God—*"To the Lord our God belong mercies and forgivenesses . . . " (v. 9).*

Proverb for Today: *"The Lord is far from the wicked: but he heareth the prayer of the righteous." —Proverbs 15:29*

September 23

Read Daniel 10–12
Family Reading: Daniel 11:36-45 and Daniel 12

The Two Resurrections

Daniel 12:2 reveals the truth concerning the resurrection of the body. The Bible teaches clearly that there will be a resurrection of those who have died. Some will be raised to everlasting life, and some will be raised to shame and everlasting contempt.

Many today think there is only one general resurrection. They have the unscriptural notion that everyone will be raised to face a judgment. At that judgment if the good deeds outweigh the bad deeds, these people believe that God will say, "You have been good enough; you can come on in to Heaven." But if the bad deeds outweigh the good deeds, they think God will say, "I am so sorry; you will have to go to Hell."

Nothing could be farther from the truth! The Bible truth is that there will be two resurrections: the first for those who have been saved, and the second for those who have not been saved. Whether a person goes to Heaven is not decided after he dies. That is settled on the basis of whether he has accepted Jesus Christ. One who has trusted Christ has eternal life. Without Christ a person is lost and will be in Hell.

In addition, Daniel 12:3 reveals that the saved person who lives wisely to the glory of God will receive special reward in Heaven. Friend, have you accepted Christ? If not, please do so today. If you have received Christ, are you living to please Him today?

Bible Truth for Today: *"Marvel not at this: for the hour is coming, in the which all that are in the graves shall hear his voice, And shall come forth; they that have done good, unto the resurrection of life; and they that have done evil, unto the resurrection of damnation."*
—John 5:28, 29

September 24

Read Hosea 1–6
Family Reading: Hosea 4:6-11 and 5:1-15

God's Judgment Coming

Hosea is the first book of the section in our Bibles that we often refer to as The Minor Prophets. The reason this title has been given is that these last twelve books of the Old Testament are shorter books than Isaiah, Jeremiah, Ezekiel, or Daniel—not that they are any less important. Their messages are very relevant for today. You could almost hold the minor prophets in one hand and the daily newspaper in another and have them fit together.

Hosea is pleading with Israel to turn back to the Lord. As a nation, Israel had been unfaithful to the Lord. Hosea had married an unfaithful wife, but he still loved her (Hosea 3). His domestic life had become a living example to Israel of her failure to be faithful to the Lord. With deep compassion Hosea was able to plead with Israel to return to the Lord.

The prophet warned the nation that judgment would come. No nation can separate from God without paying a bitter price in judgment. This judgment comes in various ways. God presents one of these ways in Hosea 5:12—*"Therefore will I be unto Ephraim as a moth, and to the house of Judah as rottenness."* Moths eat slowly, and rottenness moves slowly. When a nation fails to be faithful to God, judgment may move slowly; but judgment will move certainly unless some drastic action is taken to correct it. Finally, judgment will come another way—as a young lion snatching the prey (Hosea 5:14).

America has been in the moth and rottenness stage. Unless there is revival in America, she will move into the young lion stage.

The Cause That Produced the Sinful Nation: *"My people are destroyed for **lack of knowledge**: because thou hast **rejected knowledge**, I will also reject thee . . ."* —Hosea 4:6

September 25

Read Hosea 7–12
Family Reading: Hosea 10

Break Up Your Fallow Ground

God commanded Israel to break up her fallow ground (v. 12). Fallow ground is different from virgin soil. Fallow ground has been plowed and cultivated and has produced a crop. It has been permitted to lie idle for a time. Wheat farmers know that if their wheat ground lies fallow every other year, they will actually harvest more wheat. As the ground lies fallow, the farmer kills the weeds so that valuable moisture is retained.

God said that Israel had fallow ground. Because Israel had not been careful to destroy the weeds of sin, indifference had come. In Jeremiah 4:3 God commanded, " . . . *Break up your fallow ground, and sow not among thorns."*

In the spiritual realm we should never let the ground lie fallow. God wants us to produce fruit for Him consistently. We must break up the fallow ground and bear fruit for the Lord. The Lord will not bless any growth of thorns or weeds in the field of His service.

We can detect the time when it will be necessary to break up the fallow ground. *"Israel is an empty vine . . . " (Hosea 10:1).* When the ground is lying idle and no fruit is being borne, this is the first indication of fallow ground. God desires fruit in the life of His child.

The second indication of fallow ground is idolatry in the worship. Too often there is no life or blessing in the worship services conducted in the churches. Men have to turn to something—idol worship—as the Israelites did. God condemns idolatry as fallow ground that must be broken up.

A third mark of fallow ground is found in verse two. God says Israel had a divided heart. They were not settled with one purpose in serving the Lord.

A fourth mark of fallow ground is in broken covenants. Verse four speaks of making a covenant and not keeping it. This can be the covenant to have daily devotions or to be a tither or to be faithful in church. Let us beware of fallow ground that needs to be turned.

September 26

Read Hosea 13 and 14 and Joel 1 and 2
Family Reading: Hosea 13 and 14

God's Yearning Tenderness

The last chapter of Hosea presents the lovingkindness of our God even toward a backslider who has departed from the Lord. God manifests the same yearning tenderness our Lord Jesus Christ revealed when He wept over Jerusalem. In this chapter the Lord begs His people to return but also tells them exactly how they should go about it.

First, God invites them to return. In love He cries, *"O Israel, return unto the Lord thy God; for thou hast fallen by thine iniquity" (14:1).* Israel has proven the truth that the way of transgressors is hard. They have fallen very low, yet He who has been so grievously sinned against lovingly entreats them to return.

Then Hosea gives them the very words to use. He tells them to pray to the Lord, *" . . . Take away all iniquity, and receive us graciously: so will we render the calves of our lips" (v. 2).* This is the kind of prayer every child of God needs to learn. We must confess sin and ask God for cleansing. It is sin that separates us from God. Daily we should pray, *"Take away all iniquity."* This is the soul's longing. Sin becomes hateful once the soul is in the presence of God. It is then that the need of grace is realized. Therefore, the next part of the prayer is, *" . . . receive us graciously . . . "* Praise God that in His grace He hears the prayer of repentance and does receive us!

Hosea 14:4-7 presents the promises God gives to Israel if she prayerfully returns to the Lord. In His tenderness, love, and mercy, the Lord is ready to take a backslider back. That backslider must recognize his sin and the fact that no one else can help—not Asshur (Assyria) nor idols (v. 3). Only the Lord can save.

> *Amazing grace! How sweet the sound,*
> *That saved a wretch like me.*
> *I once was lost, but now am found,*
> *Was blind, but now I see.*

September 27

Read Joel 3 and Amos 1–4
Family Reading: Amos 1 and 2:1-5

A Bold Prophet Pronouncing Judgment

Amos is an outstanding and singular figure among the Old Testament prophets. He wrote with force and forthrightness. He begins the book by introducing himself in verse one: *"The words of Amos, who was among the herdmen of Tekoa . . . "* He had been a herdman tending sheep in Tekoa, south of Bethlehem. In Amos 7:14,15 he gives a brief biography of himself and speaks of his call.

"Then answered Amos, and said to Amaziah, I was no prophet, neither was I a prophet's son; but I was an herdman, and a gatherer of sycamore fruit: And the Lord took me as I followed the flock, and the Lord said unto me, Go, prophesy unto my people Israel."

Amos knew he was called of God. He had no doubt about his divine call. He said, *"The Lord said unto me, Go prophesy . . . "* No wonder he could cry out again and again: *"Thus saith the Lord."* Amos spoke plainly and bluntly in showing the people their sin. He was the kind of prophet-preacher that is needed all over the world today. As I read Amos, I think of these lines by Charles Wesley:

> *Shall I, to soothe the unholy throng,*
> *Soften Thy truth or smooth my tongue,*
> *To gain earth's gelded toys, or flee*
> *The cross endured, my Lord, by Thee?*

In the first two chapters one phrase appears many times. It is, *"For three transgressions . . . and for four . . . "* God is saying with this phrase that the transgressions have come to the full. He was saying they had actually become more than full—really that they had gone on too far in going on in their sin. When Israel had done evil the first time, God brought rebuke. The second time God threatened. At the third time, God had raised His hand ready to smite. But now Israel had gone one more—the fourth time—and God was going to bring judgment. God is not mocked! Cumulative sin will be judged with cumulative retribution.

Bible Command for Today: *"Therefore thus will I do unto thee, O Israel: and because I will do this unto thee, prepare to meet thy God, O Israel."* —Amos 4:12

September 28

Read Amos 5–9
Family Reading: Amos 7:14-17 and Chapter 8

Famine in the Land

God announced there would be a famine in the land of Israel—not a famine of bread, nor a thirst for water, but a famine of hearing the words of the Lord (8:11). He said that people would " . . . *wander from sea to sea, and from the north even to the east, . . .* " thereby covering the land for the purpose of seeking the Word of the Lord. And then God added that they " . . . *shall not find it" (v. 12).* There was a dreadful famine of hearing the Word of the Lord in Israel.

It has happened in America. I have noted during election campaigns that some churches turn their Sunday morning services over to debates by candidates for office. I believe in learning where the candidates stand, and I believe in taking an active part as a citizen. But I do not believe in using the church service to have a political debate between candidates. People come to church to hear the Word of God. There certainly is a famine of real Bible preaching in America today.

I can think of nothing worse than for people to be deceived in a church. They think they are going to church to learn about God, but instead some unbelieving, liberal preacher gives them everything but the Bible. Oh, the judgment that will come to preachers who fail to give their people the Word of God! They are blind and leaders of the blind. They are leading souls straight to Hell. Those who sit in the pews in front of them are unsuspecting souls, being led astray, away from God and away from salvation.

There does not need to be a famine in your life, for there are wonderful Bible-preaching churches today giving forth the whole counsel of God. Be sure you are saved and are part of a church that preaches the Bible.

Thot: Don't continue to support the Ichabod Memorial Church, where Dr. Soothing Syrup is the pastor and where he looks at his congregation through rose-colored glasses every Sunday and sprinkles ethical perfume on everybody.

Biblical Command: *"Preach the word . . . . "* —II Timothy 4:2

Read Obadiah, Jonah, and Micah 1
Family Reading: Jonah 1 and 2

Salvation Is of the Lord

"But I will sacrifice unto thee with the voice of thanksgiving; I will pay that that I have vowed. Salvation is of the Lord."

—Jonah 2:9

Jonah cried out, *"Salvation is of the Lord."* He was in the belly of the great fish, a picture of the fact that Jesus died and was buried. Jonah knew his only hope was in the Lord. He cried, *"Salvation is of the Lord."*

Salvation is the work of God alone. No one and nothing else can quicken the soul that is *" . . . dead in trespasses and sins" (Ephesians 2:1).* He saves from the penalty of sin and also is the only One who can save us from the power of sin and preserve us in our spiritual life. Christ is both the *" . . . Alpha and Omega, the beginning and the ending . . . " (Revelation 1:8).* He saves and He keeps. Believers *" . . . are kept by the power of God through faith unto salvation . . . " (I Peter 1:5).*

Do we suppose we do anything of ourselves? If we are prayerful, God makes us prayerful. If I live a good, consistent testimony, it is because He upholds me with His hand. If I have had victory over a sin or some spiritual enemy, it is only because the Lord's arm strengthened me.

Have I become a separated believer? It is only because He has weaned me from the world by His grace and power.

Do I live a consecrated life? It is not I, but Christ that liveth in me (Galatians 2:20).

Do I grow in grace and knowledge? He, the Great Teacher, instructs and leads me. As a branch cannot bear fruit except it abide in the vine, no more can I except as I trust Him (John 15:4).

Bible Principle: *" . . . for without me ye can do nothing."*

—John 15:5

September 30

Read Micah 2–7
Family Reading: Micah 5

Our Great Shepherd

In the first few verses of Micah, we find many truths concerning the eternal existence of our Lord. We note that He is from eternity, *" . . . whose goings forth have been from of old, from everlasting"* *(Micah 5:2).* This One from everlasting was to be born of a virgin in Bethlehem in the land of Judah. He who is God for all eternity has come to earth to redeem sinful men. Verse four tells of His reign as King in the age yet to come. Between His coming to earth and His reign as King, there is a time when He is rejected. *"Therefore will He give them up, until the time that she which travaileth hath brought forth: then the remnant of his brethren shall return unto the children of Israel"* *(v. 3).*

During His life on earth through the time of His cross, and during this Church Age, the age in which we are living today, Christ has been rejected. The world as a whole rejects Him today. II Corinthians 4:4 states that Satan is *" . . . the god of this world . . . "* While the world bows before Satan, there are those who have come to Christ by faith and trusted Him. Praise God!

The reign that Christ will exert in His kingdom is characterized in His reign over the Church today. It is the supremacy of a wise and tender Shepherd over His needy and trusting flock.

His reign is practical in character. In verse four we read: *"And he shall stand and feed . . . "* Our Chief Shepherd is actively engaged in providing for His people. He does not sit down but stands and feeds. The Word for *"feed"* here carries with it the idea of *shepherding.* He guides, watches, restores, preserves, and protects, as well as feeds.

Note, also, that it is in the continuing present tense. *"And he shall stand and feed."* It does not say, "He shall stand and feed occasionally." Nor does it read, "He shall one day grant revival, and the next day leave His Church to barrenness." Psalm 121 tells us that He never slumbers nor sleeps. He is ever caring and feeding, and He does it in the everlasting strength of Jehovah. Happy should we be to belong to such a Shepherd!

October 1

Read Nahum 1–3 and Habakkuk 1–3
Family Reading: Habakkuk 1:1-17; 2:1-4

Rejoice—No Matter What!

The prophecy of Habakkuk is different from other prophecies. It is not written to men but is rather a conversation the prophet has with God. He is not primarily concerned with delivering a message but rather with solving a problem. The problem that perplexed Habakkuk is one that men face today. That puzzle is this: How can God put up with evil?

In Chapter 1 Habakkuk asked the question, *"Why dost thou show me iniquity, and cause me to behold grievance? . . . " (v. 3).* In verse thirteen the prophet reminded God He is *" . . . of purer eyes than to behold evil . . . "* Habakkuk could not understand why God tolerated the evil and did not bring drastic judgment.

The name *Habakkuk* means *strong embrace.* Habakkuk believed God with all his heart and was determined to be faithful and to love the Lord regardless of the problems. He revealed his faith in God in the first verse of Chapter 2. He said, *"I will stand upon my watch, and set me upon the tower, and will watch to see what he will say unto me, and what I shall answer when I am reproved."* Note that Habakkuk expected God to reprove him. He believed that God was interested and would reveal the answer to his perplexity.

Habakkuk closed his book with a tremendous statement in verses seventeen and eighteen of Chapter 3. He said that regardless of what came, he was going to rejoice in the Lord and joy in the God of his salvation. It could be the fig tree would not blossom, the vines would bear no fruit, and there would be no crops and no animals in the stall. No matter what, Habakkuk was going to rejoice. We believers need the same attitude.

> Trust and obey, for there's no other way
> To be happy in Jesus, but to trust and obey.

Bible Command for Today: *"Rejoice in the Lord alway: and again I say, Rejoice." —Philippians 4:4*

October 2

Read Zephaniah 1–3 and Haggai 1 and 2
Family Reading: Haggai 1

The Danger of Selfish Living

"Ye looked for much, and, lo, it came to little; and when ye brought it home, I did blow upon it. Why? saith the Lord of hosts. Because of mine house that is waste, and ye run every man unto his own house." —*Haggai 1:9*

There are those who stint their contributions to their local church and to the Lord's work and missions. Such saving they call good economy. They are actually impoverishing themselves. They think of themselves and their families and neglect the house of God. Such neglect will actually bring ruin upon themselves.

The word *miser* is the root of the word *miserable.* Not all miserable people are misers, but all misers are miserable.

Haggai and Zechariah were used of God to stir up the nation of Israel to build the temple. Ezra records that the temple construction was stopped, and for fourteen years nothing was done. During this time God raised up Haggai and Zechariah to challenge the people to do the work of the Lord. Haggai repeatedly called on the Israelites to *". . . consider your ways . . . " (vv. 5,7).* They had lived selfishly and were finding they had nothing.

Haggai is teaching this important spiritual principle: *"The liberal soul shall be made fat . . . "(Proverbs 11:25).* Oh, that God's people could learn that principle. In His providence He makes our endeavors succeed beyond our expectations, or He causes our plans to fail to our own confusion and dismay. By a turn of His hand, He can steer our vessel in a profitable channel or run it aground in poverty.

I have noticed that the more generous Christians are always the most happy, and sometimes are prosperous in the world. Men trust good managers with larger and larger sums—and thus it may be with the Lord. The individual who is chintzy with God will come up short.

Bible Principle for Today: *"There is that scattereth, and yet increaseth; and there is that withholdeth more than is meet, but it tendeth to poverty."* —*Proverbs 11:24 (Also note vv. 25, 26.)*

October 3

Read Zechariah 1–7
Family Reading: Zechariah 6

The Crowning Day

Zechariah is one of the three prophets who wrote to the Israelites after their captivity. Haggai and Zechariah were the two prophets God used to stir up the Israelites to come out of their slothfulness and their self-seeking to build the temple for God. Haggai was especially used in arousing them to action. Zechariah followed with messages of cheer and encouragement. He did this by pointing them to the future and the coming of the Lord Jesus to set up His kingdom with the reign of righteousness. Saints of God will work more for the Lord when they have the proper vision of the coming of the Lord. They will also long for holiness of life. *"And every man that hath this hope in him purifieth himself, even as he is pure" (I John 3:3).*

In Chapter 6 Zechariah saw the chariots and horses go forth. He stated in verse eight, *"Behold, these that go toward the north country have quieted my spirit in the north country."* Ezekiel 38 tells us that the invaders will come from the north into the land of Palestine. Zechariah's vision presents God's control of the destructive agencies He permits in the punishment of nations that deserve His wrath. His vision was intended to give a rest of heart and confidence of mind to the remnant of Israel.

Zechariah was bidden to take silver and gold and make crowns and place them upon the head of Joshua, the son of Josedech, the high priest. As he did this, he prophesied of the future High Priest, the Lord Jesus Christ. In verse twelve he said, *" . . . Behold the man whose name is The BRANCH; and he shall grow up out of his place, and he shall build the temple of the Lord."*

Our Saviour will build a temple far more glorious than anything Zerubbabel had ever dreamed. As believers we can also look forward to that glorious time when our Saviour-Priest will be crowned King for eternity.

Bible Prophecy for Today: *" . . . The kingdoms of this world are become the kingdoms of our Lord, and of his Christ; and he shall reign for ever and ever."* —*Revelation 11:15*

October 4

Read Zechariah 8–13
Family Reading: Zechariah 12 and 13

The Fountain of the Word

These chapters of Zechariah are pointing to that day when Judah will enter the tribulation period. It will be a time of cleansing. Zechariah 13:1 reads: *"In that day there shall be a fountain opened to the house of David and to the inhabitants of Jerusalem for sin and for uncleanness."*

In Zechariah 12:10 God speaks of the death of Christ with the words: *" . . . and they shall look upon me whom they have pierced, and they shall mourn for him, as one mourneth for his only son . . . "* That points us to the atoning death of Christ.

Then Chapter 13 opens with the fact that a fountain shall be opened to the house of David. This coincides with Ezekiel 36:24-27, where God states that He will sprinkle clean water upon them and they shall be clean. In Zechariah 12 He points to the brazen altar of sacrifice. In Zechariah 13 He speaks of the laver of cleansing. This is the order of the tabernacle and the order throughout the Word of God. First, there is the blood at the altar, and then there is the water at the laver. From the side of the crucified Saviour there flowed both blood and water (John 19:34).

First, there is the blood that expiates sin before God. Then there is the water that cleanses the forgiven sinner. That water is the Word of God: *"That he might sanctify and cleanse it with the washing of water by the word"(Ephesians 5:26).*

The fountain in Zechariah 13:1 must be that fount of the Word of God that cleanses from defilement. John wrote: *"Now ye are clean through the word which I have spoken unto you"(John 15:3).* Our daily cleansing must be by the Word of God. First, we must be transformed by the blood of Christ. Then we must be cleansed daily and continuously by the application of the Word of God.

Bible Truth for Today: *"Sanctify them through thy truth: thy word is truth."* — *John 17:17*

October 5

Read Zechariah 14 and Malachi 1–4
Family Reading: Malachi 3

Our Unchanging God

*"For I am the Lord, **I change not**; therefore ye sons of Jacob are not consumed."* —*Malachi 3:6*

Our Lord changes not. The name *Malachi* means *messenger.* He was the messenger to the nation of Israel of God's judgment and the possibility of Israel's repenting and being brought back. God speaks here of the fact that judgment will be required because of their sin: *" . . . I will come near to you to judgment . . . "(v. 5).* He announced those whom He would judge.

Then in verse seven He said, *" . . . Return unto me, and I will return unto you, saith the Lord of hosts . . . "* He is the Lord who changes not. He must judge iniquity. But He is also the Lord who changes not; therefore, He must deal in mercy. If Israel had only returned, He would have been ready to return unto them.

They asked, *" . . . Wherein shall we return?" (v. 7).* Then God dealt with them about their sin of robbing God. They had failed to be faithful as tithers. He said if they were going to return, they would have to manifest it by the right stewardship principle and attitude. Then He could bless them and *" . . . rebuke the devourer for your sakes . . . "* (v. 11). God was ready to take them back, if only they had been willing to return.

They made another serious accusation: *" . . . It is vain to serve God: and what profit is it that we have kept his ordinance, and that we have walked mournfully before the Lord of hosts?" (v. 14).* God answered them by stating that He kept a book of remembrance and that it was not vain to serve the Lord (v. 16). The day would come when God will make up His jewels, and service for the Lord will be rewarded (v. 17).

How we need the message of Malachi today. There are so many of our church members and so-called Christians who live as though they were not really going to be rewarded for serving the Lord. Praise God, He changes not. His mercy is everlasting, and He will act in mercy—and He will also act in judgment.

October 6

Read Matthew 1–4
Family Reading: Matthew 3

Why Was John the Baptist a Great Man?

John the Baptist was a great man. The Lord Jesus affirmed this when He said, *"Verily I say unto you, Among them that are born of women there hath not risen a greater than John the Baptist . . . "* *(Matthew 11:11)*. What made him such a great man?

First, John the Baptist was great because he was a humble man. Our Lord laid down this rule for greatness in Matthew 20:26, 27: *" . . . but whosoever will be great among you, let him be your minister; And whosoever will be chief among you, let him be your servant."*

In John 3:30 John announced that Christ must become more and more exalted and that John himself should become less important. Peter, who had difficulty with this matter of pride and humility, in his first epistle commanded believers: *"Humble yourselves therefore under the mighty hand of God, that he may exalt you in due time"* *(I Peter 5:6)*. When the multitudes came to him, he always pointed them to Christ. In Matthew 3:11 John stated that he was not even worthy to bear the shoes of the Lord Jesus.

Second, John was great because he was faithful to the Lord and to His Word. When the multitude came to see him, he faithfully showed them their sins and their need to trust the Lord. These are two ingredients in a life that are absolutely necessary for a man to be truly great: humility and faithfulness.

Bible Truth for Today: John the Baptist said of the Lord Jesus: *"He must increase, but I must decrease."* *—John 3:30*

October 7

Read Matthew 5–7
Family Reading: Matthew 5:17-48

Christ's Law

Matthew 5–7 is that portion of the New Testament which we commonly refer to as *"The Sermon on the Mount."* It is literally the manifesto of our King, the Lord Jesus Christ. These are rules by which born-again Christians should endeavor to live today. They are also rules that Christ will use when He establishes His reign during the kingdom. The kingdom laws are particularly given in Matthew 5:17-48. They are principles of the Kingdom.

A good little outline for you to remember is as follows:

I.	Christ's Laws of Life	Matthew 5:21-32
	A. Laws of Individual Life	Matthew 5:21-26
	B. Laws of Family Life	Matthew 5:27-32
II.	Christ's Law of Lips	Matthew 5:33-37
III.	Christ's Law of Love	Matthew 5:38-48

Note Christ's Law of Lips

Words of utterance are man's highest and most distinctive gift. Yet this same gift can become his most entangling sin. Countless passages in the Word of God warn about improper use of the tongue. The child of God is to guard against swearing. In the Old Testament, false swearing was forbidden, but Christ requires there be no swearing. He speaks of oaths men take. A bad man cannot be believed even with his oath, and a good man speaks the truth without an oath. The Lord says all that is needed is a simple affirmative or negative answer and nothing more.

Then note Christ's Law of Love

He warns in verses thirty-eight through forty-one against retaliation. The child of God should let love rule in every circumstance of life. He even should go so far as to love his enemies.

Bible Truth for Today: *"For in many things we offend all. If any man offend not in word, the same is a perfect man, and able also to bridle the whole body."* —James 3:2

October 8

Read Matthew 8, 9, and 10:1-23
Family Reading: Matthew 9:16-38

New Garments and New Vessels

In verse sixteen Jesus said, *"No man putteth a piece of new cloth unto an old garment, for that which is put in to fill it up taketh from the garment, and the rent is made worse."* Then He spoke of new wine in new vessels. He was speaking in this parable of the absolute necessity of the new birth and a new life in Christ.

Some people picture salvation as just a patched-up life. They have a problem; so they get a patch. They have another problem, and they get another patch. They may patch with some good works or nice deeds. How foolish! A person who cuts up a new piece of cloth to patch an old garment is playing the fool! The garment will tear near the new patch. And one who patches up his life by some good works is making a dreadful and eternal mistake. You cannot earn salvation by doing a good work to cover up a sin. The whole fabric of your salvation will be destroyed.

Christ is not a patch, but He is a new garment.
Christ is not a helper, but He is the Saviour.
Christ is not a crutch, but He is the Physician.
Christ is not a pebble, but He is the Rock of Ages.

Christ is saying you cannot mix works with grace. Salvation comes by grace alone through faith. If there were no new garment, you might cherish the old. But there is a new garment! Throw those old soiled rags of works away and trust Jesus Christ alone for salvation.

The second part of the parable deals with new wine in old vessels. The old wine is human experience and human satisfaction. When Christ comes, He needs a vessel surrendered to Him. It cannot be mixed with the old—all must be new. Oh, yes, people will get some satisfaction out of the old world—but in time of need, in death or in sickness, that bottle will leak. Friend, today trust Christ and Him alone.

Bible Truth for Today: *"Therefore if any man be in Christ, he is a new creature: old things are passed away; behold, all things are become new."* — II Corinthians 5:17

October 9

Read Matthew 10:24-42; 11; and 12
Family Reading: Matthew 11:1-19

Be Rid of Doubts!

John was in prison, suffering from the plague of doubts. Too many of God's people are tied in the prison of doubt and are unable to do much for the Lord.

An important truth in this passage is that even so great a man as John the Baptist can be plagued with the dread danger of doubt. No one is immune from the potential of doubting. Every doubt will weaken a child of God so that he cannot continue to stand for the Lord.

John asked, *" . . . Art thou he that should come, or do we look for another?" (v. 3).* He wondered if this One would be the Messiah or if they needed to look for another to come. In answering the question, the Lord directed the disciples to go and show John the miracles they had seen and about which they could testify to others. John's disciples had come at the right time. Jesus Christ is His own proof.

We can learn a good lesson here. When we meet souls bound in the prison of doubt, we should simply tell them what we have seen Jesus do. You can do nothing better for any person than to tell of what Jesus Christ means to you and of what He has done in your life.

Let's come back to this matter of doubt. If John the Baptist had trouble with doubts, how much more will you and I need to guard against this same enemy! How do you get rid of doubts in your own life? It is simply by spending time in the Word of God and by meditating on the person of Jesus Christ. I recommend that you take time to memorize the Word of God. Faith comes by the Word of God (Romans 10:17), and it is faith that is the shield which will quench all the fiery darts of the wicked one (Ephesians 6:16).

An Assurance Verse That Dispels Doubts: *"These things have I written unto you that believe on the name of the Son of God; that ye may know that ye have eternal life, and that ye may believe on the name of the Son of God." — I John 5:13*

October 10

Read Matthew 13 and 14
Family Reading: Matthew 13:1-23

The Parable of the Soils

Matthew 13 presents seven parables on the kingdom of Heaven. The first parable, the one we have for our family reading today, is the parable of the various soils. Four soils are listed. The soils represent the hearts of men as they receive the seed, the Word of God.

First, there is the wayside soil on which the seed fell and the fowls came and devoured it up. Fowls in the Bible speak of that which is evil. It was fowls that Abraham had to drive from his sacrifice in Genesis 15:11. In this parable in Matthew 13, fowls representing evil came and devoured the seed. This was hard ground where people and animals had walked, making the soil like iron. The evil one was able to come and snatch the seed away.

Second, there is the stony soil. As I understand it, this was soil that had a hard pan of rock under it. The roots could go down just a little distance and then would be stopped. In explaining this second soil, the Lord states that the person who receives the Word does not grow because he allows persecution to drive him away (vv. 20, 21).

Third, there is the thorny ground. The Lord explains the thorns as *"the care of this world, and the deceitfulness of riches"* that choke the Word and make it unfruitful.

Then there is the fourth soil. It is the soil which produces plants that bring forth fruit.

All four soils represent lives that are reached with the Word of God today. By the way they receive the Word, individuals are identified as one soil or another. Has your life been the soil that receives the seed and bears fruit to the glory of God? May God give us grace to present the soil consistently where the seed can take root and produce fruit.

Bible Truth for Today: *"Hear counsel, and receive instruction, that thou mayest be wise in thy latter end."* —*Proverbs 19:20*

October 11

Read Matthew 15–17
Family Reading: Matthew 15:21-39

Faith in Christ

Jesus spoke to the Canaanite woman, *" . . . O woman, great is thy faith . . . " (v. 28)*. What manifested this great faith? It was the fact that she longed to know the Lord and rest on Him.

In verse twenty-two she came to Jesus calling Him *"Lord"* but also referring to Him as *"thou son of David."* The next verse states, *"But he answered her not a word . . . " (v. 23)*. Why? I believe He did not answer her because she referred to Him as *"son of David"*— the title that had significance to the Jews but not to a Canaanite. As a Canaanite she was condemned. Israel was to conquer Canaan and destroy the inhabitants. So this lady abode under the curse. She is a picture of all sinners. Before any of us were saved, we were under the curse.

But she was not to be stopped. *"Then came she and worshiped him, saying, Lord, help me" (v. 25)*. I believe she laid hold of a word the Lord had just spoken. He had said to the disciples, *"I am not sent but unto the **lost** sheep of the house of Israel" (v. 24)*. She heard that word ***lost*** and cried out, *"Lord, help me."* She admitted her lost condition. Then Jesus made it even plainer that Gentiles were dogs. She readily admitted she was a dog, under the curse, needing a Saviour.

Then Jesus said, *" . . . O woman, great is thy faith."* What was this great faith? It was that she saw she was a sinner without any hope or help in herself. Great faith comes when we finally realize our hopeless and helpless condition without Jesus Christ. Immediately this woman saw her need met. Her daughter was healed that very hour. Faith brings the power of God to work the miracles we need.

We can never have our need of salvation met until we see we are sinners. Faith comes by hearing the Word of God (Romans 10:17). That involves our hearing and receiving the message that *" . . . all have sinned" . . . (Romans 3:23)*.

Bible Truth for Today: *"For the Son of man is come to seek and to save that which was lost." —Luke 19:10*

October 12

Read Matthew 18–20
Family Reading: Matthew 20:1-16, 25-28

The Privilege of Serving Him

The Lord Jesus asks the question, " . . . *Why stand ye here all the day idle?" (v. 6).* Christ does not want His servants idle. He wants them out in His vineyard. (Note verses 1, 2-10, 4, and 7.) You and I need to be busy in the Lord's vineyard. Too often we are idle " . . . *in the market place" (v. 3).*

Christ's promise to us is that He will do right by us if we serve Him (v. 7). We need to learn that truth. Many believers do not have the faith to believe that God will do right and take proper care of them if they serve Him. But we need never be concerned. He has promised that He will supply all our need according to His riches in glory by Christ Jesus (Philippians 4:19).

In this passage the servants who worked the full hour of the day murmured that their pay was no better than those who worked only a part of the day. They received exactly according to the agreement between the lord of the vineyard and the laborers. Still they murmured and griped.

Actually, they should have thanked the lord for his good-heartedness in letting them work and being willing to pay them. The command to you and me is to go to work in the vineyard. I must be busy there in order to please my Lord. I must leave the reward with Him. Oh, how thankful I am that God has given me the opportunity of service for Him. I almost died as a young man. I thank God that He spared my life and has given me these many years of service for Him in His vineyard.

May God give us grace to be anxious to serve Him and to be faithful in His vineyard.

> *Thou who didst hang upon a barren tree,*
> *My God, for me;*
> *Though I till now be barren, now at length*
> *Lord, give me strength*
> *To bring forth fruit for Thee.*
> —*Christina Rossetti*

October 13

Read Matthew 21 and 22
Family Reading: Matthew 22:1-22

Do You Have the Wedding Garment?

"And when the king came in to see the guests, he saw there a man which had not on a wedding garment: And he saith unto him, Friend, how camest thou in hither not having a wedding garment? And he was speechless" (Matthew 22:11, 12).

Zealous to fill the banquet room, the servants were not careful about each person. The king came in and saw one there without a wedding garment. In those days, at such a festive occasion, the host provided the garment; and thus it was at this wedding feast. The king said, " . . . *all things are ready: come unto the marriage" (v. 4).*

One man came in without the wedding garment. He hated the king and he hated his son. He resolved to come to the wedding without wearing the robe of gladness. By this he manifested his contempt for the royal proceedings. He came because he had an invitation, but came only in appearance. The banquet was set to honor the son, and this man meant to eat the good things set before him—but in his heart he had no love for the king or for his son.

Others had seen him enter. They tolerated his presence, but there came a definite, solemn moment in verse eleven " . . . **when the king came in to see the guests** . . . " The king in this parable pictures the King, who has the eye that can look over all things and overlook nothing. *"He saw there a man which had not on a wedding garment."* The wedding garment represents that which is indispensable to a Christian but which the unrenewed heart is unwilling to accept.

In the first part of this chapter there were those who hated the son and would not accept the invitation, even to the harming and slaying of the servants (vv. 3 6). These were on the outside as enemies. But here was one on the inside, professing salvation. He was as surely lost as those on the outside and was also cast into outer darkness.

Bible Truth for Today: *"Examine yourselves, whether ye be in the faith; prove your own selves. Know ye not your own selves, how that Jesus Christ is in you, except ye be reprobates?"*

—II Corinthians 13:5

October 14

Read Matthew 23 and 24
Family Reading: Matthew 24:1-26

The Character of This Age

The Lord Jesus had prophesied in the last three verses of Matthew 23 that Jerusalem would face a time of destruction. He wept over the city as He announced she would be desolate. The disciples were stunned to think that the great city could be destroyed. The Lord further said that the temple would be destroyed stone by stone (24:2). Those disciples looked at the stupendous size of the stones that made up the temple. How could it be that these would be torn down! Those blocks were forty feet long, twelve feet high, and twenty feet wide. The destruction of such a building seemed almost impossible. Then the disciples asked three questions in verse three:

1. *"When shall these things be?"* — That is, when will Jerusalem and the temple be destroyed?

2. *"What shall be the sign of thy coming?"*

3. What shall be the sign *"of the end of the world?"*

In 70 A. D. Jerusalem was destroyed as Jesus prophesied. The story of that destruction by the Romans is a terrible blot on the history of mankind. The Lord described conditions that would exist at the time of the destruction of Jerusalem — and conditions that would prevail in the world until He comes again (vv. 4-14).

These conditions were not necessarily signs of the closing of the age. There will be false christs and rumors of war. But verse six states emphatically, " . . . *but the end is not yet."* False teachers and wars and rumors of wars have characterized this age.

The change to a different age takes place in verse nine. *"Then"* (after this age) shall disciples be afflicted and killed. Christ is speaking of the first part of the tribulation. What a dreadful time that will be!

Praise God, every child of God will escape the tribulation by being caught up to be with the Lord. We believe we are not appointed to wrath (I Thessalonians 5:9). We have our hope in Christ and are looking forward to the *"blessed hope"* — that day when Jesus Christ catches us out to be with Him (Titus 2:13).

October 15

Read Matthew 25 and 26:1-46
Family Reading: Matthew 25:1-22

"Watch Therefore!"

"Watch therefore . . . " (v. 13) is the message of this parable. The Lord Jesus wants us to be ready when He comes again. The parable gives the picture of a Jewish wedding. The betrothal usually took place in the home of the bride's parents. There the promises were made, each to the other. The final ceremony was generally performed outdoors, if possible on the banks of a stream. Afterward, there was a feast for seven days at the bride's house. There would be a group of girls at that house waiting to welcome the bride. These girls had rags wrapped around a piece of iron or earthenware pottery. The rags were soaked in oil and gave a bright light. They wanted to please the bridegroom with light as he came with his bride.

The picture is that of the coming of the Lord Jesus Christ. He warns against foolish virgins who had no oil. These virgins all were dressed alike, all had lamps, all looked and talked alike. All of them expected the Lord to come, and all had knowledge of some truth.

However, there was a major difference. Some had oil and others did not. The oil is the picture of the Holy Spirit. A person who is saved has the Holy Spirit. A person without the Holy Spirit has never been born again. Suddenly, the bridegroom comes; and it is too late for those without oil to get that oil. While they go out to find oil, the door is shut. The Lord is teaching that everyone needs to watch for the day when the Lord Jesus Christ will come again.

There is one tragedy in this passage concerning believers who are saved: *" . . . they all slumbered and slept" (v.5).* That includes those who had oil in their lamps. Even believers were asleep and not watching as they should have been. Let us watch constantly, *" . . . for ye know neither the day nor the hour wherein the Son of man cometh" (v. 13).*

Bible Truths for Today: *"Watch therefore, for ye know neither the day nor the hour wherein the Son of man cometh." —Matthew 25:13*

"And now, little children, abide in him; that, when he shall appear, we may have confidence, and not be ashamed before him at his coming."
—I John 2:28

October 16

Read Matthew 26:47-75 and 27
Family Reading: Matthew 27:1-24

Judas Sold Himself

We read today about Judas, who betrayed the Lord Jesus. I can imagine that maybe Judas did not expect his action to produce the results that it did. In verse three we read: *"Then Judas, which had betrayed him, when he saw that he* [Christ] *was condemned . . ."* This may have been a surprise to Judas. He had seen Christ miraculously delivered from evil men many times. When he betrayed Him, he possibly reasoned that Christ could escape any capture. He may have thought: "I will get my money for delivering Him; He will escape again, as He has done before; so what will it matter?"

When he saw that Christ was condemned, then he endeavored to return the money. He did not truly repent. He repented of the consequences of his betrayal, not of the betrayal itself. In reality, Judas sold Christ for nothing. He returned the thirty pieces of silver. The person he really sold was himself. His price was nothing—and he sold himself to eternal Hell. This is all any soul will get when he rejects Jesus Christ as Lord and Saviour—nothing on earth, and eternal Hell thereafter.

Acts 1:18 tells us that when Judas hanged himself, he fell headlong, bursting asunder in the midst, and all of his bowels gushed out. Apparently, the rope broke and Judas fell some distance, tearing his body to pieces. He fell headlong. Oh, that he might have fallen down headlong before the Lord and been saved! Today, you must either fall before the Lord in humility, receiving Christ, or you must fall into eternal Hell to suffer forever. What have you done with Christ?

Bible Truth for Today: *" . . . that in all things he might have the pre-eminence."* *—Colossians 1:18*

October 17

Read Matthew 28 and Mark 1 and 2
Family Reading: Matthew 28

His Presence with Us

"[A]nd, I am with you alway, even unto the end of the world" *(Matthew 28:20)*. How wonderful! This One, the Lord Jesus Christ, who is ever the same, is ever with us. There is one stable Rock amidst the billows of the sea of life.

My soul—do not set your affections upon things of earth where moth and rust corrupt and where thieves break through and steal. Rather let me set my affections on Him who abides forever and abides faithful. May we not be so deceived as to build our houses upon the quicksand of a deceitful world. When our hopes are founded on Him who changes not, we are grounded upon the Rock that will stand secure midst the descending rains and roaring floods.

Hebrews 13:5,6 reads, *"Let your conversation be without covetousness; and be content with such things as ye have: for he hath said, I will never leave thee, nor forsake thee. So that we may boldly say, The Lord is my helper, and I will not fear what man shall do unto me."*

He will be with us forever. Think of it! When death's black night comes to put out our candle, we have His sunlight to shine on and on. How wonderful to trust Him who will deliver us from the cold river of death and place us safely on the celestial shore and cause us to sit in heavenly places!

We believers can trust Him. He will never leave us nor forsake us. May we set all of our affections on Him. May we put all in Christ and leave all with Him. On the day I wrote this, I visited the Butchart Gardens in Victoria, British Columbia. How beautiful! But those flowers will fade shortly, reminding us of the brevity of life. Our Lord, however, endures forever, and He changes not. *"Jesus Christ the same yesterday, and today, and for ever" (Hebrews 13:8)*. Trust Him who changes not, and He will be with you alway.

Bible Truth for Today: *"Be strong and of a good courage, fear not, nor be afraid of them: for the Lord thy God, he it is that doth go with thee; he will not fail thee, nor forsake thee." —Deuteronomy 31:6*

October 18

Read Mark 3, 4, and 5:1-20
Family Reading: Mark 5:1-20

The New Creation

'Therefore if any man be in Christ, he is a new creature old things are passed away; behold, all things are become new."
—II Corinthians 5:17

This maniac of Gadara is a demonstration of what God can do in a life that is transformed by His grace. This maniac is a picture of an unsaved man outside of Christ. He lived among the tombs. An unsaved man is dead in trespasses and sins. No man could tame him. There is no possibility for a man to change the life of an unsaved man. That can come only by the power of God.

When Jesus came, the man was completely changed. The Lord manifested His authority over the demons and cast them out. Because He permitted the demons to enter the swine and cause them to drown, the people of that area asked the Lord to leave their coasts. They wanted nothing more to do with Him.

How different it was with the man who was delivered. Verse eighteen states that he prayed that he might be with the Lord. What a change—He had wanted to dwell among the tombs, but now he desired to be in the presence of the Lord Jesus. This will always be one sure mark of salvation—a desire to be with the Lord. There is nothing to a so-called conversion if a person does not desire to fellowship with God's people and with the Lord. A person truly converted has one fervent desire to be with the Lord and with His people.

The Lord told him not to stay only in the presence of the Lord but to go back home and publish what God had done for him.

By his testimony, all the region of Decapolis heard of the miraculous power of Christ. Praise God for His wonderful power to transform a life and make it over to be a great testimony for Christ.

October 19

Read Mark 5:21-43; 6; and 7:1-23
Family Reading: Mark 5:21-43

Only Believe

The daughter of the ruler of the synagogue was pronounced dead. The question was asked, *" . . . why troublest thou the Master any further?" (v. 35).* Jesus heard that word spoken, and He said to the ruler, *" . . . Be not afraid, only believe" (v. 36).*

Only believe. What a short answer to a case of great distress! This is a simple recipe from the greatest Physician. And it is a remedy that suits all cases, all states and circumstances, and fits in at all times. So many refuse to accept this simple promise. What a marvelous display of God's great love and His almighty power can come simply by believing! Do you not realize that your soul was dead in trespasses and sins and was made anew simply because you believed?

Someone taunts us, saying, "Oh, you are all for faith—nothing but faith—only believe!" Yes, that's true. We are all for Christ, nothing but Christ, only Christ; and we can enjoy Him only by believing. Remember that He reproved the slowness of heart of those two disciples on the road to Emmaus (Luke 24:25). All of our comfort flows from faith, and all of our misery flows from unbelief.

What is your need today? Are there fears? Are you groaning under trials? Are you vexed with difficult testings? What can bring relief to you, hope to your mind, and peace to your soul? Christ's words, *"Only believe,"* are the need for your hour. Only believe and you will find death to your fears and life for your joys. Only believe—that is the way to walk in fellowship with Christ. Faith will lift you above the world and above the trials. Faith enjoys Christ—and enjoying Him is Heaven to the heart.

> *Fear not, little flock, from the cross to the throne,*
> *From death into life He went for His own;*
> *All power in earth, all power above,*
> *Is given to Him for the flock of His love.*
>
> *Only believe, only believe;*
> *All things are possible, only believe.*

October 20

Read Mark 7:24-37; Chapters 8 and 9
Family Reading: Mark 8:14-38

The Healing of the Blind Man

Interested souls brought a blind man to Jesus (v. 22). This was wise. It is good always to get needy souls to Jesus. He alone is the One able to help. Thank God that the people brought this blind man to Jesus.

The Lord Jesus never performed two miracles in the same way. In this case He spat on the blind man's eyes. This pictured the fact that men would spit on Him and reproach Him so that we could be healed of spiritual blindness.

When the Lord asked the man if he saw clearly, the man said, " . . . *I see men as trees, walking" (v. 24).* He did not see clearly. This is the case of a new convert. He has sight but needs to grow so that he will have discernment and can see clearly. This requires a continued work of grace in the life. The Lord touched him, and then he saw every man clearly. For us today this involves a growth in grace so that we can develop spiritual discernment.

Far too many of God's people have been given eternal life and are no longer blinded by sin. But they still see men only as trees walking. It is the same truth that we find in II Peter 1:9—*"But he that lacketh these things is blind, and cannot see afar off, and hath forgotten that he was purged from his old sins."*

The word for *blind* here is the word that means *"nearsighted."* This is the person who does see but suffers from astigmatism. He cannot see afar off. He has not developed spiritual discernment. He must grow so that he has understanding in spiritual things.

Ask yourself the question: Do I see clearly or is my spiritual vision blurred? You will know the answer. If you recognize that you are seeing men as trees walking, then you must determine to exercise spiritually so that you will grow in the knowledge of the Lord and His grace.

October 21

Read Mark 10 and 11
Family Reading: Mark 10:23-45

The Deceitfulness of Riches

The Lord Jesus had just dealt with the rich young ruler. This young man was a good moral man, believing he had kept the commandments from his youth. He must not have really understood the commandments. There is no man who can keep them. *"For all have sinned and come short of the glory of God" (Romans 3:23).* Then Jesus asked him to sell all that he had and give to the poor. At this the young man was grieved and turned away sad, rejecting Christ and holding on to his possessions.

Jesus then spoke to His disciples and asked them, *" . . . how hard is it for them that trust in riches to enter into the kingdom of God?"* (v. 24). Then He repeated, *"It is easier for a camel to go through the eye of a needle, than for a rich man to enter into the kingdom of God" (v. 25).*

Why is it difficult for a rich man to be saved? We need to go back to Matthew 5:3 where Jesus announced the principle, *"Blessed are the poor in spirit: for theirs is the kingdom of heaven."* It is difficult for a rich man to be poor in spirit. Why? Because wealth means power, and power is far more likely to create pride than to produce poverty of spirit. It is very difficult for a rich man to become poor in spirit—not impossible—very, very difficult. Let's long to be poor in spirit so that we can enjoy the blessing of which God speaks. *" . . . for God resisteth the proud, and giveth grace to the humble" (I Peter 5:5).*

> *In the glare of earthly pleasure*
> *In the fight for earthly treasure,*
> *'Mid your blessing without measure—*
> *Have you forgotten God?*

Bible Truth for Today: *"And Jesus answered and said, Verily I say unto you, There is no man that hath left house, or brethren, or sisters, or father, or mother, or wife, or children, or lands, for my sake, and the gospel's, But he shall receive a hundredfold now in this time, houses, and brethren, and sisters, and mothers, and children, and lands, with persecutions; and in the world to come eternal life."*
> *—Mark 10:29, 30*

October 22

Read Mark 12, 13, and 14:1-16
Family Reading: Mark 12:28-44

The Secret of True Giving

We read that Jesus sat over against the treasury and beheld how the people cast money into the treasury (v. 41). Jesus still watches those who are giving. And remember, He sees not as man sees. The important word in verse forty-one is the word *"how."* Jesus did not behold how *much* people gave; He beheld *"how"* they gave.

This passage, Mark 12:41-44, is a continuation of Christ's answer. The Pharisees had failed to render unto God that which was God's. But here was a dear lady who gave her all to the Lord. How refreshing! I doubt that this poor widow even knew the Lord was watching. In eternity she will learn the value the Lord put on her gift that day.

Let me say it again: The Lord noted not *what* but *how* these people were casting into the treasury. God is not particularly concerned with the amount of our gift but rather with the attitude involved in our giving.

This widow undoubtedly gave because she loved the Lord with all her heart. Others were giving large sums and wanted other people to take note of their giving. This poor lady gave a small amount, very likely trying not to let anybody see her gift.

She loved. That is what counts with the Lord. *"And though I bestow all my goods to feed the poor . . . and have not charity* [love], *it profiteth me nothing"* (I Corinthians 13:3).

Just a little—two mites which made up one-fourth of a cent. But it was all she had. And when the Lord saw it, He said it was more than all that the others with large gifts had given together.

The Lord valued it—not because of what this widow gave but because of what she had left—nothing. The Lord does not count what we put in but what we do not put in.

Bible Truth for Today: *" . . . remember the words of the Lord Jesus, how he said, It is more blessed to give than to receive."*

—Acts 20:35

October 23

Read Mark 14:17-52 and 15
Family Reading: Mark 14:26-52

Smitten by God

"And Jesus saith unto them, All ye shall be offended because of me this night: for it is written, I will smite the shepherd, and the sheep shall be scattered." —Mark 14:27

In verse twenty-seven Jesus prophesied that all of His disciples would be offended because of the smiting of the shepherd. That smiting of the shepherd was referring to His passion when He would suffer for the sins of all men. He stated that all of them would be offended because He would be smitten. The word *offended* means that they would be caused to stumble. He was saying that before that night had passed, before a new day would dawn, all of His disciples would be caused to stumble. And stumble they did! Peter denied Him and later went fishing rather than to wait for the promise of the Father. Thomas doubted Him. They stumbled because of His death, and they thought that all hope of victory was past.

The Lord quoted Zechariah 13:7 which reads, *"Awake, O sword, against my shepherd, and against the man that is my fellow, saith the Lord of hosts: smite the shepherd, and the sheep shall be scattered: and I will turn mine hand upon the little ones."* He referred to all that was coming in His own experience, and the experience of His disciples, in fulfillment of that prophecy. As He spoke, He knew full well that Judas had gone to betray Him. He saw distinctly what He had been telling His disciples all of the time, that the end of all would be a Roman cross. But now as He came right to the hour, this reference was to His coming death. He was dying not because of the buffeting of men's malice but because of the stroke of God. His death was in the will of God.

> *Many hands were raised to wound Him,*
> *None would interpose to save;*
> *But the awful stroke that found Him,*
> *Was the stroke that justice gave.*

Bible Command for Today: *"Awake to righteousness, and sin not; for some have not the knowledge of God: I speak this to your shame."*
—I Corinthians 15:34

October 24

Read Mark 16 and Luke 1
Family Reading: Luke 1:13-38

Believe God's Promises

Zacharias and Elisabeth were both godly people. Verse six tells us, *"And they were both righteous before God, walking in all the commandments and ordinances of the Lord blameless."* They were an elderly couple and could no longer have any physical hope of having children. But while Zacharias was ministering in the temple, an angel of God appeared unto him. This angel gave him the promise that he would have a son born who would be a great man for God.

Though Zacharias was a godly man, faithful in the Lord's service, and one who honored the Lord, he was still very much a man. And as a man, he had trouble with believing God. His faith seemed to be very weak. In his doubting he asked, *" . . . Whereby shall I know this? for I am an old man, and my wife well stricken in years"* (v. 18). Is this not just like many of us? We have a promise from God but we find it difficult to believe. Zacharias and Elisabeth had prayed for years. Now they had a promise from God. Instead of saying, "Thank you, Lord, for that blessed promise," he asks, *"Whereby shall I know this?"* He is literally asking, "Can you give me a sign? What you are saying is too much for me to believe; I can scarcely think that my prayer is really going to be heard. What sign will there be?"

I say it reverently but I believe the angel was a little bit upset over what Zacharias asked. He told Zacharias he was Gabriel, who stood in the presence of God. Zacharias should have believed. Then the angel said, "You will have a sign." That sign was that Zacharias would be unable to speak until the baby was born.

Unbelief shut Zacharias's mouth. When the baby was born, the first words Zacharias spoke were words of praise and thanksgiving. He then had faith to believe. Oh, friend, let's believe God's promises and not doubt the Lord.

Bible Truth for Today: *"Jesus said unto him, If thou canst believe, all things are possible to him that believeth."* —Mark 9:23

October 25

Read Luke 2 and 3
Family Reading: Luke 3:1-23

The Ministry of John

John the Baptist was a great man. We read of him in Luke 3:2, " . . . *the word of God came unto John . . .* " This means that a particular message came to him. Here is that which makes a man a preacher. He may be well educated and well prepared, but the message has to be that which comes to him from the Word of God. John was this kind of preacher. He received the Word of God.

John was led of God to deal with sin. The need of that hour was for men to receive forgiveness of sin. So is the need of the hour in which we live. John called men to repentance unto the remission of sins. The rite of baptism in John's ministry was the outward confession of repentance unto the remission of sins. It never brought remission—it only indicated the mental attitude that would make possible the remission of sins. But John knew well that his message was not complete. His message was one that prepared the way for the One to follow, the Lord Jesus Christ. In Luke 3:16 he declared plainly, " . . . *I indeed baptize you with water; but one mightier than I cometh, the latchet of whose shoes I am not worthy to unloose: he shall baptize you with the Holy Ghost and with fire.*"

John the Baptist was not the Word of God. He was not even delivering the Word of God in all of its fullness. He was a voice, a message, preparing the way for the living Word, our Lord Jesus Christ. Forgiveness of sins can come only through Christ. John warned the nation of sin. He called the people to repentance. He begged them to flee from the wrath to come. He challenged them to bring forth fruits that would manifest repentance. In this challenge he asked men with means to share with others, he asked tax collectors to be honest, and he asked soldiers not to use their authority to harm others needlessly or falsely.

To love the Lord, we need to manifest repentance that reveals a changed life.

Bible Preaching Against Sin: *"Cry aloud, spare not, lift up thy voice like a trumpet, and show my people their transgression, and the house of Jacob their sins."* — *Isaiah 58:1*

299

October 26

Read Luke 4 and 5
Family Reading: Luke 4:1-22

Turn Your Eyes Upon Jesus

Luke 4:20 states, " . . . *And the eyes of all them that were in the synagogue were fastened on him.*" This is the Person on whom all of our eyes should always be fastened. Jesus Christ should be central in every life.

Sundar Singh was once asked by a professor of comparative religion what he had discovered in Christianity that attracted him to it. His reply: "The Lord Jesus Christ." Thinking that the Indian teacher-evangelist had misunderstood the import of his question, the professor rephrased his question, asking instead what insight into life's mysteries or what truth he found in Christianity that he could not find in Buddhism. Again came the answer: "The Lord Jesus Christ."

It is Christ who makes Christianity unique and different. There is no Christianity when we minimize who He is or what He has done. He is our message. He is our hope. He is our life.

All eyes were fastened on Jesus Christ. Why? First, because He brought His message from the Book. He opened the Book and read from Isaiah 61:1,2. He testified that He is the One who had been anointed to preach deliverance to the captives, to see blind eyes healed, to set at liberty those that are bruised, and to preach the acceptable year of the Lord. Then Jesus told them that this Scripture was fulfilled before them. He was testifying that He was the fulfillment of this prophecy. No wonder their eyes were fastened on Him. You and I must have our eyes fastened on Christ.

> *Turn your eyes upon Jesus;*
> *Look full in His wonderful face;*
> *And the things of earth*
> *Will grow strangely dim,*
> *In the light of His glory and grace.*

Bible Truth for Today: *"Looking unto Jesus the author and finisher of our faith; who for the joy that was set before him endured the cross, despising the shame, and is set down at the right hand of the throne of God." —Hebrews 12:2*

October 27

Read Luke 6 and 7
Family Reading: Luke 7:1-23

When Jesus Meets Death

In Luke 7:11-15 Jesus met and conquered death. The widow had only one son, now a young man. Jesus had compassion on the brokenhearted widow. He touched the bier and commanded: *"Young man, I say unto thee, Arise. And he that was dead sat up, and began to speak"* (vv. 14, 15).

If a young preacher wanted to know how to conduct a funeral, he could not come to the gospels to learn from the Lord Jesus. You see, every time we read of Jesus facing death, He raised the dead person to life again. Romans 5:14 states that death reigned. If you read Genesis 5, you will find the reign of death. Of one man after another in that chapter, the Scripture says, *"And he died."* Christ, however, conquered death; and during His stay on earth, He manifested His victory over the grave.

Death is the common lot of all men. In this chapter we find it was a young man who had died. In Luke 8:40-56 the one raised from the dead was a girl twelve years of age. The third case where Jesus met death is in John 11, when He raised Lazarus, a mature man. Death can come to children, youth, or adults. And it does not respect the home ties. This young man in Luke 7 was the widow's only son; the girl in Luke 8, Jairus's only daughter.

When Jesus met death, He conquered it. It is Jesus who made it possible for Paul to ask the questions in I Corinthians 15:55—*"O death, where is thy sting? O grave, where is thy victory?"*

It is Jesus who abolished death. *"But is now made manifest by the appearing of our Saviour Jesus Christ, who hath abolished death, and hath brought life and immortality to light through the gospel"* (II Timothy 1:10).

Jesus announced in John 11:25—*"I am the resurrection, and the life: he that believeth in me, though he were dead, yet shall he live."* Praise God, He has conquered death!

Bible Truth for Today: *"Precious in the sight of the Lord is the death of his saints."* —*Psalm 116:15*

October 28

Read Luke 8 and 9:1-45
Family Reading: Luke 9:18-42

The Mount of Transfiguration

In Luke 9:28-36 we have the account of Jesus Christ on the Mount of Transfiguration. In each of the gospels, Christ's transfiguration followed immediately after Jesus spoke of His own suffering and death and of the fact that disciples need to take up their crosses and follow Him. This miraculous manifestation on the Mount of Transfiguration has been given to encourage God's people now to walk with the Lord in His rejection while we wait for His glory.

In II Peter 1:16-19 Peter wrote of this incident. He stated that he had been an eyewitness of the majesty of the Lord and that he had actually heard God the Father speak from Heaven at that time. But Peter did not boast of this as though he were spiritually superior. Rather, he wrote that we have a more sure word of prophecy—God's written Word. Think of it—in our hands we hold this precious Book, the Bible; and with our eyes we can read this wonderful Word of God. This is more sure and more blessed than Peter's privilege of being on the mount with the Lord. May we love and appreciate our Bibles!

While they talked on the mount, Moses, Elijah, and Jesus spoke of the death that Christ would accomplish at Jerusalem (v. 31). Just as they spoke of it then, we who love the Lord delight to speak of it and to sing about it today.

Peter did make some blunders that day. But let us notice some things that he did which were right. First, when he talked of building three tabernacles, at least he put the Lord first. How many of us give the Lord the first place in our lives? Second, Peter did not include the suggestion of a tabernacle for himself. He asked for three tabernacles, and there were six people on the mountaintop. How many of us are humble enough to leave ourselves out and give honor to whom honor is due?

There was a cloud that day. Matthew 17:5 calls it a *"bright cloud."* Clouds that come to the Christian are actually bright clouds meant to bring us into the presence of Jesus alone. Someday all the clouds will be gone—and we will be with Him in glory. Until then, let's glorify Him in our lives and listen to His voice.

October 29

Read Luke 9:46-62; 10; 11
Family Reading: Luke 10:21-42

One Thing Needful

"But one thing is needful: and Mary hath chosen that good part, which shall not be taken away from her." —*Luke 10:42*

One thing is needful. Martha was careful and troubled about many things, but she really needed to be concerned about one main thing.

What is this one thing? It is plain that the Lord Jesus meant by this that the soul should maintain intimate communion with the Lord. This Mary did. Mary *" . . . sat at Jesus' feet, and heard his word" (v. 39).* For the one who loves the Lord as he should, everything else takes second place to this. Actually, everything else becomes but drudgery, for this one thing comprises the holiness, the happiness, and the Heavenly-mindedness of the soul.

How important it is to bring everything in life to one center point. Paul wrote in Philippians 3:13, 14: *" . . . but this one thing I do . . . "* Paul said he was a man of one purpose, one goal. What was that one thing he did? He said it was that he forgot *" . . . things which are behind, and reaching forth unto those things which are before."* He pressed *" . . . toward the mark for the prize of the high calling of God in Christ Jesus."* Paul centered everything in doing the will of God.

Mary had this one thing. Jesus said it is the needful thing. Ask yourself what other one thing can produce so many and so blessed effects on your life as close communion with your Saviour. William Mason wrote: "Is not this *one thing*, above all others, needful? Needful at all times and in all seasons; needful in the hour of prosperity and in the day of adversity. Oh, if this one thing is maintained in the soul, your sweet communion with Christ cannot fail to subject the will, attract the affections, and beget holy conformity to Him." You will not wish or dare to follow anything which is contrary to your Lord, while you live near Him and dwell in holy fellowship with Him.

Bible Truth for Today: *"But seek ye first the kingdom of God, and his righteousness; and all these things shall be added unto you."*

—*Matthew 6:33*

October 30

Read Luke 12 and 13
Family Reading: Luke 12:15-34

Beware of Covetousness

Jesus warned in verse fifteen that men must beware of covetousness because" . . . *a man's life consisteth not in the abundance of the things which he possesseth."* Then Jesus gave them a parable to drive home the truth of the danger of covetousness. This is the parable of the rich farmer whom God called a *"fool" (v. 20).*

This farmer was a good farmer. He knew how to prepare the ground, plant the seed, and cultivate the crop so that it would bring forth a bountiful harvest. His ground produced plentifully. God recognized that this man was a successful farmer.

This farmer was also a good businessman. He knew how to plan and prepare for the future. He could plan granaries and buildings. He knew how to manage well.

Nevertheless, God called him a *"fool."* God said, *"Thou fool, this night thy soul shall be required of thee . . . " (v. 20).* It was God who called him a *"fool"*; and when God calls a man a fool, he is a fool indeed. Did God call him a fool because he was a good farmer? No! Did God call him a fool because he was a good businessman? No!

Why did God call him a fool? He was called a fool because he thought he could say to his soul, " . . . *thou hast much goods laid up for many years; take thine ease, eat, drink, and be merry" (v. 19).* A man who talks to his soul like that is a fool. The soul does not live on goods laid up, nor does it live by eating and drinking. God says, " . . . *Man shall not live by bread alone, but by every word that proceedeth out of the mouth of God" (Matthew 4:4).* This man made the mistake so many make today—he thought his soul could live on material things. All of these belonged to God; and God made this very clear when He stated, " . . . *this night thy soul shall be required of thee . . . "(v. 20).*

Bible Truth for Today: *"Let your conversation be without covetousness; and be content with such things as ye have: for he hath said, I will never leave thee, nor forsake thee. So that we may boldly say, The Lord is my helper, and I will not fear what man shall do unto me." —Hebrews 13:5, 6*

October 31

Read Luke 14–16
Family Reading: Luke 15:1-24

Christ Receives Sinners

Luke 15 is a special chapter in the Word of God. It contains one parable in four parts. The parable answers the charge that the Pharisees and scribes made against the Lord in verse two: " . . . *This man receiveth sinners, and eateth with them."* Praise God that He did exactly what they charged. Where would I be today if the Lord Jesus had not received sinners? He received me when I was a poor, lost sinner on my way to Hell. *"For when we were yet without strength, in due time Christ died for the ungodly" (Romans 5:6). "But God commendeth his love toward us, in that, while we were yet sinners, Christ died for us" (Romans 5:8).*

To teach that the Lord receives sinners and eats with them, the Lord gave the following sections of this parable. First—the shepherd seeking the lost sheep. This pictures the Lord Jesus going after the lost. Second—the woman seeking the coin lost in the house. This pictures the Holy Spirit working to reach lost souls in the church. Third—the father waiting for the prodigal son to return. This pictures God the Father longing to see the lost return.

The words *"lost"* or *"lose"* appear seven times. This is the same word translated *"perish"* in John 3:16. Three times the Lord states strongly that there is rejoicing in Heaven over a perishing soul coming back to the Lord. All three—Father, Son, and Holy Ghost—are at work, reaching the lost in the world to bring them to salvation.

The Lord Jesus receives sinners.

Sinners Jesus will receive; sound this word of grace to all
Who the Heav'nly pathway leave, all who linger, all who fall.
Christ receiveth sinful men, even me with all my sin;
Purged from every spot and stain, Heav'n with him I'll enter in.
Sing it o'er and o'er again; Christ receiveth sinful men;
Make the message clear and plain: Christ receiveth sinful men.

Bible Truth for Today: *"For the Son of man is come to seek and to save that which was lost."* —Luke 19:10

November 1

Read Luke 17 and 18
Family Reading: Luke 18:1-17

A Sinner Saved

The Publican stood afar off. He did not lift up his eyes to Heaven because he did not think that he was worthy even to look toward Heaven. The Pharisee looked around and compared himself with his fellowmen. But not this Publican. He just smote upon his breast as if all his problem lay within his breast. And that is exactly where the problem existed, for Jeremiah 17:9 states that the heart of man " . . . *is deceitful above all things, and desperately wicked . . .* " Jesus said that out of the heart of man proceed evil thoughts, murder, blasphemy, adultery, etc. This Publican smote upon his breast, the seat of all evil and sin, and cried: " . . . *God be merciful to me,* **the** *sinner."* (Luke 18:13 should read *"the sinner"* rather than *"a sinner."*) This Publican recognized that he was sinful and needed God's mercy.

Jesus Christ said that the Publican went down to his house justified, rather than the Pharisee. This parable teaches that the person who commends himself, as the Pharisee did, is really condemned by God; and the person who condemns himself, God justifies. The man who confesses that he deserves to go to Hell will never go there. It is lost sinners that Jesus came to save.

John Newton had been a vile sinner, but then came to receive Christ. He knew he was saved only by the grace of God. He wrote the words to this song which is sung by Christians everywhere.

> *Amazing grace! how sweet the sound,*
> *That saved a wretch like me!*
> *I once was lost, but now am found,*
> *Was blind, but now I see.*

> *'Twas grace that taught my heart to fear,*
> *And grace my fears relieved;*
> *How precious did that grace appear*
> *The hour I first believed!*

Bible Truth for Today: *"This is a faithful saying, and worthy of all acceptation, that Christ Jesus came into the world to save sinners; of whom I am chief." —I Timothy 1:15*

November 2

Read Luke 19 and 20
Family Reading: Luke 20:27-47

Immortality

Luke 20:40 states that after the Lord had answered the questions of various people, those same people dared not ask Him any more questions. He had answered them wisely and well. The scribes, the Pharisees, and the Sadducees had asked Him two questions. The first question was a political one and concerned giving tribute to Caesar, as found in verses nineteen to twenty-six. The second question is the one in our passage for today. It was a religious question and dealt with the very important subjects of the immortality of man and the truth of the resurrection. The question was asked by the Sadducees, who did not believe in anything supernatural. They would have been the agnostics of today, trying to explain reality with the fallacy of evolution. They denied the resurrection and thus had to deny the Old Testament Scriptures.

After the Lord had answered them, we read that these men, trying to trap Christ, were completely routed. They could not catch Him in His speech. He was on His way to the cross; but His kingliness and majesty were shining brightly.

In their question about the resurrection, Jesus told them there is a difference between this life and the life after death. He affirmed that there is life after death by using the illustration of Moses. The great prophet Moses met God at the burning bush. Abraham, Isaac, and Jacob had been dead a long time. Yet God told Moses, "I am the God of Abraham, and the God of Isaac, and the God of Jacob." That means that they were not dead even then. They were very much alive. For Jesus added that God is *"not a God of the dead, but of the living."* Those who were thought dead by men were affirmed alive by God. Their personality continued beyond this life. They were immortal, and so are all men.

Bible Truth for Today: Jesus said in John 14:19: *" . . . because I live, ye shall live also."*

November 3

Read Luke 21 and 22
Family Reading: Luke 22:31-53

What Is the Difference?

In verse thirty-five Jesus reminds the disciples of His instruction in Luke 9:3, when He sent them to preach the kingdom of God. He commanded them at that time to take nothing for their journey. He now asks them if when they took no purse, money, or clothes whether they had lacked anything. They assured Him that they had lacked nothing.

Then in verse thirty-six He says, " *. . . But now, . . .* " In Luke 9 they were not to take anything with them to provide for their needs—*but now* things would be different. In this passage He commands them to take a purse and money. If one of them has no sword, he is to sell a garment so that he can buy one.

Why the difference? Verse thirty-seven explains that Jesus was going to be reckoned among the transgressors, and He was going to fulfill in His death the purpose for which He had come. Once He sent them forth with His authority, and He commanded that they should be received and cared for. Now He has come to the end of His path here on earth. Finally He is about to be rejected and crucified; and, henceforth, His disciples should expect nothing better. Once He cared for them and looked after their interests here. Now He is soon to go back to glory and look after their interests up there, and they are to take care of His business down here. Once it cost them nothing to be His servants; now it is going to cost them everything.

"Take a purse," said our Lord. "Once I paid your way; now you must pay your own way." It costs nothing to be saved—but it costs disciples much to serve Him.

> *Love so amazing, so divine,*
> *Demands my soul, my life, my all.*

Above all, for the Christian life and testimony, you need a sword—the Sword of the Spirit, the Word of God. The war is on. Buy a sword. Fight the good fight of faith.

Bible Command for Today: *"And take the helmet of salvation, and the sword of the Spirit, which is the word of God."* —*Ephesians 6:17*

November 4

Read Luke 23 and 24
Family Reading: Luke 23:1-25

Beware Joining with Others Against Christ

"And the same day Pilate and Herod were made friends together: for before they were at enmity between themselves." —Luke 23:12

A man's attitude toward Calvary determines his relationships in this life and in eternity. There were two political rulers who were at enmity with each other. They hated each other and could not get along together. Pilate despised Herod, and Herod hated Pilate.

Then a startling thing happened. They became fast friends in one day's time. The issue that brought them together was the judgment on Jesus Christ. They became friends over the condemnation of Christ.

It has always been so. *"The kings of the earth set themselves, and the rulers take counsel together, against the Lord, and against his anointed . . . " (Psalm 2:2).* Kings today join themselves together against Christ.

Today wicked men devise every means possible to defeat and destroy the work of the Lord. Men who cannot and will not agree on anything in this life will join hands in apparent agreement to stand against the Lord. Herod and Pilate became friends over their agreement that Jesus Christ should be put to death. Their hatred of God was the catalyst that brought them together. This hatred was so intense that they were willing to forget their hatred of each other and become friends. Herod was willing to become a friend of Pilate's if he could have his men of war mock and set at nought the Son of God.

As individuals, you and I need always to put Christ first and see that He is honored. We must never let any friendship be kindled that would involve any enmity against God.

Bible Truth for Today: *" . . . And let every one that nameth the name of Christ depart from iniquity."* —II Timothy 2:19

November 5

Read John 1–3
Family Reading: John 1:1-20

Receiving Him

In John 1:10, 11 we read that the Lord Jesus Christ " . . . *was in the world, and the world was made by him, and the world knew him not. He came unto his own, and his own received him not."* These are two of the saddest verses in all of the Bible. The Lord Jesus was among men, and yet men refused Him. His own people, the Jews, refused to acknowledge Him as their Lord and Redeemer. What a tragedy!

Some years ago I read the story of a young Mexican doctor. In medical school he had been very careful not to become interested in girls so that marriage would not deter him from his purpose. Now a successful doctor, he had returned to his village and had worked untiringly to be a blessing to the people. He had built a little hospital; and now that he had his practice going, he was planning his wedding in three more weeks. A man came to him with cataracts. He performed the surgery, removing the cataracts. He removed the bandages from the man's eyes and the man was able to see, but somehow the man became crazed. He attacked the doctor, knocking him to the floor. He gouged the doctor's eyes out of their sockets. One of the eyeballs was found at the side of the unconscious doctor; the other was found in the hand of the crazed man, running across a park nearby.

That story stunned me. How could a man take the eyes from the very man who had given him sight? Then I thought of these two verses. It is easier for me to understand this story than it is to understand how some can hear of the blood of Christ, know that Jesus gave everything for them, and yet go on daily rejecting Him and living in sin. Verse twelve says that those who received Him became the sons of God. Be sure today that you have received Him.

Bible Promise for Today: *"For whosoever shall call upon the name of the Lord shall be saved."* —*Romans 10:13*

November 6

Read John 4 and 5
Family Reading: John 5:1-21

No Man

The impotent man had been afflicted for thirty-eight years. He had lain a long time near the pool. Like many others, he had been waiting for a miraculous sign to be wrought. Wearily he watched the pool. No angel came, or else the angel that came did not help him. Because he thought this pool was his only hope, he kept on waiting, not realizing that there was One nearby whose word could heal him in a moment. Many are in the same dire situation: they are waiting for some emotion or heavenly vision or definite impression. They wait in vain since these do not come. No person should ever look for them but should trust the Lord and His Word.

How many there are today who are waiting for some means such as ceremonies or vows or resolutions or ordinances or works! They have waited in vain. All the while the Saviour is waiting and longing for them to look to Him and be saved. They only need to trust the Lord and see God's miraculous power flow through them to save and assure for eternity. Trusting Jesus Christ is the sure way to every blessing. Unbelief makes each person prefer the cold porch of Bethesda to the warm bosom of His love.

God wants you to know you are saved. He gives that assurance through His Word and through your believing and trusting Christ. Oh, may each reader today turn from dead formalism to trust Jesus.

The Solid Rock
My hope is built on nothing less
Than Jesus' blood and righteousness;
I dare not trust the sweetest frame,
But wholly lean on Jesus' Name.
On Christ, the solid Rock, I stand;
All other ground is sinking sand.

Bible Truth for Today: *"Neither is there salvation in any other: for there is none other name under heaven given among men, whereby we must be saved." —Acts 4:12*

November 7

Read John 6 and 7
Family Reading: John 6:22-44

What Would You Answer?

The Sunday School Times once carried a story of a man who feared he could never be saved. He came to a preacher of the gospel and cried out: "I am such a hopeless, miserable sinner. There is no hope for me! I have prayed, resolved, and tried everything. Now I am sick of all my useless efforts."

"Do you believe Christ died for our sins?" the preacher asked. And the man said he did.

"Well," said the preacher, "if He were here on earth so that you could actually see Him, what would you do?"

"Oh, I would go to Him at once!" said the trembling seeker, "and I would tell Him I am a lost sinner."

"If He looked your way, would you request Him to do anything for you?" inquired his counselor.

"I certainly would! I would fall on my knees and beg Him to forgive and save me."

When he was asked what Christ would reply, the man became silent. The preacher then turned to John 6:37 and read slowly and emphatically: *"All that the Father giveth me shall come to me; and him that cometh to me I will in no wise cast out."*

Then he asked again, "What would the Saviour say if you asked Him to cleanse you from your sin?"

At last a happy light came into the doubter's eyes as he said with confidence, "He would answer, 'I will!'" That moment he believed and his fears departed. A new-found joy flooded his soul.

Friend, are you under deep conviction of sin? You, too, can know the peace that comes by trusting Jesus Christ just as you are. He has promised: *" . . . him that cometh to me I will in no wise cast out."*

> "Whosoever cometh, I will never cast him out."
> Oh love of Jesus driving out our doubt;
> He now calls to sinners, all unworthy though they be,
> "Take my salvation—boundless, rich, and free!"

November 8

Read John 8 and 9
Family Reading: John 8:31-55

Enslaving Sin

"Jesus answered them, Verily, verily, I say unto you, Whosoever committeth sin is the servant of sin." —*John 8:34*

Sin always has a way of enslaving those who commit sin. Suppose I were to go to a blacksmith shop and say, "Sir, make me a very long and heavy chain of these dimensions. When done I will pay you." He lays aside his engagements and goes hard at work. I call as arranged and say, "I have decided to make the chain longer; work another week." Flattered with the thought of additional pay, the blacksmith labors on. I call again and still insist that the chain is too short. "But," he protests, "my iron is used up and my strength is gone. I want my pay." I urge him to add the last link of which he is capable. Then, instead of paying him, suppose I beat him with the chain and then bind him hand and foot and cast him into a furnace of fire.

That is a picture of what Satan will do. As we continue to forge the chain, he takes the chain and binds us tightly with it. Our sins enslave and capture us.

> *Live*, *vile*, and *evil* have the selfsame letters:
> He *lives* but *vile* whom *evil* holds in fetters.

Sin enslaves until the sinner is fettered and restrained from doing right. Paul wrote that the good which he would, he did not, and the evil which he hated, that he did (Romans 7:15). The drunkard often longs to be happy and respected and healthy again and vows to leave his bottles forever; but his master passion cracks his whip over him, and he goes to drink again. All the while the sinner thinks he is free, he is really enslaved and burdened with a gnawing conscience. Remember, *"If the Son therefore shall make you free, ye shall be free indeed"* (John 8:36).

Bible Truth for Today: *"For the law of the Spirit of life in Christ Jesus hath made me free from the law of sin and death."*

—Romans 8:2

November 9

Read John 10 and 11
Family Reading: John 10:1-21

God Leads

"And when he putteth forth his own sheep, he goeth before them, and the sheep follow him: for they know his voice" (John 10:4).

"The Lord is my shepherd . . . he leadeth me beside the still waters . . . he leadeth me in the paths of righteousness . . . I will fear no evil: for thou art with me . . . Surely goodness and mercy shall follow me all the days of my life . . . " (portions of Psalm 23).

Do you need guidance on your path? Then look to the Lord Jesus. He is the Shepherd who will lead and direct you. Do not look to men. Do not look to impressions you may form. Impressions can be fickle. Friends can disagree with each other.

Claim the promise that when He puts forth His sheep, He leads them. Therefore, look to the Lord Jesus Christ. Leave with Him the responsibility to lead. He has promised that He would. Claim that promise. He will make the path you are to tread so abundantly clear that you cannot do anything else but follow. Tell the Lord that you will stand still until He directs—until He puts His arms under you and carries you where He would have you be. Isaiah says that He carries the governments upon His shoulder. Do you not think you could trust Him to carry the government of your life on His strong shoulders? He knows what is best for you. Let Him execute His plan for your life.

Sometimes He leads into green pastures and beside still waters. Then other times we may have to climb some hills. Let's trust Him. He is there with His staff and crook to handle the wild animals that may attack. Oh, dear friend, can you trust Him to lead? Do so today. You will be thrilled with the rest that He gives and blessing that He bestows.

Bible Truth for Today: *"He maketh me to lie down in green pastures: he leadeth me beside the still waters."* *—Psalm 23:2*

November 10

Read John 12 and 13
Family Reading: John 12:27-50

Believing Is Commanded

The Lord Jesus is speaking in John 12 about proper faith. He states that " . . . *though he had done so many miracles before them, yet they believed not on him" (v. 37)*. The reason they did not believe was that their hearts were hardened and their eyes blinded. These men had steeled themselves against the knowledge of the Son of God.

Verse fifty reads, *"And I know that his commandment is life everlasting . . . "* From this verse we realize that believing is a commandment. God says that His commandment is life everlasting. We receive everlasting life by believing on His Son.

Today we often think of salvation as nothing more than an invitation—an invitation to come and believe on the Lord Jesus Christ. The Lord Jesus did give an invitation. He said, *"Come unto me, all ye that labor and are heavy laden, and I will give you rest" (Matthew 11:28)*. This believing, however, is actually more than just an invitation; it is also a command.

When preaching at Athens, Paul spoke about the spiritual ignorance of the Athenians. He said that God *"winked"* for a time at their sin, but now God " . . . *commandeth all men every where to repent" (Acts 17:30)*. When Peter spoke at Pentecost, he commanded, " . . . *Repent, and be baptized every one of you in the name of Jesus Christ for the remission of sins . . . " (Acts 2:38)*.

Since believing for life everlasting is a commandment, then not to believe is a sin. Belief is not optional; it is absolutely necessary for an individual to be saved. Therefore, when one fails to believe, he is not just having misfortune; he is actually sinning against God. Jesus came to reveal the Father (John 1:18). In John 14:9 He states that the person *"that hath seen me hath seen the Father . . . "* Therefore, to know the Lord Jesus is to know God. In John 12:46 Jesus said, *"I am come a light into the world . . . "* Will you accept His light and believe on Him today as the Light of life?

Bible Truth for Today: *"And by him all that believe are justified from all things, from which ye could not be justified by the law of Moses." —Acts 13:39*

November 11

Read John 14–16
Family Reading: John 16:12-33

Necessity of Prayer

Do verses twenty-three and twenty-four of this chapter puzzle you? In verse twenty-three He states, *"And in that day ye shall ask me nothing . . ."* Then He seems to turn around and say the opposite: *" . . . Verily, verily, I say unto you, Whatsoever ye shall ask the Father in my name, he will give it you."* What is He saying?

The Lord is discussing the change for the disciples after His death and resurrection. At the time He spoke, the disciples could come to Him personally and ask a question. But after His death and resurrection, He would ascend into Heaven, and the Church Age would be ushered in. During this Church Age, we cannot walk up to Him here on earth and discuss a situation as the disciples did while He was on earth. He tells the disciples that up until that time, they had not had to pray to the Father in Jesus' name. This is the reason He said, *"Hitherto have ye asked nothing in my name . . ."*

There are two different words translated *ask* in verse twenty-three. The first one means a *friendly entreaty*. Jesus said, *"And in that day ye shall not present me with a friendly entreaty."* This is what they did while He was on earth, but we cannot do it since He is now in Heaven. The second word comes in the sentence, *"Verily, verily, I say unto you, Whatsoever ye shall ask the Father in my name, he will give it you."* Ask means *to petition and to beg for the help you need.* We cannot go to Him as the disciples did, when they went as to a loved friend and presented a case before Him. We come today as a beggar in need of His grace. We come to the Father in the name of the Lord Jesus. Praise God, when we ask, we receive answer to prayer and we then have fullness of joy. As we pray and believe God, we realize the blessing of answered prayer. Beloved, let's pray!

Bible Truth for Today: *"Ask, and it shall be given you; seek, and ye shall find; knock, and it shall be opened unto you."* —Matthew 7:7

November 12

Read John 17, 18, and 19:1-16
Family Reading: John 19:1-16

Pilate on Trial

In John 18 we see Christ before Pilate. Now the situation is reversed. It is Pilate who is on trial since he must decide what he will do with Jesus Christ. In John 18:38 Pilate stood before the Jewish mob and announced, *" . . . I find in him no fault at all."* That is literally a judgment of acquittal. Pilate should then have dismissed the case, and Jesus should have gone free. But the mock trial went on.

Now Pilate is on trial. What about this Roman judge? What is God's thought of him? What does this scene reveal concerning him?

First of all, it shows him as a weakling who knew what was right and refused to do it. In the first verse of John 19, we are told that Pilate *" . . . took Jesus, and scourged him."* He had just declared Him innocent, and then he subjected Him to the most shameful and terrible punishment. That Roman scourge was made of a number of thongs in which sharp pieces of metal were placed every few inches. When the scourge was brought down upon the bare back of the victim, the flesh was literally stripped into ribbons, and blood poured forth. This was a strange torture under which to submit an innocent man.

But Pilate was a weakling, concerned about his political position. He announced again, after the scourging, that he found no fault in Christ. He subjected the Son of God to this dreadful treatment because He was afraid of the people. Verse eight says that the voice of the crowd made him more afraid. He was more concerned about holding his office than he was in doing right.

Today we have the same type of man in many a political position. Oh, that we might have men say again, "I would rather be right than be president." Pilate completely failed his trial. I trust the Lord will use this portion to make each of us say, "I will do right if the stars fall."

Proverb for Today: *"The fear of man bringeth a snare: but whoso putteth his trust in the Lord shall be safe."* —Proverbs 29:25

November 13

Read John 19:17-42; *Chapters 20 and 21*
Family Reading: John 20:1-21

Christ Is Risen

Mary Magdalene came early to the sepulcher and saw the stone taken away. She had come out of love for the Saviour, desiring to take care of the body in a way it had not been taken care of when it was so hurriedly removed from the cross. Mary was amazed to see the great stone rolled back, and she saw that the body of Jesus was removed. She immediately ran to tell Peter and John.

When these two disciples arrived at the tomb, they went into the tomb. They saw the grave clothes lying there as though the body were still in them. But they knew that Jesus was gone. In verse eight we read that John saw and believed. He knew that Jesus Christ was risen. Verse nine tells us that they still did not realize this truth from the Scriptures. They believed because they saw the empty tomb.

Surely they realized the great meaning that was associated with His resurrection. The last enemy, death, had been conquered. No longer would that one who believes need to fear death. Christ was risen and is alive forevermore. He had overcome the victory of sin and death and the grave.

> The strife is o'er, the battle done;
> The victory of life is won.
> The song of triumph has begun.

Verse ten states, *"Then the disciples went away again unto their own home."* After they stood in that empty tomb, they were no longer concerned that someone would steal the body of Jesus. They knew that stealing of the body was an impossibility. The body of Jesus had been raised from the dead.

> Up from the grave He arose
> With a mighty triumph o'er His foes;
> He arose a victor from the dark domain,
> And He lives forever with His saints to reign.

Bible Truth for Today: *"But now is Christ risen from the dead, and become the firstfruits of them that slept."* —*I Corinthians 15:20*

November 14

Read Acts 1–3
Family Reading: Acts 1

Holy Spirit Power

The disciples asked a question that seemed very important to them: " . . . *Lord, wilt thou at this time restore again the kingdom to Israel?" (v. 6).* They wanted to be part of His kingdom. Their hearts were burning with a desire to know more about prophecy.

The Lord Jesus answered, " . . . *It is not for you to know the times or the seasons, which the Father hath put in his own power" (v. 7).* A believer needs to learn to leave the future with God. It is important to study prophecy, but there is something more important: *"But ye shall receive power, after that the Holy Ghost is come upon you: and ye shall be witnesses unto me both in Jerusalem, and in all Judaea, and in Samaria, and unto the uttermost part of the earth" (v. 8).* Our business is to be filled with the Spirit and to be soulwinning witnesses for the Lord. The Holy Spirit has come to make us witnesses to reach the world for Christ.

Today may we yield to the Holy Spirit and depend on Him for power in our lives.

> *Come, Holy Spirit, heavenly Dove,*
> *With all Thy quick'ning powers;*
> *Kindle a flame of sacred love*
> *In these cold hearts of ours.*
>
> *Come, Holy Spirit, heavenly Dove,*
> *With all Thy quick'ning powers;*
> *Come, shed abroad a Saviour's love,*
> *And that shall kindle ours.*
> —*Isaac Watts*

Bible Truth for Today: *"And be not drunk with wine, wherein is excess; but be filled with the Spirit."—Ephesians 5:18*

November 15

Read Acts 4–6
Family Reading: Acts 4:1-13, 21-31

Filled with the Spirit

Twice in this fourth chapter of Acts we read that the disciples were filled with the Spirit. In both cases we note that when they were thus filled, they immediately spoke with boldness: *"Then Peter, filled with the Holy Ghost, said unto them . . . Now when they saw the boldness of Peter and John . . . and they were all filled with the Holy Ghost, and they spake the word of God with boldness" (vv. 8, 13, 31).*

From this chapter I want us to note some truths about the filling of the Spirit. His fullness is a requirement for all Christians since God gave us the commandment of Ephesians 5:18— " *. . . be filled with the Spirit."*

I believe nearly all of us would confess that we have a problem with not being bold enough in our witness for Christ. We do not speak up when we ought. We fear men, and we find it brings a snare to our work for Christ. *"The fear of man bringeth a snare: but whoso putteth his trust in the Lord shall be safe" (Proverbs 29:25).* The answer is in being filled with the Spirit. Then God will give a boldness to witness.

After they were filled with the Holy Ghost, the apostles were able to witness with great power of the resurrection of the Lord Jesus (v. 33). Oh, how we need that power. It comes only as we are filled with the Spirit. Today let's seek God's blessing in the fullness of His Spirit. We can have His power if we will believe God and obey Him. *"And we are his witnesses of these things; and so is also the Holy Ghost, whom God hath given to them that obey him" (Acts 5:32).*

Bible Truth for Today: *"And be not drunk with wine, wherein is excess; but be filled with the Spirit."* *—Ephesians 5:18*

Though we noted this verse yesterday, let's meditate on it again today. To be *"filled with the Spirit"* means to be *controlled* by the Spirit.

November 16

Read Acts 7 and 8
Family Reading: Acts 8:4-8, 26-40

Model Soulwinner

Acts is literally a book of action. We see the apostles and deacons active for the Lord. Philip was one of the deacons and was a soulwinner.

First, he was submissive to the leading of the Lord. An angel commanded him to arise and go to Gaza, and he obeyed and headed immediately to the place the angel commanded (vv. 26, 27). Then we see the Spirit directing him to go join himself to the chariot. Again he obeyed (vv. 29, 30). After he had led the Ethiopian to Christ and had baptized him, we read that the Spirit of the Lord caught Philip away and sent him on his way, preaching and rejoicing (vv. 39, 40).

Second, he was soul conscious. He looked for opportunities to reach people. No sooner had he come to Gaza than he noted the Ethiopian eunuch and ran to the chariot (v. 30).

Third, he knew the Scriptures. The Ethiopian was reading Isaiah 53. Philip asked the question, "Do you understand what you are reading?" The man answered that he needed someone to guide him. Philip was ready. He had studied the Word of God so that he was prepared to present Jesus Christ as revealed in *Isaiah 53:5—"But he was wounded for our transgressions, he was bruised for our iniquities: the chastisement of our peace was upon him; and with his stripes we are healed."*

Fourth, he brought the Ethiopian to a decision. He led him to Christ and saw that he was baptized.

Proverbs for Today: *"If thou forbear to deliver them that are drawn unto death, and those that are ready to be slain . . . doth not he know it? and shall not he render to every man according to his works?"*
—Proverbs 24:11, 12

November 17

Read Acts 9 and 10
Family Reading: Acts 10:23-48

Three Conversions

In our Bible reading for yesterday and today, we note three outstanding conversions. Acts 8 tells of the salvation of the Ethiopian government official. Acts 9 presents the conversion of Saul. Today we read of the conversion of a Roman centurion at Caesarea. All three men were apparently good, moral men; but they were all three lost and in need of the Saviour. To all three God sent a preacher to present the message of salvation and grace, thus demonstrating the truth of Romans 10:14, 15— *"How then shall they call on him in whom they have not believed? and how shall they believe in him of whom they have not heard? and how shall they hear without a preacher? And how shall they preach, except they be sent? as it is written, How beautiful are the feet of them that preach the gospel of peace, and bring glad tidings of good things!"*

These three conversions demonstrate that the gospel is for the whole world. The Ethiopian was a black man, the descendant of Ham. Saul was a Jew, the descendant of Shem. Cornelius was a Gentile, the descendant of Japheth. The spiritual condition of the three may be met by soulwinners in the work. Some are like the Ethiopian—they want to be saved but do not know how to be saved. Others, like Saul, are blind to their need because they are self-satisfied, steeped in a religion. Then there are those, like Cornelius, who only need someone to bring them the message, and they are ready to accept it by faith.

Cornelius had called for Peter to come, and Peter had been prepared by God. Peter brought a tremendous sermon on salvation. A miracle took place, and that whole crowd in Cornelius's home believed. They were baptized and went on for the Lord.

Bible Challenge for Today: *"And of some have compassion, making a difference: And others save with fear, pulling them out of the fire; hating even the garment spotted by the flesh."* —Jude 22,23

November 18

Read Acts 11–13
Family Reading: Acts 12

God's Work Moves On!

Herod was a very proud and egotistical man. The people knew that he was very sensitive to flattery. They knew that if they complimented the king, he in turn might show them favor. They set a day for Herod to deliver a speech to them. They set his throne high above the crowd. When he came out, clothed in his royal apparel, the people gave him a great reception. They clapped and shouted that Herod was a god and not a mere man.

Herod did not give God the glory. He permitted these people from Tyre and Sidon to call him a god without any rebuke. Suddenly, something startling happened. An angel smote the king. He toppled off his throne, died, and was eaten of worms. Oh, how swift and complete can be God's divine retribution! Herod killed James the brother of John (v. 2); he imprisoned Peter (vv. 3, 4); and he killed the soldiers after Peter escaped from prison (v. 19). Now, suddenly he toppled over dead, and worms crawled over his body. Payday had come! King Herod reaped what he had sowed. *"But the word of God grew and multiplied" (v. 24).*

Men may resist and fight the gospel message, but they will lie in dust and God's work will go on. In Russia and Eastern European countries, governments under communism tried to remove the preaching of the Word of God by persecuting the Christians. Yet in those lands there has been revival with millions coming to know Christ as Saviour. Revival has moved in power in some of the countries, especially Romania. Praise God, He preserves His testimony.

Bible Truth for Today: *" . . . the rulers take counsel together, against the Lord . . . [but] he that sitteth in the heavens shall laugh."*
—Psalm 2:2-4

November 19

Read Acts 14–16
Family Reading: Acts 16:16-40

The Philippian Jailer Saved

It is a blessed truth to note that Paul and Silas were singing and praying in prison. When most Christians would have been dreadfully discouraged because they were imprisoned and beaten, Paul and Silas sang the praises of the Lord. When men do this, something is bound to happen. And something did happen! The Lord sent an earthquake to free His servants. The stocks were loosed, and the doors were opened. Supposing that the prisoners had escaped and that consequently he would be held responsible, the jailer decided to harm himself with his sword. A man has no right to harm himself. He may be harmed by others, but he should not harm himself. Paul cried with a loud voice, " . . . *Do thyself no harm: for we are all here*" *(v. 28).* The jailer fell before these Bible preachers and asked, " . . . *Sirs, what must I do to be saved?*" *(v. 30).*

Why did he ask such a question? Undoubtedly Paul and Silas had been singing songs about salvation. The message had reached this man's heart, and he was ready to know this Saviour. Paul answered his question very clearly, " . . . *Believe on the Lord Jesus Christ, and thou shalt be saved . . .*" *(v. 31).* Notice that Paul did not say, "Get baptized, and you will be saved." Nor did he say, "Be good to others, and you will be saved." He told this jailer to do the one and only thing that can save; that is, to put his trust in Jesus Christ. What a glorious result came from Paul's witness! The Philippian jailer and his whole family were saved and baptized. They became the backbone of the church at Philippi.

Bible Truth for Today: *"Jesus saith unto him, I am the way, the truth, and the life: no man cometh unto the Father, but by me."*

—John 14:6

November 20

Read Acts 17–19
Family Reading: Acts 18

Gallio's Indifference

When matters of religion or spiritual interest came up, Gallio had no desire to hear. Note that *" . . . Gallio cared for none of those things" (v. 17).* Nothing can be more deadly than spiritual indifference. The world is full of Gallios today. Many are interested in everything else under the sun, but they are not interested in spiritual things—in the salvation of their souls, forgiveness of sin, judgment, or the life to come. These men often get by all right in this world, but there is a time coming when they must face God. As they stand before Him, they will realize the enormity of their sin. They will cry out for mercy, but it will be too late.

The Jews made an insurrection against Paul. They took him and brought him to Gallio, the deputy of Achaia. Their accusation against Paul was that he was persuading men to worship contrary to the law. Paul would have defended himself, but Gallio did not even permit him to speak. He stated that since it was a situation involving words, names, and their law, he would not judge. He was just not interested. Then the Jews took Sosthenes, the chief ruler of the synagogue, a man who accepted Christ under Paul's preaching. They beat this man in front of the judgment seat, but Gallio did not do one thing to bring justice.

"Terrible!" you say. Yes, it is, but the world is filled with this same indifference today. There are good people who just refuse to have any spiritual interest. It is dreadful to realize, but their indifference will send them to Hell.

Bible Truth for Today: God's judgment on lukewarmness—*"So then because thou art lukewarm, and neither cold nor hot, I will spew thee out of my mouth."* —*Revelation 3:16*

November 21

Read Acts 20 and 21
Family Reading: Acts 20:17-38

The Word of His Grace

"And now, brethren, I commend you to God, and to the word of his grace, which is able to build you up, and to give you an inheritance among all them which are sanctified." —Acts 20:32

Paul called the elders of the church at Ephesus to meet with him in Miletus. He informed them that this would be his last visit with them (v. 25). He said that in every city he had faced jail and persecution (v. 23). Therefore, he told them again of his ministry in Ephesus (vv. 18-21 and 26, 27). He then instructed them concerning certain dangers for their ministry at Ephesus (vv. 28-31).

Then Paul stated that he commended them *" . . . to God, and to the word of his grace . . . " (v. 32)*. We will note that commendation:

First, Paul stated that He commended the Ephesian Christians to God. But then he also commended them to *"his **grace**."* It is grace that saves us. Nothing but superabounding grace can blot out and hide from the eyes of God's justice our iniquities.

Note also that Paul commended them to the *"**word** of his grace."* This is that Word which brings grace into the life and communicates daily life, victory, and power to the soul. The Spirit takes the Word and seals a testimony on the conscience.

There can be no salvation without the Word of God. We are born again by the incorruptible seed of the Word of God (I Peter 1:23). Following salvation, it is the Word that gives us strength and grace for the trials we face. We can receive a promise of divine power, of deliverance from temptation, and of support through the trial. May we constantly feed on the Word of His grace.

Bible Promise for Today: *"And he said unto me, My grace is sufficient for thee: for my strength is made perfect in weakness. Most gladly therefore will I rather glory in my infirmities, that the power of Christ may rest upon me."* —II Corinthians 12:9

November 22

Read Acts 22–24
Family Reading: Acts 23:1-13, 21-35

Victory in Service

As we read of Paul's facing the Sanhedrin and their wrath against him, we can visualize that Paul could have been much discouraged that night. The chief captain feared that in the dissension on the council, Paul could be injured. Therefore, he sent soldiers to take Paul away from the Sanhedrin and put him in the castle. That night the apostle probably was depressed and concerned. However, the Lord appeared, stood by him, and spoke to him. How Paul's heart must have been lifted as the Lord said, " . . . *Be of good cheer, Paul: for as thou hast testified of me in Jerusalem, so must thou bear witness also at Rome" (v. 11).*

God said in effect, "Cheer up, Paul! I still rule in the affairs of men. I will use you further in the work." I am sure that Paul rejoiced in these words and went to sleep with a smile on his face. God was telling Paul that he was immortal until his work was finished. Paul had always wanted to go to Rome and even prayed to go: *"Making request, if by any means now at length I might have a prosperous journey by the will of God to come unto you. For I long to see you, that I may impart unto you some spiritual gift, to the end ye may be established" (Romans 1:10, 11).* The Lord now tells him that this prayer will be answered. Paul got his trip to Rome at Caesar's expense. God provides for His own in His work.

There will always be battles in the Lord's work. Paul had faced the angry mob and the Roman captain in Acts 22. In Acts 23 he stood before the Sanhedrin. After the Lord stood by him, he received word of a group of men who were plotting his death. He did face trials, but he had God's promise of victory and deliverance. Faith is the victory that overcomes the world!

Bible Truth for Today: *"It is God that avengeth me, and subdueth the people under me." —Psalm 18:47*

November 23

Read Acts 25–27
Family Reading: Acts 27:21-44

Faith Triumphing

A few years ago a New York firm offered a "canned prayer" in an aerosol can that sprayed "a fine, heavenly scented mist." On the can were listed twenty different prayers that people could pray. The label did carry a warning: "Does not contain supernatural power." Spiritual life is not gotten in any sort of bundled or canned way. It is hard work to pray.

Paul had prayed, and he believed God was going to take care of the ship and the men. Thus he could tell them that they could be of good cheer. He could conscientiously command them to stay in the ship because he believed God. He was able to invite them to eat rather than fast since he knew that God was taking care of them. All 276 men on board the ship were delivered and kept safe.

S. D. Gordon said, "The great people of the earth are the people who pray. I don't mean people who talk about prayer or those who say they believe in prayer nor yet those who explain prayer. I mean people who take time to pray. These are the people who are doing the most for God in winning souls and solving problems and in wakening churches."

Paul had been alone with God. He had been quiet a good while— *"But after long abstinence Paul stood forth in the midst of them, and said, Sirs, ye should have hearkened unto me, and not have loosed from Crete, and to have gained this harm and loss" (v. 21).* I believe that he prayed during that abstinence, and God answered his prayer.

Thot: Faith is *dead* to *doubt, dumb* to *discouragement, blind* to *impossibilities*, and knows nothing but *success.*

Bible Truth for Today: *"This is a faithful saying, and worthy of all acceptation, that Christ Jesus came into the world to save sinners; of whom I am chief."* —I Timothy 1:15

November 24

Read Acts 28; Romans 1 and 2
Family Reading: Romans 2:5-29

God's Judgment Begins with His Own

The first two chapters of Romans present the truth that the whole world is under condemnation. In Chapter 1 we read of the wickedness of the Gentile world and the resultant condemnation by God. Now in Chapter 2 we find that Paul calls into court the Sadducees and the Pharisees and arraigns them along with despised Gentiles. These are the Jews who have an outward profession of God but not an inward change of heart (vv. 21, 28, 29).

Paul draws attention to the fact that they gloried in these things: they rested in the law, made their boast in God, claimed to know His will, claimed to have discernment, were instructed out of the law, and were confident that they could guide those who were in darkness (vv. 17-20). God had revealed Himself and His law to these people as to no other, but they were wrong to suppose that their knowledge exempted them from judgment.

We must remember that God judges His own: *"You only have I known of all the families of the earth: therefore will I punish you for all your iniquities"* (Amos 3:2). *"For the time is come that judgment must begin at the house of God"* (I Peter 4:17).

Privilege increases responsibility. It does not, as the Jews seemed to think, set judgment aside. They had the knowledge of God's oracles; therefore; they should have lived holier lives. *"Unto whomsoever much is given, of him shall much be required"* (Luke 12:48).

Bible Truth for Today: *"For the time is come that judgment must begin at the house of God: and if it first begin at us, what shall the end be of them that obey not the gospel of God?"* —I Peter 4:17

November 25

Read Romans 3–6
Family Reading: Romans 5

Results of Justification

Romans is the outstanding New Testament book that presents the whole plan of God's redemption. Chapters 1–3 present the fact of man's sin and his need of a redeemer. Chapter 4 gives the fact of justification, completely by faith, apart from the law. Chapter 5 begins with the words, *"Therefore being justified by faith, . . . "* and presents these results of justification:

1. *"Peace with God" (v. 1).* The person who is justified by faith knows that his sin is forgiven. He lives and walks in a peace the world knows nothing about.

2. *"Access by faith into his [God's] grace" (v. 2).* The person who is justified knows that he can come *" . . . boldly unto the throne of grace . . . " (Hebrews 4:16).*

3. Joy in the *"hope of the glory of God" (v. 2).* The person who is justified has hope that produces joy in his life.

4. *"Glory in tribulations" (v. 3).* The child of God can glory in tribulation, *"knowing that tribulation works patience."*

5. God's love *"shed abroad in our hearts" (v. 5).* The person who has received Christ has the love of God shed abroad in his heart by the Holy Ghost.

6. Deliverance from wrath (v. 9). The person who is justified needs to have no fear of ever being sent to Hell. He is *"saved from wrath through him* [Christ]."

7. Salvation by Christ's resurrection (v. 10). Christ's resurrection pictures a priest coming back from offering the sacrifice on the altar. When the people saw him return, they knew the sacrifice had been accepted, and their redemption was pictured in the blood that was offered. We have the same assurance through the resurrection of the Lord Jesus.

Bible Truth for Today: *"And by him all that believe are justified from all things, from which ye could not be justified by the law of Moses." —Acts 13:39*

November 26

Read Romans 7–9
Family Reading: Romans 8:1-25

Holy Spirit Power

Romans 8 is one of the great chapters of the Bible. It is often quoted and is certainly the high point of victory in the book of Romans.

Someone has said, "If we had all the Scriptures, we would find Romans to be the jewel that would give us all we need, and Chapter 8 is the sparkling diamond of all this jeweled setting."

Romans 7 is the chapter of defeat.

Romans 8 is the chapter of spiritual victory.

The big difference between these two chapters is that in Romans 7, *"I"* is the important word. The word *"I"* appears thirty-two times in Romans 7; and the word *"me,"* seventeen times. The opposite is true in Romans 8, where we find the word *"I"* but once; but we note that the word *"Spirit"* appears nineteen times. When the Holy Spirit takes control, there will be victory. When the *"I"* is in charge, there will be defeat.

The Holy Spirit indwells the believer. Verse nine says that *" . . . if any man have not the Spirit of Christ, he is none of his."* If a person does not have the Holy Spirit, that person has never been saved. Every believer possesses the Holy Spirit and, therefore, can have the victory that only the Holy Spirit can give.

"For to be carnally [fleshly] *minded is death . . . "* The believer must yield all to the Holy Spirit's control.

> *Suffer, then, O noble Guest,*
> *That rich gift by thee possessed,*
> *That Thou givest at Thy will,*
> *All my being now to fill.*
> *—Paul Gerhardt*

Bible Truth for Today: *"Then he answered and spake unto me, saying, This is the word of the Lord unto Zerubbabel, saying, Not by might, nor by power, but by my spirit, saith the Lord of hosts."*
—Zechariah 4:6

November 27

Read Romans 10–13
Family Reading: Romans 11:1-14, 26-36

Future of Israel

The eleventh chapter of Romans gives us much insight into God's dispensational plan. Romans 9 reveals that God's past dealings with Israel proved His righteousness in dealing with the Gentiles as He does in this present age. In spite of the covenant which God made with Israel, His earthly people, God has the right to call those His people who were not His people (9:25). There is no unrighteousness with God (9:14).

In Chapter 10 we understand that though Israel as a *nation* has been set to one side, an Israelite as an *individual* can turn to God and receive the same salvation that God has offered to the Gentiles.

Now in verses one through six of Chapter 11, the subject of Chapter 10 is continued and brought to a conclusion. Verse one asks the question: *"Hath God cast away his people?"* By no means! Paul's own salvation proved this was not the case. He was an Israelite who had been brought by the Spirit to a saving knowledge of Jesus Christ. What was true of him could be true of any Israelite. What had happened to Paul was a fulfillment of Isaiah's prophecy that there would be a remnant saved (Romans 11:2-5).

All of this shows the depth of the wisdom and knowledge of God (11:33). To Him belongs all the glory (11:36).

Bible Truth for Today: Salvation is only by grace. *"And if by grace, then is it no more of works: otherwise grace is no more grace. But if it be of works, then is it no more grace: otherwise work is no more work."* —Romans 11:6

November 28

Read Romans 14–16
Family Reading: Romans 16

Warning About False Teachers

Paul was personally interested in every individual in the church at Rome. He was also concerned about the danger of false teachers. He gave very specific instruction concerning these false teachers (vv. 17-20). Please note some truths from this chapter:

First, those who were teaching false doctrine were not saved men: *" . . . they . . . serve not our Lord Jesus Christ . . . " (v. 18).* These are the ungodly men who have crept in from the outside (Jude 4).

Second, their goal was to divide Christians. They caused divisions and offenses contrary to sound doctrine. False teachers always bring division. If there is anything we should hate in the work of a local church, it is that which brings division.

Third, Paul commands that Christians mark those who cause these divisions. The word *mark* means *to examine closely or to scrutinize, keeping an eye on the problem-makers so as to avoid them.* In his letter to the Romans, Paul commended this church for its faithfulness to the Word of God. But, alas! This very church opened its doors to false teachers and departed from the faith so rapidly that by the seventh century, the papacy itself was enthroned in Rome. Today we must be careful to *mark* those who would teach contrary to the Word of God. *"Hear me now, therefore, O ye children, and depart not from the words of my mouth . . . Lest thou give thine honor unto others . . . And thou mourn at the last, when thy flesh and thy body are consumed" (Proverbs 5:7, 9, 11).*

Bible Truth for Today: *"And have no fellowship with the unfruitful works of darkness, but rather reprove them." —Ephesians 5:11*

November 29

Read I Corinthians 1–4
Family Reading: I Corinthians 2

The Wisdom of God

Paul said that he spoke the wisdom of God and that he determined not to know anything among the Corinthians except Jesus Christ and Him crucified (v. 2). The only message that will ever bear any fruit for eternity is the message of the crucifixion of Jesus Christ. Paul preached God's wisdom because he wanted the faith of the Corinthians to stand, not in the wisdom of men, but in the power of God (v. 5).

Paul made some very interesting statements about the message of the wisdom of God in verses seven through fourteen:

First, he said the wisdom of God had been ordained before the world. God had planned this message that Christ's death was all anyone needed for salvation.

Second, Paul said the princes of the world did not know this message. Had they realized it, they would not have crucified the Lord of glory.

Third, this message must be revealed by the Holy Spirit. Only as the Holy Spirit reveals these blessed truths can any of us receive them. Fourth, the natural man cannot receive the things of the Spirit of God. This simply means that a person cannot understand the truths of the Word of God or the things of the Spirit of God until he is born again. A natural man is one who has never been saved. He cannot fathom the things of God for they are *foolishness* unto him.

However, the person who is spiritual—that is, the one who has been born again and has walked with the Lord and read the Word of God—will be able to judge and discern all things (v. 15).

It is absolutely essential that a person be born again. After a person is born again, it is also essential that he grow in the Lord so that he can become a spiritual person, understanding the truths of the Lord.

Bible Truth for Today: *"For the preaching of the cross is to them that perish foolishness; but unto us which are saved it is the power of God."* *—I Corinthians 1:18*

November 30

Read I Corinthians 5–8
Family Reading: I Corinthians 7:1-24

The Importance of Marriage

In this chapter Paul opens a new section of I Corinthians by answering some questions this church had written him: *"Now concerning the things whereof ye wrote unto me, . . . " (v. 1).* In Chapter 7 he dealt with their questions about marriage; in Chapters 8, 9, and 10, about meat sacrificed to idols; in Chapter 11, about the place of women in the church and also the problems surrounding the Lord's supper.

In Chapter 7 Paul speaks first about the *purity* of marriage. He states that every man should have his own wife and every woman her own husband. Some might think that Paul undervalues marriage in this chapter, but that is not the case. He is saying that being single does not relegate a person to second-class citizenship. He states that it is good for a man not to be married, but it is not better. Celibacy is good as long as a person can keep himself pure.

Paul stresses not only the *purity* of marriage but also the *permanence* of marriage. He insists on monogamy (v. 2). Then he states in verse ten, " *. . . Let not the wife depart from her husband."* Note also verse eleven, " *. . . let not the husband put away his wife."* The marriage relationship is holy in every aspect, and in it there must be love, discipline, and mutual respect. This chapter hits hard at the loose ideas in our day about marriage. We believers must stress the importance and the permanence of marriage.

Bible Truth for Today: *"Whoso findeth a wife findeth a good thing, and obtaineth favor of the Lord." —Proverbs 18:22*

December 1

Read I Corinthians 9–11
Family Reading: I Corinthians 10:1-22

The Majority Did Not Please God

The first thirteen verses of I Corinthians 10 give us Old Testament history for the development of our Christian lives. These truths are given for our examples so that we may live for the Lord.

An alarming truth in I Corinthians 10 is the fact expressed in verse five: *"But with many of them God was not well pleased: for they were overthrown in the wilderness."* The word *many* in verse five literally means *majority*. With the majority God was not well pleased. That was true in the Old Testament, and it is a type of what God says concerning today. With the majority of Christians, God is not well pleased because they fail to be faithful.

All of the Old Testament Israelites had the same privilege. Please note the word *all:*

"All our fathers were under the cloud " (v. 1).

"All passed through the sea" (v. 1).

"All were baptized" (v. 2).

"All did eat the same spiritual meat" (v. 3).

"All did drink the same spiritual drink" (v. 4).

They all had the same privilege, and yet with the majority of them God was not well pleased. The sins that kept them from pleasing God were lust, idolatry, fornication, testing Christ, and murmuring. These are the sins in which believers get involved today.

Do not say, "I will never be troubled with these." God's answer is: *"Wherefore let him that thinketh he standeth take heed lest he fall" (v. 12).* The person who believes he is strong enough in himself will fall. God warns against it. Verse thirteen is a promise that every believer should take. Read verse thirteen again this morning and claim it for your family.

Thot: *"The sin you now tremble at, if left to yourself, you will commit." —Colgate*

December 2

Read I Corinthians 12–14
Family Reading: I Corinthians 14:1-22

Tongues

Today many sincere Christians are asking about the gift of tongues. They wonder if they should seek such a gift. They have heard testimonies of others who claim to have received "the gift of tongues." Should they seek this experience also? Are tongues valid for today?

The question all should ask is this: "According to the Scriptures, should I seek the gift of tongues?" Believers should desire above everything else to walk according to the Scriptures. Isaiah 8:20 says, *"To the law and to the testimony: if they speak not according to this word, it is because there is no light in them."* You see, we need to be sure that our practice is according to the Word of God. The Bible never once states that a Christian should seek a tongues' experience. In fact, the opposite is actually the case. We are told to desire love and the gift of prophecy (v.1). In the remainder of the chapter Paul mentions several times how important prophecy is.

Paul uses two illustrations. In verse seven he speaks of a musical instrument. Unless there is an intelligent use of a musical instrument, according to the notes on the musical scale, its playing is useless. Likewise, unless our language is intelligent, according to speech usage, it is meaningless. Neither language nor music is valuable unless there is some means for interpretation. Paul is saying that prophecy is more valuable than tongues because it will be understood. Notice the word *"understanding"* in verses fourteen to twenty. Understanding is more important in worship than unrestrained and unintelligent emotionalism. We must have understanding.

We need to appreciate and love prophecy (Bible preaching) as it gives understanding to our message and lives. Tongues were a sign to the early Christians and are not needed today.

Bible Truth for Today: *"Charity never faileth: but whether there be prophecies, they shall fail; whether there be tongues, they shall cease; whether there be knowledge, it shall vanish away."*

—I Corinthians 13:8

December 3

Read I Corinthians 15 and 16
Family Reading: I Corinthians 16

Duties That Bring Victory

"Watch ye, stand fast in the faith, quit you like men, be strong."
—I Corinthians 16:13

Those who believe in Christ partake here and now in His full salvation. There is no enemy who can deprive any believer of the blessing of his salvation because we are *" . . . kept by the power of God through faith unto salvation . . . " (I Peter 1:5)*.

How is it that we know we are saved? It is by the truth of the Word of God and the promises He has given in His Word. We accept these promises by faith. Therefore, since we know we are saved through faith by the Word of God, is it not equally understandable that we should accept the exhortations of the Word of God for our daily lives in Christ? Here in I Corinthians 16:13 we are exhorted to *"watch,"* to *"stand,"* to *"quit,"* and to *"be strong."*

First, God tells us to *"watch."* Through watchfulness many evils are kept back from our lives and many blessings are enjoyed. When a Christian gets off his guard and is spiritually asleep at the time he should be watching, he is exposed to attacks and to the possibility of falling at the hand of his enemies.

Second, He tells us to *"stand fast."* The idea here is that of standing solidly without compromise. It follows the command to watch. Those who watch and see the danger of evil must also stand so that they can resist the evil.

Third, the believer is commanded, *"Quit you like men."* The Lord is telling believers that they must not carry on in the energy of the flesh. Victory in Christ cannot be attained by the flesh. God wants His people to rest on Him for power and victory.

Then God commands believers to *"be strong."* Our strength must be in the Lord and not in ourselves.

Bible Principle for Today: *" . . . Cursed be the man that trusteth in man, and maketh flesh his arm . . . Blessed is the man that trusteth in the Lord, and whose hope the Lord is."* *—Jeremiah 17:5, 7*

December 4

Read II Corinthians 1–4
Family Reading: II Corinthians 1

Blessings in Trials

Paul begins in this first chapter by talking about comfort. He states that the Lord comforts us in our needs so that we will be able to comfort others who have needs. Our God is *" . . . the Father of mercies and the God of all comfort" (v. 3).* He longs to bring comfort to us in our trials.

In fact, the Lord tells us in verse five that as the sufferings of Christ abound, so shall also the consolation. You can never get so many trials on one side of the scale but that God will balance them out with His consolation. When the clouds are the blackest, then it is that the Light can shine the brightest. When the storm seems the worst, then it is that our Heavenly Captain is always the closest to the crew. When we are the most cast down, it is then we can be the most lifted up by the Spirit through His consolations.

You see, trials make more room for consolations. Great people are made by great trials. The Lord comes into our lives. He finds them full. He then begins to break our comforts and to make us realize our own emptiness.

The more humble a man is, the more comfort he will have because he will be more ready to receive it. It is when we are in trouble that we often have our closest walk with God. When the granaries are full, the farmer can get by without God; but when the drought hits, he thinks of praying. When the bank account is full and the purse is bulging, we think we can get by without praying. In my life God knocked me down so low that I had to reach up to touch bottom. It was then that I was willing to turn to the Lord.

God comforts us in our tribulations. Those tribulations can bring us to the Lord—to the very place where we will appreciate His comfort and consolation.

Bible Truth for Today: *"Beloved, think it not strange concerning the fiery trial which is to try you, as though some strange thing happened unto you: But rejoice, inasmuch as ye are partakers of Christ's sufferings; that, when his glory shall be revealed, ye may be glad also with exceeding joy." —I Peter 4:12, 13*

December 5

Read II Corinthians 5–8
Family Reading: II Corinthians 6 and 7:1

Separation: A *Must* for Christians of All Ages

II Corinthians 6 is a very important chapter for the believer. It presents a great challenge for us to live separated lives. Verses seventeen and eighteen state: *"Wherefore come out from among them, and be ye separate, saith the Lord, and touch not the unclean thing; and I will receive you, And will be a Father unto you, and ye shall be my sons and daughters, saith the Lord Almighty."*

It probably has always been true that the preacher who stands before his people and calls upon them to separate themselves from the world will be ridiculed and despised. Many people will be ready to count him as an enemy of their true happiness. They will cry out, "Narrow! Legalistic! There is no harm in it!" But a faithful preacher must do exactly what Paul did. He must warn that believers are to be separated from the world and its entanglements. The Christian life is totally opposite from the way of life in the world. Paul showed how irreconcilable the Christian life and the world are when he used the graphic contrasts of II Corinthians 6:14, 15. Look at them: light and darkness, Christ and the devil, faith and unbelief.

Before Paul called upon the Corinthians for this firm stand, he proved to them that he loved them. In verse eleven he told them, *"O ye Corinthians, our mouth is open unto you, our heart is enlarged."* Paul has prepared us for the challenge to come out from the world and be separate. He told the Corinthians how much he loved them. He went into the sufferings he endured, all because he was a minister of the gospel of Christ. In this very chapter he reiterated these truths that he had stripes and imprisonments and labors. He had faced dying for his witness, evil reports of his life and ministry, poverty, and chastisement. Why did he do it? The answer is obvious. He did all of this because he loved the people. He wanted them to know God's Word and His ways. With this love, he called upon them to be separated from the world.

Paul said that separation from the world is a *must*. If we do not have a separated testimony, we will bring dishonor to our Saviour. May God give us grace to obey His Word.

December 6

Read II Corinthians 9–12
Family Reading: II Corinthians 8:20-24 and Chapter 9

God's Abounding Grace

"And God is able to make all grace abound toward you; that ye, always having all sufficiency in all things, may abound to every good work." —*II Corinthians 9:8*

Paul has been making an earnest appeal for the Christians in Corinth to give financial aid to the saints in Jerusalem. He had boasted in many places of the generosity that the Corinthian Christians had manifested. Now he writes in a tactful way, encouraging these believers to keep their promise so that they can prove their love. But finance is certainly not the main thrust of Paul's message in this chapter. Paul is speaking of dedication to Christ, a dedication manifested by a willingness to give to meet the needs of others. From verse eight let's notice three truths today:

1. An Inexhaustible Provision
   "And God is able to make all grace abound toward you . . . " A Christian who is blessed must recognize there is a fountain from which flow all of the blessings needed for each day. Paul states that *all* grace can *abound*. These are two superlatives. Everything for a holy, godly life is provided in Jesus Christ.

2. An Inevitable Practice
   " . . . that ye, always having all sufficiency in all things, may abound to every good work." Because we receive from the fountain of His grace, we should always be full so that we can be used for His glory. *" . . . the water that I shall give him shall be in him a well of water springing up into everlasting life"* *(John 4:14).*

3. An Inescapable Principle
   "And God is able to make all grace abound toward you." Paul does not say, "God will make all grace abound"; he simply states that God is *able* to do so. The responsibility rests with us. We need to be ready receivers of His grace. May we be found in the place of surrender so that His grace can be operative in us.

Bible Truth for Today: *"And he said unto me, my grace is sufficient for thee . . . "* — *II Corinthians 12:9*

December 7

Read II Corinthians 13 and Galatians 1–3
Family Reading: Galatians 1

Beware of False Teachers

The book of Galatians gives us very important truths for today. It links intimately with the letter to the Romans. In Romans we have the fullest, most complete revelation of the grace of God that we get anywhere in the New Testament. In this letter to the Galatians we have the glorious message of the gospel of grace defended against those who were seeking to substitute legality for grace.

Paul had preached the gospel to them and many had been saved. But then Satan, who comes as an angel of light, led false apostles to come in and to endeavor to destroy the testimony of the Galatians. These false apostles told them that unless they kept the law of Moses, observed the rite of circumcision, and kept the different feasts and holy days of Israel, they could not be saved. These false teachers wormed their way into the confidence of the believers by undermining their faith. They did this by endeavoring to destroy their confidence in Paul, who had led them to the Lord.

No wonder Paul made it so clear that these false teachers should not be followed. *"But though we, or an angel from heaven, preach any other gospel unto you than that which we have preached unto you, let him be accursed. As we said before, so say I now again, If any man preach any other gospel unto you than that ye have received, let him be accursed" (Galatians 1:8, 9).*

The subject of this book of Galatians is law and grace. We are saved by grace and we are kept by grace. These that taught contrary to grace so troubled Paul that he wrote in Galatians 5:12—*"I would they were even cut off which trouble you."*

False teachers are an abomination to God. He wants us to turn from false doctrine to love Him and to serve Him. Paul loved the Galatians, and in this letter he pleaded with them to turn from heresy to love the Lord Jesus and to believe his message of grace.

Bible Truth for Today: *"I do not frustrate the grace of God: for if righteousness come by the law, then Christ is dead in vain."*

—Galatians 2:21

December 8

Read Galatians 4–6
Family Reading: Galatians 5

The Battle Every Believer Faces

"For the flesh lusteth against the Spirit, and the Spirit against the flesh: and these are contrary the one to the other: so that ye cannot do the things that ye would . . ." —*Galatians 5:17*

In every believer there is a continuous battle between the old nature and the new. Paul knew what this battle was, and he experienced it all of his life. We have no scriptural authority to suppose that this strife ever ceases in any of the saints until they get to glory. None are delivered from it while they live in this fleshly body.

In *Pilgrim's Progress* the battle between "Christian" and "Apollyon" lasted three hours, but the battle of "Christian" with himself lasted all the way from the Wicket Gate to the River Jordan. This enemy is so securely entrenched that we cannot drive him out completely while we are in this body. It is the truth presented to Israel in Exodus 17. God states that there will be continual warfare with Amalek—a type of the flesh. This is the truth taught in Galatians 5:17—there will be a battle between the flesh and the Spirit continually. It is true in my life, in your life, and in the lives of the most eminent saints. The command of Romans 11:20 is very appropriate in this matter: *"Be not highminded, but fear."*

Martin Luther wrote: "The more godly a man is, the more doth he feel this battle between the flesh and the spirit . . . It profiteth us very much to feel, sometimes the wickedness of our nature and corruption of the flesh, that we may be waked and stirred up to call upon Christ."

Though we have this enemy strongly entrenched, we also have One who stands ready to win the battle. He is our almighty helper, even Jesus Christ, the captain of our salvation, who will make it possible for us to be *"more than conquerors"* through Him (Romans 8:37). With Him as our Assistant, the newborn nature is more than a match for its foes. But remember, the last part of this verse states that we cannot do the things that we would. We must surrender all to Him.

Bible Truth for Today: *"If we live in the Spirit, let us also walk in the Spirit."* —*Galatians 5:25*

December 9

Read Ephesians 1:1–4:16
Family Reading: Ephesians 3

Unto Him That Is Able

*"Now unto Him **that is able** to do **exceeding abundantly** above all that we ask or think, according to the power that worketh in us, Unto him be glory in the church by Christ Jesus throughout all ages, world without end. Amen."* —*Ephesians 3:20, 21*

Ephesians 3:20, 21 closes a prayer of the apostle Paul—a prayer he began in Ephesians 3:14. He has been stating some great things in Ephesians concerning the work of God in the lives of believers. Then he comes to the close of this prayer and commits all unto Him who is able to do exceeding abundantly above all we can ask or think.

The usage of the term *"exceeding abundantly"* is found only in Ephesians 3:20. It is a combination of Greek words that mean *"the over and above and beyond abundance of God's ability."*

God is able! There is no limit to His power. He can and will do great things for and through those who surrender all to Him. As we face the work we have to do for Him, we face these tasks not in our own strength but in His abundant power. How mighty is God, our Champion! When we face seemingly impassable mountains that we cannot move, He can touch them and they jump at His command.

It is in the spirit and power of Ephesians 3:20 that we are to face the present world. We live in a world of increasing power and difficulty. But we must move forward as David against Goliath and be able to announce: *" . . . [We] come to thee in the name of the Lord of hosts . . . This day will the Lord deliver thee into mine hand; and I will smite thee . . ."* (I Samuel 17:45, 46).

Let's not come before God thinking it is presumptuous to ask for His power. Instead let us boldly come, praying the will of God to be done and believing that God is exceeding abundantly able to work with the power that He has given us.

Bible Truth for Today: *"And Jesus came and spake unto them, saying, All power is given unto me in heaven and in earth."*

—Matthew 28:18

December 10

Read Ephesians 4:17-32 and Chapters 5 and 6
Family Reading: Ephesians 4:17-32

The New Man in Control

Two days ago we considered the old man, the flesh nature, from Galatians 5. The title of our devotional was, "The Battle Every Believer Faces." Today in Ephesians 4:17-32, Paul exhorts the believers concerning this constant battle with the flesh. In verses twenty through twenty-four, Paul states that our knowledge of Christ instructs us to put off the old man and to put on the new man. Paul frequently makes this distinction in the life of the believer. He teaches that a genuine, born-again believer has two natures—the old nature and the new nature. In Ephesians 4 he refers to these as the old man and the new man.

The new nature is the result of the new birth, created in righteousness and true holiness. The old nature is the result of the flesh birth and is that nature which caters to the flesh. It follows the vanity of the mind with a darkened understanding and a blinded heart.

Every believer must so yield to the Lord that he walks in the power of the spirit with fullness of blessing. Ephesians 4 gives some practical results in the life if the child of God walks in the spirit and not in the flesh. God says the child of God will put away lying (v. 25), will not steal but labor with his hands to have *his* needs provided and also to meet needs of *others* (v. 28), will guard his speech to see that no corrupt communication comes from his lips (v. 29). Further, he will not grieve the Holy Spirit with bitterness, wrath, anger, clamor, evil speaking, or malice (vv. 30, 31). The new man will be marked with kindness, a tender heart, and a forgiving spirit (v. 32).

May we pray today that we will manifest God's miraculous grace in our lives by living with the new man in control. *"Therefore if any man be in Christ, he is a new creature: old things are passed away; behold, all things are become new" (II Corinthians 5:17).* Remember, if you wish your neighbors to see what God is like, let them see what God can make you like!

Bible Truth for Today: *"That ye put off concerning . . . the old man . . . And that ye put on the new man, which after God is created in righteousness and true holiness." —Ephesians 4:22, 24*

December 11

Read Philippians 1–3
Family Reading: Philippians 2:1-24

One-Mindedness

In Philippians 2 we have the fool-proof remedy for church problems. The secret is that we all be of one mind and one accord. When a church is one-minded, that church will enjoy blessings from God. The secret to the power of the church in the book of Acts is that they were of one accord in one place. They were standing together.

In Philippi there had apparently been some division among the members. In Chapter 4 Paul begged two of the members to be of the same mind in the Lord. In Chapter 2 he commanded them to do nothing by strife or vainglory. In lowliness of mind they were each to esteem others better than themselves. This type of attitude would solve many church problems. It would put a stop to the aggressive designs of "Mr. Desire-to-be-Important" and bring a sweetness and unity to the fellowship.

How can believers come to this place of blessed fellowship with each other? The formula to accomplish such a result is found in verse five, when Paul says, *"Let this mind be in you, which was also in Christ Jesus."* It is just that simple. If we have the mind of Christ, we will have the humility and submission necessary to promote godly fellowship and the unity of the spirit.

The mind of Christ is represented first of all in His self-humbling. The more we have the mind of Christ, the less we will be seeking our way and our rights. God is the One who has the power and authority to exalt someone. He exalted Christ with the Name above every name so that every knee shall bow and every tongue shall confess Him as Lord to the glory of God the Father.

> *All hail the power of Jesus' Name;*
> *Let angels prostrate fall;*
> *Bring forth the royal diadem,*
> *And crown Him Lord of all.*

Bible Truth for Today: *"[Love] Doth not behave itself unseemly, seeketh not her own, is not easily provoked, thinketh no evil."*

—I Corinthians 13:5

December 12

Read Philippians 4 and Colossians 1 and 2
Family Reading: Colossians 2

Walk in Him

"As ye have therefore received Christ Jesus the Lord, so walk ye in him" (Colossians 2:6). Here is a great verse for Christian victory. We are to walk in Him as we received Him—by faith. We do not merely have truth *about* Him—we have *Him.* We receive Him as the Saviour from our sins; but even more, as the Master, the Lord of our lives, our wills, our affections, and our consciences. Receiving Him is simply the acceptance of a gift. As the earth drinks in the rain or as the night accepts light from the stars, so we, giving nothing, accept freely of the grace of God. We believers are not by very nature wells; but rather we are cisterns, receiving the water God pours out so that we can be as wells giving forth the blessing. To receive, we must first realize our need. We must realize who Jesus is and what He can be to us. Before we were saved, Jesus was to us just a name of a great figure in history. But by an act of faith, He became a real Person in the consciousness of our hearts. After we have received Him, then we are to walk in Him by faith.

Walking implies action. We must carry out into life that which we have experienced alone with Him.

Walking signifies progress—daily spiritual progress.

Walking involves continuance. How foolish to think I can be with Jesus in the morning and then hold hands with the world the rest of the day!

Walking implies habit. When we speak of a man's walk, we speak of his habits, the constant tenor of his life. If we sometimes enjoy Christ and then forget Him or sometimes testify that He is ours and then do not continue on, we are not really walking in Him. Therefore—having received Him, continue on, trusting Him as the only Source for your daily life.

Bible Truth for Today: *"And walk in love, as Christ also hath loved us, and hath given himself for us an offering and a sacrifice to God for a sweetsmelling savor. See then that ye walk circumspectly, not as fools, but as wise, Redeeming the time, because the days are evil."*

—Ephesians 5:2, 15,16

December 13

Read Colossians 3 and 4 and I Thessalonians 1 and 2
Family Reading: I Thessalonians 2

Paul's Burden in Doing God's Will

The church at Thessalonica was a good church. Chapter 1 speaks of the characteristics of the Thessalonians that made it a great church. They accepted the preaching of the Word of God with a spiritual hunger, and they lived the Word of God out in their lives to see real fruit for the Lord Jesus Christ. They were a missionary-minded church, and a church that looked for the second coming of Christ. We note all of these truths in the first chapter.

Now in Chapter 2 we find what Paul went through to see the work established in Thessalonica. He had to suffer in order to give out the gospel. In this chapter he answers some of the lies that had been told. Apparently he had been accused of deceitful methods, but he informs the Thessalonian Christians that this was not true (v. 3). Also, his accusers said that he was a selfish man preaching for his own glory. This accusation he answers in verses five through seven.

He had given himself for the Thessalonians. He labored night and day for them and expected nothing from them (v. 9). He had lived an holy and unblameable life before them so that he could challenge them to live godly lives (vv. 10-12).

Paul had worked at soulwinning. He considered these Thessalonian Christians to be his children in the Lord. He believed God would reward his work in soulwinning. He asked in verse nineteen: *"For what is our hope, or joy, or crown of rejoicing? . . . "* And then he answered it with another question: *" . . . Are not even ye in the presence of our Lord Jesus Christ at his coming?"* The soulwinner will have the reward of fruit in the presence of the Son of God.

> *Jesus, I long, I long to be winning*
> *Men who are lost and constantly sinning.*

Motive of Paul's Life in Ministry: *"For we preach not ourselves, but Christ Jesus the Lord; and ourselves your servants for Jesus' sake." —II Corinthians 4:5*

December 14

Read I Thessalonians 3–5 and II Thessalonians 1
Family Reading: I Thessalonians 5

Always Ready

"Therefore let us not sleep, as do others; but let us watch and be sober." —*I Thessalonians 5:6*

One of the greatest incentives for godly living and consecrated service for the Lord is the prospect that our Lord will return at any moment.

A man visited a certain school and made a promise to all of the students that he would give a prize to the pupil whose desk was found to be in the very best order when he returned. He did not tell the students when he would come back. After he left, one little girl, who was well known for her messy desk and disorderly habits, announced that she planned to win the prize. Her schoolmates mocked and laughed at her, saying, "Mary, your desk is always a mess. It is never cleaned up."

She replied, "I know it, but starting right now, I'm going to clean it up the first of every week."

One student asked, "Suppose the man comes at the end of the week?"

"Well, then," Mary said, "I will clean it up every morning."

Another asked, "What if he comes at the end of the day?"

Mary sat silent for a time. Then her face lighted up and she said, "I know what I'll do. I'll just keep it clean ALL THE TIME!"

This is the way it must be with us. We must be always ready for our Lord's return.

> *When Jesus comes to reward His servants,*
> *Whether it be noon or night,*
> *Faithful to Him, will He find us watching,*
> *With our lamps all trimmed and bright?"*
> —*Fanny Crosby*

Bible Truth for Today: *"And now, little children, abide in him; that, when he shall appear, we may have confidence, and not be ashamed before him at his coming."* —*I John 2:28*

December 15

Read II Thessalonians 2 and 3 and I Timothy 1–4
Family Reading: I Timothy 1

The Gospel Defined

Timothy was the pastor of the church at Ephesus. The first epistle was written to help this young godly pastor know how to lead and direct the local church at Ephesus. The key verse of the book is I Timothy 3:15, where Paul states: *" . . . that thou mayest know how thou oughtest to behave thyself in the house of God, which is the church of the living God, the pillar and ground of the truth."*

In the first chapter of Timothy, Paul warned Timothy to instruct the people so that they would not follow false teachers. These teachers were legalists, giving instruction in the law but not understanding the truth of the law. Paul showed that the law was given to reach the unsaved, the lawless, and the disobedient.

We have in this first chapter one of Paul's best testimonies of his salvation. In verse eleven he states that any doctrine is wrong if it is contrary to the glorious gospel of Jesus Christ. Then he defines what that gospel does and the basis on which it operates.

First, the gospel transformed Paul, enabling him to perform the work of the ministry. He said he was in the ministry, not because of his ability, but because of his faithfulness. God uses faithful men. *"Moreover it is required in stewards, that a man be found faithful"* *(I Corinthians 4:2)*.

Second, the gospel transforms very wicked men. Paul had been a blasphemer and a persecutor, but God saved him.

Third, the basis of the gospel is the grace of God. His grace was exceeding abundant and brought this wicked sinner, Saul, to be saved and become Paul, the mighty apostle. Paul sums it up in a wonderful way in verse fifteen when he states that Christ Jesus came into the world to save sinners, and he was the biggest sinner of all. This is the attitude that is necessary for one to come to know Christ: he must admit that he is a sinner.

Bible Truth for Today: *"And the grace of our Lord was exceeding abundant with faith and love which is in Christ Jesus."*

—I Timothy 1:14

December 16

Read I Timothy 5 and 6 and II Timothy 1 and 2
Family Reading: II Timothy 1

Death Abolished

"But is now made manifest by the appearing of our Saviour Jesus Christ, who hath abolished death, and hath brought life and immortality to light through the gospel." —II Timothy 1:10

How can Christ have abolished death? Christians die physically and as surely and really as others. There are only two persons of all the sons of Adam who have been exempted from dying—Enoch and Elijah.

The English Parliament decreed on August 1, 1836, to abolish slavery in the West Indies, but the decree did not go into effect until one year later. During that year the slave was still under the whip of his master, and all went on as in the old slavery days. But on July 31, 1837, twenty thousand slaves met together in Jamaica. They put on white robes, and at eleven o'clock they knelt down and waited for one hour with upturned faces. When the clock struck twelve, these white-robed slaves rose up and shouted, "We are free! We are free!"

Slavery had been abolished by enactment a year before, but now it was abolished in fact. Christ in His death on the cross has abolished death, but we are waiting for the *" . . . manifestation of the sons of God" (Romans 8:19).* Death will be swallowed up in victory. It is all a settled enactment by our God. God delivers us now and eternally from the second death. We can rest in all of His promises, and one day we shall realize in fact that He has abolished death. We will then be able to shout, "We are free! We are free!" Death, then, can never touch us because our portion is life evermore through Jesus Christ.

For this reason we can realize the blessed truth of verse seven, where God promises that He delivers us from the spirit of fear and has given us the spirit *" . . . of power, and of love, and of a sound mind."*

Thank God for this blessed privilege of hearing the gospel and receiving eternal life through Jesus Christ.

Bible Truth for Today: *"Who delivered us from so great a death, and doth deliver: in whom we trust that he will yet deliver us."*

—II Corinthians 1:10

December 17

Read II Timothy 3 and 4 and Titus 1–3
Family Reading: II Timothy 4

Paul's Burden and Glory

Paul was in prison when he wrote this second letter to Timothy. He knew he would probably not see Timothy again and that he himself would soon go on to glory. Timothy and younger men like him would need to carry on the work of the Lord. He wanted to leave Timothy the best advice possible. Therefore he wrote, *"Preach the word . . . "(v. 2).* No preacher could receive better advice than this. God's Word is the seed which bears the fruit, and it is the hammer which breaks the rock in pieces. Preachers today need to heed this admonition and preach the Word of God.

Paul knew he was to die soon because he said, *" . . . the time of my departure is at hand" (v. 6).* There he sat in that little, damp, dark, Mamertine prison. He had been there for three years, most of the time with a chain on his hand and a soldier watching by his side. Most of us would have despaired at such treatment, but let us look at the apostle. His face glows with rapture, and as he writes his pen almost catches fire in the speed of its flight. We ask, "Blessed Apostle, what of the outcome? What will happen?" He answers, "That is what I am writing. I have fought a good fight; I have finished my course; my departure is at hand." "Paul, you must despair at the thought of dying." He speaks triumphantly, "Not despair! Henceforth a crown is laid up for me."

"A crown, Paul? Why, I see a soldier waiting just outside the city with a drawn sword to take off your head. And, Paul, I hear the crunching of bones and groans in the den of beasts as they wait for one more prisoner."

"Oh," answers Paul, "since you mention it, I do hear the harps of innumerable harpers welcoming me home." What a difference! This salvation that Paul had gives a joy and a light in which he steadily lived, and which we can have to make us ready for whatever comes.

Bible Truth for Today: *"For I reckon that the sufferings of this present time are not worthy to be compared with the glory which shall be revealed in us." —Romans 8:18*

December 18

Read Philemon and Hebrews 1 –3
Family Reading: Hebrews 1 and 2:1-8

God Has Spoken Through Christ

In both the Old and the New Testaments God spoke. The prophets in the Old Testament were as truly messengers of God as the Son in the New Testament. In the Old Testament the message was external and came through the mediation of men. God Himself did not enter the life and take possession of man and dwell in him. In the New Testament we have God's Son, Emmanuel, who is *"God with us."* He gives the believers an inward hope and reality of which the Old Testament was only the shadow.

Today God has spoken in His Son (v. 2). Man was created for fellowship with God. Sin interrupted that fellowship. But praise God, that broken fellowship is not forever. The silence has been broken. God has spoken and calls man back to Himself. He has spoken, and He asks for our hearing. We must listen. We can hear that voice only as we open our spirits to Him.

When a missionary is going to learn a foreign language, he works diligently hour after hour. He needs a teacher who knows the language. If we are going to understand the speaking of Christ, we must permit the Holy Spirit to teach us. In Christ there is all we need for redemption, grace, power, deliverance, and victory. As you read through Hebrews today and in the next three days, pray for a fresh view of our blessed Lord and Saviour.

Bible Truth for Today: *"No man hath seen God at any time; the only begotten Son, which is in the bosom of the Father, he hath declared him." —John 1:18*

December 19

Read Hebrews 4–7
Family Reading: Hebrews 6

Two Classes of Believers

In every work for the Lord, there are two classes of people. There are those who give themselves with their whole heart to seek and serve God. Then there are others, too often the majority, who, like Israel, are content to be delivered from Egypt and just settle down and take the Christian life easy. This class never strives for full possession of God's promises.

Paul warned both groups—those in the first part of Hebrews 6 who are careless and indifferent, and then the group who diligently wanted to serve the Lord wholeheartedly. In verse nine he states clearly, *"But, beloved, we are persuaded better things of you, and things that accompany salvation . . . "* The *"things that accompany salvation"* are given in verses ten through twelve. First are works (v. 10). Then is the need to show diligence in honoring the Lord and *" . . . full assurance of hope unto the end" (v. 11).* Finally is the admonition not to be slothful but faithful in living for Christ (v. 12).

This class of people in Hebrews had been slothful in hearing the Word of the Lord and in doing it. God wants us to be followers of those who through faith and patience inherit the promises.

In which class are you? O Christian, use the time you have to grow in grace and in the knowledge of the Lord Jesus Christ. Be not slothful but diligent.

Bible Truth for Today: *"Not slothful in business; fervent in spirit; serving the Lord." —Romans 12:11*

December 20

Read Hebrews 8–10
Family Reading: Hebrews 10:1-25

Thankful for His Sacrifice

"But this man, after he had offered one sacrifice for sins for ever, sat down on the right hand of God." —Hebrews 10:12

The Bible commands us to be thankful. One major basis for our thanksgiving should be the fact of the death of Christ on the cross. By His one sacrifice, the Lord settled forever the penalty of our sins. The cross of Christ should be our glory, but how small a share does the Lord Jesus have in the affections of believers! Disciples do not love their Saviour as they should. How little do we allow our meditations to center upon the labors of love and the agonies of body and soul that Christ suffered for us. If someone were to rescue us from certain death by drowning or in a trap of fire, how we would appreciate our kind deliverer! When we would later reflect on the danger we were in, our hearts would swell with gratitude for all that was done.

But where is our warm affection, our fervent love to our Redeemer whose heart, filled with love for us, caused Him to offer Himself willingly as a sacrifice for our sins? He set His face like a flint and headed for the cross for you and me. Why are we not more thankful for the sacrifice of Christ? Is it that we do not look at sin properly? We think sin is not too serious. Sin, how malignant is its nature! How deep is its stain! Only one thing could redeem us. Nothing but the divine blood that flowed in His veins could possibly atone for this dreadful sin.

Think of it! Our blessed Lord Jesus Christ offered His sacrifice once. It was sufficient. It covered all my sin. Jesus Christ knew His sacrifice atoned for sin forever; so He sat down at the right hand of God. In the Old Testament, though there were many items of furniture in the tabernacle, there is never a mention of a chair. The high priest was never able to sit down. But Jesus, our High Priest, after He had offered His one sacrifice, sat down forever. He could rest in a finished redemption. Thank God for His sacrifice for us!

Bible Truth for Today: *"For by one offering he hath perfected for ever them that are sanctified."* —Hebrews 10:14

December 21

Read Hebrews 11–13
Family Reading: Hebrews 11:1-22

Faith

"Now faith is the substance of things hoped for, the evidence of things not seen." —Hebrews 11:1

Hebrews 11 is the great *faith* chapter. Verse one gives us a definition of faith; then the remainder of the chapter reveals what faith has accomplished. Faith is the spiritual faculty in our lives that deals with the spiritual realities of that which is unseen. We communicate with the world around us through our senses of sight and hearing. Even so, our faith is that sense by which our soul is in contact with the spiritual world. Our senses of hearing and seeing are actually dormant until sound or light strikes the eyes or the ears. We cannot see in the darkness, and we cannot hear when there is no sound. Even so, faith is a dormant faculty until the reality of eternal impressions is laid upon it.

In fact, faith must be built. How do we build it? *"So then faith cometh by hearing, and hearing by the word of God" (Romans 10:17).* With faith we have the evidence (the title deed) of things not seen. We simply believe God that He can do great things for us. We build this faith so that we can please God by studying His Word and applying its principles to our lives. Faith is the substance (literally, the foundation) of God's blessings in their actual reality. Faith can grow into firm and full assurance. It finds its confidence not in itself but in God and His Word.

> *My faith looks up to Thee,*
> *Thou Lamb of Calvary,*
> *Saviour divine!*
> *Now hear me while I pray,*
> *Take all my guilt away,*
> *O let me from this day*
> *Be wholly Thine!*
> *—Frances R. Havergal*

Bible Truth for Today: *"But without faith it is impossible to please him: for he that cometh to God must believe that he is, and that he is a rewarder of them that diligently seek him." —Hebrews 11:6*

December 22

Read James 1–4
Family Reading: James 1

Count Trials as Joy

"My brethren, count it all joy when ye fall into divers temptations." *—James 1:2*

The believer is not to fret when various testings come but to count them all joy. This is not easy, but he will see God's blessing if he will obey God's Word. James tells us the reason for this blessing: " *. . . the trying of your faith worketh patience" (v. 3)*. God uses trials in our lives to develop us into what we need to be. When the trials come, we should rejoice and thank Him for the grace He gives. What a blessing it is to see God do a work and the Spirit of God undertake in a miraculous manner.

James exhorts us in verse four to let patience have her " *. . . perfect work . . . "* This will come as we submit everything to God's will. When testing and trials come, are you rebellious, or are you submissive? If you are rebellious, you may need to abide in the furnace until you are brought into submission. The dross and slag of rebellion must be skimmed off in the furnace before the pure metal can flow forth. Only when we come to the place of genuine submission will patience have her perfect work.

Look at Jesus. He is our example. He was in the Garden of Gethsemane with the prospect of the cross before Him. He could say, " *. . . not my will, but thine, be done" (Luke 22:42)*. Here we see the perfect work of patience in the perfect soul of our Lord and Redeemer.

If an engineer sees a loose cog or a wheel out of gear in a piece of machinery, he must adjust the defective part so that it will work in harmony with the rest of the machine. If God sees some particular grace not in operation or improperly performing, He must bring that area into harmony with His grace and mercy. When trials come, obey the Word of God and rejoice. The blessing will be yours.

Bible Truth for Today: *"That the trial of your faith, being much more precious than of gold that perisheth, though it be tried with fire, might be found unto praise and honor and glory at the appearing of Jesus Christ."—I Peter 1:7*

December 23

Read James 5 and I Peter 1–3
Family Reading: I Peter 2

Growing in the Lord

I Peter 2:2 tells us exactly what a new convert is. He is literally a newborn babe. Jesus said, *" . . . Except a man be born again, he cannot see the kingdom of God" (John 3:3).* Christ refers to him as a new baby in Christ. A baby must eat to develop and grow physically. The same is true in the spiritual realm. *"As newborn babes,* [we are to] *desire the sincere milk of the word . . . " (v. 2).*

The new birth is a spiritual birth and is analogous to the physical birth. Each person is born a baby. Growth is very normal and natural and requires time to produce physical achievements. We cannot expect new Christians to do all of the things Christians should do who have been saved for a time. Each must grow to be what God desires him to be.

Peter states that the way to grow in the Lord is to *" . . . desire the sincere milk of the word . . . " (v. 2).* He is referring to the Word of God. The new Christian can take the Word of God just as a new baby drinks his milk and gets his nourishment. He identifies the milk needed as the *sincere* milk. The word *sincere* means *unadulterated.* It should be the simple Word of God, not tainted with any of the philosophies of men. One must take time for the Word of God and let it work in his life to develop him to be a strong Christian.

Many Christians quote verses two and three very glibly, but they fail to recognize that verse one is also part of the passage. That verse states, *"Wherefore laying aside all malice, and all guile, and hypocrisies, and envies, and all evil speakings."* A person who will grow in grace must lay aside these things of the old life. So long as those things remain, that individual cannot grow. Therefore, growth depends on our taking time for the Word of God, forsaking the old life, and living according to the new life for God's glory.

Bible Truth for Today: *"That we henceforth be no more children, tossed to and fro, and carried about with every wind of doctrine, by the sleight of men, and cunning craftiness, whereby they lie in wait to deceive; But speaking the truth in love, may grow up into him in all things, which is the head, even Christ."* —Ephesians 4:14, 15

December 24

Read I Peter 4 and 5 and II Peter 1–3
Family Reading: II Peter 3

Remembering the Word

Peter begins the third chapter of this second epistle by telling us why he wrote it: *"This second epistle, beloved, I now write unto you; in both which I stir up your pure minds by way of remembrance."*

Note first of all that he said he wanted to bring them to remembrance. In the first chapter he used the word *remembrance* three times. He wanted his readers to remember truths of old. That which he especially wanted them to remember is given in verse two: *"That ye may be mindful of the words which were spoken before by the holy prophets, and of the commandment of us the apostles of the Lord and Saviour."* We must never forget the words of the Old Testament prophets nor the words of the New Testament apostles.

In verses fifteen and sixteen Peter refers to the words and teachings of Paul as writings that every child of God should remember and believe. The Bible should be our textbook, our only rule of faith and practice. All that we believe and all that we are as believers depend upon the credibility and truth of the Word of God.

Second, please note that Peter says these believers had pure minds: *" . . . in both which I stir up your pure minds . . . " (v. 1).* He is speaking to those who believe on the Lord Jesus Christ. In Titus 1:15 Paul states, *"Unto the pure all things are pure: but unto them that are defiled and unbelieving is nothing pure . . . "* We have been made pure by God, and we need to walk as pure before Him.

Alexander Whyte was so conscious of this truth that before he read his Bible in the morning, he would dress as neatly as he could, straighten his tie, comb his hair, and then sit down and open the Word of God. He made careful preparation to go before the King. Many people are more concerned about how they look to others than they are about their appearance before God.

David knew this truth because he cried out, *"How sweet are thy words unto my taste! yea, sweeter than honey to my mouth!"*

—Psalm 119:103

December 25

Read I John 1–4
Family Reading: I John 1

The Blessing of Fellowship Through Christ

Today is Christmas Day—the day when we should give thought to the coming of Jesus Christ into the world.

In this first chapter of his epistle, John verifies that Jesus, the eternal Son of God, became a man. John says in effect, "I know He came because I was with Him." Verse one states: *"That which was from the beginning, which we have heard, which we have seen with our eyes, which we have looked upon, and our hands have handled, of the Word of life."* In his gospel, John called Jesus *"the Word"* and said He became " . . . *flesh, and dwelt among us" (John 1:14).* Now in his epistle, John says we heard Him and saw Him and were with Him.

Why did Jesus come to earth? He came that He might redeem us and give us fullness of joy. Verse four reads: *"And these things write we unto you, that your joy may be full."* Christ came to earth so that sinners could be saved (I Timothy 1:15). When we know we are saved, we have the fullness of joy that God wants to give us.

Jesus also came so that we could come into fellowship with Him and the Father. A title given to the Lord Jesus by God, the Father, is " . . . *Emmanuel . . . God with us" (Matthew 1:23).* Through Him we have fellowship with the Father and with God's people. What a blessing! We can personally have fellowship with God and with those who believe in Him.

May we today rejoice in the privilege of knowing Christ and the joy there is in fellowship with Him.

Bible Truth for Today: *"This is a faithful saying, and worthy of all acceptation, that Christ Jesus came into the world to save sinners; of whom I am chief."* —*I Timothy 1:15*

December 26

Read I John 5, II and III John, and Jude
Family Reading: II and III John

Stand for the Truth

Today we look at two very short but extremely important letters. John centered both letters around **the truth**. In II John we note how important **the truth** is.

"The elder unto the elect lady . . . whom I love in **the truth** *. . . also all they that have known* **the truth***" (v. 1).*

"For **the truth's** *sake, which dwelleth in us . . . " (v. 2).*

"Grace be with you, mercy, and peace . . . **in truth** *. . . " (v. 3).*

"I rejoiced greatly that I found of thy children walking **in truth** *. . . " (v. 4).*

Then in III John you will find the same emphasis on **truth**: *"I have no greater joy than to hear that my children walk* **in truth***" (v. 4).*

In both letters John dealt with problems in the church. In the second epistle he warned them not to have fellowship with unbelievers. Those who refuse to believe that Jesus is the Son of God are not believers and do not have God. We should not endeavor to have fellowship with them and should never bid them godspeed. If we were to wish them God's blessing, we ourselves would become partakers of their evil deeds.

It is interesting that II John 8 is written in the context of warning that believers should not fellowship with the deceivers of apostasy. John wrote: *"Look to yourselves, that we lose not those things which we have wrought, but that we receive a full reward."* This verse says we can lose the reward that God would give us simply by not standing against those who do not dwell in the truth. II John speaks of men forsaking the truth by trying to have preeminence in the church. A critical spirit can harm the work of the church and its message just as fellowship with unbelievers can do harm.

Proverbs for Today: *"Have not I written to thee excellent things in counsels and knowledge, That I might make thee know the certainty of the words of truth; that thou mightest answer the words of truth to them that send unto thee?"* —Proverbs 22:20, 21

December 27

Read Revelation 1–4
Family Reading: Revelation 1

Today we are doing something different than we have done in this whole volume of daily devotions. We are giving two pages to today's devotional.

Revelation is a fascinating book. And to all believers, it should be an important book. It promises a special blessing to all who will read the book and meditate in its truths. That promise is in Revelation 1:3.

Revelation and Genesis

Revelation is the book of completion. The key number is seven, the number of completion. It presents seven churches, seven blessings, seven seals, seven trumpets, and seven vials. Thus, as the last book of the Bible, it is the book of completion. Genesis, the first book of the Bible, is the book of beginnings; and Revelation, the last book of the Bible, is the book of completion. In Genesis we find a beautiful sinless paradise. In Revelation we see a still more wonderful paradise yet to come. In Genesis the devil makes his first appearance. In Revelation Satan makes his last appearance and is sentenced to his final doom. Genesis reveals the beginning of sin, of sorrow, and of suffering. Revelation closes with the judgment on sin and the glory for believers. In Genesis we read of the first death; and in Revelation, the time when there is no more death. Genesis tells of Eve, the bride of Adam, his help meet; and Revelation speaks of the Bride of Christ, the Church, being presented to the Lord Jesus Christ. Genesis tells of man's rebellion and the beginning of Babel. Revelation gives the account of Babylon and its fall.

Let's See Jesus

Please note that the title of the book and the first two words of the book are *The Revelation.* It is not "Revelations," the title so many use, but rather *"The Revelation."* It is one revelation, and that revelation in the first verse is *"The Revelation of Jesus Christ."* This book is to reveal Him, and as we read it we should long to see Jesus. The first chapter is in reality a wonderful revelation of Him. *"I am Alpha and Omega, the beginning and the ending, saith the Lord . . . "* *(v. 8).* It is hardly necessary to explain that Alpha and Omega are the first and last letters in the Greek alphabet. When the Lord said that He is the Alpha and Omega, He was saying that He encompasses all of the alphabet. This glorious truth reveals Him as the Eternal God. His nature is revealed in all creation, all races of men, all of redemption's work, and the final victory of peace and righteousness. We all need to join with seraphim of Heaven as they chant, " . . . *Holy, holy, holy is the Lord of hosts: the whole earth is full of his glory" (Isaiah 6:3).*

He is the Alpha and Omega. From His eternal power and being, we will find all the letters and words which will take care of our deficiencies. How wise and blessed just to rely on Him!

John was alone on the isle of Patmos, banished for his testimony of Jesus Christ (v. 9). But he was really not alone. There he saw Jesus Christ in all of His splendor and glory. And what was the greatest cure for John's loneliness? It was the fact that Jesus is living. He announced in verse eighteen, *"I am He that liveth, and was dead; and, behold, I am alive for evermore . . . "* In your loneliness—in your sadness—call unto Him. He is alive and ready to be your Companion.

Therefore, as we read *The Revelation* in the next few days, let us ask God to give us a revelation of Jesus Christ. This book should do much more for us than just satisfy an interest to know the future. It should give us the blessing promised in Revelation 1:3 and a deeper knowledge of Christ Jesus. This first chapter reveals Him to us as the altogether lovely One; the Ancient of Days (white head and hair, v. 14); the Judge (eyes as a flame of fire, v. 14); the One who suffered for us in the furnace of fire (v. 15); the One whose voice is God's authority (v. 15); and the Head of His Church (v. 16). May He become more real to us as we meditate on Him in this book.

Exaltation of Jesus Christ for Today: *"Thou art worthy, O Lord, to receive glory and honor and power: for thou hast created all things, and for thy pleasure they are and were created." —Revelation 4:11*

December 28

Read Revelation 5–9
Family Reading: Revelation 5

The Worthy Triumphant Lamb

In Revelation 5:2 the angel asked: *" . . . Who is worthy to open the book, and to loose the seals thereof?"* The *"book"* is a scroll, the title deed to the world. Satan kidnaped this world and became the god of it (II Corinthians 4:4). The scroll is the title deed to the world. Only One is worthy to open the seals of this important document. This One is not a man because no man in Heaven or in earth can be found who is worthy.

The One found worthy is the Lamb, the Lord Jesus Christ. He is worthy because He paid the price of our redemption. John saw the Lamb as He had been slain. When the song was sung in Heaven, its theme was based on the redemption accomplished through the death of the Lamb.

"And they sung a new song, saying, Thou art worthy to take the book, and to open the seals thereof: for thou wast slain, and hast redeemed us to God by thy blood out of every kindred, and tongue, and people, and nation" (Revelation 5:9).

Praise God for His shed blood that has redeemed us. May we ever recognize it as *" . . . the **precious** blood of Christ, as of a lamb without blemish and without spot" (I Peter 1:19).*

He is called the Lion of the tribe of Judah, the Root of David (v. 5). It was not as the Lion that He triumphed over Satan, but as the Lamb slain from the foundation of the world.

> *Dear Dying Lamb, Thy precious blood*
> *Shall never lose its power;*
> *Till all the ransomed Church of God*
> *Be saved to sin no more.*

Exaltation of Jesus Christ for Today: *"Saying with a loud voice, Worthy is the Lamb that was slain to receive power, and riches, and wisdom, and strength, and honor, and glory, and blessing."*

—Revelation 5:12

December 29

Read Revelation 10–14
Family Reading: Revelation 11

Singing of Our Reigning King

One great blessing of the Christmas season is the music. When we think of Christmas, we almost automatically think of Handel's *Messiah*, and we hear its strains sung or played many times. Included in Handel's *Messiah* are the words of Revelation 11:15 *" . . . The kingdoms of this world are become the kingdoms of our Lord, and of his Christ; and he shall reign for ever and ever."*

Is it not wonderful that we sing so much at Christmas time? I believe one reason is that at the birth of the Saviour there was a multitude of the heavenly host praising God. When we think of the blessing of our Lord Jesus Christ, we will find a song welling up within us. And certainly when we come to know Christ as our Lord and Saviour, we have a song placed within us. The psalmist wrote it this way: *"He brought me up also out of an horrible pit, out of the miry clay, and set my feet upon a rock, and established my goings. And he hath put **a new song** in my mouth, even praise unto our God . . . " (Psalm 40:2, 3).*

No wonder Handel could write such great music when he realized the wonderful truth of salvation through our Lord Jesus Christ. Someone has said:

"Watch Christians at work, and you find a morality;
Talk to Christians, and you find a theology;
But get to the heart of Christianity, and you will find a song."

Praise God today for the wonderful songs of Christmas that make this a most blessed time of year.

Bible Truth for Today: *" . . . be filled with the Spirit; Speaking to yourselves in psalms and hymns and spiritual songs, **singing and making melody** in your heart to the Lord." —Ephesians 5:18, 19*

December 30

Read Revelation 15–18
Family Reading: Revelation 17

Judgment on Babylon

Revelation 17 and 18 present the destruction of Babylon by God's judgment. It speaks in particular of the Babylonish world religious system. That system began with Nimrod in Genesis 10. It endeavored to build its own tower in Genesis 11—that which caused God to send confusion of languages—and has continued as an enemy of God and His Word ever since. In Revelation 17:3 we read of a woman sitting on a scarlet-colored beast having seven heads and ten horns, representing nations and kings. This woman in all of her bright garments and jewelry (v. 4) is titled " . . . *MYSTERY, BABYLON THE GREAT, THE MOTHER OF HARLOTS AND ABOMINATIONS OF THE EARTH" (v. 5)*. She represents a great religious system which is in existence today and will become more and more prominent up until the coming of the Lord Jesus.

This religious system is the Roman Catholic system which has its ties back into the pagan worship of the Babylonish system. I have seen the crowns of various popes in the Vatican Museum. On every crown I have seen either the letters *"P. M."* or the words *"Pontifex Maximus."* That is the title given to the high priest of the Baal religions in the Babylonish system. The professing church was drawn into this system when Emperor Constantine professed to be converted and made the church the State Church, made the pagan temples "Christian" temples, and made the pagan priests "Christian" priests.

Today the modern ecumenical movement is the mainstay of this Babylonish system—the protestant churches are heading back to Rome and its popery. God clearly instructs believers in Revelation 18:4, 5— *". . . Come out of her, my people, that ye be not partakers of her sins, and that ye receive not of her plagues. For her sins have reached unto heaven, and God hath remembered her iniquities."*

Bible Truth for Today: *"Wherefore come out from among them, and be ye separate, saith the Lord, and touch not the unclean thing; and I will receive you, And will be a Father unto you, and ye shall be my sons and daughters, saith the Lord Almighty."*

—II Corinthians 6:17, 18

December 31

Read Revelation 19–22
Family Reading: Revelation 22

"Even So, Come, Lord Jesus!"

Today we end another year. Congratulations to those of you who have read through the whole Bible this year. As we read these last three chapters of the Bible, we learn of great and very significant events in the future. In the twenty-second chapter we hear John pleading for the coming of the Lord Jesus Christ.

No wonder John wanted Him to come. Revelation 22:3 states that because of His coming there will be no more curse, and verse five says that there will be no more night. I have visited many times in homes of believers in Communist lands. These believers have undergone severe persecution. We could not speak a common language; however, as it came time for us to leave them and go back to our homes, I have seen them point joyfully toward Heaven, indicating they would see us there.

In verse seven the Lord Jesus announced that He would certainly come. He has sent His angel in Revelation to testify of these wonderful things (v. 16). John announces that the Holy Spirit says, "... *Come* ... " *(v. 17)*. Finally, John himself shouts, *"Amen. Even so, come, Lord Jesus."* That expresses the heartbeat of every true believer—the longing for Jesus Christ to come again.

As I write this, I realize the Lord Jesus could come before we complete another year. I personally believe His second coming is very near, and each believer should look for Him every day. May we say with John: *"Even so, come, Lord Jesus!"*

Bible Truth for Today: *"So Christ was once offered to bear the sins of many; and unto them that look for him shall he appear the second time without sin unto salvation." —Hebrews 9:28*